MY LIFE IN THE STRUGGLE FOR THE LIBERATION OF ZIMBABWE

MY LIFE IN THE STRUGGLE FOR THE LIBERATION OF ZIMBABWE

J Mpofu

authorHOUSE®

AuthorHouse™ UK Ltd.
1663 Liberty Drive
Bloomington, IN 47403 USA
www.authorhouse.co.uk
Phone: 0800.197.4150

Published by AuthorHouse   09/02/2014

ISBN: 978-1-4969-8323-7 (sc)
ISBN: 978-1-4969-8324-4 (e)

DEDICATION

I dedicate this book to my late wife, Professor Emeritus Ratie Mesa Bara Mpofu who dedicated herself to building and strengthening broad family relations during 47 years of our marriage. She was a loving wife, a friend, companion, mother, grandmother, colleague and comrade in all but name.

ACKNOWLEDGEMENT

My wife, Ratie, constantly reminded me that I was in possession of a lot of information about Zimbabwe's liberation struggle that was worth bringing into the public domain, not only in the interest of future generations but also to contribute some factual accounts of the struggle from its origin. I am grateful for that encouragement but deeply regret that she did not live to read the book.

My children, Nonhlanhla, Velakude and Veronica frequently asked me questions about the struggle and when hearing my description of it, they declared that what I had to say should be put in a book.

Several comrades, including J Zwelibanzi Mzilethi, Phillip Mabena, Eli Mthethwa, Owen Tshabangu and Clark Mpofu encouraged me to write what I knew about the struggle as much as I could remember up to victory.

My friends, in academia, persistently encouraged me to write something about the anti-colonial underground network that sustained guerrilla warfare in Zimbabwe. These include Professor David Moore of the University of Johannesburg in the Department of Anthropology and Development Studies, the late Professor Lionel Cliff, former academic at Leeds University, UK, in the Department of Politics, Dr Frank Reeves, Director of Race Equality West Midlands, UK and Professor Mischack Matshazi, formerly in the Department of Education, at Fort Hare University, South Africa.

Essentially I was galvanized into sitting in front of the computer to write my story after reading publications by former freedom fighters, Wilfred Mhanda and Zwakanyorwa Wilbert Sadomba who demonstrated that guerrilla warfare took place across the country as a whole (between 1976 and 1980) against all odds in terms of the Rhodesian counter-insurgency strategy.

I thank the publisher for professional guidance in the process of making this project possible. The entire narrative is mine and mine alone in every aspect of the contents, supportive references notwithstanding.

ON THE UNSUNG HEROES OF ZIMBABWE'S LIBERATION WAR

When in 1984 I first arrived in Zimbabwe to carry out research for my doctoral thesis on the "construction of hegemony" during the country's liberation struggle I rented a house from Alfred 'Knotty' Knottenbelt, one of Zimbabwe's unsung liberation heroes. In 1968 Knotty refused to fly Ian Smith's new flag and thus was told by Rhodesia's education authorities that he could remain no longer as Fletcher High's headmaster. His next job was the warden of the university's Manfred Hodson Hall, where he participated in the struggle's 'underground railway'. When he learned of my scholarly aims he told me "all of Zimbabwe's heroes are dead", and laughed his huge and deep guffaw.

He should have known: he taught quite a few of the heroes and those counterpoised to such status during his tenure at Goromonzi and Fletcher. As the years went on, however, it became apparent that there were many heroes alive and well – but quiet, or in exile. One of them, studying in Europe until 1991, was the late Wilfred Mhanda, aka Dzinashe 'Dzino' Machingura. He was was the *de facto* leader of the *vashandi* section of the Zimbabwe People's Army, a short-lived attempt in late 1975 and 1976 to unite the two liberation parties' armies and to deepen the ideological content of the war. By 1977, Robert Mugabe, having just reached the top of the Zanu (Zimbabwe African National Union) ladder, in collaboration with Mozambique's president Samora Machel squashed Zipa. Zipa's leaders spent the rest of the war in jails – some with gardens, some not. Zipa has become a relatively well-known episode, in part because in 2000 some of its members such as Mhanda revived their opposition to Mugabe's Zanu in the aftermath of the new millennium's 'fast track' land re-orientation. Mhanda's book, *Dzino: Memories of a Freedom Fighter,* was published in 2011, so his version of Zipa's tale was preserved just about two and half years before he succumbed to cancer in May 2014. 'Dzino' was an unsung liberation hero who had started to chirp very loudly indeed.

Joshual Mpofu's *My Life in the Struggle for the Liberation of Zimbabwe* illustrates that there are indeed more quiet political heroes in Zimbabwe's history who are beginning to chant a loud chorus. He is one of them, remembering a time when the old guard of Zimbabwe, still in power after all these years, was challenged first. The most well-known of Mpofu's political moments was 1971's March 11 Movement, when a group of young and militant cadres in Zapu's (Zimbabwe African People's Union) army took their elders to account for their sloppy military strategy, ethnic regression, and unresponsiveness to questioning from below. They ended up in Zambia's jails and Rhodesia's gallows for their efforts to open up the struggle.

It's a tale that bears much in common with Zipa's fate a few years later and also with generational impasses in Namibia's South West African People's Organisation, South Africa's African National Congress, and the same country's Pan African Congress: all handled with the incredibly clumsy and brutal hands of the leaders and the hosts of the countries allowing the guerrilla fighters a base alongside their as yet colonised homes. The generational similarities bear further study: one sees 'modern', often Marxist-oriented, militarily well trained, and liberally contrarian youth in the 1970s challenging an 'old guard' of nationalist leaders lacking in most of those traits (although, as Mpofu recalls, there were many good blokes and women in the elder category who would have been much more tolerant: it's only that they did not have much power). The conflicts are repeated even today as the ones who won the battles illustrated so well in Mpofu's *My Life in the Struggle* meet an even younger generation on the turf of a new and ideologically altered post-colonial terrain. The latter could – and must – learn from the struggles of their predecessors, who combined socio-economic *and* civil forms of freedom seamlessly in their efforts to expand both beyond their leaders' narrow confines. As the old saying goes, *a luta continua* as the looting continues.

Yet cross-country comparisons can yield only structural correspondences: as *My Life in the Struggle* shows so unerringly, the differences in the histories of the actors ranging to the responses of the host countries are significant and affected the way in which these inter-generational challenges transpired. Indeed, even co-actors' interpretations of the same historical moment can differ: *My Life in the Struggle* carries a voice somewhat apart from the version on offer in Owen Tshabangu's *samizdat*-like *The March 11 Movement in ZAPU. Revolution within the Revolution for Zimbabwe* (Heslington: Tiger Papers, 1979). Personal reflections such as Mpofu's reveal the individuality of the participants in history and the particular *longue durée* of their struggles: the narration herein of Bulawayo's early underground is ground-breaking (please excuse the pun) and Mpofu's involvement therein suggests he was very far from a 'young turk' grasping for power in youthful ignorance when the 1971 moment came.

After reading the words in this very moving book how could anyone – even the sorts of people who write about the war of national liberation in Zimbabwe in Wikipedia as if it were the "Rhodesian bush war" and take seriously allegations that the March 11 Movement was plotting against the Zambian president himself – imagine the likes of Joshua Mpofu as a 'terrorist'. The characteristics that emerge from this book are those of honesty, bravery, fairness, humour, social justice, freedom, reconciliation … and the list will go on for those who read the following pages. It's hard to imagine how the conditions under which Mpofu and his comrades were raised – racial discrimination, poverty, humiliation – could produce such worthy souls (unless one takes into account some aspects of Rhodesia's education system, with more than its share of Knottenbelts' robust liberalism, publicly and in the missions; Garfield Todd being exemplary, and into the political realm too). These are the traits of many of the 'unsung heroes' I have encountered in Zimbabwe through talking with people such as Joshua Mpofu and his counterpart Dzino Machingura.

But when such 'firebrands' encounter those who think they alone embody the noble resistance tradition before they have even reached the pinnacles of the power, they will be misunderstood either wilfully or (if we give them the benefit of doubt) innocently. When I was carrying out research for my doctoral thesis, which raised some of the issues covered by *My Life in the Struggle* (and was never published because one guardian of official history advised James Currey against it: perhaps this was a small incident of 'generational' – if not ideological – struggle!) I was told by Joshua Nkomo that the March 11 Movement was full of "cowards" who were afraid to go to the front to fight. Enos Malandu told me that the movement was a CIA plot. Aaron Milner, the Zimbabwean-born home affairs minister in Zambia readers will meet in this text, was more objective: he said he was so busy '"fire-fighting" youngsters' revolts like this that he could hardly cope. When in August 2013 I interviewed Mark Chona, permanent secretary for Zambia's foreign affairs in 1971, he exclaimed of the March 11 Movement "they were going to kill JZ" (JZ Moyo, to be encountered herein). Clearly, the careful preparation carried out by the (unsung) heroes of this book was to no avail: they believed that a well stated and well publicised 'mission statement' of their intention to call a conference would be treated as they meant. Instead, to a group of politicians steeped in the paranoia of coups, double-standards and triple crossings, their honesty could not be seen for what it was. It would be perceived as tribalism, power grabbing, foreign destabilisation, intellectualist one-upmanship, "infantile ultra-leftism" (as Samora Machel screamed at the Zipa gang), or simply murderous mayhem. It's a wonder men and women of Joshua Mpofu's ilk kept at it.

Keep at it they did, even after their 'punishment' – for the March 11 Movement leaders, after three years' incarceration it included exile to the United Kingdom, thanks to the hard work of internationalists (including Joshua's wife Ratie) all over, with the chance for further education. With their return, after 'freedom' had been gained in the form of the universal franchise and the first years of the seemingly eternal reign of Robert Mugabe and his ZANU (now with the suffix 'PF', but that is a long enough story in itself), readers will follow Joshua Mpofu's efforts to make the best of a world with *Gukurahundi's* dark shadow falling over it. His work created a sliver of sun. Sometimes those slivers widen to an immense opening.

Aside from adding to Zimbabwe's political history immeasurably this book is a testament to all the unsung heroes whose struggles to free Zimbabwe *have* made it a better place – may more add their voices to what is now a literary duet – than it otherwise might be, and an inspiration to those who are carrying on the torch. Read this book and weep – with tears of joy that people such as Joshua knew innately what the word 'liberation' meant and how to act on it, and with sadness that so many with power twisted 'liberation' and 'freedom' into cynical synonyms for oppression, repression, and depression even before they started their journey into democracy's fabled 'second stage'. That this book exists carries hope that liberation's real partisans are actually winning their war.

David Moore, Phd.
Professor of Development Studies
University of Johannesburg

PRELUDE

This is an elucidation of accumulation of personal experience within the context of socio-cultural internalization in particular and the socio-political environment in general that is intended to provide some insights into a plethora of ingredients that converged and crystallized into a catalytic impetus that socially transformed my generation from village boys to highly politicised freedom fighters during the 1960s to the 1970s in Rhodesia. I have done this by tracing the footprints of my experience which show multiple stages and strands of cultural, social, political and physical determinants that landed themselves on my growth path, starting from socialization in my parents' home, all the way through the local community traditions and schooling to active service for the freedom of my country at local and national level. Here the crucial elements that moulded my social being in a very profound way have been ventilated to show when and how I became able to distinguish antagonistic differences between justice and injustice from a very early age. Proceeding from here, I have brought out how I teamed up with others whose political outlook and aspirations were identical with mine, as we all voluntarily joined the anti-colonial struggle, starting from (invisible) low intensity activism in schools and towns up to risky adventures that finished up in armed struggle within a broad national perspective.

The narrative further demonstrates the domesticity of the movements that championed the liberation struggle, as its drivers were citizens who grew up in the rural villages and urban African townships, where they progressively became aware that they were born (unlike their parents) in a country under colonial administration. In doing all this, I had to spell out how my interaction with informative social vectors brought awareness of how my country, Zimbabwe, was colonized and governed by Europeans without the consent of the indigenous natives, who showed their resentment to foreign rule by rebelling (First Chimurenga) within six years of colonization, but failed, only to succeed in the second rebellion (Second Chimurenga), after ninety years of racial domination. Furthermore, I believe I have laid bare how I became a civilian freedom fighter, together with peers of my generation, in the second rebellion, where the intolerable weight of oppression caused us to abandon non-violent methods of struggle in favour of using the arms of war to face a network of security forces led by the superb military machine of the colonial state, wherein lay formidable challenges confronting rebelling citizens. The armed struggle phase meant that fighters and their collaborators had to face those challenges in the theatre of operation. Initially they exhibited more weaknesses than strengths, and lost opportunities in the form of political support from the mass of people. The overall process of the struggle exhibited strengths and costly weaknesses, right from the civilian phase up to the armed struggle phase, with or without my participation. It was not until freedom fighters gained experience in planning and undertaking field operations that they became able to apply appropriate tactics to sustain the struggle in the theatre of operation. More importantly, the narrative makes the point that the Rhodesian colonial system was presided over by European settler leaders, who barely recognized the right of African citizens to participate in governance of the country with equal rights in social, political, economic and juridical spheres of societal setting of two main races. Exclusion of Africans from consensus on the act of Unilateral Declaration of Independence (UDI) by Ian Douglas Smith was a fundamental blunder that precipitated nationwide fury that led to a civil war in which a deprived citizen fought against a privileged citizen who was indoctrinated with the falsehood that his adversary, freedom fighter, was sponsored by foreign powers of a communist type, while the latter rightly believed that he was fighting to free his country from racially-imposed injustices of deprivation.

More importantly, the narrative lays emphasis on the creation of massive political structures throughout the country, well below the radar of legality, for the purpose of sustaining guerrilla warfare in the face of the super-professional Rhodesian security forces. In this connection, the final phase of armed struggle demonstrated to all at home and abroad that freedom fighters became significantly effective because they were politically rooted in the oppressed population, whence came their strength against superior military hardware and a 'water-tight' counter-insurgency strategy of the Rhodesian security forces. Essentially, it was that political strength, not Communist powers, or betrayal by the West, which caused all stakeholders to become willing to come to a negotiating table at Lancaster House in Britain in 1979 to settle the armed conflict decisively.

CONTENTS

CHAPTER ONE

EARLY CHILDHOOD DEVELOPMENT IN A FORESTLAND

I have to start off with mention of my parents, because it was owing to their influence that I internalized some of the fundamentals of how my country was colonized by Europeans, who had established a firm grip on the country within a short space of time after their victory over the Africans. My early childhood development, like that of any other African village boy, was characterized by performing family tasks, interacting with peers in a variety of physical games in the countryside and at school. But let me begin with my father, Mahlathini ka Mjiwa, born in 1885, at a place called eMambanjeni (where the current suburb of Bellevue is situated) four kilometers south of the modern city of Bulawayo in Zimbabwe. He was a good story teller on these matters. As the year of his birth shows, he was born during the reign of King Lobengula of the Matabeles (as the Ndebele were called in official documents). He spent his early boyhood at eMambajeni until old royal Bulawayo was seized by the colonialists in 1893 whereupon his farther, Mjiwa ka Dingimizi, and his family moved from eMambanjeni to eMatojeni (Matopo Hills), at a place known as Bhedza, now called White Water. He remembered what happened when Bulawayo (Lobengula's Royal Headquarters) was attacked by Cecil John Rhodes' invading soldiers, causing civilians to run in all directions, but mainly into the Matopo Hills to hide. In the history of my family the known key personalities were my grandfather Mjiwa, great grandfather Dingimizi, and the great-great grandfather and mother Mawondela and Majubane, respectively. According to the collective memory of elders of the extended family, Mawondela and his wife, Majubane, mark the foundation of our family tree as we know it today. I mention this because when I told my extended family about writing about my political experience, many of my uncles and cousins urged me to try to trace our tap root beyond Mawondela and Majubane but, I had very limited time to do that as it is a huge project on its own. So, in this regard, I will leave it at that.

For all intents and purposes, it is of fundamental importance to start off with my family background because I believe it is the foundation of my interest in the politics of national liberation from colonialism. For instance, my father witnessed, and got bruised running away from the very first (1893) European invading army that overran his country when he was young, and resulted in the demise of African rule overnight. Within three years, he witnessed another violent clash of forces when a country-wide African uprising (1896) took the settlers by surprise. It,, too, was crushed by the British army. He then grew up in the period when a new European administration was rapidly asserting itself all over the country with a different approach from King Lobengula's rule. Western influence began to cause change to most aspects of African culture, especially: religion, education, health, public administration,

1

taxation, justice, policing and so on. Although he grew up in the vicinity of the Matopo Hills when their natural make-up was hardly tarnished with contamination from frequent intrusions by humans, new transformative institutions emerged in the immediate neighbourhood that changed his life. He was scarcely aware that the 'new' life he had experienced would pass to his offspring as a mixed bag. In his early childhood, my father, like any other African boy, grew up under strict rules of custom and tradition, alongside transformative institutions, such as the churches, schools shops, and towns. Indeed he could not escape the impact of these powerful institutional novelties which seemed to make life easier. He went to a mission school when he was about fourteen years old (the first mission was established in 1859 at Nyathi), where he finished up with a Standard 2 (Grade 4), and then went to work at the site where modern Bulawayo was being built. He worked in an iron foundry plant which was part of a growing industrial site. In 1921, he married a girl from eNtabeni zikaMambo (Mambo's Mountains), near Gweru, two hundred and seventy five kilometres south west of Harare, the capital City of Zimbabwe. Her maiden name was Msindose ka Ndubiwa Moyo (1902 - 1970) of the Lozwi dynasty.

The couple was blessed with a girl in 1923 and thereafter eight children followed at intervals of two to four years. There were three girls and six boys and I was the eighth child out of nine, born on 30 September 1939 in the Dimpamiwa village at Nkayi District, in what was then Southern Rhodesia (Zimbabwe). From the first to the last born the line up of siblings is as follows: Lizah Ester (F), Moya Scott (M), Khandampevu Obed (M), Matshazane (F), Simetshi Alick (M), Ntombikaise (F), Meshack (M), Joshua (M) and John Msolina (M). Only the last two of us have survived the rest so far. My birth place is situated 330 kilometres south west of the capital, Harare and 160 kilometres north of Zimbabwe's second largest city of Bulawayo, in Matabeleland North Province. Nkayi District was characterised by vast forestland, with giant trees of sorts, which were punctuated by flat savannah grasslands suitable for mixed farming, especially of livestock and small grain. The thick forests were distinguished by deep green canopies and impenetrable undergrowth, subtended by beautiful green plains along river valleys in spring and summer. More so, in summer, the dotted crop fields closed gaps to complete the green cover of the entire district, making the landscape appear like a vast and well-managed botanical garden.. Another attraction of the forests was the variety of the wild fruit which survived the predation of the increasing human population and birds. There is no orchard or man-made plantation that I know which could have matched the abundance of fruit found in the forest up to the proximity of the villages and the crop fields at that time.

At the front of our home, my father had cleared the undergrowth to leave a giant tree canopy forming a natural roof above. The cleared spot was an assembly place called idale[1] where, every evening, he delivered to his spell-bound sons the unforgettable stories, legends and folklore of the past.

Parental Socialization in Matters of Nationhood

Here is an example of one of those stories.

It was one of those usual evenings when we sat around the fire at a designated spot, **idale**[1], located just out of the boundary of the home yard. The sun had just sunk behind the horizon and the sky was serene except in the west, where a semi-circular shaped golden disk, subtended by a mall of similarly colourful cloud at the point of sunset, signalled the end of the day. It had rained the previous day and the summer birds seemed to celebrate the occasion by diving in the atmosphere in spectacular formations, like jet bombers in exercise. The cows had just come home and there were no reports of some of them gone astray or damaging neighbours' crops. There was every

---

[1] *father and sons' assembly place*

2

reason for everyone to be in a jovial mood because, even in the kitchen, my mother was putting final touches to the supper of the day, which consisted of an assortment of samp and boiled ground nuts, with fresh beef on the bone, and marrow-saturated gravy for a sauce.

When my father was in a joyous mood he had plenty of folk stories to tell, with emphasis on what we ought or ought not to do as we grew up to become men among men. That day was one of those days. It was a memorable day because he talked about African kings and their kingdoms, such as Rozwi, Venda, Zulu, Sotho, Tshwana, Swazi, Xhosa, Shangaan, Ndebele, etc. He finished by harking back to memories of Matabele King Lobengula's weaknesses in contrast to Mzilikazi's strengths (Matabele kings in succession). For him, it was the former's lack of wisdom that led to the demise of his kingdom in 1893. He said Lobengula should have thought of a better plan to handle the Europeans before allowing gold diggers to come into the country without first acquiring weapons similar to theirs. He referred to King Shaka Zulu who noticed the uniqueness of white men's weapons - that they spat deadly fire from a long distance. Therefore, he suggested, Africans should first acquire similar weapons and learn how to use them in order to counter European incursions. If King Lobengula had remembered Shaka's brilliant observation and advice, he could have avoided doing battle with Cecil John Rhodes' soldiers, who were well armed with superior weapons. My father's observation on his king's weaknesses notwithstanding, it seems clear that Cecil John Rhodes was unlikely to be deterred by the lack of an agreed concession with Lobengula. He would still have used armed force, with or without Lobengula's consent, because he was determined to remove what he called "that savage sitting on the second Rand" during their planning stroll with Colonel Pennfather in front of the Kimberly Hotel, as we shall see in subsequent pages.

At the end of his illuminating presentation, we asked father how it happened that all those African Kingdoms had become extinct and replaced by European rulers who came from overseas. Especially our country (Zimbabwe) was ruled by Europeans, whose males demanded that natives should address them as "Nkosi" (King), regardless of whether they had positions of authority or not. Their wives were to be addressed as Madam or "Mesis" (Mrs), their sons "Nkosana" (Prince), and daughters "Nkosazana" (Princess). In other words, Africans were compelled to address Europeans with the aforesaid royal titles of honour. Was it just a manner of respect, or was it a compulsory acknowledgement of the power of a ruling race, that had placed itself in the position and status of our defeated kings and all royalty? My father gave an answer that never evaporated from my memory. Translated from siNdebele, these were his words:

"You boys need to know that Europeans fought and defeated your grandfathers because they used weapons that were spitting fire to strike a target (grandfathers) at a long distance. The Africans advanced in the face of that fire, trusting their numbers and speed to reach the adversary in order to spear them at close range, Tshaka style. They fought bravely but their spears were no match for the fire that reached them from afar where their spears scarcely reached European positions even if they were thrown at them with maximum vigour. Battles left heavy casualties on both sides, but the Africans were defeated with higher losses. Therefore, having shed their blood to take this country, the Europeans will never give it up without fighting. I can tell from the way they have been talking to us (workers) at work that they are here to stay in control of the country they regard as their own which they acquired by conquest. Also they

use different methods (from our own) to run the country which seem to require education to understand how they administer everything. It means that if you boys want to take this country back, you should first acquire some of their good habits and weapons like theirs which were used to defeat your grandfathers, otherwise do not try anything other than those fire spitting weapons. Even if you become educated, where will you get similar weapons? Above all you will need strong leadership to unite the Africans the like did by bringing various tribes into one nation similar to the way King Mzilikazi ka Matshobana assembled several tribes to build the Ndebele Nation (iSizwe sama Ndebele) and Mambo too, of the Rozwi, had a large Kingdom that he kept united."

So, a man of the 19th Century generation believed that there was value in a unified nation created from various ethnic groups. Clearly, he regarded nationhood as one of the fundamentals in building a strong nation to overcome any challenges, including fighting a powerful adversary. There was a gun that he called isigwagwagwa[2], which he said was spitting rapid fire like a hailstorm. I came to know this rapid killing machine as a Maxim gun (heavy machine gun). According to my father, isigwagwagwa was the crucial weapon which provided the invading army with decisive fire power and inflicted heavy casualties on the African armies in all battles and wars of his time until they were totally defeated. Historians confirm this very clearly. He went further to say that when the Africans regrouped in a unified effort after a lull of three years, they adopted a better strategy that entailed an element of surprise attack (ukujuma) on a large scale covering every European settlement in the territory but isigwagwagwa prevailed again. In spite of their numerical superiority and surprise attack, they were eventually crushed by rapid fire from "the fire spitting machine", which proved beyond any doubt that weapons on the two battling sides were grossly mismatched.

It was interesting that when my father mentioned the heroes of the second war to dislodge the settlers, he referred to that war as the war "led by Sikhonkwane and Mbuya Nehanda" ("Impi ka Sikhonkwane lo Nehanda"). Here, he was talking about the 1896 uprising, which marked the first peoples' war against colonialism in Zimbabwe. Our latter-day nationalists' talk of Mbuya Nehanda alone in this connection, yet elders of the past knew that the 1896 uprising of the Ndebele and Shona peoples was a united affair.

Interaction with peers

Forestland or not, every boy at a certain age was required to traverse the fearsome terrain when family duties called. For my part, at the age of 6, I joined my brother, Meshach, in herding my father's cattle, which were nearly one hundred in number. Herding cattle normally started at the beginning of summer, in November, and ended in winter, around the beginning of June every year. Before I went to school, my brother and I spent the whole day together in the forest looking after the herd. Initially, this was an exciting adventure, because I found so many new and amazing things, such as the beauty of large stretches of green vegetation which looked like an undulating green carpet across the valleys and hills that ran side by side but paralleled by the glassy shine of aqueous stretches of river that meandered towards and away from each other like snakes competing for a single prey. I gazed at the swinging canopies of large tall trees touching one another when a

---

[2] *heavy machine gun*

slow breeze blew steadily across the slopes of stunted hills that formed valleys between them thus exhibiting a remarkable display of corrugated green turf. The abundance of wild fruit and animals completed the magical scene with colours and shape, let alone taste. We indulged in feasting on the varieties of fruit but could never devour them all, not even in a week. In this way, we were quite close to the state of nature, not only in our green surroundings but in the food we consumed, to the extent that rural boys and girls appeared to be fitter and stronger in school sports and athletics than urban dwellers.

While the flora had its own fascinating features, the fauna too, exhibited many beautiful species such as antelope, impala, buck, kudu, eland, zebra, mountain goat as well as fearsome wolves, hyenas, cheetahs, buffalo, elephants, rhinos and others. The impala herd was noted for its speedy galloping and high jumping over bushes and trees of medium height on the periphery of the thick forest. Some of the animals, such as the snakes, were very dangerous to the cattle herders, as they always concealed themselves under the grass, or in the leaves of bushes. But we got used to all of these as we learned to observe the swaying of grass when a snake was moving, or lifting its head at the approach of an intruder. It was always fascinating to gaze at all this natural beauty when standing on top of the famous local kopje, Gande, near the local Shangane River, which runs from the Mambo Mountains to Gwai River in the North of the country.

With grazing lands quite populated with a diversity of wild life, many people may be tempted to assume the dangers faced by the herd boys, who spent almost the whole day in the bush, would come mainly from wild animals or thorny bushes. On the contrary, it was rare for animals to attack a person in the bush, because there was more than enough other prey for carnivores. During our younger days, cruel adult humans were more bothersome to herd boys than were the wild animals. There were several instances where the behaviour of adults posed a threat and discomfort to herd boys. It came in various forms. For example, one day when I was driving the cattle home, whistling in a jovial mood, I suddenly heard a hoarse voice calling me by name from behind. I looked back and saw one well-known local man, Mangena Ndiweni, running towards me wielding a stick and ordering me to come to him for a flogging. I ran away into the bush and he gave chase. I was hoping to lose him in the thicket of the forest but, instead, I fell into an ant-bear's (**aardvark**) hole. Apparently, Ndiweni was close enough to see me all of a sudden being "swallowed" by the earth. He panicked, calling my name many times and encouraging me to hold on to the wall of the hole, as he prepared to pull me out. His voice now sounded worried. He urged me not to make a move until he told me to.

Meanwhile, each attempt I made to advance up the hole, I slipped down because the texture of clay soil had no grip. It was as if I was holding on to some kind of powder. I became scared to the extreme when I saw the mouth of the hole becoming narrower far up there. When I looked down the hole, it was dark and I had no idea of what might be lying below me. Ant-bears have a tendency to dig holes and abandon them to be taken over by medium to larger size reptiles (eg pythons, iguanas, etc). The thought of things like that made me tremble and sweat as if I was close to a blast furnace. Eventually, he appeared with a long stick, pushed it down and asked me in a gentle voice to hold it firmly and shake it to signal readiness. I did. Then he steadily pulled me saying "hold on my boy you will be out now" but before I popped out, the stick snapped and I slipped downwards again. He ran to find another stick and came back very quickly to repeat the rescue operation and indeed I came out of the hole, terrified and sweating. At the time, I could not even guess how deep I had gone down the hole but later, when I was grown up, I estimated that the upper side of my body might have been about one and-a-half to two metres deep from the mouth of the hole. While in the dark hole, I could not reckon what was lying in wait for me outside the hole.

As soon he pulled me completely out of the hole, Ndiweni held me firmly by the hand and said "now that you are out of the hole, my boy, I want to teach you a lesson so that you will never bring your cattle near my crop field again." He picked up his original stick and flogged me thoroughly for allowing the cattle to pass near his field. Normally if a boy was disciplined by a member of the community for wrong-doing, he never reported the incident until the member concerned reported to the parents, who would then approve of the action. But, in this instance, I felt treated unfairly without any justification. I reported the matter to my father and once he had seen the hole, he was infuriated by the fact that Ndiweni aggravated my trauma by chasing me into a hole, only to pull me out for a beating. It was an act of extreme cruelty to apply measures that exceeded any reasonable punitive requirement to match an offence, if any. Indeed, I had done nothing horribly wrong to deserve such a harsh treatment. The man was made to apologise to me and my parents. I was twelve years old when this happened, but I never forgot the shock and trauma of falling into a hole and being pulled out to be flogged immediately afterwards. Was I to know that far worse was waiting for me in adulthood? As we shall see, in later years there were painful occasions that made me wish that I had been swallowed by the Ndiweni hole.

Nevertheless, it was not all grim in the bush. There were plenty of games which had both an entertainment and physical fitness value. Some of the games that young boys were expected to play were of a painful nature but had to be accomplished without flinching. One regular initiation was to participate in a competitive boxing game (ukuxega abafana). Another was stick fighting (intonga) with other boys, which took place every day at a chosen assembly ground. Such an assembly ground was a small open space (about a quarter of the size of a football pitch), surrounded by a thicket of trees and a body of water nearby, man-made or natural (so that in the event of bleeding or fainting, water would be useful). No gloves were used for boxing and we knew nothing of padding the hands until we went to town. We called our fighting games "fighting with bare hands." Parallel with fist fighting was the use of sticks (Xhosa style), whereby each would use two sticks, one for striking the opponent and the other for defence. Boys from different areas would assemble in groups, each under the leadership of an older boy, who was strong enough to have emerged as head (ingqwele) of a group of boys in his neighbourhood and with enough stamina to stand against bullish head boys from other areas. After emerging as a "head boy" (ingqwele) of a group of boys from the same neighbourhood, an older boy with boxing and stick-fighting skills would then train his boys in the art of fist and stick fighting to prepare them for more serious fighting with boys from other neighbourhoods. A head boy had the power to veto any suggestions from other head boys, if he thought the fight would be a mismatch. Head boys organised boys into groups and assumed commanding positions similar to a military set up. In this way, each head boy assumed authority over a group of boys whom he trained and caused to obey his orders. The head boys set and agreed on the rules of the game and managed the whole process through orders and sanctions imposed upon those who broke the rules. In most cases a head boy had an assistant or two, who would motivate their group to be ready for any encounter with other boys, without fear. Such assistants were not appointed, but emerged from the ranks through their motivational skills and knowledge of the games. Those without head boys had to be very bold to come to the assembly ground because the head boys present could pick any one of them to fight another boy. Everyone had the right to decline if they felt unprepared to fight the other person but, declining to fight another boy without making an alternative choice, ran the risk of being called a coward. No one wanted to be labelled a coward. It was more honourable to suffer defeat than to display cowardice in front of an assembly of boys. Peers would spread information to others not in attendance about the cowardice of anyone who declined to fight without making an alternative choice of an easier target. Bravery was a virtue that became pronounced throughout the community of youngsters within and outside the neighbourhood. Many boys succeeded in gaining recognition for bravery regardless of whether they won or lost in the games. Others did not quite make the grade of brave victors. In every fight there are victors and vanquished.

For all intents and purposes, these were games that no local youth could avoid except by migrating at a very young age to the town or a boarding school. The aim of the physical training given to the boys was to prepare them to face a world of fighting, hard labour and struggle. The tradition dates back to when young men, after passing through the phase of fist and stick fighting, were expected to become warriors. In reality, this was a phase of physical preparation before undergoing military training. But for our generation there was no longer a compulsion to undergo military training, as the country was now in the hands of colonial masters, who did not conscript Africans. The age range for those who took active part in these games was 6 to 15 years. In this way, the school factor and the labour market reduced the upper limit to no more than 12 years (in the 1950s) because from that age some boys would have gone to study at upper primary schools, where they would spend a full day attending classes, or alternatively to labour on neighbouring cotton farms or in the towns. Clearly the phenomena of school and labour market tended to cream off the head boys, whose upper age limit normally ranged between 15 and 20 years. Those at lower primary school would still go to herd cattle in the afternoon, during which time they still participated in the games until they left for distant upper primary and secondary schools. But, of course, after graduating from the forest games, we all felt bold to face any challenge that needed to be tackled by physical encounter, including sport. Having gone through the above-mentioned process, I did not regret it, because I eventually ended up in the military, as we shall see later, although it was several years after going through the rigours of the forest boxing and stick fighting games. After the games, no one held grudges. We remained constantly friendly towards one another until politics brought us together again as comrades and the time for us to seek our national freedom had arrived.

Our forest ventures would have been incomplete without hunting for game or wild animals for both sport and meat. Hunting demanded physical strength because it involved walking and running long distances. In this connection there was one fascinating occurrence that I witnessed during one of our hunting episodes. I was still at primary school level when, one afternoon, my two brothers and I went on a hunting venture. On our way to our hunting ground, we met a white man from a nearby gold mine, carrying something that looked like a pipe. He spoke to us in Fanikalo[3] and asked if we knew of any place where he could find game, such as antelope, kudu, or impala. Luckily for him, we were also going to a grazing area which we knew to be populated by the animals that he was looking for. We guided him to the place and indeed we found a herd of impalas. At this point he ordered us to move back and hide from the animals. He took position, aimed, fired, and one of the impalas dropped while the rest galloped away at a terrific speed, displaying their high jumping over the bush as if they were intending to fly. I saw a flash from the mouth of the 'pipe' almost at the same time as the sound of the gun and, before I could digest this, entire one impala dropped and remained still on the ground to the delight of the hunter. My brother, Meshach whispered "So this is what happened to our forefathers." At first I could not understand what he was talking about

---

3

twisted Sindebele slang

until my younger brother, John, said "that white man's pipe spat fire and killed the animal from a long distance" Oh! I nodded in the affirmative. In appreciating our successful guide to such a delicious find, the hunter gave us a packet of toffee sweets and promised to give us something bigger next time if we helped him find a bigger game like kudu. While we were still wondering how he would carry his 'boot,' he looked at us beaming with a smile that we failed to reciprocate as we were still bewildered by the bang that dropped the animal instantly and he lifted it and placed it across his shoulders and walked away towards the mine. A few minutes later, we heard the sound of a pick-up truck starting and driving away. That day became a special one because we saw a weapon spitting fire from a distance and killing an animal instantly.

The most important thing here was that I came face to face with reality to witness a rifle being fired to kill an animal from about a hundred metres away. Indeed, that was the fire my father was telling us about. Clearly he was right that the spear was no match to a "fire-spitting pipe" (impompi ekhafula umlilo) as we called it from that day. After that eventful day, we saw these 'pipes' many times in the hands of the army and the police, and eventually they became a desired tool for liberation.

Nevertheless, the fighting games and hunting adventures were part of a phase that we had to undergo as boys before we entered school and progressed up the ladder of education away from the forest. In this regard time came for me to take up something different from forest games, before I started school. **When the moment finally came to enter school, I found the games and physical exercises there varied and often enjoyable. The slow coming of my chance to enter school was now a chronic pain that occurred every January of each year when schools opened. Peers used to call one who was not attending school "isigom.[4]" I needed to be spared this name once and for all. When I saw them going to, or coming from, school, I would hide in the bushes until they all passed as they walked in pairs. When they approached our home, they would shout *"where are you* sigom?" as they ran past our home as if they were running a cross country track.**

Enter school in the midst of social transformation in rural areas

I have mentioned that Nkayi District was overwhelmed by the predominance of huge tall trees and vast expanse of virgin land, populated by an assortment of wild plants and creepers that were the envy of the sangomas[5] who needed some small undergrowth plants for their traditional healing purposes. Owing to the predominance of giant trees and suchlike natural features, many urban dwellers referred to the district as as Emaguswini amnyama[6] and its residents as Amaqaba asemaguswini[7]. Instead of regarding this as derogatory, many young people took it as a challenge that they should face head-on by overturning it and going to school. It seems that parents, too, took it that way because the period between 1949 and 1955 witnessed an inflow of tens of young men and women (aged between 22 and 28 years), qualified as teachers, to reinforce

---

4   *Slang for an ignoramus or a 'non-school goer'*

5   *Youngster **Sangoma**-traditional healers*

6   *Dark forestlands*

7   *Uncivilized people of forestlands*

or replace temporary teachers, who had no teaching qualifications, yet held forth quite well. There was almost a sudden boom of qualified teachers, who were distinguishable by their self-confidence and assertiveness on matters of teaching, sports and **change in mannerism**. Above all, they liked smart attire and immaculate bicycles, as well as neat homes. Wherever they met each other, they spoke to each other in English, but without trace of self-aggrandisement. In their behaviour they conducted themselves as an integral part of the community even if they were not locals. Their ability to combine what was new and the local customs gained them full respect from the elders and youngsters. Their general demeanour attracted many young people to follow their footsteps up the education ladder. One of their outstanding habits of distinction was that they formed an association of teachers which affiliated to a mother body nationwide, thus making it easy for information to flow throughout the country in a systematic way. All these characteristics caused them to be the envy of many youngsters as they became exemplary in respect of the quality of life that they seemed to enjoy, including their politeness to locals. Hence, they were accorded cordial hospitality and tremendous trust in the communities where they were located. They unceremoniously gained leadership as pioneers of social transformation, in terms of encouraging parents to build new schools and then asking missionaries to provide teachers for both lower and higher grades. The response was tremendous because many lower primary schools gained new grades upwards (from Grade 4 to 5) and a few were graded to higher primary level (Grade 6 to 8) as the demand for education grew with an inflow of large numbers of qualified teachers who became the agents of a mini cultural revolution in the District.

The main source of wealth of the rural Africans was agriculture, especially livestock and small grain. The standard of living of the rural teachers, unlike that of the families of their pupils, depended on the value of their knowledge and teaching skills which gave them a seemingly higher standard of living. Their comparative economic prosperity motivated parents and children to regard them as examples of successful social development and personal integrity. It was almost inevitable that this first wave of teachers, generously bearing essential and empowering information about what might be achieved through education, became the main talk in the villages. The teachers were also well informed about current affairs and other matters of social value to the community. Indeed, parents were so impressed and motivated at the prospect of the benefits of education that they even sold their cattle to raise funds to pay school fees to send their children to boarding schools so that they could gain appropriate qualifications for a better quality of life in adulthood.

During my younger days, African education in the rural areas was provided by missionaries of various Christian denominations. A major shortcoming in all of this was the absence of secondary schools in Nkayi District in spite of over 50 primary units called "lower primary schools" (Grade 1 to Grade 5) and three higher primary schools (Grade 4 to Grade 8). Under the London Missionary Society circuit, up to 1957, there was only one higher primary school called Zinyangeni Mission, drawing students from the number of lower primary schools within Nkayi and the periphery of some neighbouring districts. Another higher primary school belonged to the Presbyterian Mission situated at Zenka, twenty kilometers from Zinyangeni Mission. It also drew its clientele from lower primary schools under its Mission's circuit. The upgrading of lower primary schools put more pressure on the two higher primary schools, until two more were opened at Dakamela School, forty kilometres from Zinyangeni Mission, and at an Anglican Mission at Mbuma Mission, sixty five kilometres from Zinyangeni Mission. To be admitted into higher primary level, pupils had to pass an entry examination which meant that a large number fell by the wayside, entering the labour market at a young age. After writing mid-year exams in Standard V1 (Grade 8), the top eight were recommended for admission into Form 1 at Nyathi Secondary School.

On completing higher primary level, the eight, together with more than a hundred from other schools, took an entry examination into Form 1 where the successful eighty candidates would be admitted. The lack of a secondary school in Nkayi District, forced students to seek places in other districts, such as Bubi (Nyathi Secodary School, 80km from Nkayi District), Plumtree (Tegwane and Mpandeni Secondary Schools, 260km), Gweru (Fletcher High School, 140km) and Zwimba (Kutama Mission, 290km). As all of these were boarding schools, some students could not afford the fees, so they fell by the way side. The aforementioned schools were open to admit suitable students from anywhere in the country, or other territories of the Federation of Rhodesia and Nyasaland, only if they met criteria for admission. Actually, in the rural areas African education was provided by the Missionaries, especially in what were called the Native Reserves now called Communal Lands. The notable teacher training colleges were also quite far: Hope Fountain Mission, (South of Bulawayo, 180 km from Nkayi) Dadaya Mission (Zvishabane, 270 km), Dombodema Mission (Plumtree 260 km). The advent of trained teachers from these training colleges ignited what can be described as energising "age of enlightenment" **or** "mini cultural revolution" in Nkayi District because from then on there was a widespread realisation of the advantages of education within the communities arising from the positive reports given at social gatherings. In time, more schools were upgraded to higher primary level to meet the growing demand for education in the district. Since in my family there was a teacher in the making by the late 1940s, I became more eager to enter school much earlier than my father prescribed.

When my brother Meshach started school in 1947, I wanted to go with him but father said I was too young (at the age of 7!). So I had to bear the pain of waiting for my turn while I was being called "isigom" by my peers. I was in tears every January when schools opened because that provocative word was getting louder and louder every year and I had to hide from my peers when I saw them going to or coming from school (girls uttered the word loudest). It was not until one January day in 1950, when I saw two brand new pairs of uniform in our room and, knowing that it was only Meshach older than me, that I began to think the other pair must be mine. Indeed, a week before the schools opened my father told me to make sure to get used to cleanliness because I would be starting school in a week. To say I was excited is an understatement.

Meshach assisted me to get ready for school so that when the opening day came I was well prepared for the occasion. In the middle of January 1950, schools opened and I was enrolled at Dimpamiwa Primary School to start Sub Standard A (Grade1). From that day, no one ever called me 'isigom' again: instead it was now my joy to call a non-school-going younster an isigom. A whole bunch of newcomers were called by another clumsy name, 'madzwinyu' ('lizards'). This was accompanied by certain rites of initiation but none severe, because teachers were always close by. Our teacher, Mrs Mangqatshana Nxumalo-Dlomo, was fully charged with passionate dedication to ensuring that each individual child understood what she was teaching. I still remember all her motivating songs and amusing stories which made us enjoy school life and to expect even better things to come with higher grades. I wondered what the teachers benefited from teaching so many children with so much enthusiasm to make them internalise new things such as the alphabet which results in their becoming literate in their own language and the English language after five years of schooling. For instance, I felt so much self-satisfaction after mastering the alphabet and numbers to the point that the whole class could read and write. Physically we did drilling and exercising, manual work, (including work in the school field and garden), carving up wooden articles, as well as sports (such as football and athletics). It was fascinating to learn new things in competitive ways with classmates and school mates without inflicting pain on each other. During the school hours speaking or talking in English was compulsory for Standard 1 (Grade3), Standard 2

(Grade4) and Standard 3 (Grade5) under the watch of the school monitors. The purpose of this was to train pupils to express themselves in the English language because from Grade 5 it became the medium of instruction. The school monitors were charged with responsibility to ensure that all those required to speak the language spoke it in all conversations between themselves, or in exchanges with teachers. Any breach of this rule was punishable by two hours hard labour in a school vegetable garden. This was pretty tough because there were many who chose to stay quiet until the end of the school day unless addressed by a teacher. Some pupils seemed to enjoy speaking the language and even though grammar was hugely distorted they rambled on until they learned to speak it faster.

In 1953 a qualified teacher, Moya Mjiwa Mpofu, my eldest brother, was appointed Head Teacher of Dimpamiwa Lower Primary School. He introduced interschool competitions in sports and this brightened the school further with a variety of sporting events, when more than a dozen schools from the neighbourhood took part. Moreover, the sports offered wide-ranging competitive activities that were full of excitement in contrast to the rigmarole of the bush boxing games. Starting school at the age of ten did not exempt me from the boxing games, but I felt that I had played my part enough to "graduate", as I found schooling more exciting and fascinating than the bush games. After all, I used to cry for school every first day of the first term from the age of six. The variety of activities in the school atmosphere was better than the boxing games that we were engaged in at the forest assembly grounds. In this regard, school became the most enjoyable place out of all my experiences before I went to school. I had every reason to appreciate schooling because it delivered me from the tormenting voices of other children calling me 'isigom'. But for me, the wait to start my schooling was excruciatingly slow because up to the age of ten I missed out on the development of my personal and social skills. I was consoled by the fact that I was not alone as half of my class mates were of my age and the rest were around one to two years younger than me.

My eldest brother Moya was one of the new crop of trained teaches of the period referred to above. At the height of his successes as a Head Teacher, Moya became highly respected in the community and his fellow teachers revered him so much that they elected him leader of the district branch of their Association. I have to mention his outstanding attributes, because Moya was my key role model, as I believed that I should be as educated as I believed he was. My mother used to call him 'isikolas[8]' and she referred to his friends as 'izikolas' (plural of isikolas). We eventually got its meaning from Moya himself, who described a 'scholar' as a highly educated person noted for writing books and that was sufficient to make some of us desire to become scholars. When we came to know that the word 'scholar' referred to an academic guru, we could not figure out how mother acquired that vocabulary since she used it to describe those whom she referred to as "college boys" (izkolas zekolitshini), as distinct from school boys.

One of the outstanding features of the 'mini cultural revolution' (increase of trained teachers resulting in increase of higher primary schools) that I mentioned above, was the advent of fashionable attire at teachers' weddings which became so bright and attractive that it began to overshadow traditional weddings from that time on. Every trained teacher's marriage was firmly wedded to a flashy white wedding, whose distinguishing features included a Christian ceremony and the bride's white attire from head gear to footwear, a quite dazzling affair that stood far apart from a traditional wedding in terms of its pageantry and ceremonial march. I do not exaggerate when I say that every one of my age glued their hopes on that form of wedding. My brother, Moya, could

---

8

believed to have been derived from ***"scholar"***

not bypass the new phenomenon of a glittering wedding in European imitation (influenced by missionaries). On his wedding day, 12th March 1954, one thing that was outstanding was my father's open display of joy and excitement over his first son's momentous occasion. It was as if he was doing this for the first and last time of his life. He showed glowing delight on that day as the bridal procession entered the gate of the groom's home in a rhythmic grand march. The bride, in dazzling white satin, was accompanied by a bevy of bridesmaids with counterpoising bright velvet attire, side by side with the bridegroom's troupe on the left flank which was distinguished by swanky navy blue outfits with both sides well pronounced by these contrasting colours in parallel rows. All this was supposed to be the centre of attraction. Many expected this to be preceded by a traditional wedding but none of that happened. Unexpectedly, my father stood at the entrance and as soon as the bridal pageantry was about a couple of metres in front of him, and made an about-turn to take the lead as he danced in traditional style (ukugiya) but in step with everybody in the bridal entourage. His lone figure in front of the pageantry caused a refraction of focus away from the main actors to him in a jovial display of excitement over his eldest son's wedding. For the first time, we saw our father dance in front of the bridal procession, virtually taking the role of the bridal guide as he became the lead personality ahead of the whole drama. The 'official' leading maid led the flower girls behind him like it was a pre-arranged thing, as the procession adopted his step and followed him right round the home yard until the time of sitting down. Nothing like that has ever happened at any of the weddings that I have attended or heard about before and after that occasion. What a day for the family because that was the family's first white wedding! Two sisters were already married, but not in the way my brother had. Normally, fathers of the bride and the groom stay aloof from the bridal procession until the end of the pageantry. Excitement galvanised my father into performing an incredible dancing stunt that we had never seen him doing before that occasion. What was the significance of this?

The moment of joy that was displayed by my father on my brother's wedding day lasted for months in our memories before it was interrupted by a dark spell. My father became ill in June while the joys of the wedding in March were still the talking point. This was at a time when the youngest three of us were always talking about the wedding in terms of wanting to do the same thing when we grew up to our brother's age. We even expressed wishes that we could do better to impress our father who was so supportive and believed that he would do the same thing at our respective weddings if they happened in his lifetime. Apparently, if wishes were horses, beggars would ride, but there was nothing of the sort in real life. A sorrowful situation was beginning to engulf the family as my father's illness resisted treatment at the Mission clinic where the nursing sister tried her best to turn the tide. For my part, it was a time when I was riding high on the wave of excellent performance in Grade 5, looking forward to traversing the field of education to the highest limits. That optimum temperature of happiness and excitement dropped suddenly when tragedy struck while we were taking everything for granted. My father passed away on 28 August 1954. That day was the most devastating trauma for all of us in the family, especially for the youngest three of us: Meshach Grade 6, John Grade 4 and I Grade 5. I felt as if the sun had switched to rise from the West and set in East. In the circumstances, the future looked bleak, as everything turned tasteless and unpalatable. We were still hoping to obtain some more information about our history, as father seemed to be a fountain of undiluted knowledge about the African kingdoms mentioned at the beginning.

Following the death of my father, we thought that was the end of our schooling and loss of our main fountain of information about the African past and prospects for the future. Contrary to our fears, we were assured in a formal way that the elders (father's brothers and sister) confirmed that father told them that the cattle should be used as the source of funds to pay our school fees until we had "finished." Our eldest brother Moya was given responsibility to ensure fair management and distribution of cattle amongst all his siblings. My mother had her own cattle that remained untouched so she would benefit from them without interference from the children. For all intents and purposes, the assurances removed the uncertainty that had engulfed our minds when our father died.

Following the above-mentioned decision, we continued attending school as if no disaster had happened in the family. I proceeded to a new school and went through Grade 6, in 1955, up to Grade 8 in 1957, at Zinyangeni Mission. The Mission, also founded by the London Missionary Society (LMS) in 1916, was the centre of all the lower primary schools of LMS. Initially, I was supposed to stay in the boarding but, close to the beginning of the first term, it was decided that I should stay with relatives as a day scholar. Undoubtedly, Lower Primary School of Dimpamiwa opened a new chapter in my life by instilling a sense of optimism about success through education. The excitement that was generated by learning new things at Dimpamiwa ignited a torch of hope as it equipped me with some shock absorbers with which to take on more challenging bumpy situations. For instance, as a child I believed mainly what I heard from my parents and was cautious at accepting the sweets of knowledge from strangers but, as I progressed up the ladder of learning, teachers ceased to be strangers and learning new things was no longer frightening. Competition with other pupils in all spheres became even more exciting. I marched confidently into Zinyangeni Mission School with a dream of success at the end of the educational conveyer belt.

I was very much upbeat about the prospects of going to a boarding school because I had heard a lot of interesting things about it from my eldest brother, who was a boarder for eight years. Clearly, the change to becoming a day scholar poured cold water on my eagerness to attend the Zinyangeni Mission School

Nevertheless, I had to gear myself for the new environment and to stay with relations away from home. I focussed on what I had come to do at the new school. At the lower primary school I sailed through at the top of each class from Sub A to Standard 3 (Grade 5). In Standard 4 (Grade 6), things changed. Here, I met with many pupils from several feeder schools, who were top of their classes, too. So, there was a fierce battle for the top of the class right from the start. Our teacher, Mr Albert Malikongwa, was a born teacher in that he inspired everyone to aim high, not only in the class, but also in life. He drove the whole class of 38 to a 100% pass at the end of the year, which was quite an achievement on his part and for us. But for the first time, my class position went down a couple of steps, in spite of my having raised the bar considerably in every subject.

In the middle of 1955, I got a shock to be informed that my younger brother, John, had disappeared and his whereabouts were unknown. Yet he was so brilliant in class, always taking first position in all examinations. As if this was not enough, in October of the same year, my brother Meshach passed away after a short illness. Upon hearing about the death of Meshach, John returned in December 1955 to mourn his brother, and then went away again because he felt home was no longer the same. Indeed, it was not the same without our most beloved brother, Meshach. He was our "sergeant major" amongst the three of us at the lower end of the family hierarchy as he linked us with the elder siblings and parents in terms of the flow of vital information and instructions. Unlike a military sergeant major, he was gentle and full of humanity in his brotherly leadership style. He was able to combine decisiveness and gentility in guiding us to perform family duties both in the fields and elsewhere. Above all, he was well informed about things we were supposed to know, in such a way that we did not rely on our peers on matters of customs and traditions affecting young people of our age because he had it all from older brothers. His untimely departure left us in a void that has never been filled. So, all these devastating tragedies left me bewildered and unsure as to how many more of us were going to be taken away by a similar fate. The loss of my immediate brother was so mind-boggling and unsettling that I spent some time wondering whether there was a killer curse that had come to sweep away the Mahlathini family. Our sister, who was born two years before Meshach, had passed away more than a decade before, so my mind began to build a picture of some spell that was sweeping down the line of siblings towards the last of us. I missed my brother so much that I hardly believed he was gone forever.

However, my mother, noticing that I never let go of my brother's shadow, counselled me in the same way as she did after my father's death. She strongly advised me to get on with what I was doing without thinking too much about all these disastrous losses of father and brother. She told me about the loss of her eldest brother who died on the eve of getting married, but that tragedy had not stopped the rest of the siblings from continuing with their lives. It took some time before my mother's advice eventually sank into my mind. In any case, it was imperative to take her advice seriously for my wellbeing and the pursuit of my education.

The home where I stayed during my year in Standard 4 belonged to Mr Aaron Mpazvirio Mpofu popularly known by his nickname, 'Mafotola'[9]. He and his wife, Velina, (whom we respectfully called "Aunty") were ex-teachers of my eldest brother and sister. He earned the name of Mafotola from pupils because he always threatened to "dent" (fotola) anyone who did not do as told. In reality, he never dented anybody because his disciplinary measures never went beyond the threat. The couple owned a general dealer store and a bus service that plied the Nkayi to Bulawayo route via Zinyangeni Mission. At the same time, they owned a small farming plot in what was called the Native Reserves (Communal Lands). There were three of us who stayed in uncle Mafotola's home from different families. In this home, there were five siblings, four girls and one boy about my age. We worked in the fields from land preparation during winter and spring leading to actual planting in summer. The lady of the homestead was the "commander" of all operations, as she set a time table that we had to follow without faltering. The time table started soon after school and ended after the fall of dusk. School time finished at 16h.00 and the time for us to do our field work started at 16h15 and we were expected to adhere strictly to it. The distance from the school to the homestead was one-and-a-half kilometres. In essence, this was very appropriate training for young people to prepare them for the future. The main advantage of staying in Uncle Mafotola's home was that I gained proper skills in agriculture which contributed considerably to my constant interest in farming. Managing a family's production levels needed toughness combined with humanity, as uncle Mafotola demonstrated. In that home, Aunty was very tough in demanding measurable results of work in the fields, but generous with the other necessities of life. In contrast, Uncle Mafotola was very gentle and endowed with a motivating sense of humour when he worked with us in the field. Under his watch, we worked less than twelve hours during school holidays and weekends contrary to what the "commanding" lady of the house required, because he wanted us to rest and have time to do other things in the spare time before the end of the day. But most of the time he was away on business and so his style of management and working were scarcely practised.

Nevertheless, there were other tasks that were too cumbersome and dangerous for us. For instance, when the crops ripened, the three of us harvested and carried the produce with an ox-cart which we pulled by hand. Pulling the two-wheeled cart was the most difficult operation of the whole process because we did it on a rough surface which had already been tilled, with large boulders that constantly tipped the cart up and down in a menacing way, all the way to

---

9

    one who can "dent" a metal object with a fist

the unloading point about 200 - 300 metres distant. This was very unnerving. During the school holidays we were not allowed to go to our homes, but worked full time from sun rise to dusk every day except Sundays. In the 1955 farming season, the yield rose from just four tonnes the previous year to twenty five tonnes of grain from a plot of five hectares. That was a record yield and the highest tonnage ever in this home's farming history. There was a half-a-tonne of ground nuts - also a record yield. The two parents appreciated that marvelous achievement by three school boys who were not full-time employees. After our departure, we were informed that our record yield was never repeated. I met the elderly couple in 1998 and they confirmed that our record was still standing without and prospects of being reached. They are both deceased. The accumulation of knowledge in farming in uncle Mafotola's fields and the difference in styles of command over his workforce remained in my memory for many years and I was to apply them in some other ventures as we shall see later.

For Standard 5 (Grade7) in 1956, I was admitted to the school as a boarder, and to an arrangement in which students managed each other (through a prefect system) after school till the following morning. This was very instructive in terms of the way we did our homework and prepared for the following day without a teacher's guide. The early days in the boarding were hell fire as there was horrible practice of initiation for newcomers. We were tormented by the bullies, who used all sorts of torture, from mid- January to the end of March. On the 1st April we were "baptised" with stale gravy of beans mixed with stale soup and other rotten substances. After this we were declared duly belonging to Zinyangeni Boarding School by the leading bullies of the school. This was the nastiest experience of my schooling life. When I passed from Grade 6 to Grade 7, I thought the status of "newcomer" had been behind me since Grade 6, since I was already a pupil at that school. I was wrong because day scholars were hardly bullied as there was very little time or space for bullies to do this without the teachers noticing it. In the boarding school, the students were normally alone from 4pm to 7.30 am. So there was plenty of time and space for the bullies to have a field day over the newcomers. The prefects did not stop it because they too had gone through the same grinding mill when they were newcomers. They regarded it as a long-standing tradition of the Mission. But the following year I teamed up with three other learners to stop the ill treatment of "newcomers" and we succeeded in banning it altogether. We proclaimed that it was forbidden permanently and we asked those who were returning to the boarding facilities after we were gone to enforce the proclamation. Apparently they did, and the ill-treatment newcomers remained forbidden at Zinyangeni Mission as originally ordained by our generation of boarders of 1956 to 1957. The rationale was that the tormenting practice was a cultural abomination that should not be allowed in a place of learning as it caused so much pain and humiliation of newcomers without any reasonable justification. The majority agreed with this line of reasoning and the interaction between older students and newcomers was transformed into new tradition of harmonious relations.

A Teacher "bites" our ears

In regard to our education, we were delighted that our brilliant teacher, Mr Malikongwa, was the geography master for all classes from Grade 6 to Grade 8. That was good for us because he was such a capable motivator. Besides matters of teaching, Mr Malikongwa was a fountain of information about political developments in our country and the rest of Africa. On the western part of the map of Africa there was a country called the Gold Coast, a British colony, but during the first half of 1957, Mr Malikongwa instructed us to change that name to "Ghana" on our map because the country had become an independent African state in the March of that year. He went on to explain the process and the stages through which the country had gone to achieve its independence. In this connection, similar freedom movements were striving to achieve the same goal in the rest of the colonies in Africa, including our country, as signified by the increasing demands to become independent from our colonial masters. He cited some of the leaders in the anti-colonial struggle such as Dr Kwame Nkruma, Prime Minister of Ghana at the time, Jomo Kenyatta, leader of the Kenya African National Union in Kenya, Chief Albert Luthuli of the African National Congress in South Africa, as well as the birth of Southern Rhodesia African National Congress (SRANC) led by Joshua Nkomo and James Chikerema in February 1957.

Photographs of Ghana, its flag and its leader were pinned on the wall of our classroom alongside those of the other Commonwealth countries and Mr Malikongwa explained further that independence had not been granted on a silver platter to that country. His description of Ghana's attainment of independence injected a dose of excitement and hope about our own country, especially as there was already a movement demanding freedom as the Ghanaians had. He spoke in a manner to indicate that Ghana had triggered an anti-colonial wave throughout the British colonies in Africa. He described Dr Nkrumah as "a man of letters", which we took to mean highly educated, as it was self-evident from his title. For me, this new knowledge marked a dawn in my interest and understanding of politics of the Africans' quest for political freedom through education. At that time, I was a school prefect responsible for time-keeping in the entire school, except for the girls' dormitories, which meant I was part of a youth leadership which kept order in the whole school. In this new phase in my acquisition of political knowledge of colonisation and decolonisation, an interesting equation was beginning to emerge. At home, my father had recounted the history of the defeat of Africans by British colonialists, but in school I learned of the dichotomous picture, not only of defeat but of the efforts of the Africans in seeking to regain their countries from the colonialists. Having gone through all sorts of rough and tough situations, I had gained so much self-confidence that I was convinced that my educational endeavour was on a smooth trajectory and that made me look forward to achieving an advanced level of political understanding not just for knowledge's sake, but as a tool for attaining our freedom, if I finished school before independence. As early as at primary level we had the privilege to hold debates every Saturday evening on any subject, but there was not much depth at that level because of the limited sources of information available to us. We focused on the forced removal of people from their ancestral lands which we had witnessed ourselves, mourning our powerlessness and the loss of our most fertile ground. Our main sources of knowledge about the loss of our country to the British were our fathers. Even so, in our debates, we expressed hopes that at the point of finishing our education, the country might be free like Ghana. We even went further to count the chickens before they were hatched by telling each other what we would do in a free country. But we also debated about other pertinent issues such as culture, Christianity, and education. The students' age range in Grade 8 was 14 to 20 years among both boys and girls, which means that we were able to grasp all material issues that Malikongwa shared with us although in a somewhat simplified form. What we were told was insufficient to provide in-depth guidance on the principles and processes which drove the colonial state and the forces opposed to it.

CHAPTER TWO

HORIZON OF ENLIGHTENMENT EXTENDED AT SECONDARY SCHOOL

After passing Grade 8 at Zinyangeni Mission at the end of 1957, I proceeded to another London Missionary Society (LMS) School as it was a tradition in the LMS Missions to keep their best students within their circuit. In this way, I was admitted for Form 1 at Nyathi Secondary School in 1958 about 80 kilometres from Nkayi where I completed my 'O' Level Certificate in 1961. Its historical significance was that it was the first Mission founded by Robert Moffat in 1859 with the permission of King Mzilikazi. The school was a truly cosmopolitan institution in that it admitted students from all over Southern Rhodesia (Zimbabwe) as well as from the other Southern African countries such as Northern Rhodesia (Zambia), South Africa, Bechuanaland (Botswana), Nyasaland (Malawi), Tanganyika (Tanzania), Basutoland (Lesotho). The social composition of the students in the school was significantly pan-African in content and form. As the latter part of the 1950's to early 1960's witnessed the rapid rise of African nationalism in Central Africa, the assembling of learners from different parts of Southern Africa was also a significant phenomenon as it provided the opportunity for cross-fertilisation of ideas and sharing knowledge about peoples of the region. I do not think that the Missionaries deliberately assembled all these diverse learners to enable them to brew up a conspiracy to overthrow colonialism. But that is exactly what happened at Nyathi Secondary School and other secondary schools for many years from mid 1950s to the demise of colonialism in the British colonies in Southern Africa.

The political turbulence that was shaking the shackles of colonialism in Southern Africa in the late 1950s to early '60s, reached momentous levels of strength in organizational terms when I was at Nyathi Secondary School. That was the period during which African nationalism in Zimbabwe crystallised into a dynamic motive force of African freedom movement for a definite purpose and a definite line of action to pursue not only demands for racial equality in law, education and health but, more importantly, in the goals of self-determination based on one man one vote (adult universal suffrage). It was a form of renaissance that reawakened the old and enlightened the young to aspire to be free from colonialism by all means possible. It touched everyone in towns and villages in the countryside regardless of their age and station in life in terms of realising our identity as Africans; a black race that was oppressed by a white race on the grounds of the colour of the skin. While colonial authorities were regarding the natives as segmented tribesmen without a common cause, the Africans saw themselves as an oppressed black indigenous nation on the verge of waking up to change the power relations by attaining majority rule based on one man one vote (universal adult suffrage). Colonial authorities, who apparently did not expect unity of what they regarded "fragmented tribesmen," were alarmed by a new trend of African nationalism and felt threatened by the wave of anti-colonialism. On the other hand we, the students, were excited and motivated by the call to regard one another as Africans rather than as different tribes in themselves. The most exciting aspect of all of this was the brightening prospects for regaining our country from the colonialists as a united nation.

We deeply appreciated the fact that the Missionaries at in the LMS circuit in general and Nyathi Secondary School in particular allowed the evolution of a tradition of free expression of views through debates every Saturday evening. The tradition enabled us to develop considerable debating skills on a ranging field of issues. At the same time we gained some degree of political knowledge because we had to obtain facts from the field beforehand to feed into our debates thus, landing ourselves on the real world of complex and conflicting interests and claims concerning both the oppressed Africans and our European rulers. It was at these debates where we were able to ventilate our sentiments on any issue pertaining to how Africans lost their rights to participate in the governing of their country under colonialism. The debates took several forms for the purpose of minimising monotony in terms of presenting a variety of topics on each Saturday. There was a debate based on a selected topic whereby one panel of speakers spoke on the affirmative and another on the negative. This form of debate was popular because it was eventually opened to the floor for the rest of the time. The other form that generated lively exchange was a seminar where a couple of lead speakers delved into intricacies of a subject without formal opposing sides. It started off with presentations from a panel with an aim of reaching consensus on an issue on the table. The rest of the house contributed until a consensus was reached on the subject of that seminar. Seminal topics ranged from cultural matters all the way up to political matters in the real world. Here students could express their genuine opinions unlike in the structured debates where some participants found themselves on the side that compelled them to express views that were not necessarily theirs but for the sake of a side that they were placed on.

In all the forms of debate there were some students who excelled in all kinds of debates while others were eloquent in matters of African liberation in formal debates and informal discussions in different corners of the school. In all of these there was one student who was first among equals in terms of ability to elucidate complex dynamics concerning the bone of contention between the African nationalists and the colonial authorities. Such an outstanding political torchlight in the school was Aleke (Alick) Banda (Malawian). He was well informed and articulate on the broad issues of political freedom and justice as propounded by African leaders like Dr Kwame Nkrumah and other contemporary stalwarts on the continent. He was alert to the 'winds' of change (which were later highlighted by Mr Harold Macmillan, British Prime Minister, on a visit to Apartheid ruled South Africa in 1960) in the form of a decolonisation process in Africa. It is without doubt that Aleke's influence played a major role in contributing to students' understanding of African nationalism at Nyathi Secondary School at that time. I became delighted to come to a school where political issues of the African Continent were so hotly debated fearlessly and openly by students. This was enough to raise the temperature of my motivation to new heights together with giving full support to the cause of African majority rule project in each of the colonised countries in Africa. It was through taking part and listening to fascinating debates and informal conversations among students that my interest in the politics of freedom solidified. For me it was a pleasant opportunity to be in a school that helped me to broaden and deepen what I had acquired from Mr Malikongwa at primary school regarding African nationalist politics of emancipation from colonialism. When I was in Form 1 in 1958 Aleke was in Form 111 but at that level, his analysis and intellectual portrayal of political issues proved him a motivating firebrand in his own right yet he was just a teenager like all of us in the school. During the debates his delivery demonstrated that he had a sound grasp of how Africans suffered from injustices of colonialism in terms of deprivation and racial discrimination that created unequal rights and freedoms between blacks and whites in the same country. He had a profound understanding of the legitimate aspirations of the African people in their quest to be free from a repressive system that denied them participation in governance of the country. He focused on factual issues in a calm manner without fuming with bubbling emotions or exaggerated claims and unrealistic promises. He usually stressed the point the road to freedom would be rough and dangerous as white resistance against majority rule was powerful and strong,. Therefore, those who chose to resist oppression should be committed and courageous to challenge the mighty machinery of colonialism

When the Federal Government and the three territorial governments banned the three ANCs in 1959, they all reorganized under new names within a short space of time (Blake, 1977). Southern Rhodesian government went further and banned the Southern Rhodesia African Students Association (SRSA) of which Aleke Banda was Secretary General (I was one of the witnesses of the banning because I was a member of SRSA through our branch which was ordered by school authorities to be discontinued only to resurface in another name overnight). At that time Aleke was in Form 1V (due to complete "O" Level that year) and expecting to pass with distinctions for which he and the school would be proud and, most probable, he could have left the school with a trail of new impressive records of achievements in the School. Nevertheless, that was not destined to happen as Aleke was picked up from school by two plain clothes Special Branch detectives in one morning of a March day in 1959 and sent to Nyasaland (Malawi) for detention. The rest of the students were shocked by the arrest of Aleke, a student who was so humble and totally free from crude behaviour. What did he do to deserve arrest in front of the teachers and students? Our initial reaction was not only shock but also dismay and anger as we did not understand why a secondary school student could be arrested without having committed an offence. The arrest left the students visibly shaken and petrified by such a brazen arrest of their colleague for no definable crime except his desire for the freedom of the African people from the yolk of colonialism.

The Principal, Mr Kenneth Malthus Smith, was asked about the arrest but he took cover by saying he had no power to question the government on security matters. We were not satisfied by the answer. The arrest of Aleke Banda was a landmark in the annals of my political history as a citizen of Africa in general and Zimbabwe in particular because it gave me the impression that under colonialism Africans had no rights to ventilate their views on what they felt about being excluded from governance in their own countries. It ignited a new fire in my mind the way I began to view the ruling authorities in my country at that time. When I was at Zinyangeni Mission (primary school) many people used to refer to the Europeans as **Abezalokukhanya**[10]. To unpack the kind of light they were perceived to have brought to our country would consist of Western systems of social development such as education, health technology, agriculture, land use and management, industry and commerce, science and engineering, **Christianity, etc**. But their harsh response to the legitimate demands of the indigenous peoples threatened to quench that perception because they treated Africans without civility and decorum commensurate with civilised standards that they were applying amongst themselves. An African began to feel like a stranger in his/her country as he/she was regarded as a trouble maker (eg over 200 national and regional leaders of ANC were detained without trial in Southern Rhodesia: **African Daily News, March 1959**) who deserved no rights of any definition in the system of colonial society. Banning a student association and arresting its Secretary General for detention without trial was incompatible with definition of **Abezalokukhanya** because it created an impression that we had

---

10

    vectors of enlightenment/civilisation

no rights or freedom to say what we felt about prevailing racial domination in our country. It was an act of 'turning the light dim' that left us groping in the dark in terms of whether Africans were or were not entitled to civil liberties such as those that were being expatiated to us in our history class. Clearly whites, as a ruling race gave themselves the privileges to enjoy the freedoms and rights such as freedoms of speech, association, choice, dissent, ownership of land (through legalistic mechanisms such as Land Apportionment Act, Native Affairs Act, Master and Servant Act, etc) (Wikipedia, Politics of Rhodesia, 2013). It was deprivation of these rights and freedoms that caused us to be angry and look deeper into the injustices of the system for the purpose of challenging it. We began to think about long term issues regarding what strategy to adopt in order to contribute to a movement for attaining self-determination in our country. We swiftly took steps to discourage young people from calling whites **Abezalokukhanya** because their system was identified with repressive mechanisms (eg discriminatory legislation and exclusive governance) that demonstrated the opposite of **"ukuhanya"** (light) for Africans. This view concerning the colonial government's injustices against Africans exclude missionaries because they were noted not only for promoting education in African areas, but also for allowing young people in schools to debate freely any topic of their choice. Contradictory application of civilized standards by government on one hand and missionaries on the other was a very interesting picture in terms of which one was the source of the impetus for Africans to resent and resist the colonial system and which one strived to turn them into subservient subjects but failed.

In any case it was on the basis of this perception that I began to suspect that colonialism in its nature was a political edifice to provide and sustain privileges for European settlers to the exclusion and expense of the indigenous peoples who were denied a fair platform for peaceful negotiations for participation in a democratic system. I started pondering on whether the reason why Africans in Kenya and Algeria resorted to violence to gain their independence was because the colonial authorities were unwilling to listen to their demands. So, I thought, Kenyans adopted a violent campaign led by Jomo Kenyatta to challenge colonial authorities to come to their senses. At that time a more interesting case was in Algeria where French authorities banned a nationalist party in the 1930s but its frame went underground only to emerge as a more militant organisation, the Front for National Liberation (NLF) which formed a government in exile to launch and wage armed struggle with the support of those structures created by its banned predecessor (Wikipedia, National Liberation Front (Algeria), 2014). When I thought about these examples I felt my attitude hardening further against colonial authorities as I digested and internalised the aforesaid approaches as legitimate methods for waging a freedom struggle against stubborn repressive regimes. At the time of Aleke's arrest at Nyathi Secondary School, Jomo Kenyatta was still in detention in Kenya and we increasingly became inspired by his leadership of the Mau Mau. But we had no details of how the Mau Mau was organised to the extent of causing worries in the Colonial Office in London and Nairobi (Wikipedia, Mau Mau Uprising, 2013). The question still remained for us: if the colonial authorities did not tolerate an open campaign for majority rule, what was the option for the Africans to gain their freedom? Was it Mau Mau or the Algerian model of struggle or any other revolutionary course that could lead to freedom? We finally answered this question.

We also heard about the Cuban revolution that had just happened about a couple of months before the ANC was banned in Southern Rhodesia. Newspapers reported that the Cubans took two years of fighting to overthrow the repressive dictatorship of Batista. Some students had followed the trend quite closely until victory so it was quite interesting to hear that a young lawyer (Fidel Castro) and a medical doctor (Che Guevara) underwent military training to undertake an armed revolution to overthrow a national dictator (Batista) (Wikipedia, Cuban Revolution, 2013). When debating international affairs, Cuba was mentioned by several speakers until it became politically fashionable to highlight it as a model of struggle against dictatorship. But the details of how Cuban revolutionaries did it were too scanty for us to compare with our situation; yet on the other hand the youthful age of the leader (Fidel Castro) of the revolution was quite motivating for young people of our age. We read all this in local newspapers such as The Rhodesian Herald and the Bulawyo Chronicle during January 1959 but there was nothing that we wanted from those plain reports.

However, having discussed Aleke's arrest exhaustively, we settled down to reality. At that point we felt that the arrest added more fuel to the fire of anti-colonial activism among students in the school. We all wanted to keep the momentum of political activism going so as not to let Aleke down in this regard. So, instead of becoming demoralised by the government's show of power over its opponents, we became more motivated to take and follow Alake's ideas of the total liberation of Africa by all means possible. We came to know that none of the other leaders of the national student organisation (SRSA) was arrested for detention. The axe had fallen on Aleke Banda alone from this organisation. Apparently the colonial authorities got the information about his vibrant articulation of freedom politics from the school authorities because they never expressed disconcert over Aleke being the only student arrested in Southern Rhodesia. They should have been worried by losing one of their top brilliant students in Form 1V at the time of his arrest. The main issue that should have caused concern on the part of the school authorities was the fact that he was due to write GCE 'O' Level examinations in seven months' time from the date of his arrest. We could not see how Aleke could have harmed anybody if he was left to write the examinations in the School without official disturbance. Above all he was a reliable house prefect in terms of enforcing School rules fairly to all students with absolute objectivity, so the gravity of his case against the state was weak in terms of capability to harm anybody.

However, after the SRSA ban, its Nyathi branch had to change its name to be called the Inyathi Students' Association (ISA) led by another firebrand, Abel Chanda (from Zambia), a very fine speaker on matters of the African cause of freedom. But at times Abel would be overcome by anger as he spoke furiously about the wrongs of colonialism yet Aleke hardly spoke with anger nor exhibited fuming emotions regardless of how touching the subject was. He was always cool and calm in his eloquent expression of views or presentation of arguments during debates. He never used vulgar or threatening expressions as he always unleashed free flow of expressions that were loaded with constructive meanings whether or not he was attacking colonialism as a repressive system. There was a lot to learn from Aleke's humane methodology of using powerful expressions to express his disgust over the wrongs of colonialism without the slightest flash of derogatory smear against adversaries.

School turned into a practising ground for subterranean political activism

It is worth while taking note of the fact that in the post-World War 2 the wave of demands for freedom from colonialism was in vogue not only in Asia but in Africa, too, and this, preceded by successful anti-colonial movements in Asia and West Africa, should have made Rhodesian authorities realise that the freedom movement in that country might be part of the unstoppable phenomenon of the time to bring colonialism to an end. They were fully aware that African citizens of Rhodesia had been excluded from political power against their will since 1893. The sources of information concerning the strength of anti-colonial trends were the same for all subjected peoples in the colonies. We recall that teachers talked about these matters right in the mid-1950s signifying that ruling politicians should have been more informed in this regard. Surprisingly, colonial authorities decided to reject peaceful African demands as they deliberately brushed aside a richly motivated movement that propelled those demands. Post World War 11 quest for freedom in the colonies and everywhere was much in evidence and the colonial powers could not stop it by arrest and imprisonment of the champions of a just cause whose aims touched the masses deep and wide. African participation in the Second World War made them realize that the colonial powers in Europe were vulnerable in the light of the rise of two rival super powers, US and USSR that were anti-colonial system for different reasons (Crowder, 1975). After decolonization of India in Asia, in Africa the process began from Ghana and swept eastwards and turned south to engulf most of Sub-Sahara Africa but settlers in self-governing Southern Rhodesia, dominion of South Africa and Portuguese colonies regarded themselves as exceptions to the political trend of change because of their status conferred to them several years before. Rhodesian white settlers pinned their stance on the status of self-government of the territory since 1923. For them the final step was to attain independence similar to that granted by the British Government in South Africa in 1910. They were not concerned about problems of deprivation that were intensely felt by the masses of African people. At our age as secondary school children, we were already aware of chronic lamentations from our parents over loss of fertile land to the whites. The lamentations did not omit the very first loss of political power following their defeat by the British army that opened the way for white settlers in the country. It was at that grassroots level where ingredients of an explosive situation were located while the authorities dealt with leaders who merely provided the vents that should have alerted the authorities about a serious problem prevailing in the main body of the population at grassroots level. Instead of paying serious attention to the ventilated symptoms of deep-seated mass discount, they regarded the outspoken leaders as trouble makers who should be sent to jail hoping to quench the legitimate aspirations of the African people. My generation was part of the grassroots mass of the population.

The arrest of a student at the beginning of his development as a politician was meant to frighten all youngsters away from political involvement. But this did not work that way because soon after the brazen arrest of Aleke Banda a few of us noticed wide spread anger among students and that motivated us to be more enthusiastic in support of the Nationalist Movements. We felt that our support could become practical only if we created something that would be properly structured to keep alive the fires of freedom underground. This move actually demonstrates that the authorities descended on leadership without assessing or ignoring where the actual power lay, that is at grassroots level. The question was, how could a structured organization survive underground without risking detection and arrest like Aleke who was arrested without being involved in subversive activities? In conceiving a plan for an effective underground organisation, we did not have a proven reference framework or model as a guide of how to set up such a movement to challenge an unjust political system. We shall see in appropriate chapters, that banning of African political parties in succession seemed to have become a political tradition of the colonial authorities by which to silence the African voice. This forced the movement to go underground thus creating a situation of the need for a strategy similar to the Algerian experience.

As a matter of fact, reading from the local press, white Rhodesian settlers, like the French settlers in Algeria and Afrikaners in South Africa, had decisively resolved to entrench themselves in the country by having a firm grip on the levers of power to the exclusion of the African majority for an indefinite period of time. Their power was pivoted on economic resources that provided them with prosperity with Africans as glorified "spectators" of whites enjoying privileges and prosperity. For the authorities to ban nonviolent organisations (such as SRANC) demonstrated beyond any shadow of doubt that they were not prepared to give political space to the African majority unless the Africans gave themselves that space by other means than nonviolence. Their intransigence reminded me of what my father said about the entrenched power of Europeans in our country and that, therefore, only fire power could dislodge them.

The banning of the ANCs in the three territories of the Federation followed by arresting and detaining leaders plus a student (Aleke Banda) generated fumes of anger among all students in secondary schools. Most of the secondary school students were either in their mid to late teens or just passed the threshold of that phase of growth. Therefore they were able to understand the political trends and strands in the country. That is to say even though we were still young, we were mature enough to see no sense in the act of banning a peaceful political party and detaining its members just to clear more space for racial domination to thrive in the exclusion of the majority citizens from the apparatus of governance. It would appear that drivers of repressive systems like colonialism were too detached from reality because they did not pay full attention to what was behind real desires of the African people nor did they bother to understand their genuine discontent against discriminatory racial practice at every level of society. Their perception of an African was that of a docile person with limited intellectual capacity to distinguish between the nature of political illegitimacy of colonialism and legitimate entitlement of the indigenous peoples to regain their lost rights to govern their own country. The act of arresting a student in front of his peers without having committed a crime severely devalued the moral character of the colonial state in the eyes of young people. The arrest was seen by our generation as demonstrating that the colonial system was driven by people who were not prepared to appreciate and at least meet African demands half-way or indicate that they understood the presentation of principles that defined those demands. They did not even give some thought to the fact that such a brazen act in a school (populated by upper teenagers and above) could aggravate emotional distaste against the colonial authorities among young people who witnessed or heard about the arrest of one of their number. It showed that the authorities were either too distant from reality or they trusted use of brute force to put the indigenous peoples in line. Banning political parties and detaining people without trial created a perception of aggravated circumstances of repression that gave rise to consideration of invisible methods of resistance. In this regard, instead of just lamenting over what had happened we began to think of creating or forming something to ensure that Aleke's Pan-African approach to indigenous emancipation did not evaporate with his arrest. A few of us combined our thoughts on what to do and how.

One of my classmates and friend, Gershon Phangwana, had read about the Chinese struggle against the Japanese occupation and the nationalists (Kuomintang) lead by Chiang Kai Shek. He asked us if we had read anything about the formation of the Soviets before the revolution and how they were used by the Bolshevik Revolutionaries to drive an uprising in 1917. None of us had an idea about that until we were out of school. The Cuban revolution had just occurred. Even if it impressed us by taking two years to overthrow a dictator we had no details of how it was organised to achieve such a quick victory. We were looking for a minimal understanding of clandestine operations under dangerous conditions but without being detected. My younger brother, John, had just lent me his copy of **The Autobiography of Kwame Nkrumah (1957)** but there was not enough material on the underground modus operandi except for the political organisation and uniting mass organisations to rally behind a slogan of **"self-government now."** I had some idea about Algeria's war of independence and Nassar's coup in Egypt but no detailed information as to how they planned the campaigns. As stated above I had read an article about Algeria but it was about launching armed struggle in 1954 by a banned party that emerged as a Government in exile. That too was not clear on how a banned party prepared itself to emerge as an armed force although there were some hints on clandestine preparations. That made us interested to know more about the aspects of that clandestine preparation. I asked a friend in Bulawayo to find this information from the library or newspaper records like the African Daily News, the Chronicle' The Herald or Drum and Parade magazines. He found some reports from various sources on what was called "Algerian War" and picked up a few interesting lines and sent them to me in a summary.

The summary showed that Algeria's pre -armed struggle preparation entailed creation of underground cells by an Algerian nationalist party before it was banned by the French in the 1930s leaving the cells invisible but alive underground. The French authorities had arrested leaders, including Ahmed Ben Bella, of the liberation movement but the struggle raged on throughout the country. Such a reference was close to what we were looking for in our endeavour to form a secret political body. During our time at Nyathi School, armed struggle for national liberation was raging towards final victory in Algeria. My friend's note provided us with a useful summary that would give us some idea about an underground strategy for national liberation struggle. One aspect of the strategies that seemed appropriate to our need was the creation of underground political cells by an Algerian liberation movement which finished up banned by French authorities. After several decades a new party, the National Liberation Front (NLF), was formed to launch armed liberation struggle anchored by underground cells created by its predecessor. In this way it went further to strengthen its diplomatic front by forming a Government in exile that also had responsibility for waging the war inside Algeria. With such a status, guerrilla warfare enjoyed mass support from the populace on one hand and, at international level; they enjoyed diplomatic recognition by several governments, on the other. In our home situation, we noted the Southern Rhodesia African National Congress was banned without leaving underground cells unlike the Algerian model. So there was nothing to learn from it in this regard. For our purposes the phrase "underground cells" became of great interest to us because it defined how people could operate under some cover without being seen by authorities.

Since there was already a mainstream movement in each of the three territories of the Federation, there was no need for us to form a large scale movement. So we decided to confine ourselves to schools, if we could, to cultivate political consciousness among young people to enable them become part of the wave of national freedom movement through connecting to mainstream nationalist organisations in the three territories of the Federation. But if need be, the youth structures should be submerged below the surface politics to drive the struggle as an invisible force for action while the surface politicians remained responsible for mobilising resources for waging the struggle.

We continued to brainstorm on the nature and purpose of an underground movement until the end of 1959, thereafter, the process was adjourned until the following year. It took us nine months to reach complete agreement on the formation of an invisible movement in the school. When we returned to school in January, we were armed with a lot of ideas including Aleke Banda's Pan-Africanism and commitment to African liberation from colonialism. On this basis, we began to develop necessary justification, strategy, objectives, functional principles and organisational structure of an invisible organisation in the school. Having put together pieces of information about the Chinese mobilisation of the masses, high degree of sacrifice by Mau Mau in Kenya and NLF model of struggle in Algeria we thought the little that we had acquired gave us enough guide therefore we agreed to form an invisible organisation on the rationale that there were signs that the struggle was going to be tough and prolonged because the settlers would not voluntarily compromise their lucrative privileges with African demands for majority rule. We further agreed that the organisation should remain small without a written constitution or records of meetings such as minutes. The five of us formally established an underground movement named **"Invisible Black Stones"** (**IBS**). Its motto was: ***"The Youth of Africa Knows No Peril."***

In IBS everybody held some responsibility, as would be expected in a small organisation like it. We appointed Gershon Phangwana to lead the IBS. He was a soft spoken and unassuming fellow student but well informed and full of constructive ideas on the liberation struggle. Other founder members were James Kamanga (responsible for external affairs and information), from Malawi, a dynamic orator, with a captivating oration in debates and seminars; Douglas Tshabalala, integrated urban with rural students politically; was rich with what latter day peace builders call "none violent communication" in his interpersonal interactions whereby powerful points were coated in "diplomatic language;" Josiah Mpofu, encouraged music clubs in the school to compose and sing freedom songs, was reserved but a careful thinker, often cautious when dealing with sensitive matters, and myself, Joshua M. Mpofu (strategic matters and propagating the cause of freedom among other students), I believed in underground operations rather than glamorous or hazardous surface politics. It was necessary to be invisible because there were times of strategising on the probable use of force in the removal of colonialism. The methods of doing this had to be considered carefully without endangering the safety of the activists and collaborators.

The main objective of IBS was to clandestinely mobilise other students in a planned way to motivate and drive them to support the African Nationalist freedom movements in each of the three territories (*Southern Rhodesia* – **Zimbabwe**, *Northern Rhodesia* – **Zambia** and *Nyasaland* – **Malawi**). In this way we politicised virtually every student organisation in the school to ensure that they took the message of freedom to other youngsters wherever they were. We did all this by obtaining information from the mainstream political movements in major towns and feeding it systematically into our debates and informal discussions among the students in the school. All the topics for debates originated from IBS (behind the scenes) and fed to the Executive Committee because four of us occupied top positions in the leadership of the Debating Society. In this way IBS became the powerhouse of political information and knowledge thus playing a leading role (behind the scenes) in influencing and shaping the students' political alignment with the African Nationalist freedom movements in the Federation, especially Zimbabwe. The colonial authorities forbade the Nationalist leaders from addressing rallies in the rural areas. As a result information about the cause of national liberation tended to be scanty. In this regard, we moved towards filling what we perceived as a gap by mobilising other students to become the vectors to convey not only information about freedom but also to complement the urban working class in their link with rural peasants in political matters.

When the National Democratic Party (NDP) was formed, IBS linked up with that Party through a liaison officer, a Malawian working for the Chronicle newspaper in Bulawayo, some 80 kilometres to the south of Nyathi Secondary School. Our liaison officer constantly sent us a bunch of newspapers every week by post to keep us well informed about what was happening in the Federation in general and Southern Rhodesia (Zimbabwe) in particular. If there was extra information that was not in the papers he would write a fairly detailed letter in a report format. We made an effort to ensure that our activities were no child's play by instructing our contact person to link up with higher level of the NDP and he complied to our satisfaction by establishing regular personal contact with a member of the National Executive Committee of the NDP, Jason Ziyaphapha Moyo in Bulawayo. (Moyo was popularly known as JZ). He was informed that the body he was in contact with was operating strictly underground with the sole objective of galvanising young people to support the national freedom movement in the country. He was happy to keep it that way because the information that he got from us was encouraging as it was not some kind of an infantile political bubble in terms of strategies to cover and embrace large numbers in politicising young peoples in schools so that they could spread the "gospel" to others in the villages. His positive view of us was confirmed in the feedback from our contact and, eventually how delighted he was when I met him several years later in Bulawayo after I had joined the NDP successor, ZAPU. This link with JZ Moyo would last up to a comradely level in the armed struggle

At the end of each school year we elected the Executive Committee of the Debating Society to take their positions in the following year. Students usually chose colleagues that were debating enthusiasts. It so happened that four members of IBS were elected into the Executive Committee of the Debating Society for the 1960 school year; all of them were in Form111. I was elected Chairperson with a huge majority and so were the other colleagues in their respective positions. The rest of the members of the Executive Committee were Chemist Mawere, Deputy Chairperson, Gershon Phangwana (IBS) Secretary, James Kamanga (IBS) Critic (on language and correction of factual errors), Douglas Tshabalala (IBS) (Judge: quality of presentation and main points) Maninji Murumirwa Deputy Secretary, Miss Manguni Gwebu, and Miss Sibusiso Nkomazana were committee members. Chemist Mawere and Maninji Murumirwa were the only Form 1V students in the Executive, the rest were Form 111. Normally the Executive consisted not only of the best debaters in the school but also highly politically charged individuals. This particular one reflected Form111 of that year as the most politicised class to the extent that a few individuals Form 1Vs observed that "all Form111s think that they will be Prime Ministers at the same time." We took that as a joke because no one took it seriously but it said something about political consciousness of that class as it certainly became a political driving force in the school for the entire year. Note that four members of the Executive Committee were members of IBS thus strategically placed on the front bench to drive the politics of decolonisation through the formal and informal processes of the debates and seminars, symposia, model parliamentary debates as well as conversations at recess and leisure times. Josiah Mpofu was the only IBS member who was not in the Executive Committee of the Debating Society.

The Executive Committee of the Debating Society provided leadership in all matters of debates in the school as it planned and adopted the social timetable and topics for debates. At that time I was regarded as one of the outstanding fiery debaters in the school and most students seemed to enjoy my delivery on stage as their applause reached a crescendo when I finished debating, regardless of the topic of the day. I believe that it was my ability to capture practical facts and present them in their true perspective that earned me confidence of my fellow students as seen through the way I was elected Chairperson constantly until I asked to be rested during the second term of my final year at Nyathi Secondary School. In other clubs such as the Student Christian Movement (SCM) and Inyathi Students Association (ISA) Gershon and James held leading positions and helped to propagate a considerable amount of political flavour in those movements' debates and programmes. The SCM interacted with students in other schools on a wider scale countrywise, thus becoming a strategic networking web within student associations in the country

In my final year, we recruited and admitted more students into membership of IBS that we found to be in the same wavelength with us on political matters. When I stood down as Chairperson of the Debating Society at the end of the second term in 1961 (then in Form 1V), I was succeeded by Moffat Ndlovu (Form 111), who had just been added into the IBS membership as he had become one of the articulate young political thinkers in the school. During that year we admitted four more members to boost our strength and enhance capacity. At a point when we were cultivating Sekai Hove (now Mrs Sekai Holland, former Minister of National Healing Organ in Government of National Unity –GNU- in Zimbabwe: 2009 - 2013) we retreated before we informed her about IBS because of her attitude of ambivalence on armed uprising or revolution on grounds that she felt we were too extreme in our approach to anti-colonial struggle for majority rule. That was because one of us, James Kamaga liked to declare a slogan **"Africa for the Africans"** when opening and closing his delivery during debates. But Sekai was a live wire in her debates, especially in SCM debates. During formal and informal discussions she often took a controversial stance in political debates by expressing an opposing view on issues only at a point where people appeared to be moving towards a consensus. She would emerge abruptly from the ranks by taking an opposing intervention against a common direction of other debaters in any subject under review. In this way Sekai used to stir the tranquil waters into turbulent waves, a stance that re-enlivened the discussions on a topic of the day. But the effect of her intervention normally led to a different outcome from the one to which people were beginning to gravitate towards it before her intervention.

A clear example where people were in the same wavelength before Sekai' intervention was that since colonial authorities could not allow Africans to rise to power peacefully, leaders should begin to prepare for an armed uprising immediately. She vehemently opposed the adoption of violent methods of struggle before the neighbouring states became independent because there would be no launching pad for such a dangerous adventure. She expounded quite convincing grounds for opposing what she called "an uncalculated act, driven more by anger than by rationality" that would lead to calamitous consequences. She pointed out that those who advocated for an armed uprising without giving some thought as to how they could acquire military knowhow and the requisite resources with which to launch armed uprising were misleading others. So the outcome of the discussion was that the matter had to be put to rest until opportune time took its course.

Besides the school's tradition of free debates there was another catalyst for the development of a tradition of free political debating at Nyathi Secondary School. The school authorities permitted Fourth Form students to organise and stage a "Model Parliament" or "Parliamentary Model" that was based on the political traditions and practice of the British House of Commons. Students were encouraged to act as politicians like in the real world by forming "political parties" that competed for election of members of "Parliament." The election process was managed in a similar manner but not as in real elections as ours took a simplified format. The dormitories were delimited into constituencies where full scale campaigning behind a "manifesto" and canvassing for votes took place by aspiring candidates and their parties. A party that won with a clear majority in the "Parliament" formed a government and then presented a budget to the elected members of "Parliament" on Saturday evening in the presence of the entire audience of students, witnessed by teaching staff. An imaginary state was usually headed by a titular Head of State with an Executive Prime Minister who would appoint a Cabinet. Presentation of the Budget was followed by a robust debate between the governing party and the opposition party or parties.

For me a memorable occasion was that I found myself forming a 'political party' that was acting as close to a real one as possible in seeking election to a model parliament. In doing this I organised a team of like-minded students and, after intensive consultation and discussions, we emerged with a name "United Peoples Democratic Party" (UPDP). Gershon Phangwana formed another and James Kamanga also formed a third one. Note that the three of us were members of underground IBS but this time we were opponents. The three parties campaigned vigorously all over the student's residential dormitories. UPDP won but short of clear majority and that forced us to form a coalition government with James Kamanga's Party that enabled business of government to proceed according to a stipulated time table. The coalition enabled me to assume the position of "Prime Minister" and, in accordance with our coalition agreement; James Kamanga became "Minister of Finance." Gershon Phangwana was leader of the Opposition. A Finance Bill, tabled by Minister of Finance, would go through three stages of reading similar to those in the House of Commons but, of course all stages completed on the same day. With the fiery Gershon Phangwana leading the Opposition, and James Kamanga, master of oratory, Minister of Finance, the debate was superbly robust as both speakers pitched the level of debate to such heights that stimulated impressive and lively participation of backbenchers as they became keen to contribute and make the exchange a lively contest between both sides of the House to the delight of the audience. Some of the Teachers who attended our Parliamentary session were stunned by the calibre of secondary school students debating like serious politicians in the real world.

The imaginary state was usually an imaginary former colony that would have just won independence from Britain. We derived all this exercise from one of our text books on **"British Government and Politics"** and from an elaborate delivery by the History Master on the same topic including the historical shift of power from the monarchy to an elected House of Commons in Britain with Ministers appointed by a Prime Minister who became regarded as first among equals. This strand of history spelt out the development of democracy over a long period from the signing of the Magna Carta (1215) throughout the Reform and Parliament Acts leading to the current era of democracy in England. For us as students, the practice through a model parliament reinforced our understanding of the basic principles of a modern democratic system and how it developed to an institution that conferred and guaranteed fundamental freedoms and rights of citizens. In our debates, the colonial system failed the litmus test because it was not an embodiment of those rights and freedoms and, worse still, did not have an electoral system that was based on adult universal suffrage as propounded in the text book on British Government and Politics. Above all, most of the white settlers were of British stock therefore well cultured in democratic values yet they did not practise fully fledged democracy in Rhodesia by excluding Africans from the system of governance. They did not even place their system of governance on a progression mode towards attaining a fully-fledged democratic system in future. They closed it to themselves without considering the legitimate wants of the indigenous peoples in the country. I never understood how the Rhodesian British segment expected Africans not to raise objections to such an unjust system of racial domination which did not approximate the prevailing political traditions in their Mother country. As a matter of fact, I came to know that they were safeguarding the wealth that they had acquired by hook or crook through colonial plunder (including land seizures by settlers).

Debates like these actually connected us with the real world of political activism in the Federation in general and Zimbabwe in particular. In this regard we were able to find the difference between the practice of democracy in the UK and lack of it in the British colonies. A distinguishing feature in all of this was a racist rationale for excluding majority people from an electoral system and governance. That was then one of the main issues student associations discussed from time to time and gained a perception that colonialism was an unjust system because it gave all privileges to white people whereby they (ie whites) enjoyed a 'racially exclusive democracy' that excluded Africans more or less like Pericles' system whereby free men only had rights to participate in an assembly for governing Athens to the exclusion of women and slaves in ancient Greece. The similarity was that in Rhodesia's **"democracy for Europeans only"** was enshrined in the constitution through high voting qualifications and the Land Apportionment Act 1934 by which most public amenities before 1962 were labelled like: **"Europeans Only"** or **"Natives Only;"** to separate white citizens with full democratic rights and fundamental freedoms from deprived black African citizens. Management of public affairs like governing the country, towns and localities were in the hands of Europeans as if they were also labelled to reflect who was in power. All this left the Africans out in the cold like Periclean slaves and women, yet they were largely the suppliers of labour in the whole economy that generated wealth that sustained European privileged status.

It then became imperative upon all of us and the student associations to widen the debate so as to spread vital information on campaigning for attaining freedom from an unjust system of colonialism. Clearly our European rulers enjoyed some kind of exclusive democracy within the confines of their race colour. They hardly applied democratic principles that would have embraced all adult citizens in voting for a national government of the country as they did in their country of origin, (England) according to our text book. We were quite aware that in England democracy did not happen overnight. The process could be traced from the time of signing Magna Carta in1215 (Great Charter of the Liberties of England) when Barons caused the Monarch to accept principles that allowed them to enjoy certain rights and freedoms. From that time through several centuries of bitter struggle between social classes of progressive thought and the moribund classes of the old order eventually lead to far reaching political and juridical reforms till the attainment of democracy of a modern standard wherein all citizens enjoyed the same liberties and rights in all spheres of life. But it took a much shorter length of time for democracy to develop in other European countries and North America (because they did not spend time on "re-inventing the wheel" since the pioneer state, England, had accomplished that invention). Why was it impossible for Africans in Zimbabwe to take part in running the country, say from the early 1960s until it matured into a fully-fledged democracy where racial harmony could have become possible owing to unimpeded social interaction of races for all intents and purposes? The legalised separation of races that placed the Europeans on a domineering position over the Africans created a gap between them in which anger and animosity brewed into dangerous proportions that led to violent conflict in the long run. I could not see how double standards like those displayed by Rhodesian whites could fail to precipitate a grave situation of conflict at a certain point in time.

Issues like those stated above were recycled in conversations of youngsters as they shared information amongst themselves in and out of school. Part of the importance of discussing pertinent matters with members of students' associations was that members interacted with their home bases during the holidays, thus becoming crucial conveyors of political messages concerning support for the nationalist movements in championing the cause of African majority rule.

On their return from school holidays students gave very encouraging reports about work amongst other young people in the villages. As a matter of fact, we found that there were committees in the rural areas that worked quietly within the masses and they were delighted when we worked with them there especially to organise youngsters to support a current nationalist movement. All the student enthusiasts confirmed that in their Districts there were committees up to what was called area committees of the existing nationalist Party. This happened in spite of the fact that members of the National Executive of the nationalist movement were prohibited from addressing meetings in the rural areas. In spite of the restriction, structures of the movement were created in the rural areas during the life of the NDP, although they were not quite strong until the parallel referendum on the 1961 Constitution. Another factor that contributed to political awareness in the rural areas was the fact that most of urban workers had homes in the countryside thus making a crucial political link with the peasantry. The effect of this link was under estimated by authorities who trusted what they heard from chiefs. Some teachers also shared information with villagers as they got it from newspapers and radio broadcasts at home and from BBC.

As I was responsible for strategic matters, I had to be creative in terms of setting up a functional body that would be a catalyst in providing a wider forum where current affairs would be discussed informally. It was a question of how to stimulate students' enthusiasm to participate in such informal discussions in large numbers. For this purpose I came up with a simple plan which was readily accepted by my colleagues and the rest of the students. We formed an informal body (open to all students in the school) and called it the *Soviet Policy.* The name seemed to suggest that this was a revolutionary movement of a communist type. In practical terms it had nothing to do with the Soviet Union which was ushered in by the Bolshevik Revolution of 1917. To the astonishment of many students, its openly declared policy was about social life. Also, the political issues that were covered beneath the declared social life issues had nothing to do with communism at the time. According to its declared stance our *Soviet Policy* ostensibly focused on matters of morality and romance as it advocated for *"one boy one girlfriend"* and *"one girl one boyfriend".* This was a strategic camouflage because its underlying purpose was to attract students to assemble informally so that IBS would have an audience to motivate towards supporting the anti-colonial struggle in all the three territories of the Federation. Its "President" was a flamboyant and self-confident Agrippa Madlela, deputised by myself. The *Soviet Policy's* discussions at recess were informal but very popular and lively because they started off with matters of social life between boys and girls.

As most of the discussions were ostensibly about matters of love and romance, attendance and participation were very high and the debates were quite robust. The topical political issues could creep in as incidentals and suddenly generated live debates almost with the same enthusiasm as was the case in the romance matters. The rest of the students knew nothing about **IBS** but knew a lot about the informal *Soviet Policy* which was open to all students whether or not they agreed with a simple principle of *"one boy one girlfriend"* and *"one girl one boyfriend".* What enlivened the debate was that many students did not accept this notion in romantic relationships between boys and girls. An overwhelming majority of the boys opposed this on the grounds that it did not take into account the question of the period of "experimentation" and "searching for the right girl." To my surprise many girls argued against it too, describing it as unrealistic and superficial. This marked very sharp disagreements that generated very lively discussions during recess periods because the minority who supported the principle of 'monogamous' relationships also held strong views and thought-provoking questions that had no easy answers for the other side. The fact that this subject was discussed in a jovial atmosphere showed the keen interest the students had in the matters of love and romance between boys and girls. But the high level of participation suited **IBS'** purposes very well as it helped to reach as many students as possible. The forum became hugely popular amongst students in all the Forms in the school. Thus, becoming a crucial platform at which the students became informed about political trends out there in the country. In other words the forum delivered to us a large audience for our political topical issues during recess. Here political parties and their leaders were mentioned by their official names as well as their practical efforts to secure a constitutional conference to negotiate transition to majority rule.

For all intents and purposes whatever was the initial subject for discussion at the *Soviet Policy* gatherings, we made sure that we skilfully caused the discussion to gravitate towards the politics of freedom struggle and the whole question of lack of rights and freedoms under colonialism. For instance the question of fairness and justice was propounded by those who defended "monogamous" relationships between boys and girls. In this regard if a boy had several girlfriends with or without their knowledge by any one of them, there was an element of cheating which was regarded as unjust and unfair by some. The principles of fairness and justice could be easily used as window to bring in political issues in the form of examples of unjust practice and unfairness as exhibited by the colonialist double standard of preaching Christianity (with clear principles of fairness and justice) yet practising injustice over the Africans. Thus the debate could drift through suchlike angles towards the politics of freedom and justice in Africa which was lacking under colonialism because of the unfairness of the system to the majority. They could point out that sometimes injustices could cause fighting regardless whether between individuals or a state versas the downtrodden. In fact there were many windows through which the debate sneaked away from romance matters to political matters quite smoothly and effectively. This happened more frequently than less at recess periods. Sometimes we could let the debate dwell on romantic matters right up to the end of recess in order to avoid saturation of politics in the arena of informal discussions of the *Soviet Policy* because we feared it could lead to loss of enthusiasm in the popular matters of recess period. We were delighted that the mix of matters of romantic relationships and politics steadily shaped into a harmonious symbiosis in the fact they landed together as examples of how unfairness could hurt the adversely affected side because the other side might have abused power relationship to own advantage.

The subject of romantic love relationship had no analogical congruence with politics but it was basically a fantastic audience puller that we needed very much for informal discussions on political matters. The **Soviet Policy** was introduced by me as a motivating catalyst, having noticed that the students were enthusiastic in talking about love and romance in relationships between boys and girls. Most of them in the school were teenagers in search of knowledge on social life of love and romantic relationships and how they visualised the future from young age to adulthood. It then became clear that bringing them to the party via this subject of emotion would generate high level of participation and indeed it did. Actually it became a 'magnet' that pulled so many students into the arena where we wanted them to be: "political debates for action." Within a short period since the formation of underground **IBS** and its on-surface auxiliary, the **Soviet Policy**, the entire School was well politicised and united regardless of their diverse ethnic backgrounds or country of origin. Nyathi Secondary School became an academy of political knowledge and activism in all but name; in essence it was a practising ground for the real political battles yet to come in our different countries and localities out there. But some of the students, including Agrippa Madlela, became aware that the **Soviet Policy** had a lot to do with politics than just romantic matters. What they did not know was that there was an invisible organisation that was driving the whole process in the direction of politics.

As the political ground was already relatively fertile, there was very little difficulty in getting almost every student of the time to support the nationalist parties and their leaders in the three territories of the Federation. For example during the Sharpeville massacre in South Africa, the students paid tribute to those who were mowed down by the forces of Apartheid. Also, when the NDP leaders were arrested in Salisbury and Bulawayo, there was a mini uprising called **Zhi**[11] which swept across the City of Bulawayo like a tornado. It subsequently spread to other major towns such as Mutare, Salisbury (Harare), Gweru and Kwekwe. The students supported this phenomenon passionately to the surprise of the teachers. For instance in our class, the English lesson started late because there was an argument with the teacher about the rationale of **Zhi**. One student, Agrippa Madlela, stood up to say the cause of all of the uprising was that some people did

---

[11]

    down with the enemy

not see anything wrong with imposing themselves into "someone's home." The teacher countered his statement swiftly by saying Bulawayo was not some one's home. There was a jungle of hands raised as each students wanted to tell her their opinion. She picked the same one who made the assertion. With his voice vibrating with emotion, he said: "Africa is the home of an African and the intruder is the colonialist; that is why there is violent resistance against the uninvited intruder" The rest of the students applauded their colleague, to the surprise of the teacher. Realising that the atmosphere in the class was hyper- charged with disturbed emotions, she softened her tone and modified her attitude towards **Zhi,** as students went into some detail to explain the causes of Zhi. The atmosphere was the same in all the classes in the school, thus signifying the students' political consciousness about the injustice of colonialism upon Africans.

Before the end of my schooling at Nyathi, I was satisfied that most of the students of our period in the school would go out there and be disciples of the African national liberation movement in their respective countries during the holidays. Geshon Phangwana and I did a lot of political work at grassroots level in the villages among primary school pupils at Nkayi District. In collaboration with the students from Lupane District (120 km west of Nkayi) we formed the Shangane Advancing Students Association (SASA) that galvanised the young people and their parents in Nkayi and Lupane into activity, conscientising them on the politics of freedom from colonial oppression through education. The link person in Lupane was Johnson Mkandla, a very passionate champion for African advancement. This was to ensure that they cherished and pursued education to the highest possible level in order to liberate themselves from ignorance before looking far and wide. I was elected the first Chairperson of the Nkayi chapter of SASA, with Easter Ndiweni as Deputy and Gershon Phangwana as Secretary.

A local example of a highly educated person was Peter Sivalo Mahlangu from northern part of Nkayi. He had a BA and MA degrees in Education that elevated him to the heights of school inspector; probably one of the first African School Inspectors in the country. When I came to know about Mahlangu's achievements, I raised my ambitions beyond the level of my initial role models, the teachers that I referred to as **izikolas** when they descended upon Nkayi District in the late 1940s throughout the 1950s. Many more youngsters wanted to emulate him to reach those heights but we noted later that he was not politically inclined unlike, say, Welshman Mabhena, a holder of post Matriculation tannery certificate from Nyathi Boys Institute. Over a period of time, Mabhena would steadily develop into a formidable political figure at Nkayi District to become a local example of how an educated person had considerable depth in understanding the repressive nature of colonialism and why Africans demanded to be free from its shackles. We, too, believed that through education the young people could see the light that would give them focus towards acquiring knowledge with value to them and society. We propounded the view that becoming educated would enable them not only to carve up their careers but also share that knowledge with others to empower them to fight together for political freedom in their country. SASA was a surface student organisation whose constitution was submitted to the Nkayi and Lupane District Commissioners and they had no objection to it. So with official recognition we had a lee way to spread the message on political matters with education as a torch light of all endeavours in life. In our campaign, we succeeded in wedding education to political consciousness as two inseparable twin engines of progress for young people of "forestland."

We did all this political work before we met or saw any of the leading personalities in the African nationalist movement. We first learned about African Nationalist parties from teachers, especially Mr. Albert Malikongwa at higher primary school before we read about them in newspapers and magazines such the Bantu Mirror, African Daily News (edited by Nathan

Shamuyarira, a former Cabinet Minister in a liberated Zimbabwe), The Herald newspaper, Drum and Parade magazines. The African Daily News carried a lot of information about the National Democratic Party pertaining to the demands articulated by its leadership. The Bantu Mirror was quite brief on matters of African activism, although it was a selective conveyor of African news without critical editorial comments. The Chronicle and The Herald would report in far spaced occasions while the African Daily News had a story every day about issues of freedom for Africans. We read in the newspapers about African Nationalist speeches when they addressed rallies or news conferences to make exposition of injustices of colonialism and what freedom from colonialism would bring to the country and people as a whole. It was reports on speeches where principles and aims of the NDP were spelt out to the extent of inspiring us to support the cause of our country's liberation from colonialism, not the sight of personalities.

When the batch of our class finished at Nyathi Mission in 1961, we left a legacy of highly politicised youngsters in the school with IBS having grown larger in membership and gender inclusivity. Our successors at the School recruited more members including many girls in such a way that their gender mixed team became a formidable element in size and militancy in the school. Above all they were better informed about struggles in Africa, Asia and Latin America that motivated them to continue their political activism with enthusiasm. They left school in batches and automatically joined the main stream freedom movement in the real world of struggle in waves year after year after us. Some of the third generation of school leavers found us in the field nursing a banned organisation underground again. Quite a number of them finished up in armed struggle.

From all this I thought the Principal was not fully aware of what was happening in the school. But my testimonial, on the school report, with contrasting commendations from Boarding Master and Principal showed that the latter had observed something he did not like. The Boarding Master had written something like this: **"Joshua was one of the most well behaved boys in the school. His behaviour has been exemplary for other students to emulate"** But the Principal responded thus: **"I hate the Boarding Master's report! Joshua has been exceedingly engaged in extra-mural activities in an unacceptable manner in the school, therefore his behaviour cannot be described as exemplary"** The Boarding Master was black and Principal was white. I cannot speculate that the varying perceptions were based on race because I have no evidence of that. The only mistake I made was that I did not ask my colleagues in IBS about their testimonials. In my view, the Principal's expressed attitude towards my vocal disquiet about colonialism seemed to indicate that he might have contributed to Aleke's arrest regarding how the security branch got to know that he was the most politically hyper-charged student in the school. Contrary to the Principal's remarks, my schoolmates nicknamed me "Judge" a name by which they called me to this day.

As the quest for freedom steadily drifted towards a dangerous course for activists, it is essential to briefly revisit the origin and nature of the system that impelled us to work so hard to change it at all costs right from school days to adult life.

CHAPTER THREE

THE CONTEXT: ORIGIN OF THE PROBLEM IN BRIEF

Zimbabwe gained its independence from Britain in 1980 after a long drawn out national liberation struggle, which started off on a peaceful path in the 1950s but eventually became violent, owing to the intransigency of the Rhodesian authorities. I want to briefly revisit the creation and the nature of the colonial system that was developed from a gold-seeking company to a state driven political power house that became a guarantor of white settler privileges at the exclusion of the indigenous Africans. Literature abounds on the subject of Zimbabwe's colonisation and how the European settlers systematically developed it into their paradise as they gained political power after defeating Africans. Colonialism was not created through peaceful negotiations between invaders and indigenous peoples; it was violent as its drivers overthrew indigenous regimes by military means thus creating a system of political architecture characterised by built-in ingredients of violent conflict between the vanquished Africans and the victorious white settlers, who were legally called **Europeans** and Africans were coined **Natives.** After the defeat of the Africans, there was measurable tranquility in the country for more than half a century but, sixty years later, the tempo of resistance against colonialism intensified in spite of the growth of the state as an instrument of repression for nearly a hundred years. The accumulation of power and wealth on the part of the white settlers grew side by side with consolidation of repressive legalistic mechanisms of the colonial state and, as a consequence of this, the Africans and the colonial government finished up embroiled in a full blown warfare of liberation. What was the origin and consolidation of colonialism in Zimbabwe that became so repressive as to cause violent resistance by the Africans?

The answer to this question can be traced back from the well-known search for gold by Cecil John Rhodes on behalf of British economic interests in1890. After discovering gold in South Africa, Cecil John Rhodes, believing that there was a second Rand across the Limpopo River, hotly spearheaded the search for a second Rand through his British South Africa Company (BSAC). This way, Rhodes, then Prime Minister of the Cape Colony, heralded the colonisation of the country, for whose honour it was named Rhodesia. In his first major step he sent a team of concession seekers headed by Charles Rudd, his business associate. The territory that was believed to embrace the second Rand was occupied by Matabele Kingdom whose king was Lobengula, son of Mzilikazi ka Matshobana. With the assistance of some Missionaries who had visited the Kingdom during Mzilikazi's rule, Charles Rudd and his team entered Matabeleland for negotiations with King Lobengula. Apparently, Rudd secured King Lobengula's dubious consent to the concession in 1888 by enlisting Reverend C D Helm and John Smith Moffat, who were well known to Lobengula, to negotiate his entry and subsequent interpretation of the agreement from English to Zulu for King Lobengula. The verbal interpretation was done by Reverend Helm in both the negotiation process and the agreement from English to Zulu and vice versa for both parties. There are grave doubts that at that time Reverend Helm could have mustered enough Zulu Language to use it to interpret the legal terminology in the Concession to enable Lobengula to fully understand the principles and implications of the contents of the Concession.

For example, John Gunther (1955: **Inside Africa, Harper**) reports that Lobengula was swindled and cheated like a child. Gunther is one of those who believe that Reverend Helm may have omitted some of the key principles either deliberately or because he did not know enough Zulu to translate the full contents of the legal language of the Rudd Concession. On the part of Lobengula, neither he, nor his lieutenants, knew any phrase or clause in the English Language that could have enabled them to understand the fundamental principles of the Rudd Concession.

Nevertheless, a **Rhodesian government statement** (1978) was on the side of the view that contradicts the abovementioned assertion on Rev Helm's lack of proficiency in Zulu. The statement declares that Helm knew and spoke Zulu fluently therefore he translated for Lobengula clause by clause of the Rudd Concession. In that way, the King and his chiefs were satisfied with what they heard. The problem still remains that the material content of the Concession clearly gave the British South Africa Company (BSAC) carte blanche access to the entire territory Lobengula claimed to be under his jurisdiction. If that entire document was translated in full it is unlikely that Lobengula would have voluntarily agreed to surrender his territory and power to BSAC stock lock and barrel as we are made to believe. Herein rest grave doubts about the Rudd Concession's credibility and validity regarding whether it was a mutually comprehended document in terms of whether it was clearly spelt out in its entirety to Lobengula and his chiefs. It is highly probable that the actual agenda of BSAC remained hidden under the English verbiage that sounded as if the King and his people would benefit from the agreement, yet the main goal remained concealed under a camouflaging phraseology of English legal language that could not be translated into Zulu.

A late attempt to "rescue" Lobengula from Rudd's entanglement was made by a self-serving Edouard Lippert, who seemed to speak Zulu fluently and interpreted the Rudd Concession 'correctly,' but time was no longer on his side. Lippert's interpretation was substantially different from Reverend Helm's version. Thinking that this Zulu speaking Boer was on his side and would marshal other Boers to align with him to force the British out of his territory, Lobengula was misled into making another mistake by giving Lippert a Concession on land with which the latter finished up swindling the King by selling the concession to the BSAC, thus providing the Company, therefore Rhodes with a legal document to distribute Promised Land to members of the invading force. The Company's stranglehold on King Lobengula's territory could only be challenged by military means if ever that was feasible for the King at all. It seems that, there was no escape route for the Matabele King.

Whatever the case was, the matter was hotly desired by Cecil John Rhodes as he swiftly acquired the Royal Charter that granted him mineral rights and setting up administration in Mashonaland to run the whole country including King Lobengula's territory. Before the King realised the duplicity of the agreement, Rhodes (armed with a Royal Charter) had authorised rapid implementation of the principles of the Concession by sending an advanced team of military scouts in the name of hunting to open the way for a stealth invasion of the country. In 1890 a Pioneer Column under the command of Frederick Selous, with Colonel Edward Pennfather commanding a contingent of supporting troops entered the country without permission of the Africans. Pennfather exercised his men to be fully prepared for the task on a long march to battles north of the Limpopo River to show that Rhodes' priority was to seize and control the entire territory combining Mashonaland and Matabeleland in order to have free access to minerals and land in the entire territory. All those forces called pioneer column, hunters, Selous Scouts and the lot were part of a well organised military machine to take control of the aforesaid territory. Pioneer-driven invasion marked the actual beginning of the takeover of the country by Cecil John Rhodes on behalf of Britain in 1890. When Lobengula realised that what he was told verbally did not include a Pioneer driven scheme of things, he repudiated the Rudd Concession; but it was too late because Rhodes had obtained a Royal Charter giving the BSAC exclusive rights to mine and set up administration controlling a territory all around Lobengula's kingdom and Mashonaland. As a consequence tension developed between the King and the new authority administering the territory as defined in the Concession. Within Lobengula's army there was uneasiness and anxiety about lack of decisiveness to dislodge the settlers. Subsequently, a war broke out between the Matabeles and the colonial army in 1893. The two sides fought fierce battles with heavy casualties on both sides, but, the fire power of gun powder prevailed over the Matabele spears. This strengthened BSAC grip on the territory until a second uprising of 1896 took the settlers by surprise.

The 1896 uprising was the first people's war against colonialism in that the Ndebeles and the Shonas united for the first time to reclaim their country from European occupation. The impressive aspect of the 1896 war is the fact that when the chiefs in Matabeleland sent an emissary (Mkwati) to their counterparts in Mashonaland to get ready for anti-colonial onslaught on the settlers, he found that the Chiefs in Mashonaland, too, had reached an advanced stage of preparedness to fight the settlers. When Mukwati arrived in Mashonaland with the message for simultaneous uprising, he found the Chiefs ready and preparing to instruct their own emissary to go to Matabeleland with the same message. They were encouraged to note that there was convergence of purpose between both sides regarding planning to fight the settlers by military means. The emissary immediately returned to inform Ndebele chiefs that the Shona people were ready to attack settler institutions and settlements so the game was afoot. They, too, must attack more or less at the same time. Indeed, upon hearing the report that Chiefs and people in Mashonaland were ready to strike, Ndebeles too, became too excited to hear the good news from Mashonaland and they did not wait. The younger men swiftly stormed key settlements around Bulawayo towards the end of autumn of 1896 and the Shonas stormed Native Commissioners camps in Mazowe and Mangwende in mid-winter. Mkwati's regiment rapidly occupied Intaba zika Mambo (in the Midlands) and remained illusory for a long time before overwhelmed by devastating gun fire after settler troops recovered from shock. The surprise attacks escalated as they swept from west to the centre of the country and from the east to the centre, south and north. The shock waves sent many settlers to depart helter-skelter out of the country to South Africa. Isolated settlements were swept away by the uprising until Rhodes had to seek reinforcement from Britain when there was stalemate on the rocky mountains and hills throughout the country. The people-inspired war prolonged to 1897 until fire power of gun powder and dynamites once again prevailed over spears and bows and arrows of Africans. So the Africans were defeated again by the weapons that spat fire from a distance, thus outclassing the spear which required stabbing at close range and the arrow that could not match the velocity of a bullet towards a target. The African defeat was complete but not final.

The most striking significance of the 1896 African uprising is not just the battles against the colonial army and European settlements. It is the nature and causes of the uprising that have landed themselves to scrutiny by historians, social scientists and political analysts. Most of these academic competitors have nothing to do with finding the nature of the circumstances that brought the Africans together against a common enemy other than to exhibit their methodological and analytical skills in the field of social inquiry. For me as a freedom fighter the most impressive aspect of the uprising was the realisation by Africans that they, as black people had all lost their land, cattle and political power to the white settlers galvanised by Rhodes scheme of empire building. That brazen invasion of an African territory could not fail to attract indigenous resistance therefore it hardly needed a scientist to tell them what to do because the physical presence of settlers displayed a social setting of deprivation of the black people by white settlers. It stands to reason that the spontaneous and simultaneous rejection of European settlers on Shona and the Ndebele territory was a consequence of deprivation of fundamentals that defined who they were regardless of whether they were disjointed social entities. The fact is that besides what our elders told us, some scholars have traced and found evidence of the pain and anger over the loss of land and cattle since the advent of white settlers in Matabeleland and Mashonaland. Although several historians come up with all sorts of speculations and questions about how fragmented tribesmen could suddenly become nationalistic in respect of their apparent rejection of settler invaders, the primacy of all of this lies in an undisputed fact that Africans saw themselves as victims of the invading white race that used force to seize their territory. That is, they had lost their land, cattle and ownership of their territory and left with bare minimum resources they could call theirs. It cannot be denied that peoples of Mashonaland and Matabeleland demonstrated their rejection of the loss of their wealth and social power to the settlers. In this respect theirs was a resolute attempt to use their numerical strength to dislodge the intruders from control of their territory. As the loss was equally felt throughout the country, it seems highly probable and logical that they would want to share the task of fighting the invaders by bringing everybody on the same degree of preparedness to fight the common enemy occupying the common territory. In an article that ploughs through old and current literature on the 1896 uprising in Southern Rhodesia, titled: "The First Chimurenga: 1896/97 Uprising in Matabeleland and Mashonaland and Continued Conflicts in Academia;" in **Constellations Volume 2, No2**, (2011) Suzanne Dawson restates an understandable but academically controversial historical significance of the uprising:

"The First Chimurenga has been defined as a historical turning point in African resistance in which Ndebele and Shona groups united to rid Matabeleland and Mashonaland of British invaders." (Page 149)

Whilst many historians may suggest that academic treatment of the subject of the First **Chimurenga/Umvukela** would require empirical evidence that could support the definition of that historical turning point, many of us contend that there is enough evidence to sustain a definition of that turning point. In this connection, many authorities have demonstrated that the two ethnic groups may have regarded each other as owners of the same territory that the British had seized therefore felt that combined action could remove the occupiers from their territory. Clearly such a move, including a decision by the Matabeles to send an emissary (Mukwati) to their counterparts in Mashonaland to seek agreement on a strategy for simultaneous action only to find Mashonas ready, portrays a picture of transcendence from fragmented tribal groups towards broader black solidarity at that primary stage of socio-economic formation. The very thought to plan to remove the occupiers from their territory by joint effort underlines the fundamentals that define the causative impetus for transcendence beyond tribal identity to recognising black outlook on which all subsequent anti-colonial struggles and nation building would be pivoted.

The act of calling upon each other to rise all at once should be seen as the key that opened the harmonious lines of socio-political interaction of the Africans across tribal boundaries in Southern Rhodesia for the first time since the invasion of the country by the Pioneer Column. This was not immediately repeated until they formally converged at a better organised level in the formation of the Southern Rhodesia African National Congress (1957) that was seen as a completion of the end of fragmented tribal entities towards a formalised nationalistic mass that saw the dawn of national approach to politics of emancipation never seen since peoples' first uprising.

The 1896 history is worthy highlighting for the sake of understanding when and how Zimbabwean peoples merged and defined their interests as one common interest by shading their blood fighting for their territory in a united effort. In that unity of purpose linguistic diversity was not seen as defining the political aspirations of the people as a whole but, instead, they saw themselves as inhabitants of the same territory that was now occupied and ruled by European colonialists who deprived them of their land, cattle, political power and their ways of life as black peoples. For academics, the question of whether or not they perceived themselves as one nation is a subject for further scrutiny to determine whether there ws a centre of political power to which all paid tribute to recognize and affirm it as a point of national convergence before the invasion or at the point of preparing for the uprising and how much influence royal centres were seen as points of national convergence. The striking factor here is that simultaneous moves towards a unified effort in order to drive the European intruders out of their territory thus creating the perception that they were aware that, as blacks, they had lost their territory and control of their affairs to the white occupiers. A distinguishing factor here was the visibility of whites as victors and blacks as the vanquished in their own territory. Professor Robin Palmer: 1977 (**Land and Racial Domination in Rhodesia**) was first to bring out a scholarly but brief ventilation of the issue of the first peoples' war (**First Chimurenga/Umvukela(Uprising)**) in Zimbabwe which surprisingly the nationalists never portrayed as a phenomenon of national significance in the annals of Zimbabwean political and social history. Instead they sang about it as the first Chimrenga led solely by Mbuya Nehanda from Mashonaland. Instead, they should be pointing out that Mbuya Nehanda was one of the leading drivers in motivating the people to fight colonialism as a united people country-wide in 1896. The fact that Mkwati was allowed to return to Ndebeles to report back on the war-readiness of the Shonas indicates that Mbuya Nehanda may have approved of the united uprising. Any leader with a live sense of nation building could have highlighted these happenings unequivocally instead of propounding a poisonous narration of national disintegration. There are other authorities who also erroneously present the uprising as the second Matabele War (after the 1893 so-called rebellion). Contrary to these versions, many enlightened historical accounts show that there was not anything like that because in 1896 there was a countrywide uprising against colonial occupation which erupted at short intervals of each other in Matabeleland and Mashonaland on the basis of a consensus to fight colonialism as already stated. One of the major weaknesses was that this grand effort was not coordinated from one command centre and sub-centres that could have planted a seed for a new unifying phenomenon of African nationalism earlier than it emerged in the late 1950s to challenge colonialism in an organised way by peaceful means.

For me, a striking aspect in Robin Palmer's findings and observations was that they corroborated almost word for word of our elders' tales of African's united attempt to dislodge their colonisers in 1896. In this respect Robin Palmer's version of the 1896 "people's war" confirmed our fathers' oral narrations pertaining to a country-wide unified effort to dislodge the settlers by our forefathers. Elders who were born between 1875 and 1885 had vivid memories of what their fathers told them about the efforts of that time. Also, Professor Terrence Ranger's interpretation of the uprising is not far from our elders' narration of what happened in 1896/7. They said a lot about the 1896 conflict between the Africans and the colonialist authorities as they talked with so much passion as if they participated in all battles and communication between chiefs in their effort to cross the ethnic divide for a common cause. I suspect that most parents of that generation passed this information with pride to their children or grandchildren because they seemed to want us to internalise it as part of red letter days in the annals of our country's political history. Evidence of this (many debaters referred to their elders as sources of facts) emerged very strongly during our debates in students associations in secondary schools and at political level in the actual nationalist parties where ever people were tracing the origin of colonialism in Zimbabwe. On the part of the elders, they even wished that they were able to record what happened at the time because they were aware the only people who recorded events were European settlers and they were not sure whether their records were accurate. In some cases they recorded accurately but their interpretation of the African aspirations was nowhere near reality at every stage of colonial existence in our country. In all of this, what is puzzling is why the African nationalists in Zimbabwe did not pick the element of unity of purpose with excitement as a phenomenon of national significance that depicted a united people against settler occupation at its infancy. Such a phenomenon should have been the major point of reference that deciphered the unsung origin of the people of Zimbabwe's propensity to unite on a common cause. Maybe educated African leaders have a lower propensity to build and lead a large nation than the uneducated ancient kings in this respect. For the national leadership, united peoples' uprising of 1896 provided them with a fertile ground upon which nation\building could thrive as opposed to what has bedevilled Zimbabwe's national fabric since 1963. The May 1963 split of the nationalist movement was a mother of all splits in that its ramifications have become a devastating cancer not only in Zimbabwe's body politic but also in the social matrix of societal cohesion. The problem is that the nationalist leaders have become master strategists in divisive politics for personal survival whereby national cohesion has become anathema in their scheme of things. In this regard it may not be too far from the truth to suggest that the 1896 leadership of the uprising performed better in bringing every African on board against colonialism than our nationalist leaders of the second Chimurenga/Umvukela in their vision of Zimbabwe as the land of tribesmen rather than the land of 1896 and 1957. The aforesaid years were the land marks of national unity that have made us proud of our grandfathers for uniting for a common cause that became the fundamental point of reference for the subsequent generations. The so-called 'Patriotic History' moves nowhere near the fundamental version of the 1896 history of the first (united) peoples' war in Zimbabwe because of its narrow outlook of tribalisation of that glorious event in the annals of our country's socio-political transformative dynamics.

However, the defeat of Africans handed power in the plate of BSA Company. The Company's grip on both the political power and control of its newly found wealth showed that the whole purpose of seizing Zimbabwean territory was about seizure and gain ownership of wealth through the levers of political power, which was Cecil John Rhodes' scheme of empire building. Initially, BSAC did this by ruling the country with limited white settler participation with no African representation in the legislative council. By 1922, the white settler population had grown in wealth accumulation and political influence that gave them enough power-pressure to gain adequate access to the levers of political power. Having gained enough representation in the legislature, they put pressure for self-rule, but the British Government offered them a choice between self-governing colony and becoming a province of the Union of South Africa. There was no African representation in the legislative council as the voting qualifications were too high in the form of high incomes and ownership of immovable property of high value plus education qualifications at high grades. The all-white electorate voted for responsible self-government and they were granted it by Letters Patent from the British Government.

In the Letters Patent, the British Government conferred considerable responsibility to the self-governing colony of Southern Rhodesia. The colony's constitution provided for an all-white elected parliament with no African representation. To qualify as a voter, the white adults had to earn very high income or command a certain minimum value of immovable property and a certain level of education. At that time no African had any of the required qualifications to be on the voters' roll. There were provisions for the Governor to appoint the Prime Minister who was vested with executive powers to appoint cabinet ministers and senior state official such as commissioner of police, commanding officer of the army, etc. The Southern Rhodesian parliament was given powers to pass legislation without referring to the British Government except those matters affecting Africans. From that time onwards the settlers wanted the British Government to grant them independence on the lines of South Africa, Canada, Australia and New Zealand. Actually, they demanded a dominion status.

To consolidate white power over Africans, the settler government began to move swiftly to prepare the ground to create a firm base that would anchor their power and wealth without including Africans in their scheme of things. Initially, land distribution was haphazard and ill-defined. In response to the settlers' demands for a systematic allocation of land and to meet the promises of land to the invading army personnel, the Government appointed a Commission on Land Tenure in Southern Rhodesia, led by Morris Carter, to investigate the land tenure system and come up with definite recommendations. The Carter report came up with far reaching recommendations that spelt out racial division of land ownership and occupation that met the desires of the settlers. The Government accepted the Carter Commission's report and passed the Land Apportionment Act (1934) along its principles. The Land was apportioned thus: 207 000 Europeans (Whites) got 50%, 2 500 000 Natives (African) 33%, Urban 3%, State Land 2%, Native Purchase Areas 10% and other 2%. More significant in all of this was that the European settlers were allocated about 78 of prime land in the country. Prime land was distinguishable by being the most fertile and well watered (high levels of annual rainfall) in the country, graded as ranging from Region 1 to Region 2. Like all other pieces of legislation, this far-reaching enactment was passed without consulting the African majority, as per the recommendations of the Morris Carter Commission. The Land Apportionment Act became the main legalised framework that provided a model of racial domination and discrimination that placed the Africans at the level of second class citizens in their own country. The implementation of the provisions of this Act had implications. Millions of Africans found themselves inside the European owned farms and the "new owners" of this land resented the presence of Natives occupying "their" land. They put pressure on the government to remove them. Indeed, from1946 to1956 the country witnessed a process of massive forced removals of the Africans from their fertile land to designated areas called 'Native Reserves' most of which were sandy soils or forest land with minimal fertility and low annual rainfall. Actually the Act legalised racial imbalance in the ownership and use of land in the country. It is important to note that such a legalised racist framework accentuated conflict between the colonial authorities and the Africans until the outbreak of armed struggle.

Another European dominated mechanism that was installed by the British government, in consultation with the colonial authorities, was the imposition of the Federation of Rhodesia and Nyasaland in 1953. This followed the recommendations of the Monkton Commission Report. Sir Godfrey Martin Huggins (later became Viscount of Malvern) became the first Prime Minister of the Federation and Garfield Reginald Todd took over the Premiership of Southern Rhodesia. The ruling party in the Federal Parliament and in all the three territories was the United Federal Party (UFP), with a loosely concocted policy of partnership between the Europeans and Africans which scarcely worked in practical terms.

Meanwhile the African Nationalist movements in the three territories took formal shape as freedom organisations in the late 1950's. This was the time the Africans in the three territories intensified their resistance to the Federation because they regarded it as consolidation of colonial settler power in Central Africa without the consent of the indigenous majority. In each territory the African Nationalist movement was called African National Congress (ANC). The three ANCs demanded introduction of majority rule based on one man one vote (universal adult suffrage) followed by independence. The authorities stuck to their declared policy of 'partnership' as the only realistic way of building a multiracial society in Central Africa. Africans rejected that approach as a strategy to keep them out of power in their own country.

CHAPTER FOUR

AFRICANS UNITE AGAINST COLONIALISM SECOND TIME

The installation of the Federation on the three territories was coterminous with the rise of organised African resistance to colonialism in the three territories. For instance in 1957, the Youth League, led by George Nyandoro, James Chikerema, Yatuta and Dunduza Chisiza, Edson Sithole, etc in Mashonaland, merged with Joshua Nkomo's African National Congress (based in Bulawayo) to form the Southern Rhodesia African National Congress (SRANC). Reverend Samukange facilitated the merger as he was one of the principal founders of the ANC in Bulawayo. Apparently the formation of an African political party which united them right across the tribal divide and demanded equal rights in education, health, public amenities, voting and majority representation in the Legislature. This was seen by the White settlers as a threat to their power and privileges that they enjoyed to the exclusion of the African majority. Formation of the ANC was an act of wisdom on the part of the named leaders because they united African people against colonialism in a manner that seemed like history repeating itself (cite 1896 peoples' war), albeit on the basis of peaceful demands for equal rights between Africans and Europeans in all spheres of life in the country.

A little earlier, in 1956, Garfield Todd, then Prime Minister of Southern Rhodesia, stopped forced removals of Africans from their land and introduced far reaching reforms in education to enable the Africans to rapidly gain knowledge on a scale that was to enable them to participate in the economic and political affairs of the country within a short period of time. Viewing this as a threat to their power, the white members of the UFP felt uncomfortable about what they regarded as the "ultra-liberalism" of the Prime Minister. Some of his Cabinet Ministers resigned and made it impossible for him to form another government without them. They feared that the right wing opposition Dominion Party would gain ground on a race ticket at the polls. Consequently, in 1958 his Party, the UFP removed Garfield Todd from being Party leader and Prime Minister. The UFP feared that Todd's plan would swing the electorate to the right wing opposition Dominion Party, which was vehemently opposed to the plan of advancing the Africans educationally or otherwise. In this whole saga, there were some allegations that Todd recruited hundreds of African teachers without a budget to meet the costs of hiring them. Owing to his alleged inability to explain the apparent incongruence between number of teachers for hire and the budget, his Party lost confidence in him. On this account UFP Parliamentarians swung from the centre to towards right wing politics of the opposition and deposed him. The removal of Garfield Todd for expanding African education marked the beginning of the end of white liberalism in Southern Rhodesia. The UFP MPs came out in their true colours by behaving in a manner that showed that White settlers were on the same wavelength with regard to the question of management of African affairs. Their rejection of a plan that could have opened the gate towards African advancement exposed them to be seen as being in no mood to compromise on paradigm shift from their citadel of power that conferred a vast range of privileges which they enjoyed for over half a century. They feared that Todd's plan would lead to the Africans swamping the Whites by qualifying rapidly as voters. Noting that Africans numbered 7 000 000 and whites 250 000, they feared that expansion of their education could lift them to the level of qualifying as voters and produce a majority of voters that would enable them to gain majority seats in parliament without having to introduce universal adult suffrage.

In this respect the whites perceived two threats to their power: one, internal, consisting of the Prime Minister's plan to expand and advance African education; two, the external threat consisted in the stormy rise of African nationalism demanding majority rule based on one man one vote (universal adult suffrage). They moved fast to solve the internal threat: they sought a leader that would talk partnership while maintaining the status quo of white control of the country. They found such a leader in Sir Edgar Whitehead, who was Ambassador in the US at the time. Whitehead was a liberal who believed in a carefully managed and controlled development of Africans within the context of his party's policy of "partnership" between black and white races. In contrast, Todd's plan was meant to increase education facilities at all levels throughout the country within a short space of time to uplift the Africans to the level of their white counterparts in skills and knowledge. He thought this was in the interest of both the whites and the Africans because both would have the same knowledge as they competed for jobs and political space in the country.

It seems that Todd's thinking was that if Africans acquired the same kind of qualifications as their white counterparts, they could rapidly rise to attain the needed qualifications to vote and be eligible for election to parliament without having to lower the voting qualifications. In this case, the plan was coterminous with the establishment of the University College of Rhodesia which was multiracial, therefore poised to absorb students from both racial streams of high schools with a probability of churning out more African graduates than whites. Apparently the majority of the whites were not ready for these developments. If Todd's plan was adopted, it could have benefitted all races in Southern Rhodesia by moving towards levelling out the inequalities through increasing education facilities for Africans hoping to create a contented African middle class that could organically drive social and political development of the rest of the African people in a relatively peaceful transformative process. Probably, such a social structure could have crystallised into reality within conditions of racial interaction brought about by equal opportunities to access resources of development and livelihood. Maybe, Todd's policy could have reduced chances of violent conflict between the colonial state and the African nationalists because at that time African nationalists never called for a thoroughgoing transformation of the colonial system to a new socio-economic formation that could have required a different architecture that would possibly meet the needs of the people rather than those of colonialists.

African demands of the time would have easily led to inheritance of the colonial state in the same manner that we did at independence in Zimbabwe and, with that, they could have been satisfied with attainment of African majority rule that gave the Nationalists some comfort in the boots of our former colonial masters. Since there was no revolutionary movement, African nationalist would have become contented with attainment of majority rule and the country would have escaped a life consuming civil war because Africans could have no cause to rebel against a democratic government of their choice. The white leaders and supporters in Rhodesia had a very artificial understanding of an African's desires and fears with regards big things like self-determination. They did not think about long term effects of injustices imposed on Africans by a colonial system of racial domination and discrimination

For no apparent reason except possible fear of its growing strength across the tribal divide of the African masses in Southern Rhodesia, the authorities banned the SRANC in 1959 and detained most of its leaders except Joshua Nkomo who was out of the country at the time. A new party, named the National Democratic Party (NDP) was formed to replace the banned ANC. The NDP, first under the leadership of Michael Mawema, mobilised the masses of African people against colonialism and succeeded in achieving this objective in an unprecedented scale since the united uprising of the people against colonial administration in 1896.

In 1960, at its Congress in the then City of Salisbury (Harare), the NDP elected Joshua Nkomo as leader, Morton Malianga was his Deputy and Washington Malianga was Secretary General and Ndabaningi Sithole as National Chairman, to name but a few. The NDP was better organised, more focused, clearer in policy articulation and impressively united for the attainment of majority rule. Thus it became known and gained support faster nearly in every corner of the country, right from grassroots level up and across every stratum of African society. A Mother of all motivating slogans termed: **Mwanawebvu** or **Mntanenhlabathi**[12] proved to be a massive stimulus that elevated Africans to the level of seeing each other as one nation as it instilled passionate love for every African in the country and Africa at large. It washed away divisive ethnic identity and consciousness and brought in a new identity of African consciousness. Wherever we saw an African we saw our brother or sister or father or mother and we gave them appropriate respect as in African culture. Thus, the boundaries of tribalism melted away like ice in boiling water. It profoundly extended horizons of political consciousness beyond the limits of ethnicism and enhanced the understanding and practice of **"Ubuntu"** beyond the narrow tribal parameters of say, Ndebele or Shona or Kalanga or Shangaani. Alongside the key slogan of the time, there was a wide spread song on **"freedom now"** which became the 'battle cry' in a peaceful struggle for freedom. The **"freedom now song"** was a clear expression of the fundamental demand for emancipation from racial domination at that time. The expression was actually demanding a bundle of freedoms which Africans did not have but hoped to find them in a democratic system that would allow them to make free choices of government of the country.

The **Mwanawebvu** slogan was a phenomenon of exciting marvels as it ushered in an era of political enlightening for all young and old because it did not only provide light with which Africans saw each other clearly as nothing but Africans of the same soil. This brightened our hopes for the future of a nation united in diversity as it also created a picture of Africans of all languages interacting with each other in harmony like children of the same family. One of its marvels was that we witnessed how fast it caused the differences of ethnicity and ethnic chauvinism to disappear to the extent that only languages provided a perception of distinction within the African population. It was satisfying to know that all the African people in the country from Plumtree to Mutare and from the Zambezi River to Limpopo River were members of the same family, sons and daughters of the soil of our Motherland (Zimbabwe) and Africa. Needless to say that the leaders made it clear that the same slogan applied to all Africans from Cape Agulhas (southernmost tip of Africa) to Casablanca (the northern end of Africa) as it was translatable into all African languages in continent of Africa. Such was the culture of love for humanity propounded by the National Democratic Party (NDP) leadership and well received by the African people in Southern Rhodesia. Its motivation and unifying strengths and power were similar to

---

[12]   *Child of the soil: extended to mean* **"Sons and Daughters of the Soil of our Motherland"**

Mayibuye iAfrica[13] of the African National Congress (ANC) of South Africa whereby African identity took primacy over all ethnic identities in that country.

The slogan of **Mwanawebvu** not only broadened the political horizons of the Africans beyond the country's borders in terms of understanding that they were not just Zimbabweans, but also enabled them to realise that they were Africans in the context of continental setting in relation to other Africans because it was easy to encompass every African by saying **"Sons and Daughters of the Soil of Africa."** In this way, the slogan ushered in a progressive element of cross-tribal relations in the social and cultural spheres that diminished the attitudes of **exclusionism** and **tribal chauvinism** which are usually characterised by self-aggrandisement and self-elevation on the basis of just a tribe. Tribal chauvinism was the most degenerate social trend that fuelled hostility between ethnic communities because each one thought they were the most superior above all others in every aspect of social outlook and traditions. NDP levelled down this façade by adopting and applying constructive slogans for nation building. While the African people consolidated their strength based on national unity behind the NDP, the Whitehead Government seemed nervous about this powerful mix of advanced African "new look" on the political landscape of the country, thus tearing away the colonial policy of divide and rule. The government believed that its policy of partnership was good enough to keep all races separated on colour lines while developing slowly towards a wider democracy based on higher education and ownership of high value immovable property. This was incompatible with the African demands for universal adult suffrage as the only way to achieve self-government and democracy that would meet the legitimate aspirations of the majority of citizenry without undermining the rights of white people.

While the contradictory claims grew on both sides of the divide, tension rose rapidly between the Government and Africans who were consistently demanding a constitutional conference that would enshrine the principles of majority rule based on one man one vote or universal adult suffrage. In pursuing the objective of majority rule, the Nationalist had massive support from all African classes in towns, rural villages and working class in commercial farms. People wanted a reasonable solution to accommodate their demands, similar to the process followed in the other components of the Federation, Northern Rhodesia and Nyasaland where constitutional conferences took place and finished up with recommendations on African majority rule. Zimbabwean Africans were inspired by what happened in the other territories before they got their independence from Britain. In all the demands and expectations, the NDP had a solid social base and high morale among members. With signs of progress in the north, Zimbabweans viewed all that as a chapter of the same book wherein their chapter was next. Many people began to regard all these developments in a simplistic way by confidently thinking that freedom for Zimbabwe would just flow southwards from the North. They even became more united behind the NDP in that regard.

The serious tension between the NDP and the Whitehead government put pressure on the British Government to intervene by convening a Constitutional Conference in 1960. But the British Government's determination of the number of delegates showed to be grossly skewed against the Africans as they invited only two delegates from the NDP out of twenty five delegates who attended the Southern Rhodesia Constitutional Conference. This left many people to think that the British Government was openly siding with its kith and kin in Rhodesia in complete disregard for the legitimate aspiration of the African majority. The NDP delegates were Joshua Nkomo and Ndabaningi Sithole with Herbert Chitepo as legal advisor, assisted by T.G.Silundika and others. At the end of the Conference, in February 1961, a new constitution was announced, giving Africans 15 parliamentary seats on the B roll in the Southern Rhodesia Legislature and

---

13

Africa back to Africans

the minority whites were given 50 seats, on the A roll, in a House of 65 members. Clearly this left the African people grossly under-represented in the Legislature. The indication was that the Conference failed to resolve the conflict between the indigenous Africans and the settler authorities in Southern Rhodesia.

Apparently the NDP leadership conditionally accepted the new constitution (on the grounds of *a two fires theory*, one burning in parliament and the other outside, country-wide) hoping that the impact of the two fires would weaken the Europeans' grip on power. Thus pressure would be enough to enable a faster rise of African representation up to majority rule. Some of the hardliners (eg Leopold Takawira) in the Party openly rejected the constitution and denounced the agreement as treacherous. The leadership did a lot of explaining concerning the two fires theory and how it would work. According to the African Daily News of the time, majority of Africans did not entirely understand how that theory would lead to majority rule that the Nationalists were singing about at rallies. In the schools we all rejected the new constitution unreservedly. In the final analysis pressure was so overwhelming that they had to follow the will of the majority, as Earl St. Aldwyn reported in the House of Lords in November 1961 about the outcome of the constitutional conference on the future of Southern Rhodesia and confirmed NDP's initial acceptance and subsequent rejection of the new constitution:

"To this, all those represented at the conference subscribed, with the exception of the Dominion Party, who disassociated themselves from it. Subsequently, as your Lordships are aware, the delegates of the National Democratic Party indicated that they were no longer prepared to support the Conference recommendations."

Apparently, they had accepted the recommendations of the Constitutional Conference in the first instance. In changing their minds, the leaders justified their withdrawal of support on the grounds that the land question was left unresolved in the Conference recommendations that provided the heads of proposals for a new constitution. They then argued that the African population should be given the right to have a say on the new constitution through a referendum, even if the government rejected the move. In this way they successfully extricated themselves from their conditional acceptance of the constitution by organising a parallel referendum whereby Africans would make their verdict on it. The results of the unofficial referendum showed that Africans decisively voted overwhelmingly against the proposed constitution. But the white minority electorate supported Whitehead government's call and accepted the new constitution with a comfortable majority.

The Government, buoyed by the electorate's acceptance of the new constitution, did not give any significance to the results of the African referendum. On the other hand the Africans, too, did not recognise the results of the whites-only referendum. In the circumstances the only path open was **collision** between the government and the African Nationalists. Tension rose high again between them until the government broke the deadlock by becoming the first to strike; banning the NDP in December 1961. Like the banning of the SRANC, outlawing the NDP was totally unjustifiable because the Party was moving firmly on a nonviolent path of attaining majority rule through negotiations. The government was lucky because the nationalists were still hopeful that peaceful pursuit of their cause might yield desired results so they defied the ban by forming a new party, Zimbabwe African Peoples Union (ZAPU) within ten days after the ban of NDP. In the context of the Rhodesian politics the UFP found itself fighting in two fronts: trying to keep the nationalists at arm's length from the citadel of political power and privileges on one hand and stopping the opposition Dominion Party (DP) from gaining support from the white electorate on the other. Having campaigned for the rejection of the new constitution and failed to convince the white electorate to reject it, the DP focused on persuading all right wing white associations to merge into a united front to defeat the UFP whose policy of partnership was seen as a gateway to African majority rule. They organised intensively in the White working class suburbs and commercial farms with promises of preserving the privileges of those classes. The nationalists had no power except mass support of overwhelming majority of Africans, a politically deprived race, and not yet geared to rise against an unjust system that denied them all the fundamental rights that were enjoyed by the whites.

A positive aspect of the unofficial African referendum was that it became a huge catalyst in taking the principle of majority rule to the masses in the countryside. The organisers of the referendum reached every remote part of the country and ensured that everyone who wanted to vote did so, including juveniles. For the first time the NDP message of **"freedom now"** from colonialism became the loudest "battle cry" in the entire country thus making progressive slogans rest in the ownership of the African people as a whole. Within a short time political vocabulary concerning freedom became part of everyday expression in the African population and, it also became the ligament of holding them together as politically enlightened Africans rather than as disjointed entities of tribesmen of ancient times.

The opposition Dominion Party did not conceal its right wing stance and racism as it rejected the new constitution on the grounds that 15 parliamentary seats for the African majority were too many compared to 50 seats for whites in the House of 65 seats. They argued that the speedy rise of numbers of educated Africans showed that they (Africans) could qualify for the A roll sooner than later, thus becoming the majority to upset the white voters and this would swing the pendulum from a position of European power to deliver power to Africans in parliament before they were ready to govern a modern state. Ian Douglas Smith, Chief Whip in the Federal Assembly, resigned from the UFP and formed his own party, Rhodesia Reform Party to challenge the adoption of fixed numbers for racial representation instead of one number of seats in the assembly so that only merit would be a qualifying criterion (at A roll level) for voting and be elected to parliament. The 1961 constitution raised the temperature of right wing politics in that the DP became more determined to stop what they believed to be a basis for majority rule. They mobilised all the right wing fringe organisations and associations, including Smith's Rhodesia Reform Party, in the country and succeeded in hammering out a merger with them to form a united front of white organizations, the **Rhodesian Front**, to challenge the UFP on its policy of Partnership between Black and White

On the part of Africans, the formation of ZAPU soon after the banning of the NDP sustained the high hopes that were generated by the NDP. At this time everyone thought freedom from colonialism was around the corner because the masses of people throughout the country took the overwhelming rejection of the new constitution by Africans was powerful enough to cause the authorities to recognise African demands.

The NDP had been banned in December 1961 and immediately succeeded by ZAPU within ten day, on December 17th, with Joshua Nkomo as president. He was deputised by a brilliant medical doctor, Dr Tichafa Samuel Parirenyatwa. Born in Rusape and grew up in Mutare, he trained as doctor of medicine in South Africa. The outstanding significance about Dr Parirenyatwa was that he was the first African doctor in the country. He was appointed to work in a mining hospital, Antelope Mine Hospital in Kezi District about 100km south of the city of Bulawayo. He sacrificed his medical career for the cause of freedom for the people of Zimbabwe and at a time when African doctors were still scarce. ZAPU fitted squarely in the shoes of the banned NDP but the calibre of its leadership was now more impressive because so many intellectually capacitated personalities had come forward into leadership. Dr Parirenyatwa's appearance in the top echelons of the leadership team was particularly exciting because we believed that he could not sacrifice his career without seeing the light at the end of the tunnel. Above all, his appointment to the position of Deputy President was an acknowledgement of his quiet work in organising African intellectuals and grassroots people to join the African Nationalist movement right from the days of the NDP while he was still a practising doctor. In addition to Dr Parirenyatwa, there were many dynamic firebrands such as Robert Gabriel Mugabe, Publicity Secretary, Advocate Herbert Chitepo, T.G.Silundika, etc.

CHAPTER FIVE

MY MOVE TO URBAN ENVIRONMENT

When ZAPU was formed in January 17, 1962, I had just arrived in Bulawayo. At the time of my arrival in the second biggest city in the country, neither did I realise that I was leaving behind the rural life forever nor predict the intricate mix of things lying in wait for me in the City's socio-political environment and beyond. At the same time it was the time when African Nationalism was at its peak of success in terms gaining support of the masses of people all over the country. My departure from rural to urban life was not unique to me at that time. It was a trend that those who acquired a certain level of education automatically became creamed off to urban glamour where life seemed more lucrative than in the rural forestlands. My destination was Luveve Technical College in Bulawayo where I was admitted to a five year course of Painting and Decorating. I was delighted to be admitted in such a prestigious technical college to follow a technical course after completing GCE 'O' Level because prior to this fruition of plan B, hopes of proceeding to Forms V and Vl were dashed when my brother told me that money for further education had run out. At Luveve Technical College students did not pay tuition or boarding and lodging fees because bursaries were available for all technical students. Technical courses taught at Luveve were offered and certificated by City and Guilds in London. I regarded this as good because it was designed to produce qualified artisans, a qualification that was the preserve of the whites before Luveve Technical College was established by the Federal government. The comforting part of the course was that it had a scholarship to cover tuition as well as boarding and lodging. The first two terms were quite satisfying because we began to see what the course was all about in terms of its professional relevance in the labour market. My admission into Luveve Technical College (LTC) marked my entry into urban life of Bulawayo as well as the beginning of the end of rural life for me. The Painting and Decorating course kicked off soon after college opened in January and it kept us busy as we started by both theory and practices that gave us high hopes about its utility value as a professional course. There were second and third years ahead of us who had begun to do tread practice and most of them were already apprenticed with relevant companies in Bulawayo. As early as the first term we were all looking forward to following the course to its end. The College was located in Luveve Township in the western side of Bulawayo.

Luveve Township (otherwise known as Luveve Village) was well resourced in terms of schools, sports and recreation facilities, public transport and social amenities. More importantly College students had enough freedom during the weekends to visit relatives until Sunday evening. There was plenty of opportunity for me to interact with political activists in the townships, mainly in Makhkhoba Township (Old Location) where most of my relations stayed. I found some time to be formally introduced to Jason Ziyaphapha Moyo, who was aware that there was an underground movement at Nyathi School during the life of the NDP. I briefed him about our successes in spreading political work in the rural areas. The biggest opportunity here was that for the first time I joined a political party that was championing the cause of freedom for the African people in my country. I was delighted to be a member of ZAPU in the Youth Wing of Makhokhoba Branch. For me this was a crucial and formal entry into the gate leading to a rocky journey of liberation struggle. Fortunately I was already aware that Southern Rhodesia was a self-governing territory with what they called "responsible government" therefore different from other British colonies in terms of the fact that it was under the firm control of the European settlers not the Colonial Office in London. That was a huge challenge facing the deprived African majority in Southern Rhodesia, as we shall see in subsequent chapters.

At Luveve Technical College things appeared to be flowing smoothly at face value. We started off smoothly both in our studies and in getting ourselves organised into a Student Representative Council. The ethnic mix was no different from the familiar scenario of Nyathi Secondary School except that there were no girls. Political consciousness was average compared to Nyathi Secondary School because it was quite discernible among first years in all departments of the College but relatively lower among our seniors.

Nevertheless, in the middle of 1962, the students incidentally made a startling discovery regarding the status of the College. They stumbled on the recent minutes explicitly stating that the College was not registered as an institution of learning and the prospects of it getting registered were bleak because all the powerful white unions vehemently opposed to its existence. Apparently the establishment of the college was rejected by the powerful white unions, led by the most powerful Engineering and General Workers Union (EGWU) which demanded and campaigned for its immediate closure because they never wanted it in the first place. The EGWU was the most powerful white union in the country and it could sway the white working class to a party that opposed African development in the work place. The authorities were unable to register the college without the consent of the white unions because they had the muscle to cause public disenchantment with government's 'liberal' policy. Students stood firm on their demands to get the College registered because they felt insecure attending an unregistered college. The college was well resourced as far as staffing and needed equipment was concerned. Above all Luveve Technical College was the first and only one earmarked for Africans in the country. We challenged authorities to be decisive on this question on the grounds of promoting equality because the Whites had two technical colleges in Salisbury and Bulawayo. At the head of the negotiations on behalf of the students were Lazarus Dlakama, Meshach Chinamasa, Haddon During and myself. At the helm of this wave were Lazarus and I. We had serious discussions with College authorities but there was no solution until the College eventually closed down. Students had consistently tried to persuade the authorities to ignore these unions and get the college registered for the sake of progress in providing young Africans with technical skills for their careers and industrial development in the country. Unfortunately we had to leave the College just before it formally closed down a year later. After closure, the whole complex was turned into a High School for Africans. The closure of the Luveve Technical College actually demonstrated clearly that Rhodesian whites regarded themselves as the only human beings needing development resources because, to them Africans were not worth of uplifting to the level of Europeans. The Missionaries were the only progressive segment of the instutionalised systems that offered basic education to Africans throughout the country. But their r e s o u r c e s were not enough to sustain advanced or higher education that was required to match the standard of Europeans who were locally educated.

The fact of the matter is that if they were conscious about the rights of Africans who inhabited the same country with them, the white ruling class could have welcomed equitable distribution of social development resources to minimise dissatisfaction and anger-driven disruptive conflict.

Entry into active surface politics

Before I left Luveve Technical College I used to attend ZAPU rallies and gatherings in the townships stadia. The first ZAPU organised gathering I attended was a cultural event called "Traditional Dance" which was staged at Barbourfields Stadium in Bulawayo. Here all the ethnic groups participated in a spectacular show of traditional dance in its natural setting. It was here that I saw all the members of the National Executive Committee (NEC) of ZAPU for the first time as they were paraded and introduced one by one to the cheering audience. It was indeed a wonderful show because the performers came from all Zimbabwe's ethnic groups. There were fifteen performing troupes. At this time national unity was still relatively intact as the cultural show also reflected that social cohesive atmosphere. The show contributed to expanding my horizon of understanding the multiplicity of ways of uniting such diverse cultural entities into one Zimbabwean nation. The most impressive performers were: Muchokoyo (Chipinge), Mbakumba (Masvingo), Shangara (Masvingo), Mabhiza (Plumtree), Jerusalem (Murewa), Sitshikitsha (Tsholotsho), another from Manicaland that I cannot remember, etc. That intercultural explosion opened a new chapter whereby people began to appreciate each other's culture and recognized its value not only for intertainment, but also for its power of enhancing identity of each ethnic group in the country. The element of entertainment rose to new heights because from that day such cultural events spread and became popular in all the towns in the country.

In July 1962, I attended an elective meeting of ZAPU Youth of Makhokhoba Branch at Stanley Square stadium in Makhokhoba Township, Bulawayo, which was full to capacity. One member from the floor proposed my name and gave the meeting my brief profile which included my role in the student movement at Luveve Technical College. The audience became ecstatic upon hearing my political record in school and college. I was elected with a huge majority into the Executive Committee of the Makhokhoba Branch of the Bulawayo District. For the first time I joined the leadership of the youth at a surface level of a nation-wide political party that was the sole voice of the African people at the time. I felt empowered by the confidence shown by the people of Makhokhoba in me when I was still quite young (22 years of age). I participated in the Committee meetings with enthusiasm. The work entailed recruitment of young people to join the party in numbers. The first Committee meeting I attended we drew up a programme of action in our branch which included recruiting new members through visiting people in their houses in the evening or at weekends.

The cardinal point here is that I was now in a position not only to take part in the active politics of my country, but also observe and absorb the political and social dynamics as they interacted with or against each other in the political arena of the country. My path towards freedom struggle had its seed planted by my father's talk to us (children) about Europeans' fire power that defeated our grandparents. The said seeds germinated when Teacher Malikongwa contributed fertilizing information that he whispered to our class at primary school about colonies gaining independence from colonizing powers. At secondary school, Aleke Banda's realistic top-up pragmatism accelerated the growth of a flourishing political plantation that began to produce fruit that made sense of what colonialism was all about and why it was being challenged by the colonized peoples of Africa and Asia. The underground 'academy' of political subversion in IBS at

Secondary School provided a graduation level in preparation for the real struggle in the open field of contending political forces. All these political stages from sheer childhood socialization signify the development of an indigenous freedom fighter who inherited the problem of deprivation from parents only to find that, at reaching adulthood, there were millions of other Africans in the same circumstances. But at every stage there was one question: "what are we going to do to regain our freedom from colonialism?" At our adulthood it was even clearer that the violent loss of our country to Europeans was never accepted by our parents and our brothers and sisters, therefore it could not be accepted by us (**African generation of Mwanawebvu/Mtanenhlabathi**). It was this generation that became pioneers of armed battles in a **"stone-throwing versus fire power"** encounter with Rhodesian security forces in the 1960s. The obvious problem here was that there was lack of level playing field for the actors concerned because the system did not accept Africans as equal citizens with their European counterparts. The policy translated itself into gross human rights abuse of opponents of the system when they demanded equal rights for all citizens in the country. The system of colonialism was driven by white males with total exclusion of the African majority from the levers of power right from the beginning of European rule in the early 1890s. The pages that follow will show why, even if the majority of Africans in Rhodesia were seen as peace loving people, they finished up carrying arms of war to liberate themselves from unacceptable repression that had been institutionalised into an architecture of racial domination and injustice against the Africans. This was exemplified by phases through which the struggle passed before it reached the highest level of conflict, armed struggle. If the regime had some notion of fair play as each phase increased in scope and intensity more than the previous, they could have at least contemplated a new and reasonable compromise path that could have avoided the bloodiest conflict since the previous anti-colonial phases.

Involvement in Mass Mobilisation

Now that I was one of the leaders of a youth branch of a national freedom movement, some work had to be done with vigour but on the basis of diligent planning before any action. For the first time I participated in moving door to door in twos in Makhokhoba Township to solicit membership for ZAPU. We were delighted to find that the majority of the people in the township had already joined ZAPU and those who had not done so were willing to join on the spot or gave us a date to return for registering and issuing them with cards. The most impressive outlook of the party was the unity of the people across the ethnic lines and gender. Our leadership gave us instructions that we should not force anybody who declined to join the Party. We maintained that directive as we approached everybody with full respect and warmth everywhere we went in the Township. Bulawayo was noted for its cosmopolitan character in its demographic set up to the extent that distinguishing people by their tribe was no longer fashionable as early as the 1960s. African identity had gained ascendency over all other identities through the powerful Mother of all national unifying slogans; **"Mwanawevhu"** which was universally acceptable throughout the country as a national unifying melody that was sung everywhere possible, thus instilling a political tradition of oneness as black Africans.

The experience gained in the underground IBS made it easier for me to participate in the discussions and planning in the Committee, especially on strategic matters. The chairperson of the Executive Committee of the Makhokhoba Youth was Ethan Dube. Ethan was only a year older than me but his grasp of politics of freedom struggle and its prospects and dangers seemed too tall for his age. In all of this, he was a dedicated young man with a lot of wisdom and courage to face awesome challenges of the struggle. He also had the qualities of a mentor, especially on taking calculated risks when faced with challenges. He warned us that while the Party policy was to strive attain majority by negotiating with British Government and the Rhodesian authorities, members should prepare themselves for the failure of this approach. The latter was based on the fact that the government had closed the door of negotiations with African Nationalist therefore Africans should prepare for a hard road to majority rule. Some symptomatic indications in this connection were that several activists were being arrested and interrogated under torture as early as the beginning of 1962. Ethan Dube was one of them but he had shown very amazing bravery when arrested and tortured under interrogation by detectives of the Special Branch. He strongly drilled all of us that it was better to resist torture than to give in, because chances of avoiding prosecution and imprisonment were much higher in resisting torture than in yielding to forced confessions which could provide the court with admissible evidence likely to secure a conviction and sentence. So we vowed to avoid prosecution by all means

In mobilising the masses one of the issues to share with them was the new constitution (of 1961) which had too many shortcomings, especially its lack of providing a clear path to majority rule in short term or even medium term. Its Bill of Rights had too many exceptions which allowed authorities to exercise their powers as they saw fit even if their actions violated the human rights of political opponents who happened to be African Nationalists. Some observers were concerned about Nationalist failure to secure at least some clauses that provided for unimpeded progress to universal adult suffrage in the foreseeable future because the Rhodesian white led political parties wanted the 1961 constitution to be a basis for independence of the country without further amendments. The African Nationalists were still demanding another constitutional conference to draw up new principles that would lead the country to majority rule. Clearly after the two parallel referenda, the Black and White politicians were far apart in their perception of the constitutional situation of the country.

Such were some of the major challenges that were faced by ZAPU leadership, especially the fact that the prevailing constitution had been agreed between the British Government and the Southern Rhodesia Government of Sir Edgar Whitehead in 1961 during the life of the NDP. A serious deficiency of the constitution was its provision of 15 B roll seats for Africans in a parliament of 65 members while 50 seats on the A roll were allocated to Europeans. It was a two tier voters' rolls with A roll requiring high qualifications based on immovable property and higher education and the lower B roll minimal qualifications. The fact that the new constitution was approved by the white electorate in a referendum but rejected by the Africans in their unofficial parallel referendum was an issue with implications in terms of the extent of accentuating the conflict between the colonial authorities and the colonised Africans. The people in the townships and villages wanted to know as to what was the next step after their rejection vote against the affirmative vote of Europeans on the other hand. While ZAPU leaders were still planning a comprehensive strategy for action throughout the country, the Government also prepared to take action because it regarded the Nationalists as acting irresponsibly by first accepting the constitution and then rejecting it under pressure of the "extremists" who were alleged by the government to have taken control of the Party. In essence, the truth of the situation was that pressure came from the African majority who had expected the constitutional conference to come up with a majority rule constitution with numbers of African seats higher than those allocated to Europeans in parliament. In the eyes and perceptions of the majority the imbalance was clear as seen in the Arithmetic of the composition of the Rhodesian Legislature in the new constitution. The people did not need a lawyer or Mathematician to find a formula for calculating the numbers which clearly showed that African majority citizens were allocated fewer seats than the minority Europeans in a parliament of 65 seats. A question arose from ordinary people on the streets: on what basis could Africans be expected to accept a constitution that regarded them as a race accorded minimal rights and freedoms in contrast to a minority white segment that enjoyed rights to choose a government and power to govern without participation of the Africans in the same country? Our situation did not need an external power to tell us that we were oppressed because we experienced it firsthand.

On the basis of all of the fundamental discrepancies of the new constitution, people were urged to support the leaders in their demands for an alternative constitution based on the principles of majority rule and independence. Failure to follow this constitutional development path might make leaders decide to take a tougher line. Joshua Nkomo had the habit of declaring that if the African demands were ignored indefinitely by the colonial authorities, including the British government, the Africans would be forced to solve the problem in **"our own way."** When asked to explain what he meant by that he replied that **"our own way is our own way."** We then had to interpret this statement to the people as we understood it in terms of the fact that the moment of liberation process was no longer stoppable no matter how many stumbling blocks could be placed against it. Also we had to indicate to the masses that if the government banned ZAPU, that might be the beginning of a shift away from a negotiating table where violent conflict could be avoided.

In all of this, the government and its supporters thought they were right to ban African political parties hoping that the majority would be intimidated and finish up abandoning the cause of majority rule. It needs to be pointed out that the fact that the African nationalists formed another political party soon after the NDP was banned, delivered a clear message that they were still committed to achieving majority rule by peaceful means. Up to that time the leaders had never adopted the option of violence as a method of struggle for freedom and, in this regard, they did not give directives to their followers to resort to violence against the government during the life of the SRANC and NDP besides a spontaneous uprising **(Zhi)** in 1960 which erupted in sympathy with the arrested leaders in Salisbury. A question may be asked: since there was no evidence of planned violent activities by the NDP, what was the reason for banning it unless the reason was to preserve and perpetuate a system of racial domination by silencing the voice of the majority? It can be assumed that the government might have decided to silence the nationalists by its show of power to instil fear and despondency in the general African population so that they could see futility in supporting the nationalists. It is also likely that they still held an old British view that primitive Natives should accept their place of defeat and recognise the rule of civilised European settlers over them (Dawson, 2011).

A close observation gives clear indications that the rise of ZAPU with such an impressive team of leadership should have given the government a different view from the above-mentioned stereotype that was loaded with false assumption that a banning methodology was a tool to silence the African voice. More importantly, that was an opportunity to abandon the idea that Africans should know their place, having been defeated in 1893 and 1896 because that notion was rendered irrelevant by a measurable development of Africans in respect of capacities to participate in the governance of a modern state. An impressive display of leaders of high caliber at Barbourfields in Bulawayo in January 1962 should have given the government a clear picture that Africans were ready to assume responsibility to run the country given the opportunity to do so, such as the Gold Coast process of decolonisation in stages (from 1951 to 1957) towards majority rule and independence. In essence African parties had already shown a steady qualitative growth in organisational strength and articulation of their legitimate demands that deserved serious attention and constructive consideration from the authorities because it was clear to all of us that the majority rule project had reached an unquenchable degree of authenticity in terms of having the full support of the majority of Africans as they were legitimately entitled to demand the right to govern their own country. Above all, the movement that championed the cause of African freedom had gained their solid support and credibility as the only political saviour to deliver them from oppression. For the Rhodesian government to ban a party like the NDP that was so well organised and smooth in its functioning mode at every level of activity, was an act of gross injustice and disingenuous disregard of its political character as a genuine movement that demanded decolonisation of Zimbabwe in a peaceful way. Above all, if Zimbabweans had a tradition of violence, such an ill-advised act of banning their Party could have been a risk with a potential to trigger mass uprising considering that the NDP had gained massive support from the African population countrywide with high hopes of attaining freedom. At that time it was no longer just the urban working class supporting the NDP, it was all classes in the African population, including rural peasantry and farm workers.

In my observation, the NDP referendum was a well "oxygenated" political campaign that motivated masses of the African population in towns and rural areas to rally behind the Nationalist leaders in support of majority rule demand by rejecting the new constitution of 1961 which had no provision for majority rule. The **Daily News** too, portrayed a clear picture of a motivated African nation after the results of their referendum were announced. In addition to the effect of the parallel referendum in the African populace there were several deep moving social currents that contributed to the growth and strength of the NDP as a party of African people. For instance, Dr Parirenyatwa and other educated Africans had worked, without beating drums, behind the scenes to mobilise the African middle class, intellectuals and the masses to support the nationalist movement for the cause of national emancipation from colonialism. The ANC had scarcely reached such a massive scale of coverage during its existence as the NDP did in a period of less than two years. The NDP's motivating referendum helped to expand the scale of politicisation of the people, thus consolidating the massive social base for African nationalism that had become a significant phenomenon within seven years of its rapid rise and solidification. A party with such a powerful national base did not deserve banning for the sake of appeasing one (minority) race that was in power without a mandate from the majority in the country. The fact that this unprovoked behaviour by a racial minority government did not ignite massive violence in the country could be read as a crucible that tested and proved that Zimbabweans were not a violent people unless they became subjected to an extremely grinding situation such as the rule of the Rhodesian Front under UDI. Putting it differently the continual banning of African nationalist parties constituted a crucible in which Zimbabweans' propensity to violence was tested and found to be low at that time. This was so because the Government's contemptuous act of banning African non-violent political parties and arresting leaders and supporters constituted excessive use of power and could have precipitated a catastrophic upheaval that might have turned the much talked about Congo crisis (of the early1960s) into a child's play. There were no compelling factors that necessitated extreme measures to push such a clearly peace loving people into the brink of armed struggle, which, by all accounts was not their plan A. The 1896 peoples' uprising also showed that the people had enough of being subjected to systems (e.g. paying tax to the government) that they had no control of in their own country. It seems that the settlers never learned the lesson from that uprising (1896) as they preferred to cling to the British notion that Natives should know and take their place quietly as defeated primitives that should appreciate being ruled by an orderly system driven by a civilised "super grade" of Homo Sapience. For our part, we learned a lot from the history of that uprising by a united people countrywide: no more spears or bows and arrows!

Tragic Loss of a Leader

As the Rhodesian government had got into the habit of banning the African parties without serious provocation from them, it never stopped to think of a better option that could have avoided violent conflict. It did not even give some consideration to the possible anger that could have led to mass violent unrest by African population against harsh decisions imposed on their successive parties and leaders. As if what they were doing was enjoyable like dinner parties, another banning was in the pipeline by early August 1962. Rumours were rife throughout the country that ZAPU would be banned and the leaders detained and this impelled the National Executive Committee (NEC) of ZAPU to take the rumours seriously and they decided to send its members out in the regions of the country to inform members about the impending ban and what action to take in the event of it materialising. Dr Tichafa Samuel Parirenyatwa, the Deputy President of ZAPU was due to pass via Bulawayo to Nkayi (160 km north of Bulawayo) on this mission. The Leaders of Nkayi District, Ronald Sibanda, William Mbambo, Welshman Mabena, and Engelbeck Khanye had come to receive him in Bulawayo and then take him to Nkayi where his mission was.

On 14 August 1962, information from the police sources spread all over Bulawayo in the evening saying that one of the leaders of ZAPU had been killed by a train on a level crossing near Shangane (100 km from Bulawayo on Harare Road). Many members of the youth wing were still awake when a wind of rumours blew from the police sources about such death. I was one of them and we went to Mpilo Hospital but had no access to the mortuary. We met a police detective who confirmed that there was an accident involving a car and a train on a level crossing near Shangane and that a deceased person was certainly a senior member of ZAPU because he had seen Party papers in the car. But he declined to say any further. There were no other sources that could tell us the whole situation about that accident until we went to bed still in the dark as to which ZAPU leader had been killed

In the morning of 15 August the Federal Broadcasting Corporation dropped a 'bomb shell' in its headline report that Dr Samuel Tichafa Pararirenyatwa had been killed by train at a level crossing the previous night while being driven to Bulawayo. His driver Danger Sibanda had been critically injured and taken to Mpilo Hospital. This was the most devastating single blow to the Nation and the Party because Dr Parirenyatwa was regarded as a new additional intellectual giant that would enhance capacity with fresh capability in the Party leadership to effectively stir it to victory over colonialism. Such value added was expected to enable the Party leadership to come up with brilliant strategies and goals that would define the nature of freedom we were aspiring for in our country. The truth of what exactly happened to Dr Pararenyatwa has hardly been satisfactorily established. This is so because the driver of the car, Danger Sibanda, told the inquest that he and Dr Parirenyatwa were driving fromSalisbury (Harare) to Bulawayo when they stopped in Gweru (275 km from Harare) where the Doctor offered to relieve him in driving and he took the passenger's seat. Upon arriving at Shangane petrol service station (100 km from Bulawayo) to top up fuel and a petrol attendant came to the car but suddenly he said (in Shona) **"please excuse me, I will be with you now"** he disappeared behind some buildings for several minutes. He returned but seemed to be very slow in serving them. Eventually they left puzzled why he had behaved so strangely like that. After driving a few kilometres from Shangane, they were stopped by a group of eight white men. Three of them came to Sibanda's side and the rest went to Dr

Pararenyatwa's side and forcibly dragged them out of the car. He said Dr Parirenyatwa asked them why they were using force but they did not respond but they continued to drag them out of the car. One hit him (Sibanda) with a blunt object and he fell on the ground and lost consciousness. The next thing he found himself waking up at Bulawayo's Mpilo Hospital about 100 kilometres from the scene of the incident the following day. On gaining consciousness he asked the whereabouts of Dr Pararenyatwa and was shocked when they eventually told him he had perished in the accident. But he said there was no accident. He was convinced that Dr Parirenyatwa was murdered by the group that stopped and dragged them out of the car. To make Dr Parirenyatwa's death more vexing, the ZAPU lawyer, Leon Baron told Joshua Nkomo and Garfield Todd that he saw his body and it seemed that his hands were tied at the back (Wikipedia, Tichafa Samuel Parirenyatwa, 2014).

Nevertheless, the train driver testified that as he approached the level crossing, the car in question appeared to compete with the train as it raced fast towards crossing the railway line ahead of the train. He said he blew the horn and applied emergency breaks but the car continued until there was an impact. The train dragged the car for nearly one hundred metres from the point of impact and Dr Pararenyatwa was found to be dead on the passenger's seat while the driver was alive but unconscious on the driver's seat. The police too, confirmed that the deceased was found on the passenger's seat while the driver was on his driver's seat. Of the two versions the inquest took the train driver's version. He was described as a credible witness and his story was accepted as a statement of fact thus came to the conclusion on the basis of the same. On this account, the driver's evidence was discredited even though he stood by his story to this day. He was sentenced to do time in prison for culpable homicide on the evidence of the train driver and the police.

The death of Dr TS Parirenyatwa was the first huge loss suffered by ZAPU in its history in terms of reduced capacity at leadership level at a time of great need. After such a devastating loss it was difficult to adjust quickly to fill the space of capacity left by a leader whose first appearance in the top leadership had raised high expectations in the Africa population. For ZAPU loss of a leader of high caliber happened within its early life compared with other African liberation movements that suffered similar losses when they were mature and already in full swing armed struggle. Therefore they had developed enough cadres who were ready to move in when one of them fell in active service or through assassination by enemies. Apparently they were able to fill the space quickly without suffering severe setback in terms of developing strategies and systems of driving armed struggle. ZAPU's loss happened when it was still a civilian political party inside the country at the mercy of the colonial authorities as could be seen that, before ZAPU adjusted to operating without Dr Pari, the Whitehead government struck fast while the leaders and the whole Party were still engrossed in mourning over the loss of a key leader. There is no doubt that the death of Dr Pari took the organisation several steps back in terms of diminished capacity and capability for strategising ahead of the government. This does not suggest that he was the only thinker in the Party, it is rather to acknowledge that a leader of his calibre would have added measurable value in the Party's capacity to formulate strategies and tactics to outmaneuver the enemy camp. Nearly twelve months after his death there was a major split that caused further setbacks and devastation. All these setbacks boosted the Rhodesian authorities because we, as Africans, were weakened in the face of our adversaries who were prepared to go the whole hog to resist the onslaught against their authority. So, the period between Dr Pari's death and the formation of Peoples Caretaker Council (PCC) in August 1963 was characterised by downward trends in the tempo of the struggle against the Rhodesian government. This was so because after the tragic loss it took us a long time to accept his absence from the leadership which now looked like damaged goods.

Before we settled down to business, ZAPU was banned, so consequently, we spent time readjusting to operate underground and just after we had accomplished that, there was a split in May 1963 that gave rise to bitterness and redirection of focus against each other instead of facing the enemy head-on. Although the PCC was formed to boost the morale of the masses, still a lot of effort was wasted hunting down each other more than we did to the main enemy. We formed powerful militias that should have become combat regiments against the Rhodesian regime but to a large extent their focus was on each other because we had come to regard a member of another party as a traitor to be eliminated. But it was impossible to eliminate members of another party that was growing within the same population as the one that considered itself legitimate. So no one was eliminated therefore time was wasted on senseless violence between Africans in the face of the enemy's growing strength. When put together, the sum total of the setbacks was political devastation and strategic retrogression towards medieval social primitivism. We eventually got over it after wasting time and energy on the totally wrong target: another African.

It takes about forty days for people to mourn their deceased relative or colleague. While we were still mourning the tragic death of our leader, Dr Parirenyatwa, ZAPU was banned within thirty six days after the Doctor's death; as if the colonial authorities were rubbing some salt on the Africans' wound before it healed up. Most people had hardly recovered from the shock of the August 15 bombshell (announcement of Dr Pararenyatwa's death) when thirty six days later the Government announced the banning of ZAPU in the morning of 20 September 1962. The leaders were banished to their rural homes for three months. While we were in double mourning, we had to wipe our tears and do the best we could to take the whole organisation underground to enable it to operate clandestinely nonstop. When the restriction ended, the leaders decided to go out of the country to ask for space where they could form a "government in exile" where they would be able to create a military force with which to challenge the Rhodesian Front Government by military means. What were they going to do since our neighbours were still colonies within the Federation, although prospects of attaining majority rule and freedom were brighter for them than for Sothern Rhodesian Africans?

However, the nearest country that could have provided space for a government in exile was Tanganyika (Tanzania) because our neighbours were still colonies inside the Federation. Northern Rhodesia being the nearest neighbour on the verge of independence was the only possible hope for a launching pad from which to unleash a war of liberation. The main problem was whether an independent Zambia would be militarily strong enough to afford to anchor a project of such immense security implications for the country.

While in Southern Rhodesia political waves of African Nationalism had not caused a significant dent on the colonial state, in Northern Rhodesia the Colonial Office was giving in to the Nationalist demands for majority rule. But that did not happen without friction. For example ANC leader, Harry Nkumbula was viewed by some of his colleagues as incompetent and they broke away to form the Zambia National Congress (ZANC) under the leadership of Kenneth Kaunda, who was the Secretary General of the ANC. ZANC was more militant than Nkumbula's ANC. Nevertheless, fearing the consequences of its powerful thrust, the authorities banned it at the same time as the Southern Rhodesia ANC. In like manner, ZANC was quickly succeeded by a new party called the United National Independence Party (UNIP) led by Kenneth David Kaunda. UNIP adopted a slogan of **Kwacha Ngwe**[14]. In Nyasaland the Nyasaland African Congress (NAC) was led first by Orton Chirwa, Dunduza and Yatuta Chisiza brothers. Later, Dr Hastings Kamuzu Banda assumed leadership until it, too, was banned in the same year as the

---

14

it has dawned

others and its leader detained. But immediately, a new party was formed, the Malawi Congress Party and continued the struggle until it succeeded to take Nyasaland out of the Federation to gain its independence in August 1964 under the name of Malawi. Northern Rhodesia followed suit in October 1964 becoming known as the Republic of Zambia. For me it is very important to mention these organisations (though in passing) because while we were at Nyathi School the nationals of the Northern territories were profoundly influential in the politicisation of students in the school and the students' movement at large. Above all the named parties were allies of the nationalist movement in Southern Rhodesia because they regarded the Federation as common enemy.

It was no surprise that when our neighbours got their independence we celebrated both Zambia and Malawi because, occurring just next door, they became a huge source of inspiration and hope for all Africans still under colonialism in Southern Africa. Above all, in accordance with the principles of Pan-Africanism, it became clear to all of us that if the Rhodesian regime persisted in rejecting African majority rule, we might have to fight using the African independent states as our launching pads for armed struggle. In this regard the emancipation of Malawi and Zambia created a strategic platform for us from which to prepare for attaining our freedom by any means that we deemed appropriate in the circumstances. As a matter of facts the leaders of the three territories had cooperated with each other in their opposition to the Federation and demanding majority rule for each country. We, too, during our student days, were united by Aleke Banda et al to think African rather than Shona or Ndebele or Bemba or Chewa or Ngoni or Lozwi etc. Indeed our northern brothers and sisters did not let us down when they achieved their independence as they immediately put their independence at risk of attack by offering their countries not only as enclaves for escaping from repression, but also as preparatory ground for hard struggle ahead.

CHAPTER SIX

RIGHT WING RHODESIAN FRONT GAINS SOLID WHITE SUPPORT

In Southern Rhodesia, the ruling United Federal Party (UFP), was losing ground to a right wing united front of white associations, including the well-resourced and organised National Affairs Association, that rallied with the Dominion Party as the main framework of a new party called "Rhodesian Front," which inherited and enhanced right wing political space and stance to oppose the Federation with more vigour and astuteness. The new right wing outfit, the Rhodesian Front, wanted independence with a political system that was entirely based on White domination and control of Southern Rhodesia. As stated, a conglomeration of the Dominion Party and other right wing elements became a powerful voice that campaigned loudly against what they called 'forced integration of black and white races' referring to the policy of partnership of the UFP and the African demands for racial equality followed by majority rule in Southern Rhodesia (Zimbabwe).

For all intents and purposes, the formation of the Rhodesian Front (RF) in March 1962 marked the end of white liberalism in Southern Rhodesia and, therefore the consolidation of racism as the RF was to become a formidable vanguard of a white driven political system. Under the leadership of Winston Field, with Ian Douglas Smith as deputy leader, the RF emerged as the champion of European interests that became an impediment to African advancement in all spheres of social development. In this regard, the RF leadership propounded right wing ideas with far reaching implications in the political landscape of Rhodesia on an unprecedented scale since the advent of colonialism. The RF displayed the impressive strategy of mobilising the white electorate to gain support by the use of the press, flyers and billboards in every street in towns and all along highways and service centres on the roads throughout the country. Their messages, like the one quoted here, were short and precise without equivocation on the question of the power to remain in responsible (white) hands thus decisively relegating the principle of majority rule onto a backburner.

Having mobilised and cobbled up a merger of all right wing fringe associations and parties as stated above, the Rhodesian Front enunciated a political strategy based on fifteen founding principles, of which the key ones included the following:

1. preservation of each racial group's rights to maintain its identity;
2. preservation of proper standards by advancement through merit;
3. uphold and adhere to the Land Apportionment Act (which formalised racial imbalance in ownership and distribution of land);
4. no forced racial integration;

5. job preservation for white workers;
6. separation of amenities for different races; (Wikipedia, Politics of Rhodesia, 2013)

These and nine more RF principles defined its 'vision' of a racially divided society by legalised compulsion that was pivoted on the Land Apportionment Act (1934) which categorised land on racial lines in respect of land use and human settlements. Although the aforesaid Act was replaced by the Land Tenure Act (1969), the fundamental principles were retained; only terminology changed such as Native reserves replaced by Tribal Trust Lands, etc. The RF was a coalition of white working class trades unions and associations allied with the rural white white commercial farmers. Clearly, the working class, with the promise of job preservation swung decisively to the RF while the rural bourgeoisie had a powerful influence with regard to the preservation of the Land Apportion Act which served their interests very well. Industrial and commercial bourgeoisie largely stayed with the UFP for a short time until the RF came up with a firm promise of independence with or without British consent. Confident that it would secure a mandate from all white class interests to consolidate the edifice of racial domination over the Africans, the Rhodesian Front was by no means prepared to consider negotiating with the African Nationalists concerning African political advancement. The fifteen principles of the RF did not even allude to the possibility of any slightest movement towards African majority rule because they believed it would be prejudicial to their 'sacred' principles that defined a 'vision' for a society based on separation of a civilised race from primitive tribesmen (as allude to by one of the principles of the UDI proclamation – see in lower pages). The fifteen RF principles were designed for perpetuating the power and privileges of a white race in a system that condemned the African majority into a subservient race in their own country. They concentrated their campaign on convincing the white electorate that their future lay in the hands of the RF because it was the only party that would uphold the status quo on the basis of its founding principles. In a short space of time the Rhodesian Front had grown in strength and influence in the white population, especially gaining support of white working class and white farming bourgeoisie.

Many distant observers still thought that the Rhodesian whites, being largely 'Englanders,' could not support right wing extremists of the likes of the Rhodesian Front. This observation was a huge misreading of the political barometer of the white Rhodesians of the post-Garfield Todd period. The signals of moving to the right began to flash when a liberally inclined UFP of which Todd was leader and Prime Minister of the country, rejected his intention to uplift Africans through education to enable them to participate in the economic and political system of the country. From then onwards, as African nationalism grew stronger and effective as a national liberating movement, white rightwing politics also grew exponentially which showed the white's unpreparedness to accept Africans as equals in any sphere of life in Rhodesia regardless whether they were 'civilised' or not.

On the part of the African leadership, it was a surprise that, initially, there was not much indication that the advent of the hard-hitting Rhodesian Front in the Rhodesian political landscape induced a matching paradigm shift in terms increasing the density of counter pressure in the form of strategic resistance to the apparent consolidation of white domination by that manifestly right wing party. If the Nationalists had revised their political strategy to match or outmatch the extremism of a new right wing government in Rhodesia, armed struggle could have begun quite early enough to counter the UDI project. They did not believe that RF could win a general election on a racist ticket. Above all they banked too much on the British Government as the colonial power with ultimate authority to intervene and compel all stake holders to come to a table conference to craft a more democratic constitution than the 1961 document. With this notion in their scheme of things, they continued to use old methods that were designed to pressurise the government to come to the negotiating table. They were not aware that a new imponderable could not be tackled by the old methods of struggle such as hard-hitting speeches at rallies and threats at news conferences or riots as well as calling upon the British Government to convene another constitutional conference and suchlike methods. All these were rendered obsolete and irrelevant in a situation of fast growing entrenchment of white power in the country.

At the time of entry of the Rhodesian Front into the arena of Rhodesian politics, the UFP, too, had clearly shifted to the right as it began to adopt an uncompromising stance against the African Nationalists. In this respect the UFP was no longer treading on the negotiating mode with African Nationalists because they realised the RF was gaining substantial support from the European electorate as its growth in popularity amongst whites was seen as an unstoppable threat to the ruling party. Faced by a probability of electoral defeat the UFP tried to reassure the white electorate that they were done with the African nationalists by distancing themselves from their demands on negotiating the transfer of power to the African majority through one man one vote. This stance was no match to the RF's fifteen principles of preserving white domination and privileges in the country. As a show of toughness against Nationalists, the UFP took tough action against the Nationalists to impress the electorate, so that they could be returned to power. They went a whole length to show their uncompromising rejection of African demands for majority rule by banning ZAPU three months before elections based on the new constitution of 1961. Clearly this action by the UFP was meant to boost its electoral fortunes to outflank the advancing anti-African "hurricane" of the RF. Even so the UFP's show of toughness against the African Nationalists failed to impress the White electorate that was apparently more impressed by the well-articulated fifteen principles of the RF were designed to perpetuate in a system that condemned the African majority to being a subservient race. Developments that followed proved that Prime Minister Edgar Whitehead's harsh decision on ZAPU did not stop the white electorate from abandoning his party for its misty policy of 'partnership between Africans and Europeans' without unpacking the phrase as the RF defined their strategy clearly enough to capture the electorate in an amazing way. Indeed on the elections of 12th December 1962 the RF shocked observers, the UFP and the African Nationalists, when the white electorate decisively swung to the right by giving it a clear majority of seats in the Rhodesian parliament. The swing to the right of centre became discernable from the day UFP members of parliament removed a progressive liberal minded prime minister, Garfield Reginald Todd, from power in 1958.

Several pundits and observers were stunned that Rhodesian whites would be so illiberal as to vote for such a right wing extremist party characterised by treading close to the footsteps of the National Party in Apartheid South Africa. In explaining the white swing from the centre to the right, some observers have attributed the move to the arrival of large numbers of white immigrants fleeing from the Congo following a post-independence crisis there. In its campaign the RF made good use of the helter-skelter flooding of whites from Congo and convinced the electorate that the UFP's policy of partnership might prematurely lead the country to majority rule resulting into chaos similar to that in the Congo where Europeans found themselves on the run for their lives (Conversation with some white Zimbabweans in Cape Town). This observation is held by some historians (Baxter, 2011) who regard the Belgian Congo's white flight from "chaotic" majority rule as one of the major influences on Rhodesian whites to fear majority rule. Above all they were convinced that the British government was going to reward them by granting independence for gallant participation during World War 11. In the post War11 period, the Rhodesian whites had no perception of the global metamorphosis that ushered in an era of decolonisation and abandonment of empires in favour of free democratic states. This placed the Rhodesian government of RF and the British government on different political wavelengths in terms of intentions regarding the constitutional status of Rhodesia. A complex matrix of internal and international trends pushed the Rhodesian white population to some form of laager mentality whereby they felt unduly pressured to surrender what they gained in 1923 therefore took the challenge by supporting a party loaded with uncompromising principles against majority rule. Peter Baxter identifies the tragic implications of the Rhodesian whites' solid swing to the right wing Rhodesian Front:

"The second key trigger that pitched the colony in the direction of war was an abrupt swing to the right of white Rhodesian electorate in the face of such change and uncertainty. From this emerged the Rhodesian Front, a powerful, white nationalist political front, headed in the first instance by a somewhat (British) collaborationist Winston Field and then by the hawkish, uncompromising and highly charismatic Ian Douglas Smith." (Baxter, 2011)

Winston Field was a British born gentleman who preferred banning leaders rather than proscribing a political party because he believed that African leaders were the principal makers and drivers of trouble in the country therefore instead of banning their party he would ban or detain them to leave their party "headless". Most members of the RF objected to Winston Field's "soft" approach to African nationalists because it was seen as similar to that of Whitehead who banned the NDP but left its leaders free and able to seize the opportunity to swiftly form a new party, the Zimbabwe African Peoples Union (ZAPU) within days after the ban of NDP; a move that helped to maintain the African momentum of political activism unchecked, as we shall see later

The leading hardliners who drove home the ideology of racial domination as a safeguard against such 'chaos' were Clifford Walter Du Pont, William John Harper, Desmond Lardner-Burke, Ian Douglas Smith, John Gaunt, Ian Dillon and P.K. van der Byle. These eloquent gentlemen were the most outspoken with regards relentless demonising of the African Nationalists and portraying the UFP as too weak to stand the powerful whirlwind of African Nationalism that was being propelled by what they called a minority of African *"extremists."*

Hearing speeches from these gentlemen and a few others strengthened our resolve to hold on to our combative stance against the Rhodesian government before they declared unilateral independence. Within the leading right wing leaders, Walter Clifford Du Pont was the most eloquent and uncompromising firebrand on issues of maintaining separation of races in the country. He became Minister of Law and Order in Winston Field's government where he had the opportunity to demonise African nationalists as extremists, self-appointed demagogues who were bent on causing trouble in the African population for their own ends. He would analyse African Nationalist speeches in detail and unmask points that he claimed contained elements of inciting Africans to violence. When Joshua Nkomo expressed the view that if majority rule was not attained through negotiations, his Party would solve the problem by "our own way" without elaborating any further as to what he meant by that. Clifford Du Pont promptly charged that the phrase was loaded with sinister motive for unleashing social unrest in the country therefore the champion of such words should be countered with swift retribution because his words implied resorting to unlawful acts. His vitriolic attack on the African nationalists made his name well known in every African household. As he amended the Law and Order Act to include a hanging clause for politically motivated armed violence and possession of materials that could endanger lives, we nicknamed him the **'Hangman.'** The aforesaid law was introduced by Reginald Knight who had been Minister of Justice in previous government of Prime Minister Edgar Whitehead but, when the RF came to power, they perfected it into an effective and politically stifling entanglement (against African political activists).

At its formation, as stated above, the Rhodesian Front was led by Winston Field who became Prime Minister when the RF won the elections that shocked the majority of the citizens in Southern Rhodesia in December 1962. To the majority of leading RF hardliners African Nationalism could be quenched by banning African parties and arresting the cream of their leadership to clear that deck. On this question, Winston Field believed in banning the leaders rather than the parties and he moved swiftly to implement his policy by releasing the remaining detainees who were part of 200 people arrested when the SRANC was banned in 1959. They were top leaders that included James Chikerema, George Nyandoro, Henry Hamadziripi, Maurice Nyagumbo, Edison Sithole, Paul Mushonga et al who were detained under the Preventive Detention Act (1959). But the rest of RF membership thought Field's policy could not contain the powerful wave of African nationalism in the country because banning leaders and leaving the party to function could not solve the problem of the dreaded winds of change towards majority rule. In addition to this white perceived weakness of Winston Field, his position became untenable when the majority of members strongly felt that he had failed to bring independence to Rhodesia as per Desmond Lardner-Burke's motion passed by Parliament the previous year. Field was forced to resign to be replaced by his belligerent deputy, Ian Douglas Smith as leader of the RF and Prime Minister in April 1964. Smith was deputised by a key hardliner, Clifford Walter Du Pont, noted for being a hard-hitting speaker against African majority rule and a passionate stiff-necked politician in the preservation of European standards through racial segregation in Rhodesia. In the African population he gained notoriety for being the champion of a hard line against full blown democratization of the Rhodesian political system on the grounds of racial incompatibility.

Ian Smith's strategic move to merge with the rest of the right wing forces can be seen in his placement near the apex of the RF from where he sprang to the top at an opportune time where he was in a position to propound the RF principles with gusto. Unlike Clifford Du Pont, Ian Smith was hardly a captivating speaker in the Legislature or in public before he rose to the Premiership of the country. But as soon as he became leader his style of leadership was seen through the accelerated tempo of right wing politics as he rapidly gained eloquence in systematically articulating the RF fifteen founding principles through which he claimed to stand for the preservation of Western civilisation and standards. On this account his supporters regarded him as a champion of Western civilisation and a motivating force in the preservation of white rule on the basis of the content of the Rhodesian Front's founding principles. As Prime Minister of Rhodesia, he propounded his desire for an independent white ruled Rhodesia with or without the consent of the British Government. His principal stance was that his Party was the only one able to prevent African majority rule which if allowed to happen, would destroy civilisation and lower the standards to the level of anarchy and chaos reminiscent of the Congo crisis soon after independence in 1960. In all of this he decisively ruled out any possibility of majority rule in Rhodesia, not in his life time and not in a thousand years. For Smith, this position was not negotiable. Such bold declarations by a leader of a government representing a minority race in the midst of the politically and economically deprived millions of Africans startled the latter and subsequently pushed them towards one option of liberating themselves from white domination.

Meanwhile the ruling Rhodesian Front members expected their leader to move swiftly towards attaining independence without majority rule. In response to the expectations the government took a hard line against the Nationalists after replacing the "politically soft" Winston Field with a more belligerent hardliner, Ian Douglas Smith, and the Rhodesian Front government showed its new leaf by mobilising the white population to support a declaration of independence if the British Government refused to grant it. In Britain, while the Conservative Government was in power Smith was optimistic about getting independence. Indications were that the Conservatives were willing to consider granting independence to white ruled Rhodesia provided the government would not amend the constitution to impede eventual majority rule in the foreseeable future. But when the Labour Party under Harold Wilson came to power the fortunes for him changed because the new government in Westminster would not approve independence before majority rule. As Smith continued to pursue the independence issue, he was convinced that unilateral declaration of independence was not going to attract drastic action from the British as it was going to be a **"two day wonder in the City of London."** After that no one would want to do anything about it as there would be no desire on the part of the British to fight their fellow "British" in Rhodesia. Apparently Smith was right in this observation. So, the ball was in the African leaders' court in so far as what options were available to pursue the majority rule project.

What was I doing when all this was happening right in front of my eyes in the country? My move from the rural area to Bulawayo marked the end of infantile perceptions of the real world in so far as political challenges were concerned.

CHAPTER SEVEN

AFRICAN RESPONSE TO RIGHT WING WHITE POLITICS

The banning of ZAPU meant that from 20 September 1962 there was no longer a legally operating African mass political movement to challenge the government. By banning ZAPU the government intended to silence the African voice, thus quenching further serious challenges to its rule. The labour movement, African Trade Union Congress (ATUC) was the main organised force that had mass support amongst the working people in towns. But it was largely an urban based labour movement whose membership did not include the farm workers and the rural peasantry who constituted the majority of the population in the country. In this regard the organised labour did not provide an adequate coverage of the interests of the population as a whole, although strategically it was a force to reckon with as they were politically conscious because most of them were members of banned ZAPU.

In response to the ban, a leaflet titled: **General Hokoyo**[15] circulated in the Bulawayo and Salisbury townships urging branches of ZAPU to go underground and keep the Party alive at the same time it warned the Government that banning ZAPU was unwise because it would lead to mass unrest in the country until the demise of colonial authority in our country. None of us actually knew the level of leadership from which the leaflet was authored except that the phrases used on the leaflet were familiar enough to make us think it was an official ZAPU call for action. Likewise, most structures made concerted efforts to drive the entire framework of ZAPU underground throughout the country. But most of the officials at local level had operated on the surface during the legal existence of ZAPU, therefore, they were susceptible to constant surveillance by the Rhodesian Special Branch. A new approach had to be adopted whereby each branch had to be divided into several small cells of three to five operatives coordinated by one person (Liaison Officer– LO) who linked up with them through one contact who liaised with each one of five or more cells and the rest never saw LO and he did not see them either. The link men met LO on a one-on-one basis for instructions and feedback. A structure like that did not make it easy to mobilise the masses at short notice for demonstration or to cause an uprising but it was suitable for clandestine action-packed operations against the colonial authorities. In order to get some clarity on driving a large national organisation underground, I revisited the Algerian model of creating cells for liberation purposes when I was working in Bulawayo and I understood it much better than I had done when I was a secondary school student.

Algerians formed the Party of the Algerian People (PPA) which was banned by the French in 1937 but political cells remained functioning underground (Windrow, 1997). Those cells had an

---

15

Hokoyo means beware

enormous use value as they became the foundation upon which the struggle was anchored with significant successes in the liberation struggle. At that point of our search for strategy, Algeria had just got independence after eight years of waging a bitter guerrilla warfare which finished up with victory in 1962. The importance of this experience was to learn how underground cells could function for a long time without surface or above ground structures. For instance the PPA in Algeria was banned seventeen years before the National Liberation Front (NLF) emerged with weapons with which to launch armed struggle in 1954. It was underground PPA that took the lead in uniting various factions into one liberation movement, NLF. The latter's military operations were performed by forces relying on the support of the aforesaid underground structures established by PPA nearly two decades back. For me, this was quite impressive and worthy of application in our own situation.

It seemed to me it was a feasible proposition to create underground cells from the structures of banned ZAPU because they were physically there except that they were no longer legally allowed to function on the surface. Here we were dealing with people who wanted their country to be free, so it was possible to motivate them to continue operating but in a different mode under different conditions of organisational structure and functions. There was a challenge on the table for us.

In my branch of Makhokhoba, I was the link man between the LO and several cells of five operatives each. Each of the five operatives would recruit as many others as possible and maintained a link with them on a one on one basis thus establishing a network of underground structures. Here I had to remember the IBS experience in the student movement during the school days. Clearly the time had come to apply that experience in the practical situation of the struggle. Our LO was the former Chairman of Makhokhoba Branch, Ethan Dube, a very astute and security alert young man. His commitment to the liberation struggle was made of steel and his leadership qualities were an inspiration to all who worked with him. One of the hyper-active cells was made up of Shadreck Nkomo from Buhera, Gordon Butshe from Plumtree, Clark Mpofu and I both of us from Nkayi. Before the ban, the four of us were part of an eleven member committee of our Branch of ZAPU. We held on to our clandestine activities against the ban and made sure that the pursuit of the cause of freedom lived on in Makhokhoba Township and the environs by delimiting ZAPU's existence into underground cells.

Many of us began guessing a possible interpretation of 'General' Hokoyo's message that we should start with low intensity but wide spread violence on government property and economic targets. To us this sounded like a call for a warning campaign as a precursor to a more intensified struggle intended to have far reaching implications for the government. We were worried that if we started with low intensity violent campaign against the colonial authority there was a danger that any acts of violence might cause the government to regard it as a serious threat and unleash its mighty force on a large scale to crush the campaign before it developed into a second phase. Such a weak threat to the country's security would cause the government to strengthen its security machine beyond challengeable levels while we were still crawling at night to throw some petrol bomb or light some crudely concocted explosive device to throw at some structure of the state. Above all, we could be dislocated and left weaker and vulnerable as the overwhelming power of security forces could grind on our infantile fighting framework. On these considerations, we then argued that if we adopted a strategy of warning the government through low intensity but wide spread violence, the security forces might take the indications seriously and apply heavy counter blows while we remained powerless. As early as that time many young people already had a perception that the Rhodesian Front government would not yield to small time challenges as stakes were quite high for Rhodesian whites evidenced by their electing the Rhodesian Front on the basis of 15 principles that promised continuation of white rule undiluted. On this account I was one of those who felt that African youths should be sent out for military training in friendly countries. But not so fast, said the leaders. All members of my cells supported the idea and even persuaded many more comrades to buy into the idea of military training as part of preparing for armed revolution as in Algeria. Here we were putting a more militant interpretation of 'General' Hokoyo's call to fight colonialism as we argued that 'General' Hokoyo's proclamation was a 'military' signal calling upon us to warn the authorities by fighting not threatening them with wishy-washy bangs. Some raised the point that a General was a military chief above all officers, therefore use of that rank to declare hostilities with the government should not be taken with a lackadaisical effort. Whoever created 'General' Hokoyo must have some military aspects of the struggle in his intention to call for a country-wide social unrest in a prolonged and ever intensifying disorder. We took this as meaning fighting not just frightening the government. We all agreed.

However, the Youth Wing of Bulawayo District Committee partially agreed with our line of thinking saying that the struggle should be in phases with the first one at low intensity tempo to show wide spread discontent in the country. Therefore we should stick to what was manageable at the time to show the authorities that there would be no peace until majority rule was achieved in the country. If they did not come to their senses regarding majority rule, a second phase of the strategy would be adopted that would lead to more destructive violent conflict. So the phase of 'General' Hokoyo was a phase of sabotage which was characterised by use of explosives to destroy physical infrastructure like bridges and bombing police stations, etc, petrol bombs were to be used to burn white farm infrastructure (including farmland enclosures and stock feeds) and if necessary economic units such as factories or wholesales or warehouses. In the rural areas the destruction included dip tanks, sale pans, schools, official rest camps, etc. Natural missiles like stones could be used at the discretion of the crowd in action at a point in time but not necessarily as a planned mode of fighting. Stone throwing used to occur spontaneously in running battles with police or any other related force threatening Africans in a demonstration.

Several forms of disturbances of the nature described above were supposed to happen on a wide spread scale to cover the whole country in order to shake the power of the government. In this connection some comrades suggested that therefore, to shake the power of the government, many people should be trained to use explosives so that there could be mass scale destruction of strategic structures countrywide in frequent waves until the government machine became strained or even fractured at strategic nodes. All Party branches were required to break up into small cells covering the entire branch and then create militias that would be directed to definite tasks as described above. To sustain such a massive violent campaign there was a need for appropriate skills to do it properly with constant supply of materials to enable relentless blows on government targets. The phase started in 1962 to last up 1964, when PCC and ZANU were banned.

Executing a mission of sabotage required skills similar to those in the military but we did not have those skills yet. We certainly went underground with organisational experience but no skills to undertake an effective non-peaceful course of action in the form of an appropriately calculated and coordinated campaign of destructive sabotage. The move needed proper training followed by setting up relevant coordination and command structures to direct trained personnel to perform their tasks with profound effectiveness. An outfit like that would require a reliable supply of resources in terms of materials, tactical moves and camouflaging systems to avoid detection during operations and afterwards. Having agreed that a call by 'General Hokoyo was a fight, not a child's play, we then drafted a note spelling out the need for military training involving masses of young men from all over the country. Comrade Joburg Zwelibanzi Mzilethi was in the forefront to present the paper to our higher echelons. The official who read the paper while we were waiting stood up when he finished reading it, looked at us with a stern face and gave comrade Mzilethi a strong smack on the cheek, destroyed the piece of paper and ordered us never to repeat anything like that ahead of the top leadership. This encounter was baffling because our effort to explain that it was a suggestion was rebuffed by the official in question who ordered us to leave immediately. We went away disappointed but without abandoning our resolve to pursue a military option.

In spite of the above mentioned disappointment, my contribution in the first place was the creation of under-ground cells that would operate clandestinely linked up with semi-surface officials who mobilised resources for the struggle. Amongst us, Ethan Dube was quite strategic in thought and approach because he stressed the need to acquire information before acting on anything by whatever means. He gave a directive from the Bulawayo District Youth leadership of the Party that a minimum use of force against the government could be undertaken by attacking police stations, police patrols (selectively), infrastructure and other significant strategic pillars such as bridges, telegraph poles, etc. He stressed that people should spend more time on information gathering and verification than on actual operations. In the first place planners should know the major and minor pillars of the state that could be targeted if appropriate resources were adequately available. In that regard, all possible targets had to be thoroughly reconnoitred before any plan of action was conceived and carried out. Action always happened like lightning to avoid arrest on the spot in action but the preceding reconnaissance took much more time to make sense of what and how action should take place on a chosen target because it was important to identify the security and vulnerable features of a target. As I later found out, all this was part of military parlance concerning intelligence gathering from an identified operation zone. Ethan had it on his fingertips already as a civilian at his young age.

We made an enormous effort to adhere to Ethan's guidelines and advice in all our operations. At the same time my experience on the underground planning and operations with IBS became relevant and invaluable in this practical situation of the struggle. The main difference was that in the IBS we were handling information only and used it to politicise the students verbally, whereas in the field of reality we were in practical action involving the use of destructive materials against the state, which was fraught with danger to our lives. Also in school we knew everybody that we had to shield ourselves from. In the practical situation we had a crop of regular police, the British South Africa Police (BSAP) and a cobweb of secret agents of the Special Branch around us therefore there was no guarantee for our safety even though we were more cautious and vigilant. The comrades in all branches readily accepted the principle of operating below the radar screen of the security forces. In public we conducted ourselves as if we had given up the struggle. In this connection, Nelson Mandela describes this kind of life appropriately that under a white dominated repressive system *"a black man lived a shadowy life between legality and illegality, between openness and concealment"* (Mandela, 1994). This is similar to what elders in the villages warned us that **"amangamabi, kodwa mahle epoliseni"** (*lies are bad but they are good when told to a policeman for personal safety*) to be safe from prosecution. In an effort to enhance concealment of my illegality in pursuit of freedom, I had to find a job that would make me appear like a politically harmless person who conducted himself in a normal way like any other humble young African with a good job in town. In the face of the power of the white race the truth could stir trouble for whoever stood up for their rights. The evidence is clear in the arrest and detention of the African leaders whose only crime was that they publicly demanded recognition of legitimate rights of Africans for self-determination. Following a nationwide swoop of leadership, their followers had to go underground to ensure that African nationalism stayed alive and fighting for freedom without singing about it anymore.

In this regard, I got formal employment in a Federal Government Central Hospital in Bulawayo. I worked tirelessly to strengthen and fine tune the underground networks in preparation for clandestine activities. With assistance of my colleagues, we created all sorts of camouflaging systems that provided cover to what we were actually up to. Some of the very simple ways of doing this entailed creating social groups like we did at school where we formed a forum ostensibly to discuss romantic matters yet the objective was to cover our political mission. In the real world we adopted what fitted the social environment and formed **'drinking clubs'** that would sit openly in taverns or beer-halls (where African beer-*umqombothi*-was sold in open 2litre containers) ostensibly for drinking in small groups but the purpose was to discuss political matters or plans to avoid detection. The drinking clubs were fluid in terms of the rotating attendance of members and location to cover large numbers in a given time. One of the key issues concerned the unpacking of the orders of 'General' Hokoyo and the Youth District Committee so that we all knew that it was not an empty threat as government officials seemed to regard it. Drinking clubs also played a significant role in providing youth leaders with the opportunity to listen to the contributions and observations of grassroots activists and then assign them to perform appropriate tasks in or out of town. Such groupings always appeared innocent as they displayed the behaviour of drunken people before and when they dispersed one by one or in twos.

In these camouflaging drinking clubs, more than half of the participants were not drinking beer; they merely pretended to drink by putting the beer container to their lips without sipping it. I was one of majority who did not drink but had to pretend by all means demonstrable. The drinking clubs were actually a forum of political discussion groups brainstorming about what people should do to keep the momentum of liberation politics alive and active in the absence of a legal party framework. A lot of highly valuable plans emanated from these clubs because there was full participation of branch leaders, operatives and ordinary members from the cells. The Special Branch could not have suspected the clubs without information because they had become accustomed to being informed about meetings behind closed doors in the townships. As a matter of fact only the tried and seasoned core activists took active part in the drinking club discussions thus, excluding any one with the slightest suspicion of being a security risk. Special Branch had come to believe that as we wanted to stay away from them we would only meet in hidden places such as houses. But of course the more dangerous materials were not handled in the clubs. These clubs were very political in content (mainly for planning strategies and how to implement them) and social in form (as camouflaging screen) but they hardly handled specific materials associated with violent campaigns. Those were handled right in the townships or bush hide-outs. The clubs' form was meant to conceal their illegal content, not entirely different from that described by Mandela in his experience when he literally became invisible to both the apartheid authorities and society. The difference was that he was operating at national level whilst we were operating at the level of a branch, therefore his volume of responsibility was much more enormous and complex than ours. But his principle that **"The key to being underground is to be invisible"** remains valid at all levels of underground work if it has to be effective in terms of achieving intended objectives without interruption or detection and disruption by security agents. An underground operative may remain personally visible but once he begins to do underground work, he automatically becomes a double personality, one invisible in respect of concealing all his/her illegal activities against repression by becoming incapable of attracting suspicion from the security agents, and another leading normal a life in his surface activities. For quite a while Mandela drove around, stopped at police roadblocks but, because he had made himself invisible, the police did not recognise him on several occasions. The main difference between Mandela's invisibility and ours was that he literally disappeared, together with his activities, from the eyes of society and the Apartheid regime while we remained visible on the surface yet we concealed our activities only as exemplified by the aforesaid drinking clubs which at face value they looked innocent yet were deeply involved in illegal acts intended to undermine the colonial system. As we sat in the pub or tavern, we could be seen and identified by anyone but no one who was not part of us knew what we were up to except to assume that we were enjoying ourselves in drinking beer.

The ANC operatives, led by Nelson Mandela, were physically concealed from the torchlight of the security forces while we remained above ground only to keep our operations off the security forces' radar screen. At certain times trained personnel from outside the country attended some of the drinking clubs (without revealing their status) where they explained what we should do to be ready to provide support to freedom fighters when they waged the armed liberation struggle and how to avoid easy detection by security forces in that situation. They came in ones on different days and they were introduced as visiting colleagues from other districts in the country that came to share invaluable information with us. They brilliantly addressed the question of managing a large force operating underground and all matters to do with technical requirements in coordinating field operations. The visitors always left the comrades upbeat about the knowledge they gained from their presentations. In the event of a non-member joining us, we changed the subject completely away from politics.

In forming the drinking clubs, I had recalled that during our student days at Nyathi Secondary School we concealed IBS with a jocund social outfit, the Soviet Policy, that ostensibly propagated romantic matters yet the objective was to enable us to carry out activities which focused on political mobilisation of the students to support freedom movements. In both cases we worked successfully for a long time and no one knew their true mission except those who were involved in political activism. The drinking clubs also provided a fantastic cover for important things to be 'cooked' under that cover and delivered to the operatives and other live cells as feedback between the semi-surface officials and underground operatives. I really appreciated what we had done at Nyathi Secondary School because the experience gained in the IBS made it possible to adapt and apply underground system without members having to disappear from the surface or relocate into hiding. This model was repeated in many branches until armed struggle took hold in the countryside with full support of civilians who did not hide themselves but their activities remained unknown to the enemy unless betrayed or caught in the act. We shall see more examples in subsequent pages where people had to wear different 'caps' for different situations.

For the sustenance of our activities and operations we organised fundraising through Mr RK Naik and Mr M K Naik in Lobengula Street in the City. The two Naiks were businessmen who staunchly supported the liberation struggle right from the onset in 1957. We had to bring all the expenditure supporting vouchers to whoever gave us the money. Most of the money we raised covered the costs of transport, production and distribution of leaflets, and other needed materials. But for certain things where records were considered dangerous (e.g. purchase of inflammable liquids), only verbal report would suffice.

Signs of Desperation in Seeking Effective Ways of Fighting Colonialism

At some point we brought back the subject of a military driven struggle for a quick victory. We asked our Liaison Officer whether time had not yet come for armed struggle of the Algerian type (Mandela suggested armed struggle as far back as 1952). Ethan advised us to talk to Akim Ndlovu (Bulawayo Youth District Chairman) about going for military training. But before he dispatched us to Akim, he pointed out that armed struggle should be preceded by thorough preparations at home and abroad. There were many imperatives to take into account in preparing for waging war and directing it without being detected by the enemy, he pointed out. For instance there was the question of the weaknesses and strengths of the organisation in terms of human and other material resources for waging a war. All of this entailed assembling a strategic model from which to derive operational plans for surface, semi-surface and underground operatives and fighters. Above all it was important to assess whether the struggle should be in phases or in one storm. This way, Ethan was trying to alert us that waging war was not like hunting buck and rabbits. By telling us all this, we got the impression that the subject had been discussed before therefore some thoughts might have been tossed around in that regard.

Our encounter with Akim Ndlovu on the question of military training was brief and to the point because he always wanted things to be called by their names straight away. In his response to our question about whether the time had not come for military training of the youth, he asked us whether we had used any device such as a petrol bomb before. Our answer was in the negative and then he responded thus: "You better go and learn how to make and use it, then come back to me after successfully using it on any government target but not on a crowd of ordinary people. You should plan very carefully before you act".

We had not expected that kind of an answer from our District Chairman but we had to do what he said because he was our senior. At least he did not drive us out of his house like the previous official (who was more senior than Akim), he listened and appreciated what he called **"youthful patriotism"** thirst for action. In any case, it was in our interest to know the elementary methods of waging the struggle before we clamoured to handle fire arms. We went back right away and bought five litres of petrol, obtained some bottles and got some pieces of clothes to push them into the bottles like a wick in a paraffin lantern. We poured petrol in one of the bottles. We had identified a lot of targets in town. One evening we hired a taxi that took us to Bulawayo Central Police Station in Fife Street where several police cars were parked. One of us held the bottle filled with petrol and a wick dipped inside and the other lit the wick with a stick of matches while the other two provided security cover. The blazing device was thrown on to a parked police pick-up, hit the bonnet of the vehicle and rolled over it and landed on the opposite side of the vehicle without setting the target alight. We escaped undetected but our first mission was a failure. We tried again on several occasions on different targets until we succeeded on one of them. But not before something went horribly wrong resulting from the way the device was managed.

In above pages I referred to hideouts in the townships or bush where dangerous materials were assembled and dispatched. One of such hideouts was right at the centre of Makhokhoba Township, between 5th and 6th Streets and between 8th Road and 9th Road, where the Bulawayo Municipality was undertaking some renovations of houses and ablution blocks. The residents of that portion of Makhokhoba were removed from their houses for renovations into temporary "shack-like" dwellings. So we took advantage of the situation and set up a similar structure alongside the temporary dwelling structures of the rest of the displaced residents of the neighbourhood called our structure the **"Dose House"** which looked like any other temporary dwelling structure in the neighbourhood. Under the guise of a temporary dwelling structure the Dose House became part of the rest of the temporary dwelling structures in the area. In this way our Dose House was seen as part of the social and physical environment in the entire neighbourhood. In actual fact, unlike the drinking clubs, the Dose House had a hidden function whereby all plans were hatched and all action materials were put together, be they leaflets, home-made lethal devices, etc. The Dose House was not immediately visible from the streets either side of it, and no one suspected that anything clandestine was happening in there. The four of us acted like any other resident by all accounts in our everyday activities.

When things went wrong in handling lethal devices there was anxiety regarding safety of the users and the community. For example, one day Clark Mpofu was assembling a petrol bomb to be used at an identified target in one of the security establishments within Bulawayo. The device caught fire from a paraffin lantern inside the Dose House and burst into flames, thus attracting attention from the neighbours because he had to throw it outside for personal safety. One diligent neighbour took a large bowl, rapidly filled it up with soil and poured it on the raging fire thus making it easy to quench. Then he chided Clark thus: "If you have never used a paraffin stove before, don't dare touch it because you will be burned up alive" He turned round and faced the onlookers and said: "This boy has just come from rural areas where they know nothing about paraffin stoves, that is why he caused this terrible fire" While this statement eased off some curiosity, the smell of petrol persisted. The man too continually talked loudly about the paraffin stove "accident that resulted from ignorance of a rural boy." The man who talked like this was respected by all in the neighbourhood. Everybody appeared to believe his assertion that the mess was caused by a paraffin stove accident. After the small crowd dispersed, the man came closer to us and said with a low but hoarse voice: "You boys, why do you assemble this kind of a thing here? You should go to the bush where there is no fire and no witnesses. I guess the device should be ignited properly at the point of attack, not here. You are lucky that people seem to believe that this is a paraffin stove accident."

The handling of petrol close to a naked flame was fraught with huge risks of burning the entire neighbourhood including those handling it. If the fire had developed into a burning inferno out of control, the residents of Makhokhoba Township could have been shocked and demoralised to the lowest point. From our group, the surviving assemblers of the device could have been arrested and sentenced to death for using an inflammable liquid to burn a residential dwelling. The rest of the colleagues would have had little sympathy for the culprits for causing anguish in the civilian population. Our saviour of the evening, Aleck Dube, actually saw that it was a petrol-filled device which was badly managed. He swiftly rose to the occasion to defuse the situation by describing our mess as "paraffin stove accident" caused by a country boy who had just come to town for the first time. Dube's first action was to quench the fire fast and then make loud pronouncements that assured the community that the device was a paraffin stove that was badly managed. This was an act of ingenuity on the part of Aleck Dube which saved the operatives and the community around the Dose House. The Dose House accident is an example of many tragic occurrences arising from the handling of lethal materials with expediency rather than appropriate skill and knowledge. But the call of duty in the struggle was such that everything appeared to need quick action to challenge a well organised, well-armed and well-resourced regime. Such half-baked knowledge in the handling of lethal materials in the hands of civilian enthusiasts caused a lot of injuries and damage with "boomerang" effects. Some of the skills were imparted for a few minutes and the recipients would proclaim themselves ready to use the device in question. The Dose

House accident was the consequence of that kind of hurried process of skills transfer. Many more accidents occurred as time went on but they never dampened our resolve to traverse the hazardous terrain of freedom struggle.

The use of rudimentary devices to wage the struggle looked laughable compared to sophisticated weapons in the hands of government security forces. It actually tells the story of desperation but determination in seeking methods of freeing our country from repression by any means available. It underlines the fact that we had internalised resentment of oppression by our fellow European citizens in our own country of ancestors. As we rose up the education ladder, we learned that history confirmed what our fathers told us around the evening fires that the country was originally ruled by Africans who were overthrown by the Europeans who had fire power flying from the **"mouth of a pipe".** The desire to get our country back in our control as Africans drove some of us to go to any length, no matter how risky, to try and find means of removing illegitimate rulers who forced our forefathers out of power by their firing pipes only to rule us with arrogance and repression. But in reality we were still as militarily weak as the heroes of 1893 and 1896 in terms of grossly disproportionate armament in favour of the Rhodesian security forces.

In all the effort that we put towards causing damage to government infrastructure we were using devices that had fire but could not throw the fire at the velocity of a bullet from the gun that defeated our forefathers. Our home-made devices were only an expression of anger against injustice but lacked the automated mechanism that the rifles and machine guns had, yet we just went ahead using them trying to burn police cars and other installations with minimal success. This means we were still far from what our fathers advised us to acquire if we wanted to defeat colonial masters. Practice showed clearly that no matter what we did we were more or less on the same level of capability as our grandfathers who tried to spear an army that had superior fire power to 'strike' them from afar. Actually, it may be argued that they were even better because in 1893 they were under a state with a head, the King, complete with structured military formations and clear lines of command. We were nowhere near that in our organisational outlook because the national executive leadership of our organisation was in detention and the much needed resources were scarce. One marked difference was that our method of attack was to strike an isolated target and disappear fast whereas they faced the enemy armed forces head-on with spears and bows and arrows but, unfortunately they perished from superior military hard ware. A Molotov cocktail bomb could not be a match to modern fire arms, as it lacked automation to unleash its flame at high velocity like a bullet or a motor shell. The 1896 uprising had a profound impact on the enemy within days of the onslaught because our forefathers had military formations with command structures and motivating spirit mediums to boost their morale, even if their weaponry was still the same as in 1893. During the uprising, their best strategy was the involvement of the whole country with an element of surprise but, unfortunately, without fire power. In our case, we were complete civilians with none of all those things to make us better equipped to have a similar effect on the government as the spears and bows and arrows had done on the aforementioned occasions. Our device could cause damage only on an isolated standing target like a building or stationary vehicle but not an advancing armed force.

So, what kind of war were we fighting with such weapons of gross limitations? In all of this effort was 'General' Hokoyo's proclamation causing a dent on the enemy's forces? Yes small size acts of sabotage and arson were wide spread enough to cause alarm in the security establishment because they were always on their wheels looking for "saboteurs or trouble makers." But in terms of reaching our objective to cause the government to come down to meet African demands, we were still very far. What else could we do at that point in time except keep going until we reached a moment of definite steppingstone to the next phase of national liberation struggle?

Besides lack of appropriate resources for freedom fighting, the entire effort by civilian activists was faced with a huge impediment: the Special Branch which was the first line of contact as they frequently clashed with us as a frontline force ahead of all the Security Forces because they had to gather intelligence, assess whether it could be tackled by the police or the army. They were determined to defeat the civilian activists at that primary level by infiltrating all the underground and semi-surface structures so that their agents could be located at the planning and operational levels of the struggle inside the country. At that phase, the survival of the regime was in the hands of the Special Branch not the army per se. The most important element they needed but did not get was the support of the oppressed African majority. Therefore if this powerful branch of security began to experience a severe drought of vital information regarding the progression of the struggle, the government would be heading towards its demise. With the tentacles of the Special Branch everywhere, civilian freedom fighters were in danger of tripping into a death penalty clause of the LOMA which could send them to the gallows. On the face of such a life-threatening challenge the IBS slogan of **"The Youth of Africa Knows No Peril"** was applicable to show that we were not deterred by the possibility of becoming hanged if we were caught in action with lethal objects for political reasons. While we were well aware of the consequences of running counter to draconian legislation, we never considered abandoning the struggle because we could not see any other avenue that would lead our country towards democracy. In another level of operation, a militarily trained freedom fighter was also fully aware that if he lost the initiative in battle he could be put down by enemy fire but he was not deterred by that possibility in the same manner that committed civilians were not deterred by the LOMA's hanging clause.

Place of employment became a suitable cover for underground activities

While we were kept on our toes by the tempo of the struggle, I took advantage of some gaps in the mornings to write applications for jobs. The move paid dividends as several responses were favourable. But one of the first ones finished up in an explosive drama. I was due to be appointed as a School Secretary at a Mission school outside Bulawayo but, a Schools Inspector responsible for recruiting staff for schools suddenly burst out thus: **"I understand that you were making yourself a junior Joshua Nkomo at Nyathi Secondary School! I am sorry we have no place for Joshua Nkomos in our schools."** As I walked away from the Inspector's office, if the Inspector was able to read what was in my head, he would have wished me shot dead. My mind was battling to understand as to why white Rhodesians regarded us as trouble makers merely for speaking out against obvious injustice against Africans? Were they merely safeguarding their privileges or was it the ideology of racial superiority that made them so politically stiff-necked? Whatever the answer would be, I went away wondering what would happen if all those who were denied jobs because of their political affiliation, grew in numbers and formed an army to fight the white dominated system that did not count an African to be anything in his own country. History would tell. The next offer was by the Department of Information where I was required to explain the Rhodesian Government policy to the rural people at a time when we were condemning those policies especially on land distribution. The job was well paying and very tempting. But how could I go out in the country to tell the elders to accept the policy of forced land seizures which had just taken place (from 1946 to 1956) throughout the country? I turned the offer down. My relatives became furious when I told them that I had rejected a lucrative job in government. They did not even want to appreciate the predicament of being an activist and at the same time propagating the policies of repression to the oppressed. The land question was the key bone of contention in the rural areas because a large number of Africans were removed from their fertile land between 1946 and 1956. Part of the job was to pacify the rural folk by persuading them to accept destocking and demarcating the land into smaller plots thereby streamlining the villages and grazing areas in tandem with the said smaller arable plots under the Land husbandry Act of 1952. This is exactly what the villagers did not want to hear from officials let alone from their own number.

However, my application to Mpilo Central Hospital (a Federal Ministry of Health hospital) in Bulawayo paid dividends. In January 1963 I got a job at Mpilo Central Hospital as a clerk in the Main Stores. The job was very suitable for the purpose of carrying out underground work unnoticed because it was a government health facility which would provide a good cover provided I was able to conceal my activities. Indeed the Hospital job was ideal as I was a government servant there and would be minimal suspicion by security forces. Indeed, over a period of time I was able to set up structures of action linking Mpilo Hospital staff and surrounding townships which were officially called "Bulawayo African Townships" (BAT) encompassing Barbourfields, Mzilikazi, Mkhokhoba and Nguboyenja, named this way because of their proximity to the City in relation to the rest. We further ventured into the suburbs to mobilise domestic servants, the gardeners and nannies. We gained access to the suburbs through the outpatients who worked and lived there as domestic servants. Their residential and work addresses were recorded in the outpatients' register so it was easy to follow up by cultivating friendship with one or two as they frequented the hospital reporting to the same clerk in most cases. Initially the process was slow but as soon as we bumped on some of the staunch supporters of the African nationalist movement, the gateway to the Bulawayo European suburbs widened beyond our expectations. Luckily, we found that most of the domestic servants were staunch supporters of the African nationalist movement. This opportunity opened the way for us to create the necessary structures of the movement in the suburbs and within a short space of time we had established branches there which had to be confirmed by the District Committees as official structures of the Party.

My job was not well paying but good enough for me at the time because I was able to make a living and support my mother and other relatives in rural areas. It also enabled me to buy a small car, a ten year old Standard 10 (Austin). Even if the material conditions for working people were satisfactory due to a low cost of living, the fundamentals of human rights, dignity and basic freedoms were denied us, Africans, in our own country. While I enjoyed owning a car for personal needs, this was also an opportunity to provide transport for all our political activities. The Standard 10 became readily available for all our ventures during the day and at night. The car enabled us to connect with the suburbs and rural hinterland of Bulawayo to facilitate the formation of militia-like structures which would be called upon to act as required by freedom fighters.

CHAPTER EIGHT

AFRICANS RETREAT FROM FIGHTING

COLONIALISM TO ATTACK EACH OTHER

The National Executive Committee (NEC) of ZAPU had a provision for a structure called Department of Special Affairs located within it as part of the structure. Special Affairs Department was actually designed to enable the leadership to use any method of struggle as they deemed fit in the circumstances, including armed struggle if ZAPU was banned (1962). On this account they sent a senior member of the National Executive, the Rev Ndabaningi Sithole as a Representative in Dar es Salaam for the purpose of arranging with progressive governments concerning training saboteurs who would return home after training to carry out acts of sabotage to force the Rhodesian government to succumb to the demands of the Africans. During that period a number of youths were sent out for training in China and returned to the country but the Special Branch of the time did mount surveillance on them without closely harassing them for quite some time during the Whitehead government. They returned before ZAPU was banned in 1962 but they did not do a lot that we could evaluate. They stayed quiet until ZAPU was banned and some of them returned to exile for further training in guerrilla warfare.

After ZAPU was banned, many people had the impression that the leadership was preparing to go out of the country and form a Government in exile to challenge the government by military means if it banned the Party. We had hoped that Rev Ndabaningi Sithole may have made some headway in preparations for that purpose in the event of the ban of ZAPU. That could have been a plan B to take the stage in the form of a government–in–exile with powers and authority to mobilise resources to prepare for and wage war of liberation the Algerian style. Before the ban information was rife in senior ZAPU circles indicating that Tanzania was willing to host such a government. We thought it was a wise idea to take that step. We began to strengthen the structures that had gone underground so that they got ready for proper training to sharpen the onslaught on the strategic colonial structures of power. The Algerian liberation movement submerged itself underground to link up with structures that were created before their movement was banned. That formula (see early pages on students underground at Nyathi School) served them very well because they did not start from scratch to mobilise human resources for support when they launched armed struggle in 1954. We thought ZAPU leaders had learned hints from Algerian experience when they started talking about forming a government in exile based on the Algerian model. But it is not clear what happened when they got out of the country because no such government was announced at all until it was overtaken by unwelcome events. We did not even know what Rev Ndabaniningi Sithole was doing in Dar es Salaam while he was representing the Party there in preparation for armed struggle if need be. We had originally believed that Rev Sithole was actually making serious preparations whereby if the authorities banned ZAPU, he would instantly press a button to unleash a fire-powered challenge to the colonial authorities. Nothing like that happened until we heard him being announced as champion of a new party. It would appear that he was there preparing to form a new party.

In politics of expectations twelve months is like twelve years if the period is marked by confusion, non-action and back and forth movement at leadership level. The people at grassroots level were increasingly becoming disenchanted and demoralised as they heard the propaganda of the victor only. The Rhodesian Front regime, being the victor, went all out to vilify the African nationalists and they had no means of putting an alternative view. Those of us who continued with the under-ground work found ourselves being slowly reduced to smaller numbers than we had six months after the ban. Nevertheless, some of us persevered until at the onset of winter in 1963 rumours sprang up and spread to all townships suggesting that a new party was in the pipeline. The people in the forefront of the "new party" were named as Enos Nkala, Edison Zobgo, Leopold Takawira et al. Accompanying the rumour, information circulated in Salisbury and Bulawayo to the effect that Robert Mugabe was against the formation of a new party as he thought this might destabilise national unity thus weakening the thrust of the struggle on the colonial authority. He was understood to prefer the replacement of Nkomo with another leader to make him deputise the new leader to maintain national unity behind a united national movement. People were relieved to hear this because, Mugabe and Sithole were considered as part of high caliber elements in the leadership of ZAPU and, if the splinter group was without those two, it might lack significant political magnetic pull effect to draw support from the masses. Above all, with the gap created by the death of Dr Parirenyatwa, ZAPU could not afford to suffer a further loss of intellectual capacity at that time of need.

Nevertheless, just before the dissident NEC members announced their intention to break with ZAPU, winds of rumours were blowing everywhere saying that Robert Mugabe had finally agreed to be part of a new party. Indeed, one May day, in the evening, his voice was heard announcing from Dar es Salaam, in Tanzania that an illustrious leader had "emerged personified in the Reverend Ndabaningi Sithole" to replace Joshua Nkomo. Many people were shocked by the announcement especially to hear the names of Mugabe and Sithole being part of the key leadership of a dissident group. There were fears that, if not carefully handled, the split could take ethnic lines thus damaging the cause of national liberation by putting the mass support base in disarray to the advantage of colonial authorities. People asked anxiously as to which side of the crack was JD Chikerema, GB Nyandoro, J Musika, TG Silundka and JZ Moyo. They were consoled to hear that they were firmly holding on to ZAPU forum.

For some of us the split was like bomb falling on an open pick-up on which we were back passengers. I personally constantly harked back upon what was ushered in by the NDP in the early 1960's and the impressive team of ZAPU NEC introduced to us in Barbourfields Stadium before the death of Dr Parirenyatwa. I could not entertain the thought of a new team that was without some of those I thought provided enough intellectual capital required for systematic crafting of a feasible strategy to resolve the colonial problem by any means possible. The loss of Dr Parirenyatwa was too much of a national set back of immense proportions by any measure. But a further exodus of some of that impressive quality of leadership was too ghastly to add to my already "disturbed" memory. The thought that they were no longer together was too harrowing to entertain because it meant the struggle would enter into a reverse gear for a foreseeable future.

Indeed the split pushed the struggle into a fast mode of the reverse gear as hostility between the two warring factions generated so much heated anger in the population to the extent of regarding and calling each other enemy, **Tshombe**[16], etc. Yesterday we called each other sons and daughter of the soil of the Motherland. But suddenly a political split made us to see each other as enemies to be lumped together with the real enemy, the colonial regime. Why? Because many people never believed that a person who was not a traitor could split the nation to the advantage of the enemy in our backyard. The splitting faction charged that Joshua Nkomo was indecisive on essential matters of strategy to drive the struggle forward. Each side did not appreciate the concerns of the other side no matter how much the issues at stake were elucidated.

However, Joshua Nkomo reacted by saying that his colleagues had not committed a cardinal sin; they had just gone **"out of step"** therefore should not be condemned (Unkown, 1963). But the split caused so much anguish and consternation amongst the ordinary people to the extent that they drew daggers to have a go at each other with ferocity. There are some people who say that Nkomo made a mistake by suspending the likes of Mugabe and Sithole for becoming rebellious because initially they were opposed to the split. If this was true, it would suggest that Nkomo's miscalculation drove these two out of ZAPU, although ZAPU officials of the time countered this by saying that the five rebels took the initiative to announce Nkomo's replacement by Rev Ndabaningi Sithole without consulting the rest of the NEC. In an effort to retain as much of the original support as possible while the dissident leaders were still in exile, Nkomo called a national conference and invited his dissident colleagues to attend; but they did not come. The conference was held at Cold Comfort farm, just outside Salisbury. At the conference one of the key developments was the formation of what they called the **People's Care Taker Council (PCC),** which became a **"regent"** of ZAPU or a surface structure representing a banned organisation which was forced to go "underground". Joshua Nkomo was elected president of this caretaker outfit. There was no position of deputy president. Instead there was Secretary for Presidential Affairs, a position that was taken by James Dambadza Chikerema, (former Deputy President of the banned Southern Rhodesia African National Congress). A totally different National Executive Committee emerged from this conference and most of them were former members of the SRANC Executive Committee, from JD Chikerema, George Bonzo Nyandoro, Secretary General, Joseph Musika Secretary for Youth Affairs, Willie Musarurwa, Publicity Secretary, JZ Moyo Treasurer, Josiah Chinamano Secretary for Education, TG Silundika, Information, Munhuwepasi Munodawafa, National Chairman, etc. But most ordinary members remained furious against those who were regarded as having "gone out of step." They felt that the split would weaken the struggle against the determined and uncompromising settler regime of the Rhodesian Front which was rapidly consolidating its power within the white population, preparing them to be ready for a unilateral declaration of independence (UDI).

However the formation of PCC was an act of ingenuity as it brought back the politics of surface activities inside the country whereby the structures were revived under a new name. Accompanying this was regeneration of morale amongst the supporters who had gone dormant and disillusioned. The elected structures ranged from branch to District, Regional and National Executive levels. That is, after the Cold Comfort Conference election meetings took place everywhere to establish the appropriate PCC structures that entered the shoes of the banned ZAPU. The re-surfacing of the political structures throughout the country revived considerable levels of optimism among the people. In the process of electing new committees, I was elected Chairperson of Makhokhoba Branch when Ethan Dube was assigned to a new mission outside the country.

---

[16] *traitor*

Following this, a District elective conference elected me to a position of Youth Deputy Secretary for Bulawayo District. At that time the indications were that PCC had inherited an overwhelming majority support from the banned ZAPU followers throughout the country as was indicated by mass rallies addressed by PCC leaders, especially in the Mashonaland regions in the north east, east, south east, southern, central and western; this included Manicaland and Masvingo. In those regions attendances at PCC rallies were higher than in any place in Matabeleland and Midlands regions. As a matter of fact, underground ZAPU structures were the ones that emerged on the surface to attend the Cold Comfort Conference where the National Executive was elected.

In August of the same year, the splitting members formed a new party that immediately held its congress in Gwelo (Gweru) and was named Zimbabwe African National Union (ZANU) headed by the Rev Ndabaningi Sithole with Robert Gabriel Mugabe as Secretary General. This meant that the split was now complete and final. The question of whether the rebels had gone out of step was answered clearly by the formation of the new party as mentioned above. What was the social cost of the split?

The ramifications of the split were far reaching as their fierce competition for mass support from the African population led to violent clashes that resulted in unprecedented bloodshed between Africans themselves. A despicable wave of violence between the supporters of the two organisations became a daily occurrence, especially in towns. Members of each party were fuming with venomous fury in complete disregard for the fact that this was a mere disagreement between the same sons and daughters of the same Motherland. So the harmony that was created by the NDP and prevailed during the life of ZAPU suddenly evaporated through the huge crack of the split like a tyre that had lost its pressure by running over a sharp blade placed along the road. Animosity between the two camps became very intense and potentially harmful to the very roots of national cohesion that we had become used to taking for granted. Indeed the violence between the supporters of the two parties increasingly approached epidemic proportions as the focus on the fight against colonialism became a peripheral issue if not parked away in the cold for a while. There was so much witch hunt to the extent that some people spent most of their active time hunting down political opponents, who happened to be other Africans. Any freedom fighter who witnessed such an abominable political duel between Zimbabwean freedom movements felt very ashamed to be part of that generation.

It was a matter of time before the foundation of the fabric of African nationhood that was laid by the SRANC and consolidated by NDP was torn asunder by violent clashes in the urban and rural areas to the political advantage of the Rhodesian Front government. In this fiasco, many people were arrested for burning each other's' children and houses instead of fighting the government or beating each other instead of fighting the security forces. **Mwanawebvu** slogan and its socially constructive derivatives were relegated to the dust bin of political insanity as African threatened to slay another African on account of artificial political differences. The virus of political hatred and intolerance infected people with misdirected militancy in their minds thus causing them to perpetuate antagonism between the two political parties throughout the period of the better part of national liberation struggle except few instances of cooperation for strategic reasons during the armed struggle (eg formation of Joint Military Command, Zimbabwe People's Army, Patriotic Front, etc). Even so a harmful tradition of political hatred between ZAPU and ZANU exhibited itself as a retrogressive trend that ripped African unity apart as if they were foreign to each other. That was a clear indication that the two parties' political hatred of each other was entrenched within each of them and permeated into societal structures wherein the virus has translated itself into a hard-to-cure political "pneumonia" that has bedeviled the wellbeing of society as a whole in terms of perpetual gross abuse of human rights on the grounds of political differences, even if the other party is no longer ZAPU in modern Zimbabwe. In essence the origin of political violence and hatred on account of political differences were triggered by the split in ZAPU when some of the key national leaders broke away to form another party, Zimbabwe African National Union in May 1963.

During or about the time of the formation of ZANU in 1963, the two African Nationalist parties were not the only culprits against themselves in the country. A new political front that came into being in 1962 with anger and animosity against a constitution that introduced few parliamentary seats for Africans was the Rhodesian Front. With opposite reasons to those of Africans, right from its inception, the RF decisively rejected the 1961 constitution which it saw as an open roadway to African majority rule. Its anger fuelled its determination to stop any slightest movement towards African majority rule therefore, in its hard line stance, it adopted and internalised political intolerance as demonstrated by its practice in detaining the African Nationalist leaders and their key supporters indefinitely without trial when it came to power. Their only crime was to champion the cause of majority rule in Rhodesia through universal adult suffrage. Its legacy has a trail of African blood no less than the two liberation movements in their share of dispensing with African life as a cheap commodity since the split in 1963. Such is the historical misfortune of our beloved country that has left an indelible mark of turning African life into a cheap commodity for elimination without a price (Sachikonye, 2011).

CHAPTER NINE

POLICY OF RACIAL DOMINATION DRIVES AFRICANS TO VIOLENT LIBERATION

The political intransigency of the Rhodesian Front government was an indication that there would be no majority rule without a hard fight. Such indicators like its founding principles and the boldness with which they were propounded to the public made the African youth become more militant and eager to fight the regime, no longer with stones but with fire. The most instigating statement was when Ian Smith said:

"If in my life time we have an African nationalist government in power in Southern Rhodesia, then we will have failed in the policy that I believe in." (Daily News, 1963)

After declaring that there would be no majority rule in his life time, he went on to add that "Not in a thousand years". Here the policy that he believed in was outlined in the founding principles of the Rhodesian Front which were clearly designed to perpetuate racial domination and discrimination in the country. The statement was a clear declaration that Africans should forget about ever attaining freedom in their own country of birth unless they used force. That was the time during which we witnessed the Rhodesian whites swing decisively from the centre politics to the right of the political spectrum. The swing to the right made many young Africans feel that there was no other option to achieve freedom other than by war. This is not to say adults did not feel the same, it is rather to point out that youngsters did not see any future under a repressive system where they had no opportunity to participate in the political and economic activities of the country as free citizens with equal rights with whites. If youngsters became hardened by the political behaviour of the Rhodesian Front government, how would seasoned politicians calculate the stakes in relation to overall national development in a country of a racial mix? Indeed, African leaders, too, moved away from moderate political ambivalence towards a hard line against the regime because they were totally marginalised by both the UFP and RF governments.

There are many people who say that if the white electorate had not voted the Rhodesian Front to power there would have been no war in Zimbabwe because the UFP government was not as ruthless, contemptuous, arrogant and politically stiff-necked in driving a system of racial domination like the RF regime of Ian Douglass Smith. The problem with the political behaviour of the latter was that they propounded the principles of racial domination and applied them in their management of public affairs of state and society as if the presence of Africans in the country was a mistake therefore they had to be disregarded in every sphere of social action. The RF principles did not only irritate the Africans rampantly, they also galvanised them into counter activity that translated into violent resistance against the regime. The Africans felt extremely undermined by the RF's contemptuous bulldozing of its way towards UDI without paying the slightest attention to their legitimate aspirations as an indigenous majority of citizenry in the country. The regime approached the chiefs to hoodwink them to support the UDI project knowing well that they no longer enjoyed popular support that the African Nationalist enjoyed because they had become paid servants of the regime. Any chief who supported majority rule p was deposed and detained (eg Chief Mangwende, Chief Mathema, Chief Tangwena, etc). Ian Smith, intelligent as he was, did not bother to fully inform himself about the genuine wants of the African people concerning the question of social and political advancement. According to the 1961 constitution of Rhodesia, becoming Prime Minister placed him in a position of leadership of a nation of racial and ethnic diversity with responsibility to adopt a political formula of how to harmonise rather than antagonize peoples who already had a record of lack of trust of each other since 1890. For him to adopt the superfluous approach of involving powerless chiefs was an attempt to be seen as reasonable and responsible' yet as leader of a nation with diverse races he should have known that twentieth century Africans of all ages had much broader aspirations than those of a chief in respect of basic freedoms and citizen rights. He should have been aware that Missionary schools taught a broad history dating from pre-Jesus Christ to modern times including land mark revolutions and the development of democracy from Greek City States to the current period. In that history Rhodesia was not mentioned as a democratic country, but it was highlighted that it was a white ruled self-governing colony since 1923. Therefore it was height of folly for a leader of that level of responsibility to pretend that such knowledge did not exist in the African population, especially the youth and middle aged. Above all, some major revolutions had occurred in his lifetime all over the world including Europe, overthrowing oppressive regimes, yet he pushed the country deep into a repressive racist system hoping that he would be an exception in History because "Rhodesians were a special brand" incompatible with all others.

Garfield Reginald Todd, who was a Missionary from New Zealand, seemed to have perceived that African demands for racial equality in all spheres of public policy were pivoted on knowledge of what was prevailing in modern systems of governance because when he was Prime Minister he attempted to make plans for social advancement of the Africans but, that caused disaffection of his colleagues as they did not share his vision of racial inclusivity. From that occasion (of Todd's dismissal from Premiership) the country began to gravitate rapidly towards the hands of white right wing extremists and finished up with the Rhodesian Front at the extreme end of right wing political spectrum in the country. Prime Minister Ian Douglas Smith and his government grossly misread the mind of an oppressed African by thinking that Africans would stand idle while the country was being ruled by a regime that excluded them indefinitely. This common sense error of African omission from governance sounds simplistic to give credence to the fact that it was one of principal causes of irreconcilable conflict in Rhodesia. A ghastly option of racial exclusivity begot a painful struggle that became a price Africans had to pay to gain freedom yet it could have been avoided if the Rhodesian whites supported Todd's social transformative plan. In line with Todd's thinking, the African Nationalists started off on a peaceful path of demanding equal rights in all spheres of societal public affairs as a prerequisite for peaceful and orderly change towards majority rule. But their call for a civil process of smooth political development to real democracy was decisively blocked through banning African peaceful organisations to the extent that they had to choose an option to which they were forced by the white electorate that swung from the centre to vote for the Rhodesian Front's poisonous narration of racism as outlined in the fifteen founding principles that generated excitement and high hopes in the white population but delivered dejection and glum upon the African people as they saw themselves subjected to racial domination and deprivation for an indefinite period. That was so because those principles became pillars of white rule that effectively excluded the majority of the inhabitants of the country from any responsibility in management of public affairs in the Rhodesian scheme of things. I have often wondered as to what reasonable basis did the Rhodesian whites let the Rhodesian Front regime adopt a political framework that excluded the majority of citizens, Africans, thus placing them on the periphery of the Rhodesian system of governance and economic development. They virtually became victims of a repressive system as they were denied basic democratic rights and freedoms in their own country. What did they expect the long term outcome of racial domination of the majority by the minority would be? If anybody suggested that Africans should take their place in a primitive political catacomb and allow civilised whites to rule them, they ignored the fact that to be ruled by whites has never been the right place for Africans no matter how primitive they were. Their right place was to rule themselves free from racial domination.

However, all the challenges of repression had to be faced by the oppressed citizens because they were the ones who felt the pinch of its injustices. The simple question was, how could banned nationalist movements stop white domination from continuing for a thousand years, as pronounced by the Prime Minister, Ian Douglas Smith? This was a crucial question to which every politically conscious person had to find an answer as to whether or not they were on the side of national liberation. Before they were banned, PCC (ZAPU) and ZANU had sent some of their senior leaders out of the country to set up structures and cultivate possible sources of weapons for waging liberation armed struggle in the event of failure to negotiate a just settlement. ZAPU activated the Department of Special Affairs, located in the National Executive Committee right at its formation. It began to play its role slowly before the split by training saboteurs during 1962. During the period of training saboteurs, Ndabaningi Sithole was in charge of the mission in Dar es Alaam, in Tanzania before the split (Sachikonye, 2011). After the split, ZAPU in exile set up a Military Administration complete with appropriate oversight structures based at the military headquarters in Lusaka. The senior commanding structure consisted of the Commander-in-chief, Chief of Staff, Chief Political Commissar, Chief of Intelligence, Chief of Personnel and Training, Chief of Security and Reconnaissance, Chief of Operations, Chief of Logistics, Chief of Communications, etc. The Military Administration was accountable to a War Council or High Command consisting of five members the NEC two of whom were in exile. The military wing was called Zimbabwe People's Revolutionary Army (ZPRA) regimented into detachments that consisted of platoons and sections at the point of deployment and in the camps where a camp commander was in charge. At the same time ZANU too set up what was called **Dare Rechimurenga**[17] consisting of five senior members of the Central Committee.

Meanwhile the Rhodesian Front regime was amassing more White support for its intent for UDI, preparing its electorate for the actual event. For our part as surface and semi-surface functionaries, we continued to strengthen our underground structures in preparation for the struggle. Part of our tasks included mobilising the masses for action and recruiting personnel for military training outside the country to build a guerrilla force that would counter UDI with armed resistance. All the youth branches formed special groups organised like regiments with definite command structures such as commander and deputy. This regimental group was called

---

[17]
War Council

Zhanda (**Gendarmes:** from DRC during political crisis in the early 1960s: refers to members of a military force with police duties within civilian population. The word became politically fashionable in the mid-1960s at the same time when Moise Tshombe was dubbed an African traitor for being implicated in the murder of Patrice Lumumba, the first Prime Minister of DRC). From then on, anyone who was believed to be a traitor was called 'T**shombe**.'

The rise of **Zhanda** militias happened in all branches with a commander and deputy both appointed by the Youth Executive Committee. **Zhanda** regiments emerged first in the townships of major towns like Salisbury (Harare) Bulawayo, Mutare, Gweru, Kwekwe, etc with the rise of PCC in 1963. The commander was appointed by the youth branch committee and therefore accountable to the same. The Special Branch got to know about **Zhanda** and they started to pay attention to its leaders. In Makhokhoba Branch, we maintained Zhanda as a semi-surface action-packed group, meaning that they were active mainly at night not during the day. That is to say, Zhanda performed both surface and underground tasks as deemed necessary by the Youth Branch Committee. Noticing that the Zhanda was becoming too large, we came up with the idea for the formation of a special group that would operate underground with more specialised operations than Zhanda was tasked to do. To this end we assigned Mbonjeni Mlilo, who was a commander of the Zhanda in Makhokhoba Branch, to identify suitable candidates for such a militia group. He quickly assembled a very large group of committed youngsters suggesting that they should form the nucleus of a secret army. We assembled them under a moon light within tall grass on the banks of a ravine running between Makhokhoba and Mzilikazi Townships. Seeing the size of the group presented to our Committee by Mlilo, Sam Dumaza remarked, **"what a formidable force!** Now we need a military person to train them as a secret army." But I was not convinced that starting a secret army without sanction from the NEC was a wise idea, so I suggested that we should keep the group for tough assignments as well as prepare them for future military training once we got a green light from above. We then named the new group **"The Formidable Force"** otherwise shortened to **The Formidable.** In this connection, I recommended that we keep the **"The Formidable"** as a clandestine operations militia regiment and the Branch Executive Committee approved the proposition. The Formidable, like Zhanda, was a regimented group with a commander and deputy both appointed by the Executive Committee of the Youth Branch and accountable to the same. We appointed Edward Tshuma, a quiet fellow but thoughtful and brave activist. Tshuma was a man of action but not keen on publicised activities in politics. He would hardly be suspected (unless sold out) in the eyes of the police. Being a shebeen proprietor gave him some camouflage because those days shebeens were not a priority for the security police because most of the proprietors were not active in politics, although some politicians liked drinking from there. Tshuma preferred to be active at night or in a situation where there was no possibility of publicity therefore this task suited him very well.

Initially, The Formidable was structured like an army, on the advice of some colleagues who seemed to have some knowledge of military formations. They were members of Zhanda who were now assigned to The Formidable, but instead of encouraging them to introduce strict military discipline to the group, we decided on a loosely structured organisation understood by untrained people for action rather than introduce a formal military structure. But the leader was a commander and a deputy commander to denote that they were on the road to become soldiers of freedom. On this account we structured **The Formidable** into subgroups with each group based on its street where members resided, headed by a cell leader. There were eleven streets in Makhokhoba Township plus Burombo Hostels which was regarded as one unit but too large to be a cell. The Hostel had to be divided into two groups each with a cell leader. The problem with such a segmented structure was that numbers were so uneven from street to street. The largest cell in Makhokhoba streets had fourteen members and the smallest five members. In the suburbs, each suburb had its own cell under a leader. Khumalo and Parklands combined had the largest number with ten members and other suburbs ranged from four to seven. When put altogether, the Formidable could have formed what is normally called a "reinforced company" (above 90 members) in military parlance. So subdividing the group into small units made it possible to manage them because we could meet just their leaders not all of them in an assembly format.

The cell leaders were answerable to the overall commander of **The Formidable** who was accountable to the Branch Executive Committee together with his deputy. In Makhokhoba, with eleven streets and eleven cells of **The Formidable**, another challenge was how to keep them apart at a time when it was no longer advisable to know what each one of us was doing in the struggle except members of the same operating cell. Streets were only separated by houses and joined by roads that ran across them. The suburban comrades were left to be autonomous because they were as many as the Makhokhoba strength and, above all, they were available only on Sundays, which was a common feature for most domestic employees residing in the European suburbs. Since they knew each other fairly well, they were asked to elect their own leader and make sure he had qualities for a tough job of operating secretly at all times. They all settled for one popularly known as Sekuru Sithole who was quite a hardliner but very thoughtful in approaching every problem situation. Sithole and his deputy attended Makhokhoba Youth Branch Commanders' meetings for ease of management. By 1967 Sekuru Sithole asked to be relieved from the struggle on the grounds that he had "a call from ancestors to become a **nyanga/sangoma**[18] in Chipinge District. In his request to be excused he stressed that it was imperative for him to comply with the ancestral call. Sithole was a dedicated freedom fighter of a high quality in terms of bravery and tact in all actions. He had brilliant contributions during strategic planning meetings. He actually suggested that the suburban contingent be treated as a reserve force that could be called upon to distabilise the suburbs if there was massive unrest that engulfed African Townships and Industrial Sites. The suggestion was accepted but no such mass uprising happened so the reserve force was never called to act because there was no uprising in the City until it just melted away over a period of time.

When Sekuru Sithole mentioned his call back home, many comrades remarked that maybe his ancestors could "protect" us from detection by the security forces. There were some who urged Sithole to return and join armed struggle with ancestry powers to provide a shield against detection as they believed that it was possible. The rest of us, while not openly dismissing the claim, we did not believe that Sithole's ancestors alone could keep us safe without taking appropriate and practical precautions to cover ourselves. In his own right, Sithole could have become commander of the Formidable as a whole but his departure robed us of a fine soldier of freedom, an untrained soldier who never ran out of ideas on tactical approach to thoroughgoing activities in the struggle.

Assembling all these 'troops' in a secret meeting was no longer feasible at all; that is why they had to be subdivided into small manageable units. Some suburbs were unable to participate in this format so they were free to come to Mkhhokhoba if they had time. Suburban numbers of the Formidable rose phenomenally to nearly equal to the total number in Makhokhoba during the life of PCC. Each street or suburban cell had to focus on underground activities of a militia nature in respect of being prepared for much needed action or support to freedom fighters as they had already begun to trickle in. Street cells were supposed to meet at their convenience where ever it was safe. When PCC was banned the units were further subdivided into small cells of no

---

18
traditional healer

more than five members per cell with one member as liaison person to link up with command structures of The Formidable. The Commander of The Formidable met with all street cell leaders at the drinking clubs or at his (shebeen) house once monthly. But after the ban on PCC, the meetings had to be on a one- on-one basis (except on a few occasions when larger meetings could be convened) and he in turn reported to the Branch Chairperson.

The description depicts a picture of full time business in the underground activities. Indeed we were busy every day after work and during weekends and public holidays. The unemployed members were the busiest regarding reconnaissance and intelligence gathering. That was why that, when we got arrested, we had to find a credible alibi when being questioned about our movements and interpersonal interactions on specific days after work and it was a very critical situation to come up with convincing answers to the interrogators. The advantage of keeping alive underground cells was that it provided a reliable supportive infrastructure for armed liberation struggle from the mid-1960s to the cease fire in 1979 (Sadomba, 2011).

The kinds of militias described above were strongest in towns and weak in the rural areas where branches had small numbers of Zhanda. We had to establish links with rural areas because it was there that plenty of natural cover for the fighters was in abundance. Most of rural youngsters had migrated to towns and that included some of us. So we had to advise rural leaders to create structures similar to ours in towns even if there were limited escape windows except towns when cornered by security forces. So, if they came to town they could find a hideout and a window of escape when faced with danger of arrest. In our situation in towns, the rest of branch committee members were members of the Zhanda and the Formidable, but all concealed from the Special Branch as much as possible. While they put their surveillance agents on the Zhanda, the Special Branch did not seem to have a clear picture of the Formidable or its distinct form and function from the Zhanda. Rural colleagues created their Zhanda and assigned them functions that were appropriate for rural environment with consideration that such structure had to provide an essentially crucial pivotal base for recruitment of freedom fighters. The rural militias became more pronounced in burning rural infrastructure such as dip tanks, schools, rest camps, homes of identified agents of security forces, etc. Rural colleagues basically maintained their executive committees from the level of branch to district because during armed struggle these were the structures that made themselves available to the freedom fighters and they were officially known as semi-surface officials of the party. They recruited Zhanda to join combat forces or assign some members to carry out some duties to service the struggle as **courier**s or conveyors of necessary supplies of any description. On the other hand in towns cells remained quite strong and able to link with rural structures for needed supplies in operational areas.

Zhanda had multiple functions in the struggle but its primary role was to mobilise the masses door to door for action such as demonstrations, riots and civil commotion in reaction to some police provocation such as arresting of national leaders, etc. At times it clashed with the anti-riot police and waged running battles using stones and any other missile they could land their hands on. But they did not confront armed police because experience had shown in 1960 (**Zhi riots which turned violent**) that police did not hesitate to shoot at a rioting crowd. After the split there were some ugly scenes where Zhanda patrols clashed with ZANU youths with serious consequences in terms of injuries inflicted by either side. But in Makhokhoba Branch I took responsibility to forbid the use of violence against ZANU supporters. In this connection it was agreed that the Zhanda should never touch a ZANU member or supporter without extreme provocation (such as assault) and all this should be reported to the branch Chairman. This worked well as our members found no reason to report to me because in Makhokhoba Township

ZANU support at the time was insignificant therefore very limited incidents of violent clashes occurred. Above all our members knew that I needed convincing reasons for attacking anyone of our opponents. That policy did not help bring down the level of anger against the split among colleagues because people felt that the colonial authorities would thrive unscathed while the Africans spent a lot of time and energy quarrelling and fighting over which leader was legitimate and which one was a traitor. Actually in the rest of Bulawayo there was low activity of violence with no fatalities or serious injuries on both sides. As much as I was disappointed by the split, I never saw any sense in beating those who were no longer prepared to be in ZAPU. It was their choice. That is why I find it totally unnecessary for present day ZANU PF to employ vicious onslaught against a totally nonviolent party like the Movement for Democratic Change (MDC).

When I was elected to the District Executive Committee as Deputy Secretary, John Mkandla took over as Chairman of the Youth in Makhokhoba Youth Branch. During my chairmanship, John Mkandla was Secretary. Both of us were instrumental in the formation and defining the role of the Formidable in Makhokhoba in the struggle. John Mkandla, like me was keen on clandestine operations more than on open activism. The Formidable force, being our baby, was kept safe from detection even if there was no guarantee on long term safety. We decided that we should create an informal channel to obtain information about the deployment of informers in the township. Our first attempt was successful because we discovered that some one that was trusted in the branch from the onset of ZAPU was a police informer. This encouraged us to make the informal channel a semi-formal one to keep ourselves informed about leakage of information from our structures

Under PCC, the female youths also elected their executive committee. The Chairperson and Secretary attended the meetings of the youth branch executive committee as ex-officio members and the main branch of the Party on the same capacity. They could participate in the Zhanda but in small numbers as they proved very good in persuading the masses for demonstration as well as recruiting new members for the Party. As their regiment grew in numbers it was placed under the charge of their chairperson and they were named **oMakhulunhloko**[19] derived from their Chairperson, Gladys Ncube, who earned the name, u**Makhulunhloko** (literally means "big head" but in this context it simply means **leader)**, because she excelled in both ideas and practical action in the field as she distinguished herself with brilliant contributions during planning meetings in Branch Committees and cell meetings. Under her leadership these young women became a nervous system of the branch in terms of detecting moles and sensing vital areas of strengths and weaknesses within our structures. They virtually became the first line of contact between us and all hostile pockets in the townships as well as in the British South Africa Police (BSAP). In this connection, they knew the BSAP patrol system and their change-over times, differences between a Riot squad vehicle and a regular police patrol pick-up. They were the first to discover and pronounce that most African members of uniformed regular police were not hostile to majority rule project because they believed that an African government was inevitable and they were looking forward to promotions by such a government. More importantly **oMakhulunhluko** excelled in the mobilisation of the masses for whatever action was on the agenda. It was fascinating to see them moving from door to door and talking to people politely with some polished language of respect and humility. Seeing the successes of **oMakhulunhloko** in their work, some parents encouraged their daughters to join them because their image impressed the Township residents in Makhokhoba during the life span of PCC. On a large measure they were reliable in matters of security and safety. For example they knew the safe and unsafe shebeens and beer-halls as they

---

[19] *leaders*

pinpointed those that were heavily infested with detectives or their agents and those that were considered detached from mainstream current of political movement. This helped us to identify streets that had become Party strongholds and those that were weak and which areas were suitable for our operational 'bases' or hideouts in the townships.

Nevertheless, **oMakhulunhloko's** numerical strength at a later stage was affected by some members getting married to men who lived in faraway districts which meant that their departure created gaps. For instance the Chairperson married in Harare at a time when she had begun to handle hard ware of the struggle. Her Deputy, Rhoda Bhebhe, married a man from Buhera (165 km from Harare) who worked in Bulawayo so she took over as leader and continued underground work throughout the period of the struggle until independence. Once organised this way, the cell was structured in such a way that its members met in small numbers but did not attend large meetings of the branch frequently. Rhoda Bhebhe successfully led her cell for a long period until it was succeeded by Sibusiso Mazibuko who linked the cell with fighters through a supply chain of needed supplies in the field operations. They met with cell leaders either in threes or on a one on one basis, for security reasons. If any member or more became suspicious that she was under surveillance by the Special Branch, she would be rested to stay put for a while until leaders were satisfied that she was safe again. The same method was applied to members of the Formidable whereby a member subjected to surveillance would be removed from the area and exported to Zambia if there was a danger of prosecution or exposure to such danger.

A striking element concerning **oMakhulunhloko** was that they seemed to be ignored by security branches because they were rarely arrested for prosecution or detention yet they were active on surface and semi-surface politics, especially mobilising people for mass rallies or any other public meeting before the party was banned. Above all they were a very strong motivating force in mass mobilisation for demonstrations or action packed activities which were declared illegal by the police. That meant that the organisers of such demonstrations could be prosecuted if found yet **oMakhulunhloko** were slippery from arrest yet they were as active as all of us as well as effective in getting people to support any event of the Party. Side by side with **oMakhulunhloko,** the **Formidable** regiments grew in the Makhokhoba Branch and that meant we had three youth militia regiments to command and coordinate their operations. It became very problematic to keep them separate until we decided to merge the **Zhanda** and **Formidable** into one militia regiment. We were quite aware that **Zhanda** was popular in Makhokhoba but because we had encountered some difficulties in managing them, we had to merge the **Formidable** with **Zhanda** into one militia regiment retaining the name **Formidable** while the rest of the townships kept the **Zhanda** as the militant arm of the Party. By merging the **Formidable** and **Zhanda** into one regiment, we created a massive reserve militia from which to recruit young men for underground operations or assignments inside or outside the country. Consequently the numbers of members of cells increased in every street. In essence some of them were oriented to be ready for any tough action, including undergoing military training inside or outside the country. By the way many of the members of these regiments were employed in various occupations in the City, like all of us in the Executive Committee. That means we performed our national duties at our spare time after work or during weekends and public holidays.

A notable fermenting desire to take an active part in the struggle at that time was regenerated and motivated by formation of the People's Care Take Council (PCC) which revived active surface politics amongst the masses in general and the youth in particular. It also revived some hopes in the possibility of the success of the majority rule project. During the life of the PCC the **Formidable,** as its name suggests became a formidable force in the Makhokhoba and Mzilikazi branches thus requiring requisite skills to direct them to execute their tasks appropriately. It was important to reorganise such a large militia regiment into small operational groups that did not mix throughout their time of existence and activity. As stated above, in Makhokhoba we resolved the confusion by combining the two regiments into one and retained the name **"Formidable"** under Edward Tshuma as commander. Mbonjeni Mlilo, former commander of the Zhanda, and others were sent out of the country for military training. The Formidable retained the structure of formations that were divided into small units for security reasons and for ease of command and management. But some within the Formidable continued the functions that they carried out in the former Zhanda such as teaming up with oMakhulnhloko for mobilising the masses for any event in hand.

The underground role of the **Formidable** became intractably linked with the use of home-made devices to attack soft targets in and around Bulawayo. By soft targets was meant government installations such as post offices, small bridges, isolated police stations or patrol vehicles, telegraph poles, sub-power stations, isolated farm infrastructure such as fences, livestock enclosures in the farmlands, etc. Members of the Formidable were trained one by one to handle home-made explosive devices including hand grenades and dynamites. They were given strict instructions that they should not attack civilians including whites whether in their houses or on the roads. Indeed, in our operational zone there is no record of a civilian who was killed by our operatives under orders. In compliance with Ethan Dube's ingenuity on making freedom struggle as destructive as possible but only in a "selective way," in terms of avoiding acts that could be lumped together with common criminality outside the realm of politics. I personally discouraged our activist from ordering any of our members to commit something that would look like a common crime, like murder or robbery or anything that was outside legislation that was earmarked to suppress political dissenting activities. They had to avoid acts that could be legally located in the non-political category of crime if they were arrested. No member of the **Formidable** was to face allegations of murder because that would make the whole thing sound outside the domain of freedom struggle therefore provide the enemy with an advantage for demonising the organisation that championed the cause of majority rule. John Mkandla and I explained to comrades of the Formidable the difference between common crime and politically driven violence whether or not there was loss of life. More importantly, destruction of anything or loss of life should never fall under the definition of common crime or murder because because it could devalue the cause of the freedom struggle at home and abroad. Any illegal action that contravened provisions of the Law and Order Maintenance Act (LOMA) or Subversive Activities Act or Unlawful Organisations Act or Preservation of Constitutional Government Act would be regarded as politically motivated in respect of its objectives and merits.

If investigation of a crime was carried out by detectives other than the Special Branch, it could be difficult to define it as politically driven and therefore indefensible in terms of removing the pursued person from the country unless his background was within the sphere of the freedom struggle. Political violence was to be directed to structures of the state and other strategic pillars of the regime's power such as security forces themselves and other state institutions. Factories and large departmental stores were not included as targets but if an operative felt it would make a strategic difference in terms of weakening or causing disquiet in the enemy camp, or boosting the morale of the African population, they could be targeted. In this respect economic targets were left to the judgement of operatives who necessarily relied on public opinion judging whether they could be excited when they heard the news after the act. The example of Lancaster Steel factory having been razed to the ground by fire was cited by many comrades as having generated a lot of positive comments from the masses who wished for more such acts on economic targets.

Also the weapons of attacking any target should not fall outside the provisions of any the above-listed legislation outside the sphere of politically motivated crimes. Burning down a structure with Molotov cocktail bomb would fall under the LOMA but a stick of matches could change the material content of the case into arson unless a political motive was identified during trial. The weapons that were available to us in all of this effort were military hand grenades and home-made explosive devices which we called **"amagadi"** (mud-moulded boulders ranging from the size of a tennis ball to a pawpaw) consisting of 'home-made hand grenades, primed land mines and dynamites' therefore were appropriate for political targets that would define the content of the act whether or not an operative got caught by the police. In any case, every operative had a commander; therefore during trial all this would come up as part of defining the nature of the deed. In all of this a civilian could be killed accidentally but that would not make an operative a common criminal because the motive could be ventilated by the identity of the target and the motive as well as the weapon used and the origin of command.

CHAPTER TEN

CULTURAL CONSTRUCTS APPLIED TO SAFEGUARD UNDERGROUND ACTIVITIES

Linked to the distribution of war materials out in the country was an effort to beef up the mechanisms of underground work both in urban and rural areas. After the banning of all African nationalist political parties in the country, many leaders had been swept away to detention throughout country. A remnant of the underground structures asked me to help them with methods of concealing their activities to continue the struggle. Pondering over how to create a simple and watertight system of keeping secrets, it dawned to me that in the rural areas people understood the concept of clandestine activities if and when some cultural constructs were used to emphasize how to keep secrets to conceal cultural rituals and activities. All matters pertaining to ancestors are often concealed behind a cipher that can be deciphered only by designated elders or **sangomas** (traditional healers) without sharing the knowledge on the technique of the cipher. The rural folk who invited me to their meeting wanted to be advised how best they could operate without being detected by police or chiefs in their District. I was accompanied by Zwelibanzi Mzilethi to meet them in a forest densely populated by huge trees and almost impenetrable undergrowth. I had to think along such cultural constructs that defined concealment of sensitive cultural rituals for whatever purpose. I had to think of something simple but closest to their knowledge regarding a situation where the alleged performers of a particular ritual never admitted or bragged about their secret activities in that connection. On this basis, I thought of something well known to be anathema to society yet its practitioners have never announced themselves in fear of being either banished or eliminated. I had to select a situation that depicted socially perceived adversarial relations between society and those who were seen as being on the wrong side of the cultural line. At that time anti-colonial activists were seen by authorities as the ones on the wrong side of the law. Those on the wrong side were activists who continued to struggle for freedom. Their activities were regarded by authorities as harmful to the country as they promoted disorder. Therefore, when caught they could be prosecuted or removed from society into oblivion. In the communities whose activities were anathema to society yet they have never been seen or caught by anybody?

I then asked the meeting whether any one or all of them knew of a practice that was always talked about in the villages but practitioners had never been seen or caught in our life time. Everybody lifted they hands and when one of them gave the answer as "**witches**" all hands stayed down. I then asked whether they were sure that there were such people as witches within the communities. Everybody said witches definitely existed and were bewitching people but they had power to conceal themselves and they did not talk about their activities in public. Why? The unanimous reply was that they could not talk about killing people because they feared that the community would stone them to death. That was exactly the answers I was looking for. To reassure myself, I asked again whether anyone present had heard or seen a **witch or wizard** announcing or bragging that he or she was a successful practitioner in witchcraft because she/ he was responsible for unleashing a bad spell in the community. They all answered with a no in a chorus. I then asked if they believed that witches were there in spite of the fact that they have never been seen or identified in public. They all affirmed that they were certain that they were there in the communities. I then proceeded to amplify this example of **witches** who, according to customary folklore, never admitted that they practised witchcraft under all circumstances unless "caught in the act." I proceeded to advise them that with regards to operating clandestinely and keeping their actions secret they were acting against the laws of the colonial government therefore in the eyes of the government they were like witch doctors because their activities were directed at destroying a system that gave joy to colonialists. Since, to their knowledge, the witches performed their nocturnal rituals of witchcraft in complete secrecy and never admitted nor bragged about being **witches** even to their children or spouses or any other person who was not part of them, how could they be found out? Even **sangomas** found it very difficult to pinpoint a culprit of a perceived a spell of death in the community or in a family. I went further to remind them that in olden days, if a **witch doctor** was caught red handed bewitching anybody or **"sniffed by sangomas,"** to have harmed any family, he/she would either be condemned to death or banishment with family to a distant forest for the rest of their lives, if they survived the appetite of the carnivores. Similarly our actions and activities against colonial authorities should be kept in complete secrecy in the same manner of perpetual denialism characteristic of witchcraft practitioners. If our political activists were caught in illegal action by the authorities, they could be sent to jail for life or hanged, depending on the mode and extent of destruction caused thereby. So participation in an activity of liberation struggle by means of breaking the law of the enemy was never a talking point in families or friends for security and safety reasons. Only people who participated in any destructive operations would have to keep the secrets of the underground work to themselves until freedom was attained because, I stressed: "in the political eyes of the regime, activists could be likened to **witches** who should be eliminated once detected and caught by the Special Branch who are the **"sangomas"** of the regime." I talked strongly as if I believed that witchcraft was real in the life of an African as I emphasized that all of us should emulate such a method of acting in complete secrecy to keep deadly use of lethal devices invisible from the enemy. We then all agreed that **umuti**[20] of a freedom fighter was a military weapon but since in the group no one was militarily trained, homemade lethal devices and explosives would make up the stock for civilian operatives. A witch was believed by society that he or she operated on selected victims effectively at night while people were asleep. For us, too, operating in darkness on our selected targets was the safest time to cause damage to the infrastructure of state, because we could wake up in the morning looking innocent like any other person who did not do anything but sleep during the night. This was well taken. I was pleased by the degree of enthusiasm and almost celebration for what one middle aged man described as **"the best guide that will enable us to destroy the colonial system to rabble without beating drums till victory."** One of them passed a joke saying that there could be some witches in the group but they could not voluntarily expose themselves in fear that "we could lynch them". Another remarked: "I hope you do not become witches in the true

---

20
    killer medicines

sense of the meaning of the word!" Another said "why don't we find witches to train us how to bewitch the colonial authorities starting with those we know?" All these were purely mythical expressions which ignored practical reality.

All those present in the meeting were so elated to hear all this and vowed to adopt the advice and adhere to the principles of secrecy as strictly as the witches were believed to do. In this way, underground activities were concealed by clandestine operations that were protected by complete silence about the action and returning to normal day to day activities in the family or community as long as the enemy was still in power. We then suggested the formation of appropriate structures for that kind of work and how the structures would relate to each other to avoid detection. It was similar to ours of small cells linked to the higher ones through one person and so on. It was interesting to find that most of them adhered to the **witchcraft approach for concealing operational secrets** until independence in 1980. The few who are still alive sometimes joke thus: "be advised not to annoy some of us because we were turned into witches by Mpofu to bewitch the Smith regime and therefore we are now seasoned witchdoctors."

The application of methods of secrecy similar to those of witchcraft might appear sinister yet this was not to suggest that underground operations were synonymous with witchcraft in terms of content and practice. Here I merely facilitated the adoption of a method of secrecy that was simple and close to what was familiar to the rural folks. Adopting an example of a well-known culturally detestable situation that people heard so much about it but never saw anyone who admitted that they practised it, was very appropriate in the circumstances. So, if it was actually there, it meant that its practitioners were perfect at keeping their identity concealed from the public because they never voluntarily announced themselves nor leaked their secrets to anyone yet they are believed to be there causing havoc in the communities without being detected. In our meeting, everyone believed that witches were active in communities but they thrived on denials about their involvement in witchcraft.

Above all witches, mythical as they are, in the rural communities they are most feared and hated everywhere by everybody who believes in their existence. In like manner any fighter who used weapons of destruction against the colonial government was a resented trouble maker to be either arrested for prosecution or eliminated on the act as a dangerous terrorist. But a freedom fighter was real and not mythical because his/her actions of destruction could be objectively measured not only by contravening provisions of the law but also by causing physical damage on targeted objects. As far as witches are concerned, people go on guessing and speculating without actual knowledge based on verifiable evidence of their existence and practice that could allow us to determine who they are and the extent of their physical damage to individuals or community in a measurable way. Even so, they are still believed to be capable of operating in a totally invisible concealment. The rationale was that if using the witchcraft method could enable activists to operate in a similar blanket of secrecy, chances of detection by the security branch could have been eliminated. Believing and adherence to such a line of operation did help civilian rural operatives to keep their mouths shut to avoid emission of evidence that could implicate them through talking about their clandestine work in public, except physical errors during action. In this regard it was quite easy for the villagers to understand this method because they grew up hearing about witches but never saw or heard them bragging about their practice because they could incur the wrath of the community with serious consequences.

In the whole situation of conflict, Rhodesian authorities resented freedom fighters, whether they were civilians or military cadres because they were threatening to destabilize the government's authority of by violent means. Every freedom fighter had to know that there were undesirable in the eyes of government like the community hated witches as they were regarded as killers of people. Therefore, to ensure the continuation and sustenance of the struggle, operatives needed to make their activities or operations invisible until they gained adequate power and strength to defeat the regime. The principle of keeping secrets, pertaining to breaking the laws of the Rhodesian Front regime, was the case in point at briefing meetings with rural colleagues where the same "ritual of invisible activities" was repeated in several sessions. It is worthy to note that even during the first phase of the struggle some freedom fighters who passed beyond the Rhodesian security forces' "search and destroy" line of defence succeeded in establishing contact with organised underground cells of ZAPU thus, becoming difficult to spot as they rapidly created a system of intelligence and counter intelligence within the masses.

Clearly, underground work was not confined to Bulawayo District Townships only nor the modus operandi confined to a single catalyst. In addition to rural areas such as described above, networks were established in other regions in the country and deliberately linked up our network with the Salisbury underground on our own initiative. The young people who came forward to join the **Zhanda** and **Formidable** militia formations were mobilised by Committees of the Youth Wing and organised into operating formations by the same. For instance we went to Salisbury (Harare) to discuss the possibility of coordinated mass action on any suitable targets throughout the country including the rural areas. We also agreed that demonstrations on unacceptable government celebratory occasions should be organised in a coordinated way in all towns including small ones. The only thing that we excluded in our activities was adopting full scale secret military training without top authorisation. Instead of adopting the option of an armed uprising, we agreed with the Salisbury underground group that we should strengthen or create structures that would be of value in terms of empowering the operatives to become pillars of a military powered struggle. This notion entailed gaining the ability to provide support to freedom fighters in waging a war of liberation when it got underway in the country. In doing all this we mentioned the successful struggle in Algeria and many of our counterparts were aware of the Algerian liberation struggle, therefore it became easier to adopt that proven formula for our purposes. Some comrades actually had the idea that in Algeria the structures of a banned party in 1937 went underground only to be useful when armed struggle was launched in1954. Such knowledge enabled us to structure ourselves in readiness for action so that we did not have to wait for the armed freedom fighters to arrive, we went ahead to use any crude devices we already had to cause confusion for the regime's security forces until the actual armed struggle took shape, as we were convinced that it was in the pipeline.

One of the interesting ways that enabled us to operate underground between Bulawayo and Salisbury was a link with a church. The main link person between the underground cells in Bulawayo and Salisbury was Mrs Thenjiwe Lesabe, a key member of the Episcopal Evangelical Church (otherwise known as Ethiopia Church by ordinary people). Within the Church system, she took advantage of any available opportunity to create a viable cover for underground channels for valuable information sharing between Bulawayo and Salisbury underground cells of ZAPU. She was a high profile leader who preferred to work at operational level with foot soldiers with amazing success. She was especially skilful in planning clandestine operations and how to camouflage them together with operatives. For instance she set up a network within the Church linking Bulawayo and Salisbury with or without the knowledge of the top echelons of the Church. Her contacts in Salisbury identified suitable people to work with clandestinely without being detected by security or noticed by those who were not involved. The unsung champion of this link organised several secret meetings under the guise of the Church's functions. We travelled to

Salisbury like members of the Church, attended services as visitors under pseudonyms and in the evening met our counterparts in Highfields Township (still in the guise of the Church) to discuss real business of how to work in cooperative ways. It was essential to hold such secret meetings so that whoever saw us could not think of the other side of our mission than attending the Church Service. So we frequently attended Church Services during the day and held secret meetings at night on several weekends in Highfields, Salisbury. Comrades from Salisbury could visit us in the same manner. The Church-aligned current became stronger and well managed in terms of remaining a reliable and safe entry into the broader underground that connected Bulawayo and Salisbury African Townships. Even if Lesabe was under the eye of the Special Branch, she managed to sneak away from their sight so that they were unable to uncover the political link of the Church with the struggle until she went to exile in the mid-1970s where she joined General Head Quarters of ZAPU. We travelled to Salisbury by the night train on a Friday and returned on a Monday morning at the end of the weekend. We did this because we wanted to be on the same rhythm with the Capital. Above all we were quite aware that ZAPU had more numbers in Salisbury and Mashonaland regions than anywhere else in the country, therefore it was imperative to keep pace with the majority of members as much as possible to rest them assured that we were on the same wavelength in terms of activity and aspirations. These meetings gave us the impression that Salisbury was quite militant and well organised both at semi-surface and underground structures. Therefore it was imperative to march on the same tune with them.

It was interesting that, contrary to what I have observed in our liberated Zimbabwe, in the mid-1960s from the first time we were in Highfields Township our colleagues urged us to speak with them in siNdebele because they wanted to learn it. Above all, they said, they would hear everything we said. Indeed they understood the content of our presentation, judging from their comments and questions they asked afterwards. When it was their turn to speak, we also asked them to be free to speak in Shona so that we could learn it faster. Indeed, we heard everything they said. That is, we conducted our discussions in our languages with each other without interpreters throughout the period of discussions which took several hours. This became a common practice in our regular meetings and it certainly helped us to take the language learning aspect very seriously. By this tradition, we both gained a lot from each other's language and some interesting idioms which we still enjoy to hear and use today. But these days many people tend to say "I do not understand your language, please speak in Shona/siNdebele" depending on which language the respondent speaks.

The purpose of creating a massive underground network everywhere was to reinforce the semi-surface officials in the 'branches' with a concealed social infrastructure to provide much needed support for trained fighters when they arrived and ready to operate. Semi-surface officials were those that were publicly known to have been active before the ban yet being able to service underground activists at opportune times. They behaved as if they had given up the struggle yet their pro -struggle activities remained alive and concealed, especially their link with the underground structures and activities were vibrant but invisible when they interacted with those who never operated above ground during the legal life of the Party. The term "semi-surface" was coined by ZAPU Lusaka office referring to those of us who were officials in the Party before it was banned and then went underground by concealing our activities while we played innocent in the eyes of government officials and security branches. The term implied that even if we went underground, we were visible to the security forces thus rendering us unable to enjoy full concealment from them. The underground structures were expected to play a crucial role in supporting and serving armed freedom fighters to make it easy for them to 'graze' in the battlefields with confidence in the masses knowing that all their needs would be catered for at the flick of a finger. In his studies on war veterans in Zimbabwe, Z W Sadomba grasped this phenomenon very well when he found that:

> **"The origins of the War Veterans movement are located in the early 1960s, as the culmination of the civilian nationalist struggle, when both the Zimbabwe African Peoples Union and (ZAPU) and the Zimbabwe African National Union (ZANU) were banned in 1962 and 1964, respectively they formed underground organisations and recruited for the war mainly young men exiled in Zambia"** (Sadomba, 2011)

It was important for fighters to find the masses politically conscious enough to understand their responsibility to support guerrilla warfare in full since that was the only path to "the land of milk and honey."

While ZAPU went underground as far back as 1964 when PCC was banned, ZANU, too, adopted a similar strategy and objectives to create underground structures. The only difference is that ZANU leadership decided on this important mattering exile when they recognised how essential it was to work within the masses clandestinely in preparation for a sustainable armed struggle, as Noel Mukono, head of ZANLA (1969/73), was reported to have stated thus:

> **"In 1969 it was decided to operate silently .... We worked underground training, stocking equipment and regrouping inside the country. Special Branch could not find out what was going on and that we were preparing for a continuation of the struggle. Much contact was maintained with the local population to review the terrain. In July 1972 ZANU called together all its forces and met in the bush in Mozambique and reviewed the situation. We were satisfied that the preparations were enough and that enough arms and food had been stashed in the bush and that we could restart the onslaught"** (Cilliers, 1985)

This is exactly what we did as civilian activists inside the country for several years up to the time armed struggle became a reality in our own hands. Virtually everything that is in the above-quoted statement covers what should be done either by the structures of the party inside the country or the guerrillas themselves before they unleash combat operations. Noel Mukono's statement shows that ZAPU was not alone in operating underground in preparation for armed liberation struggle in Zimbabwe. But we were ahead in doing this because our structures became firmly established underground before the ban during the life of PCC.

In this regard, ZAPU fighters were always briefed about forward contacts and those contacts were expected to alert key members of an appropriate cell as soon as combatants arrived in their sector of operation. The fighters who succeeded to get to the interior of the country without contact with security forces enjoyed ready-made support of the structures that were established in preparation for armed struggle. Before I left the country I played a critical role in creating underground cells for the purpose of supporting freedom fighters by connecting them to the support cells that would supply the material needs and intelligence concerning activities of enemy forces. A large number of members of The Formidable were engaged in this formula to play a variety of roles including gathering intelligence, supplies, courier services and recruitment of new fighters to be trained internally or externally. Here the support base was fairly solid for fighters to rely on for their crucial needs. Such a ready-made social infrastructure relieved fighters from the task of mobilising the masses for support on arrival in the country from training, so, this gave them freedom to focus on getting well established within their sector of operation before they started their combat missions. In towns, many of the members of the underground cells were ordinary workers in various companies or public institutions and that was their crucial cover from security branches because they conducted themselves like people who just wanted to work for their families with loyalty to their employers. The same attitude was displayed to chiefs when they visited parents in the countryside. The pretentious behaviour of Africans described here created a false impression that freedom fighters had no support in the African population. I will dwell into this in subsequent pages.

Supply source of home-made explosives

The underground organization was not created only for keeping political structure alive or on standby for armed struggle to intensify but also for constant destruction of reachable structures of state infrastructure. As civilian operatives, we laid our hands on anything that could cause damage to the Rhodesian regime as severe as it could be. We were quite aware that the regime was strong with security forces that were made up of various specialised units within the Army, BSAP, Para-Military Units, Air Force and Reserves. As we shall see later, with the war intensifying, many more units were created, thus making the Rhodesian Security Forces one of the most formidable counter-insurgent military machines in the world. But did Zimbabweans become deterred from pursuing the cause of their freedom and justice by that formidable fire power and massive intelligence network? No.

However, at civilian level some of the items used must have made elements of the security branch laugh with contempt. There were several devices that were made in a secret factory inside the country masterminded by Abel Siwela (former Mayor of Bulawayo in the 1990s). In the ZAPU structure Abel Siwela was Bulawayo District Chairman (during PCC) therefore a surface to semi-surface official which means in the eyes of the Special Branch he was a high profile politician liable for constant surveillance. Siwela was an extraordinarily shrewd strategist on clandestine operations and a fearless freedom fighter who was driven by the love of his country to sacrifice his life for its freedom. Siwela was a man of few words but a lot of actions in active service for the liberation of Zimbabwe. An accountant by profession with management skills, he could have been suitable to command ZIPRA from the onset because he had the qualities of a well politicised leader rich with ability to drive complex and potentially dangerous missions. It is difficult to bring out everything that Siwela did as a self-developed freedom fighter without formal military training.

Siwela was responsible for setting up a secret factory that manufactured the home-made devices, including hand grenades. He started off with a planning committee namely, Mavava Khumalo, Joel Luphahla, Lazarus Dlakama, and Willie Mgqibelo all of whom were high profile politicians at Regional level. He organised personnel with skills in mixing and assembling explosive devices. He created secret lines of procurement of materials of manufacture and delivery of home-made devices to various operating cells in the Bulawayo Townships and rural hinterlands. In doing all this, the team managed to make their work invisible to ensure that underground operations remained undetected by Special Branch and other security forces. Preparations for undertaking this kind of work took time because it was not just delicate and risky. It also required skills to handle explosive materials, especially the mixing and assembling them into usable and destructive objects with safety for users. The latter two of them went out of the country for military training and Siwela continued his work with assistance of the remaining two colleagues.

After operating for three years in this field of underground work, Siwela was arrested several times but he never revealed his knowledge of the factory or the names of the people that he worked with in the manufacture and distribution of the devices. So, the manufacturing plant of home-made explosives remained uncovered by the Special Branch for many years until armed struggle got into full swing. The Special Branch seemed to have put him on top of the list of suspects in this regard but they were unable to pinpoint the core of his work - the explosives factory. The operatives who used the devices never knew where they came from and who made them. Theirs was to use them without asking questions.

My link with the underground factory was to receive the devices from Siwela and distribute them (on a one-on-one basis) to the operatives in my cell. There were several cells similar to mine that also received the items from the factory. Each operative had to identify a target before he indicated his readiness to act. It was important not tell me or anybody about the nature and location of the target. There were strict instructions that such devices should be used the same night they were received and should never be kept in the house overnight under any circumstances unless a mission was aborted due to some compelling security impediments. I also conveyed instructions from Siwela that there should be no attack on civilian dwellings and social amenities, including schools, churches, buses, passenger trains and taxis. Some comrades were not happy about exclusion of white civilians from targets because they were the ones voting for repressive regimes therefore they should be dealt with until they came to their senses. Siwela might have read military science where the question of civilian situation was addressed because he did not compromise on this directive. Most operatives adhered to the directive.

While wide spread use of described rudimentary devices kept the security branch busy daily, they caused little physical damage to the regime except their persistence in occurrence. Whether they were damaged or not, the targets for the Formidable consisted of the pillars of the colonial system's power as follows:

1. Bridges were easily accessible and most of them around Bulawayo were attacked but the available explosive materials were no match to the strength of the gauge of construction mixtures therefore our explosives caused insignificant damage on the structures

2. Uniformed police patrols were easy targets but they had to be excluded from the list of targets due to their perceived non-hostile stance towards African politicians; but detectives were targets, unfortunately they patrolled in unmarked cars therefore difficult to distinguish them from ordinary civilians; but as the struggle intensified, they became easy targets

3. Police reservists were targets but most times they patrolled together with the exempted uniformed civil police; our Salisbury comrades were ahead of us in succeeding to deal with police reservists; that tended to discourage Africans from joining the force in fear of getting torched

4. Support Unit (paramilitary force) were targets but they were more of a military than police force; only a military force could tackle them with matching skills and weaponry

5. Isolated police stations were targets (charge offices) but were found to be too far from the fence behind which an operative took position to through an explosive device (from 50 metres)

6. Communication and supply lines, e.g. roads, railway lines, telegraph poles and wires were easy targets; some of them in town could be too exposed by street lights therefore they

needed dynamites with a long detonator that could be lit while hiding from a distance; during full scale war they were regularly targeted

7. Post offices were targets; but some of them were within the circumference of the flood lights in the townships and security guards after the interior of Bulawayo Main Post Office was extensively damaged by commercial explosives

8. Military barracks were legitimate targets but our half-baked operatives were no match to the Rhodesian army with its complex structures of specialised units attached to specific tasks and roles; a proper military campaign was needed to destabilise this core of the Rhodesian armed forces; subsequently, freedom fighters succeeded in overstretching the intricate Rhodesian killer machine to the extent of rendering it increasingly less effective than ever (1975-1979)

9. Elements of the Rhodesian Security Forces (including the deadliest Selous Scouts or "Pseudo Guerrillas") on patrol in active search for freedom fighters in the field and villages were legitimate targets for armed freedom fighters not civilian operatives until they were able to plant land mines on enemy routes to slow down their advance towards areas infiltrated by trained freedom fighters

10. Some white civilian males acted like 'master policemen' when they suspected that an African was "loitering with intent to commit crime." They could either flog the fellow with a sjambok (**a whip from a hippopotamus hide)** or call the police or even take him to the police; but targeting them would have turned our operatives into terrorists which is the opposite of freedom fighters' mode of operation; so we shunned tackling them head-on to avoid to be regarded as common criminals;

11. Rhodesian Front rural support base (commercial farmers) were extremely hostile to African Nationalists and well-armed enough to deserve targeting but, instead, we targeted their infrastructure, such as farm fences, heavy duty vehicles and tractors, livestock enclosures, farm equipment, storage systems, workshops, stock feeds, dams, reservoirs, dip tanks, etc.; full scale guerrilla warfare regarded them as legitimate targets because they were ready to shoot on sight what they called "terrorists"

12. Military bases in the bush

13. The sum total of the above outline of target matrix gave us a clear picture of the physical power of the Rhodesian regime which every freedom fighter had to face whether he was a civilian operative or a military cadre. Several attempts at selected targets were made with varied fortunes and misfortunes. The target matrix became more intricate and deadly as the process of liberation also became better organised and effective. Before reaching the level of effective organisation, the movement experienced serious setbacks both in civilian and military field operations. At civilian level there were several cases of horrific accidents that occurred at the point of attacking a target.

Self-Acting Cells

It is important to mention that the rise of the Zhanda and the Formidable was mainly the result of the self-acting current within the Party consisting of people who were convinced beyond any shadow of doubt that the Rhodesian Front government was not at all interested in negotiating with the African nationalists for loss of its power. There was no occasion when the Nationalist leaders gave us a well calculated directive of how to set up an underground apparatus with militias complete with command systems, communications and the work to be undertaken thereby. Even the 'invisible' 'General' Hokoyo did not suggest formation of militias or functional structures of the kind that we formed in Makhokhoba Township and other townships. The militias grew from the drinking clubs that developed rapidly after the advent of PCC and reached their peak at the point of its banning in the middle of 1964. Before we formed such structures, we discussed their function and status in relation to the Executive Committee of the Branch. We discussed these matters in detail ourselves and came to the conclusion that we should adopt and apply everything possible to destabilise the country by any means we could command without waiting for the leaders to give specific instructions. Actually, acts of violence usually occurred as protests after a political party was banned or some leaders arrested. During the legal functioning of ANC, NDP and ZAPU there was insignificant acts of violence in the country except the 1960 **Zhi** which was sparked by the arrest of NDP leaders in Salisbury and Zhi finished up with high casualties in Bulawayo. It was not planned by the leadership of the NDP. It was people's expression of anger against the arrest of their leaders. In our time it had to be an ongoing process that should continue to increase in scale and effectiveness until armed phase of the struggle got properly organised and launched. This does not suggest that we became independent of the leadership because we kept them posted about Zhanda when it rose in every Township in the country. But the transformation of Zhanda into an underground militia named "The Formidable" was our innovation in Makhokhoba Branch assembled in preparation of sending them for military training inside or outside the country.

The Formidable force as a functional part of the Party was hardly communicated to those who had no link with this militia formation. Our leaders and Government officials knew a lot about Zhanda but not about the Formidable which was entirely our baby.

CHAPTER ELEVEN

SPECIAL BRANCH: A MAJOR CHALLENGE TO FREEDOM FIGHTERS AND UNDERGROUND ACTIVISTS

On the other side of the racial divide the supporters of the Rhodesian Front were disenchanted by Winston Field's failure to bring independence for them and they replaced him with Ian Douglas Smith as leader and Prime Minister in April 1964. Within a short time after assuming the Premiership of the country Smith took a decisive move to declare a state of emergency first in Highfield and then the whole country followed by banning both ZANU and PCC in August1964. The cardinal sin at that time was that PCC and ZANU were still wasting much of their energies and time into tearing each other apart through violence that they hardly directed to the principal adversary (Rhodesian Front regime) in most parts of the country. Highfield Township was the hardest hit by interparty violence. The two nationalist parties' involvement in interparty bloodshed gave the Rhodesian regime an easy loophole for erasing them from the official register of organisations. They overplayed their cards in violently competing for space in the political arena in the country in a relentless bruising duel for control of the African masses. In this regard, A. J. A. Peck confirms (1978 p93):

> "Each of the two banned nationalist organisations in Rhodesia – the PCC and ZANU – claims to represent All African People and yet a large number of the "security offences" in Rhodesia have been committed in the course of clashes between rival organisations." (Peck, 1966)

This statement sums up a tragic period that some of us witnessed as we struggled very hard to turn our members away from burning their fellow Africans and concentrate on destroying the pillars of the regime's power. Actually, some authors, including Peck, say the two organisations were banned because of relentless violence against each other rather than against their common enemy, the Rhodesian Front regime. There is substantial empirical evidence to support this assertion (**Sachikonye, 2011**) but it needs to be added that there were many PCC leaders at grassroots level who quickly redirected members towards the original course of action against our formidable adversary, the Rhodesian government.

However, now that surface party machinery for action for us was swept away by a 'new broom' of the Rhodesian Front regime and our leaders arrested and detained without trial, what next? So, we had to submerge our structures **deeper and systematically.** As a matter of fact the Formidable was not a surface structure therefore it meant that we had to recruit some more cells underground and redefine their appropriate functions in the circumstances. Having showed his supporters that he was made of sterner stuff Ian Douglas Smith solicited support from the entire white population throughout the country for declaration of independence if the British Government could not grant it. He called another general election on the ticket of UDI and got full support of the white electorate by winning all the A roll (white) seats in the Legislature. So the die was cast for the perpetuation of racial domination in Zimbabwe. Those who had remained free from arrest had no alternative except strengthen the underground by tightening organisational structures and cells as well as get them linked up with a central command organs. The road to armed struggle became a wide open option in the circumstances because we had large numbers of the Formidable who were thirst for serious action to challenge the regime. The time for throwing stones was over so was that of burning things and crushing some structures with explosives without denting the power of the regime. More importantly the time had come to desist from violence against our fellow Africans who had joined the new party, ZANU.

At this time another leaflet circulated in the townships of Bulawayo and Salisbury titled: "General' Bayawabaya declares war on the Rhodesian Front regime." Unpacking 'General' Bayawabaya's leaflet starts with the name which means a hunter kills game during a hunting episode; in that context General Bayawabaya meant fighting to defeat the enemy security forces. That is how we understood General Bayawabaya's declaration which meant that the phase of sabotage had failed to soften the enemy enough to bring him to the negotiating table. Therefore time had come for ZAPU supporters to brace themselves for a hard fight, where fire would be answered with fire, not stones against fire any more. The Leaflet issued by 'General' Bayawabaya was taken seriously by many of us as we began to prepare in anticipation of a war of liberation. Some of the earlier trained fighters briefed (short of training) us on what guerrilla warfare was all about in form and content. We had to propagate the principles of 'General' Bayawabaya to make all structures of ZAPU aware and ready for harder work than we had been doing in the Zhanda and Formidable. Clearly the Smith regime was aware of what ZAPU and ZANU were up to in exile so they did not take that leaflet lightly except that they were confident of crushing any force that would cross Zambezi River with an objective of waging a liberation war or try to cause an uprising internally.

Before the anticipated unilateral declaration of independence by the Rhodesian Front government, we did a lot of work at both the surface and underground level of the struggle. In our activities, it would seem that some of my movements attracted the eyes of the Special Branch somehow, either through a half informed tipoff or a fuzzy surveillance. I say so because some of their questions sounded like what the lawyers call "fishing expedition." They came to pick me up from my work place before PCC and ZANU were banned. This was the first time to have a visit of this kind from the Special Branch since I became involved in active political struggle in 1962. As they drove towards my residence, with my guidance, one of them asked me if I had ever played with fire arms. I actually laughed before I answered the question and two of them smiled back. Another came back and said they had received information that I was in possession of fire arms and ammunition as well as explosives. When we stopped in front of my dwelling cottage they interrogated me a little deeper in their vehicle and during their search inside the cottage about whether I had ever played with guns and explosives because the information in their possession was that I received these items from Northern Rhodesia (before Zambia got independence) and stored them in my dwelling. They even warned that keeping explosives unprofessionally was dangerous because they could explode and kill many people. They talked as if this was the main item that

I was alleged to be in possession of. In any case my answer to every question was negative and, having drawn a blank from a thorough search, they took me back to work. I survived the first round. The truth of the matter was that some weeks before security detectives picked me up for questioning I had received about half a dozen hand guns and ammunition but not explosives. So their information was partially correct and that gave me both worry and confidence that their information was incomplete as it included guessing about explosives in their investigations. The inclusion of explosives in questioning me about a consignment of materials and the way they were brought to me were not accurate. So the details of the delivery and composition of the materials were distorted. Whoever informed them had a hazy picture of what he or she saw. The question of who informed them about all this has never got an answer. My big worry was that they were accurate on the hand guns but not their quantity nor their make. So, half of the information they received was true about arms and ammunition except how I got these items and the container they were delivered in. The weapons in question were buried deep in a metal trunk in the backyard garden below two flowering pumpkin plants. The detectives actually dug all over the small garden but did not touch the pumpkin plants. Two weeks later I removed the trunk and transferred it to Queens Park East (a European suburb) where they were kept below the door step of the house without the knowledge of the owners of the property until they were collected by their users four weeks later. The receiver and keeper of these items was a domestic gardener, John Mpofu, employed in this household that turned into an 'arsenal' instantly without the knowledge of the property owners, who were white. The new "logistics chief" was a member of the Formidable like dozens of other working youngsters in the City. This experience opened a new chapter of how we had to be constantly creative to survive by avoiding use of the same method of camouflaging storage of sensitive materials before they were used. That this place could become an arsenal was unthinkable unless the keeper of the materials began to brag about it or some accident occurred. We had to do things in so many ways to avoid detection. We did not wait for big brother from Gonakudzingwa or Lusaka to tell us how to manage matters of struggle under extremely dangerous conditions.

For me a visit from the Rhodesian Special Branch detectives was a stark warning of things to come because, even if the their information was exaggerated, somehow, they had got the wind about fire arms and ammunition and I could not pinpoint the informant in that case. Even if they drew a blank, that information made them aware that I was active in the political arena enough to be placed on their radar screen permanently. From that day onwards I began to be more secretive in my movements and contacts. I immediately became selective on numbers of people I trusted. My concern was that, having got into their list for surveillance, I could become an easy subject for tracking down until they caught me on the act. Being a PCC Chairman of the Youth in Makhokhoba Branch and liaison officer for clandestine operations in respect of overseeing the work of the Formidable, there was a danger that one of these lines of operation could burst open one day. Activism in a situation of multifarious functions poised huge challenges that were fraught with risks of arrest or getting killed by security forces or agents. However the visit by these gentle talking security men did not instil fear in my mind. Instead I increased the volume of clandestine work in the PCC in terms of creating several lines of operation and involving only trustworthy people so that if I had to be taken away, the work of liberation could continue in earnest without me. The safety situation was weakened when I was elected Deputy Secretary for Youth Wing in Bulawayo District as my visibility to Special Branch was inevitably enhanced. Therefore a well thought out strategy on the side of invisible activities had to be hatched out soon.

Clearly, on the first arrest, I was not subjected to gruesome grilling by the Special Branch. But with so many activities, activists were being hunted down and arrested and as part of the active functionaries, it would be a surprise if I had escaped the dragnet of the Special Branch any longer from this point. They had a network of agents outside and inside the semi-surface structures which were once functioning on the ground and then tried to go under-ground when the PCC was banned. So the network of agents seemed to supply the Special Branch with accurate information that made the force believe they were on top of situation in terms of denying the Nationalist movement any breathing space with regards subversive activities. The fire arms that got me into questioning by detectives were brought to me by an externally trained fighter, Mbejelwa Moyo, to keep while he assembled his comrades for deployment. After several weeks in a suburban 'arsenal' I collected the cargo from there and handed it to Mbejelwa at a convenient time and point. We then hatched out a new strategy of distributing such materials for use by comrades.

In spite of getting a visit from Special Branch I continued my link with infiltrating freedom fighters that were trickling into the country in small doses undetected. For instance, a few months after the above described incident, I became deeply involved in receiving trained personnel from Zambia (after the fall of the Federation of Rhodesia and Nyasaland) and arranged their safe hideouts and helped them identify suitable personnel for training.

At first the comrades were in hiding but when they became well established they tried to lead 'normal' life in the townships under pseudonyms. To be well established meant that the fighter had become ingratiated into the socio-cultural milieu of the area of operation to the extent that he would not be seen as a stranger by any member of the community. They began their operations in and around Bulawayo as soon as they achieved acceptability in the community. The arrival of comrades from Zambia seemed to be in line with 'General' Bayawabaya's declaration of war. For example the guerrilla legend, Mbejelwa Moyo, arrived well ahead of the rest to assess the situation and creating opportunities for more to follow in order to carry out their assignment. Those who joined him included some of former members of the Zhanda who were now trained guerrillas, such as Clark Mpofu, Steven Mareza, Patrick Sibanda, John Maluzo Ndlovu and Walter Mbambo. Mbejelwa Moyo was one of several colleagues that I sent out of the country and when he came back he prepared his operations from my premises around midnight. He and his comrades planned their initial strategy from my cottage in Makhokhoba Township. Now that I had some experience in keeping small fire arms and ammunition I was prepared to keep any consignment of a similar nature but not in my dwelling premises. In doing all this, we were all aware that no more military materials should exchange hands or be kept in my residence. Fighters gave me an assortment of their war materials for storage and distribution when required according to agreed safety measures but destinations were left to me. They first read the rules of how to manage explosive devices and their detonators as well as fire arms and their ammunition. These included primed land mines and anti-personnel mines, which could be used by trained personnel only. A full package of materials that were sought from me by security branch officers several months before finally arrived in full strength during 1964. Handling of war materials as a civilian was a very delicate and dangerous task that I had to take with full enthusiasm but with great caution in terms of what camouflaging systems were to be employed in all of these situations to avoid detection or accidental/premature exposure.

The movement of the comrades had to be concealed at all times. One of the covers here was a "informal sector casino house" opposite my cottage where people started to play around 22h00 every night up to 05h00 am in the morning. We were duly advised by **oMakhulunhloko (female youth underground)** that the casino house was hardly visited by detectives of any sort. There was

105

constant movement of patrons in and out of that house every evening day in and day out. Next to the casino house was a shebeen (informal tarven) house which also had patrons most part of the night. So with all this human traffic it was easy for the comrades to come as if they were going to and out of these houses but their destination was my cottage. The owners of the houses were staunch supporters of ZAPU during its existence and after. They thought human traffic in and out of my cottage involved members of my committee or Zhanda and they warned me of any visit by detectives before it happened. The casino and shebeen owners seemed to have connections in the police force, especially CIDs other than the anti-African freedom Special Branch. As a matter of fact they got information in advance of such visits which was far between in the form of checking if they could net some common criminals in the shebeen. The detectives that did this kind of checking usually focused on common crimes such as homicide, theft, robbery, etc.

During or about mid- autumn of 1964, Special Branch had sniffed Mbejelwa's presence in Bulawayo and that he and Clark Mpofu were alleged to have carried out some of the bombings that included Bulawayo Main Post Office. He was one of eight trained freedom fighters who had been in the country for about one year before Mbejelwa's presence leaked to Special Branch. We also got the wind about SB's suspicion in this connection and we stopped the comrades from coming to my place altogether. But after several days the detectives raided my premises around 04h00 am while I was out of town. It was a weekend and I had visited a friend out of Bulawayo when the Special Branch pounced into my cottage and arrested two cousins they found asleep there. Upon my return on Sunday my diligent neighbour, Aleck Dube, intercepted me and advised against going to my cottage. So I went to my younger brother John who stayed with his employers in the suburbs. I stayed there overnight and in the morning I proceeded to my work place at Mpilo Hospital. On my arrival I told all those that I trusted that I was going to be arrested and advised them to convey the messages of warning to the appropriate cells. Likewise, within thirty minutes of our opening of offices, two African Detectives of Security Branch arrived. Their names were Detective Sergeant Nzangani Mkhethwa and Detective Constable David Sikhuza. They first informed the Hospital Secretary (Administrator) that they had come to pick me up for questioning in connection with my link with what they called "saboteurs." Then they proceeded to my office in Main Stores where I worked and told my manager they have been cleared to pick me up. So they did.

When we reached Fife Street Central Charge Office, they asked me about Mbejelwa and others. I admitted that I knew him but had not seen him around for more than a year. They sent me to the office of Detective Chief Inspector Peter Tomlinson who talked to me with a broad smile and friendly voice but I could not help him at all in this connection. I was then sent to Detective Superintendent Brian Chalk who warned me that no one had left the police offices without having told the truth. He too did not display hostile attitude but warned me that if I did not spill the bins, his ADs (African Detectives) would "grind" on me until I sang like a bird. I replied that I was telling the truth and denied the whole Mbejelwa story. At that stage they had not yet heard about the other comrades who were part of Mbejelwa's Section. Superintendent Chalk then handed me back to Chief Inspector Tomlinson who handed me to his ADs who were keen to have a go at me. Many more detectives came in that office one by one and asked me about the whereabouts of Mbejelwa Moyo who stayed with me and two cousins. They claimed that the cousins had admitted seeing Mbejelwa in my cottage but I denied all that. They became furious and ordered that I be taken to the Security Camp (a torture centre at Rhodes Camp). Sergeant Mkhethwa and Constable Sikhuza were joined by Detective Constable Siyatsha Ncube and Detective Sergeant Ntabende Mahlangu. At the Security Camp I was placed in a small room with a desk and two benches. I was ordered to sit on the floor. Then serious interrogation started. Clearly they had some information but it was incomplete and I had to exploit that blank side by denying everything except admitting that I knew Mbejelwa before he disappeared more than a year since then.

I could not deny knowing Mbejelwa Moyo because the detectives knew that his three brothers lived in my neighbourhood and we chatted from time to time, even before he disappeared. The torture started in the form of beating with claps and fists and kicking. Then they resorted to suffocating me with my shirt which they pulled over my head, twisted and tied it above the head, threatening to finish me off if I did not talk. They pushed me to the ground and forced me to balance on my hands and toes to keep the rest of the body suspended more or less like a suspended bridge and ordered me to do a push-up exercise. On this occasion, they placed their lit cigarettes under and burned my abdomen when I went down due to tiredness. I tried to roll away from their 'fire' but they pushed me down and pressed me to stay directly above the amber-like cigarettes. They did this repeatedly until I was utterly exhausted but, as I remembered Ethan Dube's mentoring, I felt that it was better to die under torture than to confess only to be hanged after staying without pain for many years after the sentence was handed down. So I stood firm against all forms of torture at the Security Camp. The torture continued for four days from Monday morning to Thursday late afternoon. On that Thursday afternoon, a white officer of the Special Branch (never introduced himself) entered the small torture chamber and asked the detectives: "is he talking?" A sergeant major replied: "not yet Nkosi but……" The officer ordered all the four African detectives to leave the two of us alone.

He made some ice-breaking by throwing one or two jokes about life of a young man in general with broad smile to which I did not reciprocate well because of pains all over my body. I thought the men had come to finish me off without witnesses. But I banked my hopes on his outlook in very smart attire with a milky white shirt and a navy blue blazer on a grey pair of trousers befitting a proud inspector of schools. I then thought that no one in that immaculate outfit would be so violent as to splash himself with blood stains. Nonetheless, I still summoned my courage and geared myself for the worst from him. He offered me a bottle of cold drink (fanta) and I was too thirsty not to accept it. He took a bunch of keys and used an opener to open the bottle. Above all, the man was quite gentile in his initial approach. I was very careful not to allow his gentility to make me a good boy to be lured to a trap. The time of jokes passed soon after my first sip of fanta and his face became stern as he started a very intensive interrogation which lasted two hours nonstop. It was a skilful approach with carefully worded repetition of questions from different angles or rephrasing them like a prosecutor's cross examination in court. I had to be fully alert for traps to maintain consistence of answers. It was the kind of interrogation that could easily cause one to contradict oneself and get trapped. From start to finish, I had to remember Ethan Dube's brilliant guidelines on how to confound interrogators through consistency and avoiding self-incrimination. I did all this by sticking to very precise and concise statements. In the end the interrogating officer called his detectives and ordered them to release me right away. The African detectives replied in a chorus: "No **Nkosi**[21]" this is one of the most dangerous elements in the country." Their Sergeant Major added: "he is the mastermind of all the troubles here, Nkosi. Please Nkosi leave him to us till tomorrow, we will make him talk" The officer insisted on his orders for my immediate release. Just before sunset I was taken by a police vehicle to my place of residence so exhausted that I had a difficulty in walking and standing upright.

---

[21]   King

Since that time I have chronic back pains which defied all physiotherapy treatment in more than four countries including hospitals in the former USSR, UK and Zambia. In all the torture that I went through under the Special Branch, white officers never touched me in the form of physical or psychological torture except straight intensive interrogation. It was always the African detectives who applied maximum physical brutality and use of derogatory language they could find in their vocabulary. Also their interrogation technique was rough and noisy. They created a situation of fear to the subjected person in an effort to extract a confession. The white officers used carefully constructed questions and repeated them in different versions or phrasing in a relentless tempo up to where they wanted to stop. I found their method dangerously confusing especially on matters of detail about use of time during the period under review in respect of how a suspected person used that time and interpersonal interactions that took place inside that period. I had to think deep before answering their questions and be careful about what I had constructed to skip prosecution and what was concrete, to make sure that I held onto them both as the truth because an artificial construct could slip out of memory and that was where danger was. But they also issued threats, especially about consequences of concealing information from the police concerning subversive activities and harbouring dangerous elements.

Mixed Fortunes in the underground activism

After the "Mbejelwa experience" we had to review our ways of operating and covering our tracks. We were actually looking for any space that might allow us to change the mode of operation again. In this regard, we had to redesign our mode of how to conceal our activities that would keep us safe as we proceeded with more caution and tact in every step we took in our clandestine operations. Our drinking clubs were still intact but our activities were no longer fully camouflaged because we were on the radar screen of the Special Branch through their agents. They were right in warning that the consequences of involvement in violent activism would be dire if we were caught back-footed by SB. We then seriously focused onto the issue of how Special Branch got information about our supposedly clandestine work. We were very worried about leakage of accurate information to Special branch. In an effort to counter the leaks, we decided to set up our own **counter -sb on a bigger scale than the Makhokhoba branch response to informers**. We established a network of friendships with some uniformed members of the British South Africa Police (BSAP) at the level of Sergeant, selecting those we found to be friends or acquaintances of some African detectives in the Special Branch and even asking some of them to try to be close to white officers there. One of the apparent encouraging signs was that the uniformed regular police were not as strongly hostile to political activists as detectives were. We succeeded in getting some of them to help us by alerting us about any moves by the Special Branch in connection with our activities and possible raids. The friendship became so strong from informal to formal level to the extent that these police friends were able to get valuable information from some Special branch detectives concerning police informers in the townships, especially inside our operating structures. We called this channel **Amabonela khatshana** [22] and if one of us had received valuable information he would say a code which we borrowed from Nyanja (Zambian) language **zimachuruka zoga**[23]. It is interesting to note that Nelson Mandela also mentions that some black police men were sympathetic to the anti-Apartheid activists. One of his examples was a black

---

[22] *distant observers*

[23] *loads of information*

sergeant who used to tip Winnie Madikizela-Mandela about impending raids by security police. The tipoff was always accurate because the raid happened as reported by this patriotic sergeant but their victim would have gone into hiding. It seems that the trend may have been common in the colonial environment. The only branch of police that was ruthless was the Security Branch or Special Branch. The uniformed policemen (including a few white officers) were often reasonable in treating and interacting with political activists in custody or in any compromising predicament. It also happened with some informers who confessed to the Party officials about their role as police informers saying they felt uncomfortable to work against their people in the struggle for majority rule that would embrace them, too, when achieved. Here there was an element of realisation that there was a distinct possibility that Africans could eventually achieve their goal of majority rule therefore it was not safe to reach that goal while on the wrong side of the racial divide.

In addition to the above method of attempting to counter the SB infiltration into our structures, we decided to expand our counter-offensive against information leak to the ubiquitous Special Branch by encouraging **oMakhulunhloko** to join the BSAP as women constables. Many girls with required qualifications tried their luck but only five were accepted, trained and attested to BSAP as women constables. Fortunately they were deployed in Bulawayo stations with two of them at Bulawayo Central. At that time there were already some women constables scattered in various stations. We encouraged our own to be friendly to other women constables with the aim of turning them over to the side of the struggle and encourage each other to be friendly to the security branch in order to find out who was pouring information to the SB from our branches to cripple the struggle. One of the girls succeeded in cultivating friendship with some detectives in the security branch but it was not easy to get anything of usable nature until she got information about the structure of the entire organisation of SB in terms of division of labour such as the investigative and intelligence unit on one hand and the arresting detectives who received information from the former, on the other. She was able to identify personalities in these divisions, including the hierarchy of commanding officers. So those who were torturing us were on the labour of execution within the branch while those who interrogated us in a cross examination style without lifting a finger constituted labour of conception of the security branch, the real Special Branch.

With regards our link with some sergeants, we were pleasantly surprised to find that our police sergeants were staunch supporters of the cause of African majority rule. They identified quite a number of Special Branch informers located within our structures in the townships. Actually information showed that a 'plantation' of informers covered several semi-surface structures of the banned ZAPU but quite rare in the Formidable. In some cases names known to us were mentioned in this connection, thus making the information credible. Above all the Special Branch was well informed about the meetings and decisions of the Bulawayo Youth District Committee and some of its branches. The information we received by no means covered the entire network of informers in Bulawayo. But it was enough to help us to change our ways of operating. Even so, the Special Branch continued to get information about us in spite of cutting out those who were identified as agents in our midst. We asked **oMakhulunhloko** to try to shadow some Special Branch detectives to find out who they were interacting with because we had information that some people were seen with detectives in the morning hours of the day on the other side of the main railway station or near European high schools. **Omakhulunhloko** sent some of their number to observe these interactions and confirmed that they saw movements at the suspected times and places but could not identify the actual persons as they were always in a car. The extent of infiltration by Special Branch demoralised some of the comrades and they drifted away in fear for their lives, considering that we were now handling "death penalty" materials of war. In spite of the fact that our friends did not supply all names where informers were known to be in place, the majority of the stalwarts stayed on and prepared to face any eventuality.

As reports from our police friends and oMakhulunhloko showed that Specail Branch was well informed about political activism in the Townships, the disenchantment took its toll in the Branches. Those that continued to function in full strength were Mkhokhoba, Mzilikazi, Barbourfields, and Mpopoma North and Njube. The rest were operating at half capacity due to either mass arrests or retreat of comrades from the heat of political activism under constant surveillance by security branches. Mpopoma South was severely crippled by mass arrests that almost swept away both the Executive Committee and Zhanda leadership. Owing to the fact that cells were quite alive underground they organised a secret meeting of cells where a new leadership was chosen in Mpopoma South. In doing this, efforts were made to involve people who were not suspected to be connected with SB and it seemed that they were bypassed because the new leadership successfully picked up the pieces and marched forward to continue the national cause full steam as if nothing had happened.

CHAPTER TWELVE

WE ASSISTED COMRADES TO ESCAPE FROM PRISON

The political situation had virtually become part of our lives in such a way that we became immune to fear of the Rhodesian government's spider-web of the security branches. It was now a sort of an instinctive impetus to constantly desire to reach the sought-after goal of national freedom from colonialism. All the efforts that we made in our search to find the optimum strength to effectively challenge the regime, we did not hesitate to plan and proceed as we saw it fit to do so. After establishing what we believed was a scoop in linking our comrades to a trainer soldier, we began to think that our dream of developing the Fomidable into a fighting force was on the verge of becoming true. In this regard we decided to venture into how we could get every town to have military trainers like the one we had just put in place.

However, before embarking on such a grandiose secret campaign, we decided to test the safety of another of our new approaches by picking up a second seemingly unsafe project. Four of us decided to test reliability of our latest mode of excluding some suspected colleagues from our planning and implementation team so as to create a detour away from the screen of the Special Branch. Like the recruitment of a soldier to train our comrades at Llewelin Baracks, we excluded some colleagues from a delicate operation which required careful planning. The plan entailed excluding all those whom we suspected of passing valuable information to the Special Branch. Of course there were many good comrades that we left out merely for ease of management, not that we did not trust them. After creating the by-pass system, we tested our system by undertaking another top secret mission. The mission was an operation carried out by one of our cells to assist some waiting trial ex-guerrillas to escape from Gray Street Prison. We called it **"pick up landing astronauts"** because we were going to wait for them to land themselves at a designated pick up point behind Mpilo Hospital, where United College of Education is situated now. (Note that this was the early phase of an exciting age of spaceships with man on board in the USSR and US). The Prisoners were Kay Nkala, Moffat Hadebe, Clark Mpofu and Elliot Ngwabi. They communicated to us their desire to escape through our colleague John Mkandla and we immediately started planning the operation. The planners were led by myself with John Mkandla, Daniel Ndlela and Phillip Mabena who was known as **Ntsu**[24] (because most of his tasks were done in darkness) participating. We carried out reconnaissance operations on the pickup point and the "drop and make a U-turn point." We then established a watertight communication channel in terms of free flow of information in a two-way channel and materials to and from the comrades in prison without detection or causing suspicion. We kept our ears open on the direction of our police

---

24

SeSotho for black

111

friends in case they could hear something about this "spaceship -like landing" project. After satisfying ourselves about all aspects of the operation, we bought a metal cutting pair of scissors and civilian clothes and sent them to the inmates (by channelling a small parcel at a time until every needed item was in their possession). Our internal agent was a trusted prisoner who used to be sent to town by prison officers without being guarded or searched outward and inward bound. In Rhodesia there were some prisoners who earned trust of senior prison officers who issued them with immunity from security checks when sent to town on official errands unguarded and not to be searched on their return to the prison. Our comrades in prison identified one such a prisoner as reliable and linked him up with us through John Mkandla to whom they suggested the idea of escape when he visited them. Upon receiving the report of this nature we discussed the matter and decided to create a small structure to drive the escape project. One trusted member of the Formidable was designated to be our external agent to link up the internal agent (the prisoner) and then sent to the comrades (inmates) in prison to arrange a system of communication between them and us through their appointed courier (free-lance prisoner). The process took shape following our external agent's visit to the comrades. Our external agent was employed at OK Bazaar store but of course the employer did not know that he was a member of an underground militia. He brought information from the inmates giving details of how communication would be carried out between the two sides. We gave the free-lance prisoner a pseudonym of **Sigonki**[25]. But of course the man in question was not at all a dangerous character by any means that is why he was trusted by the prison officers. The word was a convenient name since it had no political connotation in case someone picked up our conversation. It was widely used to refer to a member of a sub- culture group in the City. **Sigonki's** time out into town was communicated to Mkandla verbally to enable us to synchronise our collection time with the dispatch time between us and **him**. In the arrangement, information to and from us would pass through our external agent we named **Mfanekhaya**[26] at OK Bazaar where **Sigonki** would receive it verbally, thereupon he left the reply from the comrades in prison through the same channel. Mkandla obtained the information from **Mfanekhaya** at an opportune moment. Civilian clothes were sent through this established channel as described above. We bought a metal cutting pair of scissors and placed in a dust bin in a sanitary lane on an agreed date and time for **Sigonki** to pick it up after getting information from **Mfanekhaya** . He picked the instrument at a convenient moment soon after it was deposited in a designated dust bin. The date and time for pick up from landing site were agreed upon and the game was afoot. On the evening of the appointed day we went to wait for them at the designated landing and pick up site at Old Victoria Falls Road where the present United College of Education is situated (before it was built). The time was supposed to be 22h00 but the "astronauts" never landed until we gave up at 03.00 am. At 04.00 am Dan Ngwenya (former Governor of Matabeleland North Province in independent Zimbabwe) knocked at my door and said **"get dressed now!"** I woke up quickly and went to wake up Phillip Mabhena, who was named **Ntsu** had a Zephyr Zodiac, a very fast car of the time.

The comrades found that the route to the designated landing site was too bright with street lights so they manoeuvred all the way from Gray Prison to Tshabalala Township at the railway line opposite the grain storage silos. Dan Ngwenya guided us to where they were hiding. Apparently when they got to this point, they sent one of them to Ngwenya's house in Tshabalala Township. His mission finished when we found the men waiting for us. The original plan was to drive them

---

[25] *slang for a dangerous* **tsotsi**

[26] *homeboy*

right up to five kilometres from the border with Bechuanaland (Botswana). But we were already running behind schedule. We gave them provisions. Since it was already after dawn **Ntsu** and I drove the comrades along the Plumtree Road at a racing speed until at nearly sunrise, about ten kilometres from Plumtree, we dropped them and wished them safe journey through the jungle to Francis Town. The escape was not discovered until the wake-up time at 06.00am. A manhunt operation was unleashed around 08.30 am using helicopters and other fast moving vehicles. The comrades successfully crossed the Rhodesian border into Bechuanaland (Botswana) and handed themselves to the Tsetsebe police station in the then Bechuanaland Protectorate. The police decided to return them to Rhodesia. But one of them, Moffat Hadebe, bolted out and successfully returned to Zambia where he returned to armed struggle. Unfortunately the rest were handed back to the Rhodesian authorities. Now that they were experienced in escaping from prison, they escaped again later.

On his return to armed struggle, Comrade Moffat Hadebe was appointed commander of a large detachment that was deployed in the North East of Rhodesia (Zimbabwe) to open up a new front in 1968. The detachment camped in the mountains for three months before it was detected by agents of the Rhodesian security forces. Their security patrol was spotted by an agent who followed them back to one of the six bases and dashed back to alert elements of the security forces who sent a spotter plane that they saw fly above the main base. Apparently the spotter plane confirmed the presence of guerrillas on the mountains. A massive air raid was launched resulting into a six hour battle that became known as "The Sipolilo Battle". The Sipolilo battle is a long story on its own because it has strategic elements with implications for the down fall of ZAPU as countrywide national movement. If Sipolilo succeeded, ZPRA would have been able to infiltrate deep into the north east, eastern and southern regions. At the same time the Wankie and Kariba detachments, if properly done tactfully, would have created indestructible operational sectors in the southern, north and western part of the country. A tactical deployment should have yielded different outcomes in the entire theatre of operation because no frontal attack would have taken place essentially at the initiative of the comrades. Sipolilo was almost successful except that the comrades were controlled from Lusaka rather than by their commander in the field. The Kariba deployment was reckless as it lacked tact and foresight in terms of intelligence regarding the enemy alertness along the Zambezi River. Wankie battles too were at the initiative of the enemy because of premature detection by security forces. The detachment was meant to split into smaller units and establish themselves in the west and south west so that when Sipolilo and Kariba launched tactical strikes, south west would guide MK fighters southwards to cross to the border to RSA and then entrench themselves in the Matopos

However, the prison break itself was an outstanding piece of clandestine operation below the radar of the ubiquitous tentacles of the Special Branch. The pseudonyms stated above were meant to alert us if they were picked up by our uniformed police friends if Special Branch might have got the wind of the operation and its operatives. Apparently not even one of them was mentioned so this was an indication that information on the master minders of the prison break never reached Special Branch and also the fact that we were not arrested for interrogation confirmed non-detection of the operatives. The danger here was that it was expected that such an operation would emerge with a bang upon the discovery of the absence of the prisoners and that would be followed by intensive search and investigations and possible arrest of suspected individuals. Those of us who were involved in it felt a great sense of success because the process was delicate from its beginning to its actual execution both by the inmates and ourselves outside. From this experience we learned that careful planning by a limited number of strategists in underground operations was an essential imperative. While doing all this, we set our ears at highest alert on the channel with our friends in uniformed police without telling them what it was all about. Maybe when the news finally broke the silence they might have sensed something but we did not hear their comments to that effect.

The comrades who were recaptured decided to pick on one cruel African warder who was the most notorious sadist and outspoken anti-freedom fighters in Gray Street Prison as having helped them escape. All the work that was done by the trusted prisoner was piled on the warder in question. Initially the authorities could not believe that their trusted man could do such a thing. The inmates stood their ground until the authorities had no alternative but to dismiss their trusted warder for a crime he did not commit. The senior officers were so shocked by the allegation in such a way that they did not trust the African warders anymore. The man was always quick to ill-treat political prisoners physically and through vulgar language. The allegation that a cruel warder assisted freedom fighters to escape caused so much tension as the Africans began to be sympathetic to freedom fighters because they did not want to be beaten by a person they knew how deep he hated freedom fighters. His sudden 'turn around' into a hero ahead of them for allegedly assisting the so-called "terrorists" to escape made African warders feel eager to do better than their cruel colleague turned patriot by default. Was it a good weapon to shift blame to a traitor when one was caught with an illegal 'cargo' in one's hands? Yes, provided the traitor was within the embrace of circumstantial evidence in connection with the item in question. Here, the authorities lost twice; the actual culprits (four of us out there) stayed free but their trusted person lost favours as he was discredited by his handlers for a crime he did not commit against the state. Our hero prisoner remained safe until he finished his sentence without being suspected that he helped freedom fighters to escape from prison. The comrades escaped again. So we were satisfied that our by-pass strategy placed us out of the reach of the SB radar. This operation was one of those that we carried out successfully but never told anybody about them until Zimbabwe was liberated.

CHAPTER THIRTEEN

UNILATERAL DECLARATION OF INDEPENDENCE (UDI) AND ITS IMPLICATIONS

While we were busy with perfecting underground work, the Rhodesian Front Government rapidly reached an advanced level of preparation for the proclamation of UDI if the British Government did not grant the independence on Smith's terms. Several meetings were held between the two governments without reaching agreement. In 1964 the Labour Party came to power in Britain with Harold Wilson as Prime Minister. Many Africans had hoped that Harold Wilson, a left winger in the British political spectrum, would not compromise with the right wing Ian Douglas Smith. Initially, Wilson came up with a policy of **"no independence before majority rule" (NIBMA)** which was decisively rejected by Smith. Meanwhile in the legislative Assembly Mr Desmond Lardner-Burke moved a motion proposing that Rhodesia should declare itself independent if the British Government failed to grant it as requested by the Prime Minister. The Lardner-Burke motion was approved by the Legislature. It was in the backdrop of this motion that Ian Smith was beaming with confidence that if Rhodesia declared UDI there would be a two day wonder in the City of London and things would return to normal thereafter. The British Government would not send troops because no "British" would want to kill "British"

The Rhodesian Front government laid the ground for UDI by declaring a state of emergency in order to give powers to the security forces to detain people as they saw fit for a period of time throughout the country. True to his word, on 11 November 1965 Ian Douglas Smith broadcast to the country declaring independence for Rhodesia under white minority government. It was around midday and I was listening to the radio at work. To demonstrate that the Rhodesian Front government did not consider Africans as citizens with rights in Rhodesia, the principles of UDI were deliberately framed to depict Rhodesia as a Europeans' country without other races with rights equal to those of the ruling Europeans. They decisively excluded Africans by explicitly highlighting the importance of the link between Rhodesian Europeans with their English relatives thus:

"That the people of Rhodesia having demonstrated their loyalty to the crown and to their kith and kin in the United Kingdom and elsewhere through two world wars, and having been prepared to shed their blood and give of their substance in what they believe to be mutual interests of freedom-loving people, now see all that cherished about to be shattered on the rocks of expediency"

As I have said in the previous pages, the above-mentioned quote from UDI proclamation underlines Ian Smith's political view that Africans did not count as citizens of Rhodesia on an equal basis with Europeans on whose behalf he made that proclamation. None of the eight principles of the UDI proclamation indicated the Rhodesian government was leader of all peoples of Rhodesia and that it acted in concert with the aspirations and desires of all races in the country. The mention of loyalty to the crown and to their kith and kin is self-evident that he was talking on behalf of Rhodesian Europeans who constituted a segment of British stock. After reading the principles of UDI how would a reasonable African think in terms of his status as an indigenous inhabitant of that country whose 'leader' hardly hints on the social composition of the society that consisted of black and white races all of whom were supposed to enjoy equal citizenship with equal rights and freedoms in every sphere of life? Concerning the whole question of UDI, Africans were not consulted in a serious and objective search for a common ground. But the regime had the audacity to declare that **"the people of Rhodesia fully support the request of their Government for sovereign independence but have witnessed the consistent refusal of the Government of the United Kingdom to accede to their entreaties."**

Clearly those who fully supported the Rhodesian Government were the whites not the Africans as evidenced by lack of the latter's mention in the proclamation of principles of kith and kin between Rhodesians and Britons. By UDI proclamation Rhodesian whites translated their fifteen founding principles into a basis upon which UDI was anchored to ensure a complete victory of racism over the legitimate aspirations of the African people in Zimbabwe. This implied that such racial domination was to last for over a thousand years as propounded by Ian Douglas Smith. For the deprived and second class race to undo a UDI victory needed a powerful social upheaval to overthrow the regime either by a short powerful storm or a long drawn out armed struggle. The uncompromising principles of UDI could have caused any indigenous peoples to go to war for being treated like they did not exist in the light of the fact that Europeans were given prominence as owners of the country with Africans relegated to some mythical objects of political ridicule (always described as trouble makers therefore their right place was prison). Put together the fifteen founding principles of the RF and the eight principles of UDI proclamation could not fail to cause war on account of their lack of recognition of national diversity and thin on definition of how diverse aspirations and concerns could have been addressed fully to ensure racial harmony without domination and repression.

November 11 1965 was a dark day as hundreds of us were dragged out of our work places or houses within thirty minutes of the declaration speech by the Prime Minister of Rhodesia, Mr Ian Douglas Smith, a fellow Zimbabwean by birth who separated himself from us on nothing other the differences of skin colour. To ensure that those who were called trouble makers were removed from society as he ordered the Security Forces to act swiftly take them away and make sure that there were no demonstrations against UDI. The Special Branch, the frontline elements of the Security Forces, knew who should be taken away to deliver the peace that the Prime Minister wanted to prevail throughout the country. They arrived at my work place in a jovial mood and picked me up into a pick-up which was already full of some of my comrades from other parts of Bulawayo. We were taken to Fife Street Central Police Station where we were served with thirty day detention orders by which we were to be held incommunicado.

Under these conditions we received no visitors even though they brought us food. Initially we were not allowed to bath or exercise in open air until we complained strongly to the Officer Commanding the Province. In less than two weeks' time things began to change with regards our requests. The people who were detained here with me were: Gin Ntuta, Vote Moyo, Maswazi

Tshongwe, Daniel Ndlela, Todd "Shastri" Khumalo, Judah Dube, Cleopas Nhlabano and Jaeguru Chimombe. The majority of our colleagues from all the Bulawayo Townships were detained in sub-district police stations within Bulawayo. After thirty days, Gin Ntuta, Daniel Ndlela, Judah Dube, Vote Moyo and Todd Khumalo were served with detention orders to Gonakudzingwa (a designated restriction area within a vast isolated National Park). The remaining group was released into a UDI country in the middle of December. We were surprised that comrades like Daniel Ndlela and Judah Dube were sent to Gonakudzingwa yet the depth and extent of their involvement in the struggle was the same as that of the released lot by all measures of evaluation. The separation of our group that way worried us as we began to suspect a possibility of a trap lying out there for those who were released.

That black day of November 11, 1965 witnessed almost total creaming off of the surface leaders of banned PCC and Zhanda throughout the country. Many people had expected widespread action or demonstration against that blatant contemptuous act with impunity by Ian Douglas Smith and his government. Unilateral Declaration of Independence (UDI) by the Smith regime was a **crucible** in which the capability of the African nationalists to challenge racial domination in Zimbabwe was tested. At grassroots level, the event was a challenge to the structures that we had set up: the Zhanda and the Formidable in terms of their ability to spring to action at instant extreme provocation such as UDI which was an unacceptable height of political abomination that was characterised by use of force to legitimise its existence. The minority regime clearly acted in contempt of the legitimate aspirations of the majority of the African population whose demands for majority rule were loud and clear.

For Africans, the act of UDI was the highest degree of political damage inflicted on race relations between Black and White races driven by the Rhodesian Front regime. On this account the latter could not escape the responsibility for generating conditions that provided fertile ground for a war of resistance by the offended race, the Africans. Clearly the steady rise of unstoppable violent resistance by the oppressed people of Zimbabwe was precipitated by that act of excluding African citizens from the configuration of UDI in all its aspects. We recall that African leaders had warned that if the regime resorted to violence to aggravate African discontent: "We, the Africans, will resolve the problem in our own way." Asked by journalist what they meant by that, they replied: "Our own way is our is our own way" (Joshua Nkomo). The rest of us thought that "our own way" entailed operations designed to counter the regime's extreme grind on the people. A foundation was laid by the declaration of white independence on November 11 1965. In this regard it meant that the Africans were forced to adopt their own means to free themselves from racial domination and this entailed operating outside the laws of the regime for the purpose of bringing it down in a counter**vailing** power triggered by an irrational act of UDI. Although at the point of UDI there was no nation-wide mass riots against UDI, there were sporadic protest activities far in between on the following day but not strong enough to dent the main body politic of colonialism in the country. Essentially, UDI was a **crucible** that tested African majority on their determination to reject imposition of racial domination in the manner that Ian Smith did. In this connection most people were fully aware that the white population was hardening its attitude against compromise towards majority rule as exhibited by their overwhelming vote for the right wing Rhodesian Front to power in the second (white dominated) general elections in 1964. The above pages have shown that the early part of the freedom struggle was laughable as it looked like a child's play by using stones, petrol bombs, homemade rudimentary devices, etc. in an effort to exhibit anger against injustice. But, as we shall see later, violent resistance against racial domination progressively grew from such rudimentary methods and materials as they were phased out and replaced by well organised and resourced armed guerrilla forces that made the whole process of armed liberation struggle unstoppable.

As a matter of fact, from 1960 it had become clear that the Rhodesian whites wanted independence on their own terms as evidenced by their reaction to the 1961 constitution which left 250 000 Europeans in control of the country yet they felt 15 out of 65 parliamentary seats in the Legislature were too many for representation of 7 000 000 Africans. So they voted for a right wing party that vowed to stop any further movement towards compromising with the African nationalists on majority rule. The white electoral behaviour exhibited a clear signal that a peaceful resolution of the Rhodesian conflict was over as far back as during Sir Edgar Whitehead's government which banned three nonviolent African Nationalist parties: ANC (1957/59), NDP (19660/61) and ZAPU (1961/62). Surprisingly in the series of acts of banning African parties, leaders had no plan B that they should have adopted instantly upon provocation by an illegitimate act of UDI. People expected to wake up to hear some pronouncement about plan B at the stroke of the act of banning PCC and ZANU by the government in 1964. Such a plan could have entailed concrete preparations for armed challenge to the colonial state in the event of its unconstitutional act such as UDI.

As the signs of right wing shift in White politics were in evidence as far back as the early 1960s, it should have dawned to African leadership that plan B was desirable especially after the ban of the most peaceful NDP or during the life span of ZAPU. When ZAPU was banned there were several independent African states (eg Ghana, Egypt, Algeria, Nigeria, Ethiopia, Morocco, Liberia, etc) that were supporting the nationalists; therefore there was a distinct possibility of gaining support from them to allow our leaders to prepare for armed struggle in their territories. At the end of 1964, after Zambia's independence they could have transferred their bases to that neighbouring ally having reached an advanced stage of preparedness. By 1965 there would have been enough guerrillas to challenge and destabilise the regime and frustrate its UDI project. But none of this happened in spite of our efforts to build Zhanda and the Formidable into a large secret regiment ready to feed into the creation of an armed guerrilla force. In all of this we were close to the phases proclaimed first by 'General' Hokoyo and second by 'General' Bayawabaya in terms of phases for intensifying the struggle in tandem with the hardening of white political stance in the Rhodesian political landscape. We believed that the leaflets that contained declarations of war purporting to come from 'Generals,' were designed from the top echelons of ZAPU therefore we had to plan in anticipation that we would be reinforced by trained forces in numbers in the countryside, to start with. Of course trained freedom fighters began to trickle in Bulawayo and Salisbury in small numbers as early as 1963. But many were captured soon after crossing the Zambezi River and the rest were detected several months deep inside the country.

Nevertheless, when UDI became thirty days old, half of detainees were released and another half were served with medium to long term detention papers in Gonakudzingwa. Those released from Fife Street Central Police Station in Bulawayo included Maswazi Tshongwe, Cleopas Nhlabano, Jaeguru, Todd Khumalo and I. Gin Ntuta, Daniel Ndlela, Judah Dube were served with detention orders signed by the Minister of Law and Order, Mr Desmond Lardnerburke. We found the outside world quiet with life going on normally as if nothing drastic had happened. For our part, at first we suspected that those who were released, while others were sent away for longer period of detention, were set to get into a more deadly trap of some sort. So we agreed to make a strategic retreat and lie low while observing the situation under a UDI regime. We had to do just that as we did not know what criteria the Special Branch used to take some of our colleagues to detention while we were released unconditionally yet the density of our work underground was the same.

CHAPTER FOURTEEN

MEET A WONDER GIRL

After my release from detention many comrades came to my place to congratulate me on my unexpected release from detention. Comrade Sam Shoko (Mpopoma South Branch) sent his cousin to find out how I was doing after having been held incommunicado for thirty days in a police cell at Bulawayo Central Police Station. His cousin, Munyaradzi Shumba, was accompanied by his sister, an upper 6 student at Goromonzi High School waiting for her 'A' Level results. During my active involvement in the struggle I had seen a lot of nice girls but rarely did they strike me with a dazzling imprint of a kind that touched my heart from this Shumba girl. She ignited my interest with a first stroke of sight that generated a sort of a magnetic field between us with a pull effect of an emotionally compelling desire to see more of her all the time. In fulfilment of this desire I visited Shoko's house in Mpopoma Township more frequently than usual soon after that day. Initially it was all about cultivating friendship with her in order to establish some understanding of each other, especially on matters of common interests such as political awareness, etc. I had to ask my colleagues to let me completely "loose" in order to have time and space to respond adequately to the irresistible attraction to the girl of the moment. One friend could not keep quiet about what he observed concerning my excitement about the girl and he openly expressed his surprise that I wanted to scale down my activities to spend more time with a girl I had just met in town and he asked for some details about her. I told him that her name was Ratie Shumba, a high school girl of normal height, with amazing complexion of a mixture of black and brown, the eyes were black and white with a piercing look; her physical stature was elegant yet tending towards a plump shape with well figured feminine architecture from the toes to the face with velvet-smooth skin. Her extra-ordinary pretty face tended to be lit up with electric smile that could trigger automatic reciprocation even from a hard-hearted man who normally had no time for women. Her entire stature instantly registered in my heart and mind, thus depositing an unforgettable portrait of her well figured framework. Hearing this description, my friend exclaimed: "Ah! She must be a **'wonder girl'** to cause you to suspend politics for her!" Yes, she was a wonder girl who made me suspend my activities out of the struggle 100% to pay attention to her lest I miss a golden opportunity that comes once in a life time. Indeed, I asked her out several times and I was so delighted that we gelled so fast into a couple of jovial friends.

How Ratie Shumba became Ratie Mpofu

Ratie (a name shortened from **Ratidzai**) was born on the 4th August 1945 in Mberengwa District, Midlands Province, Zimbabwe. She is the first child of Mr Mesa Bara Shumba and Mrs Veronica Murerusi (Gumbo) Shumba of Jena Village, Mberengwa. The other siblings are Sandra Siyengiwe (Shumba) Skhakhana, Jester Doreen (Shumba) Mazarire and Dicksen Shumba. Luckily, with the full support of the parents, all of them became successful in professional development. Both parents are now deceased. Sandra and her daughter survived her husband who passed on in February 2012 and Doreen and her three children have survived her husband who passed on in 2008. Dickson has two children, a boy and a girl. Ratie grew up in the hands of a broader family of Gumbo uncles, aunties and grandparents where she picked up dynamic cultural values that constituted a sound foundation upon which she built her own model that enabled her to carve up a vision for indivisible commitment to human development. Her interaction with maternal uncles (Gumbos) in particular influenced her to internalise the culture of hard work that instilled a strong dose of courage to confront complex challenges in spheres of conceptual and menial labour. She attributed her colossal achievements in her life to the wisdom of her parents and the love of her uncles, the Gumbos, whom she regarded as the foundation of all families whose grandfather was Kufa Gumbo. She went to school when she was only five years of age but acquitted herself brilliantly right from the lower grades through to higher grades. She was the first girl in Mberengwa District to reach and pass General Certificate of Education 'Advanced ' Level (GCE 'A' Level) at Goromonzi High School in 1965. Her ambition was to read for a University degree as soon as possible after completing the aforesaid level. Before proceeding to degree level, she became a temporary teacher at Matopo Secondary School (40 kilo meters east of Bulawayo) in 1966. As already stated above, it was just before she started teaching when I met and dating her in Bulawayo.

After several outings we fell for each other and that was the greatest thing that ever happened to me in my socially marketable years of my life. Besides her dazzling beauty, she was politically alert and intellectually rich with general knowledge. None of the previous girls had all of what I was looking for like Ratie had. These outstanding qualities suited me squarely and I began to inform all my relatives and friends about her exciting qualities, not only as a beautiful girl but also as a young woman with immense potential to reach an apex in any field of her choice in life. Above all, she was my first girlfriend to call me "sweetheart" and "honey" before I called her by those titles of intimacy. She expressed her love for me openly with emotional sincerity in a manner that had never happened to me before. Meanwhile the 'A' Level results arrived from the post office in my presence and she was so happy that she passed. Subsequently she got a job as a temporary teacher at Matopo Mission, just 40 kilometres to the south east of Bulawayo. That was the time I learned all the roads from Bulawayo to Matopo Mission and from the Mission to the Matopo Hills. Within a short space of time we engaged. I could not wait in case I got arrested without a wife of this impressive calibre, who combined beauty and intellectual ingenuity. As we shall see later, I was right to think like that.

In September, 1966, I took another retreat from activism in order to nurture my germinating domestic affairs. That is, I felt that I should focus a little more on preparations for getting married to my wonder girl before I was whisked away into the gaping mouth of prisons. The preparations had been punctuated by activism and arrests described above. But in spite of all those painful punctuations the relationship between my girl and I had reached a height of steamy affection that was endowed with love and joy. Above all she was a staunch supporter of national liberation struggle by any means we could command. Actually, her political soundness made me more excited about her because she proved beyond all shadow of doubt that she was committed to the cause of freedom from racial domination in our country. Indeed she was perfectly positive in all that the nationalist freedom movement stood for and how it went about it to achieve majority rule. So I was so delighted to find a girl of that calibre therefore I did not hesitate to propose to her to marry me. Instead of engaging her with a ring, I did so with a very nice Swiss wrist watch which became the envy of many girls who saw it. Fortunately she accepted the watch and so we engaged and took all the necessary steps to get married by going through all the traditional procedures to seek acceptance and approval of the girl's parents. It took two weeks to complete the process at her home in Mberengwa (560 km south of the capital, Harare and 430 km east of my natal home, Nkayi). After accepting me as their son-in-law, Ratie's parents further approved our request to fast track the legal formalities through a Priest and Justice Department as antecedents to the marriage ceremony and wedding. All these and other related procedures went on smoothly for us and we were delighted with the cooperation of my-in-laws.

On the 16th October 1966 we got married in the Lutheran Evangelical Church at Njube Township, Bulawayo. Our wedding day in the Church and outside was so marvelous in every respect with its contrast from a police station. I was 27 and she was 21 years of age. Some members of the Special Branch attended the wedding ceremony in the Church. But they did not do anything except conduct themselves in a civil manner as uninvited guests.

Soon after the wedding I returned to invisible active operations in our cells. The first significant act was to print and distribute leaflets which, unfortunately led to our arrest and detention incommunicado for one month in solitary confinement. We escaped imprisonment because the state's star witness repudiated his sworn statement to testify against us, so we were set free in mid- January 1967.

While we were still in a situation of recovering from the pains of detention and torture Ratie and I were blessed with a baby girl, on 23 January 1967, whom we named Nonhlanhla (**lucky girl**). She was very lucky to be born while I was out of jail and still in the country when things had become extremely dangerous for activists. Indeed I was exceedingly excited that this delivery happened when I was still a 'free' man. The wide spread arrests throughout the country in the period from UDI to the end of 1966 convinced me that there was a high probability that if I did not abscond, I might be caught back-footed and be sent to prison or detention without trial. Now that I had a wife and child in my name, I found myself with more courage to fight harder and face whatever came against me. Some relatives advised me to retreat or lie low for a while in order to nurture my brand new family with appropriate cultural nourishments as a husband and father. I thought of my comrades who had been sent to jail leaving their families behind and, therefore, found the advice to be out of tune with reality of the political situation of our time. For me fighting for my country was as good as fighting for my family because they were part of Zimbabwean nation that was under a repressive system. Above all I was not the only one in a situation of that nature in the country. Other peoples' sons, daughters, husbands, wives, fathers, mothers, brothers and sisters were out there seeking the 'kingdom' of freedom and justice for the whole nation.

Rekindled Motivation

The sight and dignified demeanour of Ratie Shumba gave me the impression that I found a girl with whom I could share so much love that would be hardly quenchable for a life time. Even though the discovery happened when I was busy with dangerous political activities of pursuing the cause of freedom by illegal means, I was convinced that at personal level I had found something of cardinal importance to fight for. I therefore upped my hopes that one day or another I would be in a position to bring up a family happily in a social setting of national harmony and equality in all aspects of social action in a liberated Zimbabwe. The dream (vision if you like) made me put all citizens of my country in it but at that time it was still a mirage as the space for freedom was occupied by the repressive colonial system. Pleasant time with a beloved one was always socially and psychologically devalued by the oppressive conditions of colonialism. So it was imperative to remove the system first if the dream of a joyous family life was to come true. I then saw more clearly that there was a steak for my generation to fight for, the steak would only be available to African families when every citizen enjoyed equality in freedom and justice. Therefore there should be no going back until victory so that we could bring up families under conditions of freedom, peace, economic prosperity and social justice. At this point I felt that my thinking was that of a mature person in terms of commitment to face all forms of challenges regardless of possible consequences for me personally because I was not alone in the pursuit of the national cause of freedom for my country. That is, if I fought as a family man, the stakes would be high because if I perished in active service my family would remain behind to witness the peoples' victory to freedom on my behalf while they became part of a free nation without me but my name as a national freedom fighter.

Above all, I consider myself the luckiest child of my father and mother because getting married to Ratie was the best thing that ever happened to me and my family because she was clever, intelligent, creative, sharp-witted, patriotic and saturated with love not only for me but for my relatives and her own. Right from the time I knew her she exhibited impressive qualities of maturity in understanding broad issues of life which some girls of her age hardly displayed. For instance she was well politicised and culturally astute in respect of appreciating what her parents had taught her as an African girl and connecting this with her future aspirations as an educated woman. In the context of family matters she rapidly ingratiated herself into my extended family to the extent that she became the centre pin of the whole extended Mpofu family inside and outside Zimbabwe. In all of this she was able to intertwine the Shumba familywith the Mpofu family in a manner that all the related families interacted as if they were one family without boundaries between them. In all of this they loved her and she loved them all. The most fascinating part of all of this was the way she regarded her maternal uncles as the foundation of the Shumba, Ndlela and Maphosa families whose mothers were of Gumbo clan thus regarding them all as one entity, product of maternal grandfather **Kufa Gumbo**. Out of all her Gumbo uncles and their families, she had higher adorence for "Sekuru baVuka" and "Mbuya baMuhwa" (husband and wife) for the way they cultured her to understand life in general and *Ubuntu* in particular as she observed Mbuya baMuhwa playing some kind of leadership role of the broader Gumbo family while Sekuru baVuka was at work in town. She did more or less the same thing with my family where she connected with virtually all the branches of Mpofu extended family and then enlivened our relationships with our maternal cousins (Ndubiwa/Moyo) to the extent that the whole lot of the families mentioned here became a closely knit inter-cultural architecture with her 'presiding' over it as active facilitator for ensuring sustainable harmonious relations between them all. In my memory, there is no Daughter-in-Law who embedded herself into her husband's family in such a way that she functioned and related with everybody as if she was born in that family like what Ratie did kwa Mpofu.

For me, Ratie was everything in respect of being a loving wife, a faithful companion, a reliable friend and a formidable comrade let alone a most caring mother and grandmother. She was always abreast with developments in all spheres of cultural, professional, social, economic, political and technological settings in so far as they rolled out novelties or retrogressions that impacted on human lives.

Ratie Mpofu Becomes an Academic Guru

As will be seen below, at some point I was forced to flee from Rhodesia to exile in Zambia via Botswana. Ratie remained with our daughter in Makhokhoba Township in Bulawayo. Like Mbuya va Muhwa, she picked herself to ensure that her 'single' parent family survived by finding means of livelihood against all odds including persistent molestation by Special Branch who locked her up from time to time demanding that she should tell them where I was hiding. She swiftly connected with the rest of my broader family and relations some of who were helpful. My struggle colleague, Phillip Mabena was outstanding in this regard because he virtually became my brother in all but name up to this day. They survived until in 1969 Ratie got a scholarship from the Alfred Beit Scholarship Fund to train as a Physiotherapist at Royal Orthopaedic Hospital in Birmingham, UK. The daughter Nonhlanhla remained under the care of Ratie's parents in Mberengwa, kwaShumba. Ratie completed her course in 1972 She proceeded for further training as a Physiotherapy Teacher at a College in Wolverhampton which she completed in 1974. Meanwhile she studied Bachelor of Arts degree in psychology with Open University which she obtained in 1977. One of the remarkable things between Ratie and I was that when we got married in 1966 we had just GCE certificates of which she held 'A' level standard and I had 'O' level which means we had no university education. But while in the UK we both finished up with two university degrees each by 1980. More importantly, Ratie became a qualified Physiotherapist and teacher in that profession as well obtaining a BA degree from Open University.

Equipped with these skills she returned to Zimbabwe after independence (1980) to Lecture at the University of Zimbabwe (UZ) where she became instrumental in designing an intermediary course for Rehabilitation Assistants. She led a team that planned and established a college to train Rehabilitation Assistants or Technicians. Having accomplished this feat, she returned to the UK to read a Master's degree in Rehabilitation at Southampton University for fifteen months from 1984. Upon her return to Zimbabwe, she continued lecturing at UZ until in 1993 she went on Sabbatical at the University of the Western Cape (UWC), South Africa, where she lectured in the Department of Physiotherapy. Her specialist qualifications on Rehabilitation in addition to Physiotherapist stood out to be a capital demand for capacity development of departmental staff at UWC and, on this account, top management asked UZ to release her to UWC. That was done at a cost to UWC thus galvanising her to apply herself with full commitment to UWC. She became Head of Department of Physiotherapist in 1995 to 1997. At the same time she registered for a PHD focusing on curriculum development. In 2000 she graduated with PHD degree and reappointed as head of the Department for second time. Following this academic achievement, she rose phenomenally as she became Associate Professor and soon rose to become a fully-fledged Professor whereupon she was appointed as Acting Dean of Community and Health Sciences

Faculty for two years. When applications were opened for the post of substantive Dean she applied and successful became Dean for five years. At the end of five years she showed interest to continue and she was reappointed for another five years as Dean.

During her Deanship she propounded and pursued a vision for developing the Faculty of Community and Health Sciences by focusing on staff development and curriculum development. She raised the bar by ensuring that staff should strive to attain higher degrees such Masters and PHDs in order to beef up research and teaching skills that elevate the quality of both research and teaching in the Faculty. In Curriculum development and enrichment she started off with introduction of Community Based Education in all Health Science subjects in the Faculty. The University has a record for being one of the champions of the anti-Apartheid movement inside the country throughout its existence. Ratie became instrumental in taking UWC to the communities in the Townships of Cape Town by introducing community-based education intended to produce health personnel with knowledge of holistic, socio-economic and cultural settings in the communities to enable them to work in any social setting in the country when they became qualified.

Above all she further became instrumental in establishing inter-university partnership with Belgian and Dutch universities intended to assist capacity enhancement at UWC. She presided over the project in the partnership with those international universities that became a catalyst in staff and student development through attainment of Masters and PHD degrees in the Faculty. This way she successfully drove the project towards developing academic staff through acquiring higher degrees that would provide them with proficiency in research skills and quality of teaching. For her these capacities in research drastically distinguished a University from looking like a glorified high school to one of the highly rated universities in the country not only in knowledge but also in the quality and volume of that knowledge as well as its utility value in society.

Ratie's academic proficiency encompasses the following:

1. Physiotherapy
2. Rehabilitation
3. Community based Education
4. Curriculum Development in Health Sciences
5. Inter-professional Education for Collaborative Health Care
6. Supervision and mentoring postgraduate students

On a wider scale Ratie Mpofu expounded a concept of professional collaboration in heath teaching and clinical work.

When she was due to retire in 2010, no successor was found until December 2011 when she finally retired with dignity as shown by a spectacular display of her collage depicting a massive trail of success professionally and personally. Her academic achievements at UWC are distinctly appreciable in quantitative and qualitative terms.

Her legacy at UWC is significantly profound in terms of transformative aspects pertaining to curriculum development, enrichment and the quality of academic staff with special emphasis on research skills for academic staff. The university honoured her by conferring her status Professor Emeritus Ratie Mpofu. Paying tribute to her for her achievements, the Faculty wrote in a pamphlet dedicated to a project that she drove with amazing success (UWC 2014):

"Professor Ratie Mpofu had a wonderful gift and that is she was never conflicted as to who she is. She was proud being a woman of Africa but even prouder to be a visionary charged with pioneering the way forward. She never accepted that things cannot be done and fought with everything she had to accomplish what others saw as impossible"

After retirement, two Universities, UWC and KZN contracted her to do some supervision and mentoring of their postgraduate students. When she was rising towards a peak on this work, she fell ill while visiting Canada in June 2013 and returned to South Africa after two weeks in hospital. In Cape Town she was admitted at Christiaan Barnnard Memorial Hospital where she was hospitalized for three months. On the 19th October 2013 she passed on at 09h40. So the mountain had fallen therefore the shade of comfort, a fountain of immeasurable knowledge, a galvanizing power of transformation and a freedom champion had vanished just like that thus leaving behind devastated family, relatives, colleagues and friends.

Ratie is survived by me, husband and three chidren, Nonhlanhla, Velakude and Veronica Murerusi and two grand children, Nhlanhla Marley (6) and Matida (1year and 8 months)

CHAPTER FIFTEEN

RECEIVING AND DISTRIBUTION OF WAR MATERIALS IN BULAWAYO AND HINTERLANDS

However, after so many arrests of activists, some of us still out could not feel lucky to be out of prison yet a quarter of our colleagues at leadership level had been sent to detention in Gonakudzingwa, near the Mozambique border, and Wha Wha, near Gweru many more had gone to exile for military training. So it was imperative to come out of self-imposed political quarantine and start thinking of how we could adopt new ideas and plans that would place us well below or away from the SB radar screen while we were still out of prison. We felt obliged that we should intensify the struggle in tribute to our colleagues who were now looking to us to get their freedom. It was clear that we were no longer "**invisible warriors**" any more. We had thought that we could create large numbers of militia formations leading to armed struggle level to drive the struggle from underground like the FNL in Algeria. We had thought that our Formidable would grow into a formidable army nationwide, armed with modern weapons to challenge the Rhodesian security forces militarily, initially as guerrillas and finally as regulars (Mbejelwa and Clark had propounded to us the role of guerrilla warfare as first phase of armed struggle). The odds against us seemed to indicate that such a scheme had not yet developed to the levels of our expectations. After some careful consideration of several options, we adopted a new modus operandi whereby once a cell was silenced by arrest, other cells would act either simultaneously or in succession in a show of support for the arrested comrades. This was meant to enable the struggle to continue with or without us as well as reassure the rest of the people that the struggle was still 'fire under the smoke' until the guerrillas established themselves in the country in terms of gaining a firm support in the population and the extent of militarily overstretching the regime's security forces.

In our planning we had to review our strategy in order to come up with the best way to utilise explosive devices without causing civilian casualties and what could be main targets for these. Some of them were home-made rudimentary devices which were preferred by comrades because their mechanism allowed longer time to detonate the grenade than the commercial ones. All this happened in spite of the fact that there were so many imported devices buried on the City outskirts. The reason for such a situation was because the civilian activists were still in the majority amongst the field operatives. Properly trained personnel were trickling in during 1966 but most of them were captured before they got to their destination or rendered inactive by being detected before they established themselves in their operational area. Even the operation by the Crocodile Gang of (ZANU) hardly left a dent on the regime. It was not until the Chinhoyi battle raised the bar a little bit because it became quite a fierce encounter by a group of guerrillas from ZANU and this became a talking point in towns until the Wankie bombshell dropped in 1967 with higher casualties on the Rhodesian security forces than in any of the previous encounters. More about this later

At the beginning of 1966 ZAPU leadership began to take armed struggle seriously in terms of adopting long term planning and training large numbers of guerrillas in Algeria, Cuba, Tanzania and Socialist countries because they had realised that the Rhodesian security forces could not be shaken by sporadic shooting and explosions at long intervals. One of the major factors that induced ZAPU to take full responsibility to wage full scale armed liberation struggle was the British Government inability to compel the Rhodesian regime to comply with the principle of "no independence before majority rule." As a matter of fact, at that time ZAPU was still commanding massive support of the African population so it was possible to mobilise human resources for military training to raise enough fighters to cause a complete breakdown of Law and Order in Rhodesia. Before the big bang of 1967 we had received loads of weapons in preparation for armed struggle to be waged by properly trained personnel. The idea was that trained comrades were going to train the locals before launching an offensive that was to be synchronized with the arrival of more detachments in the country. In administering the delicate matters of secrecy, the Lusaka Office would send somebody to me or Thenjiwe Lesabe or any other designated comrade with a code or password to identify myself when a delivering driver would bring the cargo. The couriers bringing codes did not give a time frame meant that I had to be on standby during the week in question until the cargo arrived. Regarding contact with trained freedom fighters I was supposed to be ever ready for any of them coming to me in the evening or at night to report their arrival in the city or neighbouring districts. The delivery of cargo hardly faltered but arrival of personnel was a different story. In all cases of failure comrades were captured before we got a signal of their arrival instead we got a signal of their capture near the Zambezi River. The capture rate close to the crossing point worried us a great deal because it meant that the weapons would not be in the hands of properly trained personnel. The management of the weapons was also cause for concern because improper handling could be fatal. It would appear that further away from the urban hinterlands, especially the border peripheries, the masses were not fully politicised enough to understand their role in relation to a war of liberation carried out by soldiers of freedom. In the earlier phase of armed struggle this problem affected large detachments of guerrillas in such a way that they hardly reached the interior of the country without being detected. Some authorities (Moorcraft: 2008 and Cilliers: 1985) found that the difficulty of lack of population along the Zambezi River border and the worst part of it was that those few villagers at the periphery were not politicized enough to support freedom fighters therefore they were prone to reporting them to the security forces upon spotting them. This enabled the Rhodesian security forces to create a "search and destroy" zone which gave them a crucial advantage to maintain a strategic initiative by which they swiftly surprised the guerrillas and pushed them to a killing ground. The scarcity of supportive villagers along the northern border and lack of political readiness for armed struggle for the few at the periphery had to be managed through a political strategy. Otherwise the few fighters who filtered through the military screen grid of the Rhodesian security forces could not be easily spotted once they reached where there was plenty of "political oxygen" in the form of politicized population in densely populated areas and towns.

For us at that time, it was hard to understand how the weapons succeeded to reach intended destinations by road yet their users hardly passed through the first line of security entanglement close to the Zambezi River. Inside the country many people had suspicions that there might be a mole within ZAPU's Head Quarters in Lusaka. But no one could be certain about the cause of the problem. The operatives left Zambia by crossing the Zambezi River by boat or some other hazardous method such as a rope across a narrower part of the river. What was even more puzzling was that weapons originated from the same source as freedom fighters yet suitcases stashed with weapons or explosives were carried by trusted drivers of long distance freight lorries or vans carrying commercial cargo between two countries arrived safely. To my knowledge no lorry driver was ever intercepted at the border or police roadblock carrying a suitcase full of fire arms and ammunition or explosives and their detonators. They filtered through and delivered to a designated point with correct identification codes for the recipients. From the recipient point of view, the discrepancy between the successful delivery of war materials and the relative failure of arrival of deployed personnel who were supposed to find them inside the country was extremely worrying until we got there to experience the real impediment to personnel movement across the Zambezi River. As already stated above, Moorcraft and Cillier confirm the nature of the impediment in the form of a "search and destroy zone" near the Zambezi River.

In respect of what is being described on preceding paragraphs, by the middle of 1966 we had received many boxes of small fire arms, ammunition and explosives with their detonators. These were supposed to be used by trained personnel from outside the country as indications were that people trained as guerrillas would enter the country for serious training of locals and fighting. We decided to dispatch most of the war materials to the countryside for safety reasons and in anticipation of arrival of comrades to use them. The social infrastructure for freedom fighter support was strong and viable but trained personnel could not pass through the security grid close to the crossing points as explained above. In the distribution of such materials, we involved unsuspected individuals to try to make sure the process was safe from SB eyes. To ensure that the distribution remained invisible we approached choirs, women, buses, delivery vans, etc. The first team we approached was **a traditional music choir,** consisting of four members. The key member here was very politically alert and he was the *lead singer* of the choir. He did most of the transportation of materials from town to the countryside. The weapons were carried in "bags of maize meal" on the buses from Bulawayo to the remote countryside. Sometimes buses were searched by the police but bags of maize meal were not suspected as long as they did not look suspicious.

It was amazing that materials reached town quite easily and left again without being detected in spite of a network of security agents and informers. The weapons were meant to come in advance of their users and to lighten the loads carried by fighters from hundreds of kilo metres from Zambia across the Zambezi River to the interior of the country. In some cases the trained personnel were re-united with their weapons but, in most situations, they did not because the potential users were captured before they went deep into the country. The Rhodesian security forces were preoccupied with hunting down personnel than looking for their weapons because they expected them to carry them along. They expected them to cross with their materials and indeed if they captured the fighters in possession of weapons. The free flow of weapons from Zambia into Rhodesia seemed to suggest that the security forces had not yet got the information about such a flow of military hard ware being transported by long distance freight haulage vehicles. Later we were informed that most of the captured comrades still carried weapons because those that came in advance were mainly meant for locals who were to be trained by the comrades once they were well established within the theatre of operation. That is why we became eager to have our Formidable Force trained and incorporated into a military regiment ready to fight alongside other fighters. All such desires did not materilise the way we wanted them to.

The country bound materials needed appropriate structures to manage them safely according to instruction from the freedom fighters. So, we had to break down into small cells of two or three members per cell to keep the weapons in a cool safe place in the bush or mountains or any appropriately dug bunker in which to place a container trunk. Rural recipients who were assigned such tasks stored the materials as advised. The keepers checked them not so frequently because they were well oiled and greased to prevent moisture and rust. The best people to keep such war materials were very mature people, between ages of 30 and 55 years of age. One of the old men who played this risky role for five years is still alive at the age of 100 years in Kafusi, Khezi District. The discrepancy between the free flow of weapons and failure to arrive by freedom fighters lead to a saturation of "buried" military hard ware in the outskirts of Bulawayo and Salisbury and hinterlands. Some suitcases were accidentally excavated by civilians on the outskirts of Bulawayo and handed over to the police who conducted an extensive investigation that touched everybody who was on the SB list. But it would not be a surprise if some more trunks could be lying dangerously in the shallow pits underneath Entumbane Township and Bulawayo United College of Education.

Some of Our Major Operational Blunders

Some of the activities in the underground did not go well like the Dose Hose accident but with far reaching consequences to the operatives concerned. Some of our activities and blunders continued to occur until I left the country. Ratie Shumba came to my life when I was deeply involved in handling materials considered by government as subversive which inherently carried serious legal consequences if and when discovered by security branch. She automatically regarded herself as part of the invisible movement of our cell. As early as before UDI our struggle had entered a phase of using deadly lethal materials just after Ethan Dube had been deployed to a strategic post in Dar es Salaam in Tanzania. I had taken over his role inside the country as a Liaison Officer with Abel Siwela as "chief of operations" in Bulawayo and the hinterland. This was the most dangerous phase during which the struggle was driven by civilian operatives using lethal materials under the efficient radar of the Special Branch. The danger was not only in the mishandling of the materials of destruction, it also lay in the Law and Order Maintenance Act (LOMA) whose draconian provisions included death penalty if found guilty of possessing or using explosives and fire arms for political reasons. In spite of the fact that we had dispatched many colleagues out of the country, the operational field was still heavily populated by **civilian** operatives handling all sorts of materials for which they were not fully trained to handle. Many more had to leave whether or not they were already on the Special Branch list of suspects. In essence we were a secret army of civilian freedom fighters who were driven by the desire to attain freedom for our country at any cost. Clearly in our handling of some of the lethal military materials was extremely risky. In this connection there were many mistakes and accidents that happened.

Actually, as we gained experience in the whole game of underground politics of '**destroy and runaway**,' we found ourselves in a situation of hide and seek between the Special Branch and ourselves. Some of the work became qualitatively significant but some not at all as many comrades were succeeding in causing measurable damage to their targets others not at all. The duel between the Rhodesian Special Branch and the underground civilian operatives could be described as "clash of the warriors behind a veil of secrecy" because the public never got to know how these forces were tracking down each other and the consequences suffered by the weaker side.

It was not all in vain nor was the slate of activists washed clean by security branch because there were many incidents that happened successfully where no one was arrested in that connection. In our branch there was no planned incident that resulted in the death of a civilian which meant that comrades did not operate out of the terms of reference of Branch's adherence to Party policy.

As I said above, some activities in which I was involved happened simultaneously with preparing to get married to Ratie as she was already part of my life from late 1965. The question of finding the time for struggle and space for my girl required a balancing act. From the time of my release from detention in 1965 certain activities in which I was involved continued during the time of preparing for our wedding and, in all of this, Ratie gave us full support every step of the way beyond our wedding day. But we still lived with lack of requisite skills to use devices of a military nature that came our way. In spite of much effort to acquire better skills in field operations, we continued to encounter setbacks not only through arrests but also from our own blunders. A few examples given below will show clearly that our operations were undertaken by locally half trained personnel for the purpose of maintaining the momentum of the struggle inside the country by causing damage and bangs where ever possible. But in doing this, there was always a danger of the half-backed operatives making basic errors that compromised their invisibility and lives.

For instance one of the cases involved a colleague who had "graduated" from the use of homemade devices was introduced to the real hand grenade and drilled on how to operate it from the container box up to the target. After the training he identified a target and was assigned to it as soon as he proclaimed himself ready. A serious mishap happened through improper handling of the hand grenade in question. He had found where a group of four top Africa Detectives of the Special Branch sat almost every evening. At the point of throwing the device, the operative forgot to remove the safety pin which controls the detonating mechanism of a hand grenade. After straightening the holding brackets of the pin on the opposite side of the neck of the grenade, he held its ring, instead of pulling it out and hold a flap that controls the detonator, he threw the grenade towards the target holding the ring side of the safety pin. Unfortunately, it landed closer to him than to the target. This was because the pin did not release the grenade smoothly to allow it to 'fly' fast towards the target. Consequently, the shrapnel sprayed his entire abdominal area and chest, thus reducing his clothes on the front and abdominal skin into shreds. In that shredded condition, he emerged in to the light bragging that he successfully attacked a group of Special Branch African detectives who were sitting in an open site of a beer hall. But he was lucky that the skin on the abdomen was torn by shrapnel without reaching the internal organs below the skin. I was shocked to see the man merging from darkness with shredded clothing full of blood from the neck to the toes. The fact of the matter is that his grenade never reached the intended target as it landed closer to him causing serious injuries on his abdomen leaving the detectives unscathed. If he had succeeded, he would have eliminated a core of African detectives involved in brutal torture of political activists. Above all, that would have been the first loss of life inflicted on our adversaries since we embarked on the use of lethal materials. The injured colleague was treated by one of the most dedicated doctors of the liberation struggle Dr Desai.

The second case of the most serious errors occurred when some such half-baked operatives carried out some bombing on the Victoria Fall Road Bridge north of Bulawayo. The ramifications of the error shook many strategic structures in the Formidable and led to an irreparable political damage which was in the form of some essential drivers of the movement removed for security reasons. The blunder in question happened when two comrades had attacked a target and one escaped into the dark but the other walked along a main road to the City, thus disregarding security precautions that he should have observed. He walked in front of an oncoming car which stopped immediately and the motorist asked him if he saw the perpetrators of the crime near the bridge. He played innocent by saying he saw someone running way into the bush and the motorist suggested that since both had seen a man running away, they should go to the police station to report the incident of crime as both of them partially witnessed the incident. The comrade agreed and the man drove his car to the police station with a passenger whom he regarded as a suspect. Apparently the motorist was familiar with the smell of explosives because when they got out of the car he pulled an iron bar from under his seat and brandished it triumphantly as he walked behind the comrade like he had arrested him. He handed him over to the police as citizen's arrest and reported the incident as he saw it. Thus our comrade was arrested because he was fooled into believing that the motorist did not see what happened. His first mistake was to walk in front of an oncoming car after 'bombing' a bridge while the motorist was approaching. The comrade was caught by a passerby who tactically got him to "voluntarily" accompany him to the police station with his hands smelling the very substance that he used in trying to blow a bridge. Clearly the motorist must have been convinced first time that he had found an armature saboteur on the act of sabotage (because the bridge was not extensively damaged). The second comrade was picked up at dawn the third day, a sign that the first comrade tried to deny responsibility for the incident for thirty six hours. Clearly, with such irrefutable evidence, the Special Branch had a field day, thus giving him no chance to deceive them this time.

At that time the police wanted the planners or "commanders" of the operation because, even if the bridge was not badly damaged, they were anxious about use and possession of explosives in town. With pressure from torture taking its toll in the form of pain on the two arrested comrades, they sent out word that their handlers should be exported out of the country quickly because their survival from torture and heavy sentences lay on admitting that they were sent by John Mkandla, Sam Sibanda and Joburg Mzilethi under duress. So they should be sent out of the country quickly before they could be implicated in the impending confessions. This was because torture was unbearable for the two youngsters. We acted swiftly by removing the comrades from their residences to a hiding place. After they were assured that their handlers were safe enough the boys confessed by placing all responsibility for bombing the bridge on the shoulders of John Mkandla's mentioned team after four days of gruesome torture. The Special Branch pounced in their houses but did not find them.

In apparent desperation, the SB went for us: Maswazi Tshongwe, Samson Shoko, Thenjiwe Lisabe, Cleopas Nhlabano and I were arrested. They picked us up at 04.00 am demanding that we should produce John Mkandla and his "gang." We were interrogated separately and thoroughly beaten up to the extent that most of us finished up with heavily swollen up faces. The substance of their interrogation indicated that detectives were guessing that we were suspects hoping that if any one of us knew something about the case, he/she might breakdown and spill the beans. In fact we all knew about the whole story about the Mkandla team. The SB had got the right people but the questioning showed that, in other words, they were on a "fishing expedition" and hoping for a catch on good luck but none of us gave them that luck until they set us free. As soon as we got out we had to fast-track the escape of the Mkandla team and we did this by setting a planning subcommittee under the leadership of Mrs Thenjiwe Lesabe, Maswazi Tshongwe, Cleopas Nhlabano and I. Upon our release we communicated with their keepers to take them to another secrete place from where they would proceed to Botswana.

There was a long standing plan (dating back from the days of the Federation) that enabled us to 'extract' colleagues from danger and dispatch them out of the country. According to the plan, safety hide-outs were identified in the western and southern routes from Bulawayo to Botswana. The head of the household in a hideout was designated as a contact person who would be activated only when an emergency occurred. All designated contact persons were not to be involved in any other activity of the party on the surface or underground except in hiding and moving people out of danger. Another essential part of the network for moving people out of danger, were buses from Bulawayo to the rural areas. In every bus route to the remote rural areas had a courier, either a reliable bus conductor or driver himself. To pass information to the rurally based contacts, the courier system would convey the message to the recipient about the arrival of, say, "clothes from the dry cleaner" or bag of maize meal or suchlike parcel from a son in town. Then the contact would wait for them at an identified bus stop on an appointed date in the bush. If the fleeing persons were hotly sought by the Special Branch they would be transported by private cars, or vans or lorries or a government vehicle driven by a government employee who would be a secret operative of the movement or any persons unknown to the Special Branch. One of such persons was Phillip Mabhena, otherwise known as Phillie whose car was widely used for most clandestine operations without being detected. On few occasions Amos Mkhwananzi's car was used for transporting fleeing persons out of town to the north during the Federation days. Lately, Mkhwananzi (former MP for Tsholotsho, Zimbabwe) emerged from underground to surface activism thus rendering himself unsuitable for this delicate task. Roger Ncube (**Gwamkwam**) had a taxi at the movement's disposal for all clandestine operations. But the SB began to suspect him to be connected with subversive elements when his taxi was spotted by security agents zooming almost every night till dawn. He had to be 'exported' to Zambia before SB picked him up. Thomas Ngwenya was a driver of a delivery scooter for a pharmacy and in the process he was a very reliable courier for any consignment, especially distribution of leaflets at designated points in the townships within Bulawayo city centre. He also fled to Zambia where he joined ZPRA and finished up as a Colonel in the National Army after independence.

The mission to dispatch the Mkandla team was carried out successfully under the direction of Thenjiwe Lesabe. Mrs Lesabe was a semi-surface official of the banned PCC and very much under the watchful eye of the Special Branch. But she was such a shrewd tactician who was always able to put a cover over what was sensitive and dangerously risky. Quite a lot of operations planned by Lesabe happened during day light using the least suspected 'conveyer belts' and sources such as rural bound wholesale delivery vans and government vehicles driven by underground activists in government employment (eg ambulance drivers, public works drivers and, quite rarely, some police vehicles driven by African uniformed police). The John Mkandla group had instantly become a high profile group for the Party because they were in charge of many underground cells in Bulawayo and rural hinterland. As Chaiperson of Makhokhoba Branch, John Mkandla was overseer of all the militia regiments, including the Formidable and oMakhulunhloko. In this respect, they could have been a valuable catch for the Special Branch because they were part of an invisible core engine driving the struggle in Bulawayo at the time. Therefore their forced migration to Zambia had to be undertaken diligently all the way until they reached their destination. The principal planner of transportation of the Mkandla mission, Thenjiwe Lesabe, was, in her own right, a high profile politician yet she was able to come down to the ground to plan and undertake dangerous missions with us successfully. After our release, she is the one who produced a well thought out communication plan to dispatch the "fragile Mkandla parcel" out of the country. We did it cautiously via Kezi, south of the **Matopo Hills** into Botswana by a mixture of ordinary buses and a lorry at the end of the relay configuration. All four of them joined armed struggle in Zambia, trained in the USSR and were deployed in the North East of Zimbabwe for operations.

John Mkandla and Sam Sibanda fell in active service in field operations in the North East of the country. Jo Zwelibanzi Mzilethi and John Phece Ndlovu survived and they are war veterans. Mzilethi has retired from public service where he occupied several senior positions in Government. The John Mkandla cells survived all blows caused by loss of leadership and were some of the most effective in Makhokhoba right through the period of armed struggle till cease fire in 1979. The cells we created while we still could, became the main supply chain for the freedom fighters in terms of intelligence, supplies and life supporting requirements in the Bulawayo rural hinterlands up 170 kilo mitres to the north, east, west and south. Mackenzie Ncube was part of the survivors of the onslaught of the Special Branch throughout the period of liberation struggle.

It was mainly under the above-mentioned Act that the Special Branch arrested activists, detained and, if they saw it fit, prosecuted them after gruelling interrogation. But during the earlier occasions their material bases of interrogation showed that they were not fully informed about who was involved in the possession of fire arms and explosives and the manufacture of home-made devices. They did not have a full picture of how the operatives were deployed and their command structure. But as time went on, they began to be better informed about some underground activities of the movement. There was a fierce battle between the operatives vs Special Branch not in terms of physical battles in a battlefield but in hide and seek game. He who had the sharpest eyes and ears to see or hear the whereabouts of the other in hiding took the initiative over the other by either arresting or fleeing depending on which side they were. The SB had the advantage of resources to reward their agents for reliable information as a result they succeeded in excavating some of the secrets that we thought were closed behind airtight veil. Their methods of obtaining information from our structures included planting informers within our structures, or recruiting some of our members to work for them as agents or they became friends of our neighbours or very close acquaintances. In some cases errors by operatives caused them to be arrested on the act in which case the Special Branch would gain full information during interrogation as the person caught in the act could be forced by circumstances to spill the beans thus providing the SB with crucial information about the nature of operations and the people driving them. There are examples of errors whereby an operative was caught in action by a pro-government passerby or by a Special Branch agent. In such a situation, they would confront their suspect with firsthand account of the operation and credible information on other suspects. If he denied they would grind on him until he confessed. If a subjected person felt that his only survival was to make a confession, he sent a word to those outside stating the names of linkmen who should be removed immediately because he would mention them in his confession. In such situations a cell responsible reacted swiftly to remove the named leading personnel of the cell out of town and eventually out of the country.

In those circumstances we had to manage the confessions to minimise two things: the first was to diminish the severity of the accused comrade's sentence and the second was avoid the damage to the struggle that would be caused by mass arrests of implicated comrades resulting from confessions. After managing the situation of **"confessions to escape severe sentences,"** an ok would be given for such confessions to be made implicating the absconded comrades for 'safety' reasons. All of this would happen within twenty four hours. As soon as the "birds were flown", the accused persons could be free to transfer and pile all the responsibility for their actions upon the persons who would have absconded to safety. The move would mitigate the possible sentence beforehand for the confessed accused. To my knowledge none of the known cases that were handled like this received a death sentence or life imprisonment because the content of the confession shifted the material density and merits of the case to those who were at large. The accused person would extricate himself by telling the interrogators that he was ordered by them to do it on the pain of death. The onus would be on the Special Branch to catch those implicated principals. The fact that they did not find them in their houses compelled Special Branch to rely on available confessions for submission for admission as evidence for prosecution in court whether or not they might have suspected that they were largely false. The fact of the matter was that confessions of that nature effectively shifted a large proportion of the responsibility of the act of sabotage to the absconded men. The accused persons would portray themselves as pawns driven to commit the crime under duress, thus hoping to escape long term sentences. When presented in court the statements were the only material veracity of the case; accordingly, the blameworthy of the accused persons would lose its true content considerably as the core of the case would rest with the absconded men. Thus, the confessors escaped a life or death sentence in this regard. The swift removal of the suspected key persons from the link of the affected cell enabled the Formidable to survive and continue to grow to supply personnel to the armed struggle and internal activities of sabotage. This is exactly in the situation of Makandla team when their colleagues were arrested.

It may be a surprise that soon after removing all the wedding regalia and fanfare, I resumed active underground activities with intention to rekindle the spirits of hope amongst colleagues and Party supporters. It was important to remind people that there was still some life in the hidden structures of ZAPU. To this end, Tshongwe, Nhlabano, I and many others printed and distributed leaflets throughout the City of Bulawayo and townships to show that ZAPU was alive in 'hiding.' The leaflets were written in language close to that normally found in the Holy Bible as follows:

> "**Mr Ian Douglas Smith,** *Thou shall not rule this country without the consent of African people because they are majority race who are the original inhabitants of the country;*
>
> *Thou hast no right to arrest and detain innocent citizens of this country for demanding the removal of chains of injustice;*
>
> *Thou hast no right to impose thy racism upon the Africans to make them second class citizens in their country of birth;*
>
> *Thou shalt not hang those who demand freedom and justice because theirs is a sacred cause; Thou shalt be a leader of honour* **only** *if ye and thy government freeth all political prisoners and invite the British Government to convene a constitutional conference to draft a newconstitution based on majority rule in our country*
>
> *Thou shalt ignore African demands for freedom and justice at thy regime's peril together with thy allies"*
>
> **"Ye Africans**, *thou art the original inhabitants of this country therefore ye art being called upon to pick the sword of justice and cut the chains of colonial bondage to set thy selves free from the shackles of colonial repression*
>
> *Thou shalt fight for freedom, which is thy birth right, till victory that shalt open the gates for ye to enter the land of milk and honey that is nigh:* **a free Zimbabwe**
>
> *Thereupon thou shalt bare the flag of freedom as ye march triumphantly on the ashes of colonialism whence shalt emerge and flourish the aforesaid land of freedom for all citizens on equal basis."*

The above is a reconstruction of contents of the original leaflet, otherwise the latter's text covered the full page of the A4 sheet. The lines of the actual text may not be entirely accurate because now we are depending on memory but, even so, there might be very little variations in wording not in content due to the length of time scale since that time. I believe that the above stipulated lines are close to the gist of the original themes of the leaflets that almost sent us to jail for fifteen years.

Distribution of leaflets went very well in the rest of the Townships except Mpopoma North where one colleague ignored the rules of secrecy and distributed leaflets in a tavern at Mpopoma Township, Bulawayo, in full view of the patrons and detectives thus leading to his arrest on the act. Under gruelling interrogation, he sang like a bird implicating Maswazi Tshongwe, Cleophas Nhlabano, and myself, Joshua Mpofu as authors and dispatchers of the leaflet. Special Branch detectives moved swiftly to pick up all of us who were mentioned by our colleague for interrogation. I was arrested by three plain cloth officers led by a white Chief Inspector all of whom I had not seen before. They all looked at me with stern faces and menacing body language. I felt that the end had come because those detectives looked like a firing squad ready to do the job at the stroke of an order. It was on the 13th November 1966, just four weeks after Ratie and I got married and many people became anxious that my arrest might mean a long term separation from each other if found guilty. Chief Inspector wondered how I afforded to buy a car with a clerk's salary. I told him that there were hire purchase facilities in the garages and other shops in town. He retorted that he would not be surprised if his investigation showed that it was purchased by Lusaka office of ZAPU. Initially they took me to West Commonage Police Station, west of Bulawayo City centre. When they found that I could not tell them anything about the leaflets, they handed me over to the Fife Street Central Police Station where the familiar torture squad of detectives was based. I met Maswazi Tshongwe and Cleopas Nhlabano at Bulawayo Central Police Station and they too were picked up the same day as me. After I was handed over to the familiar Special Branch detectives, I was taken to the security camp again for painful interrogation. The torture process was back. This time they took three days of torturing us and then served us with thirty days detention orders. I was detained incommunicado at Hillside Police station without receiving visitors. They allowed my wife to bring food for me but never allowed her to see me. Here there was an African Sergeant Hombe who was very supportive of African self-rule. He came to my cell and told me that the Special Branch gave a list of stringent conditions to the Member-in-Charge of the Station to keep me in solitary confinement. He said that he advised his boss that political detainees should not be treated like common criminals because they stood for better life for millions of people therefore could not be treated the same way as common criminals who committed crime for selfish narrow interests.

Apparently the Member-in-Charge indicated willingness to the sergeant that he might consider making things better if I requested him to do so. Indeed I sent for him and he came and confirmed that there were restrictions imposed by Special Branch officers but he listened to my request attentively and at the end of the conversation he accepted my request to relax most of the SB imposed restrictions except one that forbade talking to visitors. From there onwards the situation was relaxed, with open air exercises, a morning shower, soft porridge and coffee in the morning, lunch and supper and a ventilated cell. It was interesting to note that a day before the end of thirty days the Officer-in- Charge re-imposed the tight regime of rules whereby I was locked in a dark room the whole day with a small window until the SB officers arrived to take me to their station to be charged. This was an indication that the uniformed police at Hillside were not happy with the harsh treatment of political prisoners. Once again in the hands of the SB Nhlabano, Tshongwe and I were taken to court to be formally charged for printing and distributing unlawful leaflets in Bulawayo. We were remanded at Gray Street Prison in Bulawayo, but after two weeks we were out on bail pending trial within five weeks.

Concerning the case we were facing with my colleagues, the prosecution had pinned their hopes on our colleague who was caught red-handed and confessed that he was given the papers by us. He was then turned state witness against three of us and was promised freedom from prosecution. But with heavy pressure from party supporters in his own branch, Mpopoma North, he withdrew from the witness list and the case collapsed because he was the star witness. The potentially crucifying witness unexpectedly became our saviour by changing his mind. He decisively rejected his original statement and refused to testify against us saying he was forced to make a false statement by the police. He was sent to jail for nine months for committing perjury while our cases were withdrawn on lack of solid evidence against us. So we were set free, only for the time being. This was one of those narrow escapes that I will never forget especially because I was on the brink of long term imprisonment after I had just got married. The clause under which we were originally charged under the Law and Order Maintenance Act carried a maximum of fifteen years imprisonment with hard labour. I was aware that there was always a possibility to be arrested any time as long as I continued to do some work pertaining to the struggle. But the way we printed and planned to distribute the leaflets, should not have been easy for the SB to identify the authors and distributors of the stuff if it was not for our colleague who was arrested as he made a mistake by breaking the rules of clandestine distribution of the leaflets. He exposed himself by openly distributing them in a tavern in full view of the patrons of the place including informers and detectives. In the rest of the other places in the Townships and City of Bulawayo the distribution was successful because it was carefully done in dusk and in the absence of witnesses. Actually, all this shows the risks that all civilian freedom fighters faced in their attempt to launch a violent campaign without appropriate skills of engagement with security forces in the field.

As I went through all the episodes of severe torture, I felt so suffocated that I recalled that when I was a boy I was once chased by a very strong man with a stick until I fell into a hole where I feared that he might bury me alive. Similarly in the hands of the detectives I began to feel that Ndiweni's hole had come back in another form, especially when the detectives were suffocating me with my clothes until I could see stars and rainbows in front of me. The latter experience revived the Ndiweni nightmare to the extent that I wished I should have died in that hole than go through such physical severity again. But I quickly consoled myself by considering that I was not alone in suffering for national freedom yet in the Ndiweni saga I was alone and my death could have been wasted life compared to dying for a national cause. I said to myself, "if I survived the Ndiweni trauma at that young age, why can I not stand firm on this one now that I am a man among other men marching together for freedom in defiance of danger?" Then my mind settled down and my courage strengthened. I had to absorb the severity of torture that I was going through at the time and became prepared for any eventuality. In other words, a positive aspect of my experience in a suffocating hole was a recollection of it that lifted me up to feel grown up enough to bear worse pain than the Ndiweni saga inflicted on me at a younger age. How could I have handled the security camp situation if I had grown up in soft and smooth conditions?

CHAPTER SIXTEEN

A NEW CHAPTER OPENS IN THE DENSE FORESTS OF WANKIE (WHANGE)

From 1964 to 1967 a large number of young people were recruited into the Formidable, some being shipped away for their safety and self-motivated individuals had also gone to exile to join armed struggle. By early 1967 many people began to ask difficult questions concerning the slowing down of destructive operations in the struggle thus creating a situation of malaise and disenchantment. This followed their earlier expectations that the phenomenal rise of the Formidable would lead to a countrywide uprising shortly after UDI to overwhelm the Smith regime on a wide scale of social unrest. In this connection people were discomforted by the continuous successes of the security forces in arresting so many people in action or when they were about to act or soon after action. Trained personnel from outside the country were also intercepted close after the crossing point or arrested after some weeks of arrival deep inside the country. All these and many other factors tended to slow down the progression of the tempo of the struggle waged by civilians who were expecting to be reinforced or fully trained by militarily trained freedom fighters from outside the country. The low level of waging the struggle appeared to be sporadic thus lacking coordination and showing no qualitative change in terms of sharpening the capability of the Formidable to cause havoc behind the backs of the Rhodesian Security Forces.

However, at a time when disenchantment was threatening to take its toll in the populace, a bombshell dropped just after the middle of 1967. On a certain August morning we woke up to reports of fierce battles raging in the Wankie area between the Rhodesian Security Forces and the freedom fighters. Hopes were rekindled by the vibrations from the Wankie battles as volumes of information reached the whole country when some of the wounded soldiers landed on our hands at Mpilo Hospital. We quickly assigned those who were totally off the SB radar screen to "milk" information from the wounded soldiers in the wards. Indeed the soldiers sang like a morning bird about what happened in the battlefield. The significance of the Wankie battle was that it dropped like a bombshell at a time when many people were slumbering away from activity in the struggle because of lack of motivating bangs. But the battle woke everybody from slumber with such a bang that created an impression that war against the UDI regime had begun in the eyes and ears of everyone in the country. The Wankie battles were not the first shootout between freedom fighters and the Rhodesian security forces (e.g. Crocodile Gang and Chinhoi (Sinoia) battles, both by ZANU). The Wankie battles of 1967, demonstrated that ZAPU had woken up to take armed struggle seriously as this was the first well organised military engagement with the Rhodesian

Security Forces in pitched battles. More importantly the encounter generated a profound positive effect on peoples' morale by inflicting significant and visible casualties on the Rhodesian Security Forces in such a way that the regime could not conceal the factual consequences of the clashes. The event drastically changed the peoples' perception regarding the invincibility of the government forces. The popular perception was that the battles swung the pendulum to the side of a possibility of African victory pinned on the revived trust that guerrilla warfare had begun to propel the struggle to a successful victory over colonialism.

The Wankie battles were waged by combined forces of ANC of South Africa – MK – and ZAPU of Zimbabwe - ZPRA under the command of John Dube (ZPRA, popularly known as JD) and Chris Hani (MK). The detachment quickly discovered that they had been spotted at a point where they had not planned to do battle with the Rhodesian army because they were southward bound. Thus they were forced to prepare for battle prematurely thereby avoiding a complete surprise attack. Their original destination was the Matopo Hills in the south of the country where they were going to separate with the ANC comrades who were southward bound to South Africa. In the north east of Rhodesia, in Sipolilo, another detachment commanded by Moffat Hadebe and Francis Choga had established bases for supplies and rear bases for launch and retreat but were also spotted just before they dispersed for action deep into the country. Their mission was bound for north east and east of the country. But they took too long to launch their operations until the Rhodesian Security forces were tipped about their presence. The Kariba detachment was the worst dislocated by the enemy forces because they suffered a devastating surprise attach soon after crossing Zambezi River. After that the survivors split into two groups with one of them surviving until they crossed into Botswana. Its mission was central north of the country.

Some famous words of one of the wounded soldiers that remained in peoples' lips for a long time were: **"vakomana vanogona kuridza pfuti[27]"**. These words became a major morale booster because people were interpreting them progressively in various ways and versions with joy as if they meant that freedom was on the horizon. Even those who did not speak Shona memorised these words and transmitted them to others as they were explaining their meaning which became so varied, depending on how well one understood Shona. There was no more whispering in the work places, beer halls (taverns), street corners, weddings, churches, buses, schools and in every gathering of people in towns and villages. What happened in the battlefield itself was one thing but its powerful waves that spread rapidly nationwide were another thing in terms of reviving hopes and rejuvenating the determination to give full support to those who sacrificed their lives for the cause of national freedom. Away from the battlefield some enthusiasts exaggerated numbers of casualties of the government forces and combined this with a wounded soldier's famous **(vakomana vanogona kuridza pfuti)** words to create a source of celebratory amusement as people sang about impending demise of the Smith regime. But we had no access to white hospitals to hear what the wounded soldiers there were saying about the quality of fighting and casualties. We relied on the African soldiers who were apparently willing to give information on what they saw and experienced in the battlefield. We did not press them too hard fearing a backlash and resistance.

However, we were excited and reactivated to prepare for the 'militarisation' of both the urban and rural areas, by smuggling arms and ammunition spreading them everywhere and preparing the people to support armed freedom fighters in the villages. We further succeeded in establishing links with a few ZPRA freedom fighters on various missions. There was Sam Dumaza Mpofu's unit operating in Tsholotsho but captured in its entirety in a surprise attack by Rhodesia security

---

27

these boys know how to fight with guns

forces; Lazarus Dlakama and Moffat Ndlovu's unit which entered Bulawayo undetected until they were caught after several months in the townships. John Maluzo Ndlovu and Walter Mbambo's unit, which also covered abroad area consisting several provinces. They operated for a long time before they were captured. Eliot Ngwabi's unit also entered Bulawayo only to be captured after several months in the City. Mbejelwa Moyo's unit survived longest period until he and some of his comrades returned to Zambia but Clark Mpofu, Moffat Hadebe, and Kay Nkala were captured, Meshach Mnethwa's unit was captured in Bulawayo after several months of operation. Adolphus Mwene and nine comrades were capture still amassing weapons in Mashonaland. All these mishaps happened between 1964 and 1967. During this period security forces seemed in total control of the security situation because most of the comrades were detected while they were still preparing to launch their offensive. Even the subsequent big battles like Wankie 1967, Sipolilo 1968 and Kariba 1968 the enemy denied them any chance to take the initiative.

In all of this, there was an advanced reconnaissance and intelligence unit led by Tomy Ndebele to pave the way for JD's detachment in the south of the country. They had prepared all the necessary logistics and identified the well camouflaged areas and all requirements for a combat force that was due to be well away from the supply source north of the Zambezi River. Tomy Ndebele's unit had succeeded in caching fire arms and ammunition for the JD mission if he had reached the south of the country. They were some of the most successful in reaching that part of the country with a consignment of weapons. Apparently the weapons were delivered in advance, like all others, by a lorry. Tomy covered a vast territory establishing contacts and laying supporting social infrastructure for sustenance of combat forces and identifying not only suitable terrain but also suitable water bodies in advance in the entire southern part of the country. After being in the country for nearly eight months, three months before the Wankie battles, the Special Branch got information about Tomy's presence in the country. He, too, had a reliable line of information that alerted him that SB were preparing to search his home and capture him. The security forces surrounded his home before they entered hoping to capture him but he had slipped away two days before they arrived. His family was such a strong cell because they never betrayed him under any circumstances. They vehemently denied that he ever stepped his foot in the home since he left the country in 1964. In the southern part of the country Ndebele recruited hundreds of youngsters to join armed struggle between 1966 and 1976. It is believed that Ndebele perished in a recruiting mission in the mountainous area of Beitbridge District during or about the winter of 1976. He is one of those unsung heroes who worked tirelessly in the struggle starting off as a young civilian activist in the late 1950s up to a trained freedom fighter operating underground from1964 to 1976. Tomy Ndebele never rested at any point of the struggle since the rise of African nationalism in the country. He started off as an organiser at branch level and finished up as a fully-fledged freedom fighter specialised in intelligence gathering in the field nationwide. He is one of the struggle stalwarts that became my role models by their exemplary selfless and unflinching commitment to the liberation of our country from colonialism. He was one of those who left their children and wives to participate in active service for the liberation of Zimbabwe with high morale at all times. With so many Tomies setting example of fearless patriotism how could I not emulate them, especially being a product of **Invisible Black Stones** of Inyathi secondary School.

Tomy Ndebele's feat in the national liberation struggle always reminds me of other selfless freedom fighters who grew up with and in the Nationalist freedom movement from the onset. The first one in my ratings is Henry Hamadziripi who became active during his youthful age from the formation of the Southern Rhodesia African National Congress in 1957. He was still young when he was detained with J D Chikerema et al in Gokwe following the ban of the

ANC from 1959. He joined NDP and its successor, ZAPU while he was in detention. When some ZAPU leaders split to form ZANU he joined them and went to exile in Zambia where he was active in armed struggle as a member of **Dare reChimrenga**[28] that drove the ZANLA fighting machine until independence in 1980. For some of us, Hamadziripi was one of a sample of some Zimbabwean patriots with incredible credentials of dedication to national liberation in practical terms. Of course they are not the only ones who left behind a remarkable record of highly appreciable sacrifice for their country in the very early phase of the struggle as they tore through the virgin terrain of national freedom struggle to pave the way for those of us who came to the party a little later. There are many more: Barbylock Manyonga (jailed for transporting weapons across the country single handed in the 1960s), Mishack Makena (detained indefinitely for clandestine operations 1963) Adolphus Mwene (for storage and distribution of fire arms and ammunition after receiving military training with ten others 1964), Benjamin Madlela, (a wizard in organising and administration but died young in exile), Misheck Velaphi, (first guerrilla caught in action in the Matopo Hills 1964)., Bernard Mutuma (the most capable morale booster that I have ever seen in Zimbabwean politics1962), Isdore Kumire (injected calculated militancy in the youth movement during our time in Salisbury1962), Dumiso Dabengwa (a national liberation warrior), Report Mphoko and Gordon Butshe both grew up with the struggle), Ethan Dube, a mentor and leader in matters of how to wage and sustain the struggle against all odds, etc. These were some of the many ground breaking pioneers who traversed the virgin land of civilian driven struggle before they trained as freedom fighters during preparatory stages of the struggle to establish appropriate infrastructure for sustaining armed struggle. They faced the unknown political terrain that was infested by security agents and low level of political maturity in some segments of the African population. In this regard, they were some of the pioneers who navigated through complex political situations with courage and determination yet they have become forgotten heroes in our official scheme of things. In Zimbabwe today, there are many political elements that have been declared heroes yet they hardly contributed either their intellectual or physical labour in the liberation struggle let alone to nation building. Some of them are known to be champions of degenerative politics in their life time.

Recruitment of Rhodesian soldiers to support national Liberation Struggle

Buoyed by the Wankie Battle, we felt that the time had come for us to be well skilled to handle and use the military hard ware that had fallen into our hands but lie buried under the ground. So, having amassing a considerable amount of commercial explosive materials and some hand guns and ammunition, we decided to seek ways of getting someone to train members of the Formidable in the use what we had acquired. In the whole process of activism, the kind of operations that we were involved in had become complex and demanding in terms of skills for administering and managing military materials that had fallen on our hands yet we were not well trained to handle them accordingly let alone use them effectively. We were no longer using petrol bombs because UDI had changed the nature of challenges in the entire field of operations. We had to chop and change strategies and tactics to depart from use of older and ineffective forms of struggle such as petrol bombs and sabotage alone because the materials we possessed indicated the need for change but not many were ready to use them effectively. In brainstorming, we recalled that we had evolved a tradition or habit of internally designing our own strategies and driving them with our home brewed resources, including procuring deadly materials and use them. Such

---

28
War Council

a tradition (of independent creativity) started during the days of Ethan Dube, Abel Siwela and Willie Mgqibelo. All started off as trial and error outfits some o which failed to produce needed results but that never discouraged us from adopting new methods that proved to be better than the previous ones. In other words a lot of these attempts could be described as experimental endeavours because some of them had to be improved drastically during the course of experience.

The time had come for us to slow down amassing explosive devices and, instead, seek appropriately trained personnel to use them. Clearly there was pressing need for such a shift and after careful consideration we decided to make a move into the military barracks to assess the attitude of the African soldiers towards the question of attainment of majority rule in our country. We already had gained considerable understanding of the civil police force in uniform as distinct from the security branch. In the Rhodesian army there was a force called African King's Riffles (AKR) dating from the First World War. Its rank and file consisted of Africans commanded by white commissioned officers. We decided to investigate the possibility of infiltrating this force or to recruit some of its members into our underground cells for functional purposes.

I recalled that there were several former school mates who joined the army during the late 1950s and early 1960s. I enquired around and got information about one who finished Standard V1 at Nyati Primary School in 1958 and I visited him. First time I found him on duty but second time I found him and he welcomed me very well and introduced me to his friends. From then on I frequented Llewellyn Barracks near Bulawayo until I got to understand that African members of the African King's Rifles were just like everybody in the wider African population in terms of some being very politically alert, others moderately, some extremely and the rest mild or jut detached from politics. After establishing firm friendships in the Barracks I found that they were not afraid of the Special Branch but they feared the Military Police (MP) very much. Armed with positive findings, I approached Edward Ngwenya, a freedom struggle stalwart who was noted for being a silent hard working underground strategic planner in our midst. Edward Ngwenya, had retreated from semi-surface politics to a level of full scale underground operative soon after PCC was banned. He made some extensive search for reliable personnel in government employment for recruitment into our operatives without leaving their jobs. A man of such credentials could be reliable to get him involved in dealing with a dangerously delicate matter concerning military personnel.

Ngwenya and I cultivated some soldiers as friends and, after satisfying ourselves that we had actually struck gold at Llewellyn Barracks we made a move to cobble up a simple plan to transform friendship with some soldiers into comradeship. We subsequently succeeded in isolating one friend as most suitable for recruitment to be a trainer of members of the Formidable in small units and supply them with appropriate materials in addition to what we had. Our selected soldier-friend was a well-placed serving sergeant of the African Kings Riffles. Politically, he told us that he was a member of both NDP and ZAPU before they were banned and continued to support the demand for African majority rule. He was not only alert about African demands for African majority rule, he also had basic understanding of political trends in the country and Africa. He was well positioned because he was responsible for dispatching training materials, recorded them out and returned remainder. We carefully introduced our story to him but he responded with a lot of chalking questions concerning the extent of the proposed training and supply and the objectives of the training in relation with the overall operations planned from the Head Quarters in Lusaka. We tried the best we could to answer the questions unsure as to whether we satisfied his expectations. But after three days of talking he agreed that he would do the job. He said that with extra caution it would be possible for him to supply materials under certain conditions.

His level of education was standard 6 (Grade 8) which was a recognised lower limit in qualifications for some diplomas in teaching and other lower level qualifications such as State Enrolled Nurses, Medical Assistants, police constables, junior agricultural assistants, etc. It was therefore not surprising that he was assigned to handle delicate materials like explosives. He had tried to join the BSAP but was too short for the service therefore he turned to the army where he rose from the ranks to a non-commissioned officer (quite high for an African during colonialism).

Essentially, his job included safe keeping of and issuing training materials such as explosives and hand grenades. He recorded the distribution, and at the end he recorded the expended and the unused materials. He looked relaxed and confident that as long as we kept our mouths shut it would not be difficult for him to deal with us seriously. We recruited him to be our supplier of materials from his stock since he could record them as expended and others that he could find from other sources. As stated above, before he agreed, he asked us a many key questions of trust and reliability of operatives and whether his contribution would be synchronised or linked with guerrilla activities in terms of demand for supplies, personnel training and deployment because he wanted the weapons to be expended soon after supply as he advised against obtaining them for storage for future usage. After prolonged discussions with us, he agreed to supply us with hand grenades only for immediate use without storage because that would be a security risk. He added that he would train two trainers who would become trainers of the rest in small numbers in safe hide-outs. He further suggested that since his first task of training trainers was completed, his second task would entail supplying materials through a well trusted and reliable person. He also agreed to start training Ngwenya, one liaison person and myself in basics of military skills. He strongly advised that there should be a command structure because in military operations there should be a commander to take responsibility for everything military, especially that the group was expected to grow into an operating military force. We assured him that one of the externally trained comrades was available to be commander of locally trained personnel regardless of whether the functions entailed combat or sabotage operations.

We brought forward a thought that once came to our minds during 1963 regarding the question of training the Formidable Force as a secret army. We had shelved the idea at the time but we began to toy with it following the slow influx of trained comrades in the country which was a strong indication of the beginning of serious preparation for guerrilla operations. He strongly advised against such a move before guerrilla warfare engulfed the countryside on a significant scale. He then suggested that we could raise an "urban secret diversion force" to divert security forces from focusing on guerrillas in the bush and he could help with a plan concerning where and how to deploy such a force as well as how to gather intelligence ahead of any operation. He emphasised that urban secret army should be complementary and diversionary in its purpose as its utility would be appropriate when combat operations escalated in the bush.

We therefore suggested that for the time being the first group should get basic military know how so that they could train other operatives in the use of some concealable devices such as hand grenades, primed land mines, antipersonnel mines and dynamites before establishing an urban diversion force as proposed. He had no problem with this provided their operation would be spread far apart to minimise congestion of activities that might be easily eliminated by security forces. He warned us very strongly to be extremely cautious in every step we took to make sure that our operatives never clash with security forces which meant that they should avoid getting caught in the act. The tactical operations should entail disappearance immediately after an operation. We were already used to this therefore we had no difficult to comply. He even suggested that if a trained unit grew in numbers, he could add into the programme two of his colleagues who were as politically committed to majority rule as he was. That was a bonus indeed. There was complete agreement on every point with the soldier. For me this was the most exciting arrangement in which I was involved as it was getting closer to what I had been craving for since my school days: formation of a secret army organisation to subvert the colonial power structures.

As we were not entirely out of the SB radar screen, we brought one of our colleagues, Mackenzie Ncube, from the Formidable and directed him to select suitable comrades for training. Once the linkup between our soldier and Mackenzie Ncube was established, Ngwenya and I withdrew from our new line of operation to avoid jeopardising its fragile security and exciting prospects for the struggle at its infancy. Mackenzie was assigned to take charge of the group of comrades selected for training together with him being the linkman with the sergeant. After training, the comrades would be placed under the command of an externally trained comrade who was part of Mbajelwa group. Our agreement began to roll out action-packed programmes within a short space of time. But the training was confined to the use of hand grenades and explosives to start with. A full scale military training was to start in earnest with guerrilla war fare becoming intensified in the country as indications were pointing towards such a probability with externally trained freedom fighters showing up beyond the Rhodesian first line of defence along the border. There was a medium term objective for this programme: to raise an urban diversion fighting force that could grow in tandem with the escalation of guerrilla warfare countrywide as agreed in our meeting with the soldier. We left it at that and as it looked like our "aeroplane was taxing full speed for a take-off"

After independence, curious to know how successful this project was, I traced and found Mackenzie Ncube who told me that the sergeant's cell was not detected but it did not grow more than a section (ten men) because the commander eventually fell under SB surveillance therefore he had to flee back to Zambia leaving his unit without a trained commander. So the comrades remained at the level of minimally skilled operatives specialised in the use of explosives and hand grenades, which means they were saboteurs not soldiers. I only knew our soldier as Sibanda and his pseudonym was Thwala. Mackezie told me that Thwala was transferred in the mid-1970s to Inkomo Barracks near Salisbury (Harare) and the link with him disconnected then. As the struggle intensified the ten comrades joined the main stream of guerrillas in the bush while he remained in his cell in Bulawayo. Attempts to trace Thwala were not successful because we did not have his real name in full and we could not trace the whereabouts of the comrades that he trained and let them join the armed struggle.

When we introduced Mackenzie to our sergeant we asked them to create pseudonyms right away and arrange how they would communicate when they had to meet or plan their operations. As Sibandas' pseudonym was Thwala, Mackenzie gave himself his father's name, Masaka. When the urban diversion project fell apart due to circumstances described above, Mackenzie maintained his underground cell that initially used Abel Siwela's home-made explosive devices and finished up collaborating with freedom fighters in recruitment of personnel and supplying them with vital necessities.

CHAPTER SEVENTEEN

DRAMATIC ESCAPE OUT OF THE COUNTRY

With regards the amassing of fire arms in and around Bulawayo hinterlands, we followed the same model of creating a cell and left it to function without our close involvement. The critical factor here was that if we took too long to detach ourselves from a functioning cell, it became easy to fall within the circumference of the SB **'flood lights'** because we were no longer wholly out of it ourselves. This was soon confirmed when some comrades who were arrested in mid-September 1967 sent word warning us that the situation was very grave because the Special Branch had all the information about our activities and it was a matter of time before they swept us away from society to prison. Apparently the SB was in possession of incriminating information that enabled them to pinpoint with precision as to who was responsible for what in the whole matrix of activities including mobilising resources for armed struggle. The main culprits in all of this were Maswazi Tshongwe, Cleopas Nhlabano, Joshua Mpofu and seven others in Bulawayo African Townships (BAT area only).

The reports from the comrades were confirmed by our police sources who added that about ten of us were due to be picked up on the 30th September 1967 and be confronted with the evidence of our involvement in illegal possession of fire arms and ammunition, and explosives as well as commanding people to cause trouble in Bulawayo. We met and decided not to sleep in our houses, but one of us said he was prepared to face arrest. Indeed at dawn on the set date detectives pounced but found most of us absent from our houses, except one who opted to sleep in his house. At daybreak they went to my work place and waited for me in vain. I hid in Ben Mholi's house, a long standing friend and a stalwart of the underground activism, in Barbourfields Township. I stayed in hiding for two weeks and then sneaked into my flat to discuss a personal survival plan with my wife in the presence of a colleague, Phillie Mabena. Feeling the gravity of the situation to be the heaviest to date, we agreed that the only way out was to try to sneak out of the country via Botswana to Zambia. A strong warning from our friends in the regular police force confirmed that the information in the hands of security detectives was quite incriminating for me and several others. The density of the information was enough to cause me to leave the country without hesitation. As I was identified as key to all of this, I felt very unsafe to face arrest in the circumstances. As I said before that the Rhodesian Special Branch never dismounted their surveillance machine from one they considered dangerous until they were sure he had gone politically dormant or they caught him for detention or prosecution. In this regard, for me, there was little chance to survive the SB's "final act on dangerous elements."

For all intents and purposes, during the period between 1963 and 1967, I was instrumental in removing comrades who were in danger of arrest and exporting them to Northern Rhodesia before Zambia's independence and after the latter attained independence. Before Zambia gained independence in 1964, travelling between two Rhodesias did not require a passport. A Registration Certificate (*isithupha*) was the only document of identity for Africans therefore was acceptable at the border. The document had no photograph of the bearer, thus making it easy to obtain a forged one with a false name of the absconding person. So it was equally very easy to despatch people out of danger quite fast with forged registration certificates. But after 1964, the path to Zambia became zigzag as people had to pass through Botswana

For me, during or about the spring of 1967 a dark cloud was hovering above me in the form of the security branch closing in on me and my colleagues slowly but surely. It then became our turn to be whisked out of the country to avoid arrest and possible prosecution. On the eve of our wedding anniversary, instead of celebrating the occasion, I left Bulawayo in Phillip Mabena's car that left me at a bus stop on the Solusi Mission Road. I boarded a bus headed to Ndolwane, Tsholotsho, northwest of Bulawayo.

During the troubled times, I normally had a beard, moustache and spectacles. But that day I was smooth shaven without specs, with a hat on my head. At the next bus stop two African detectives entered the bus. One stood near the driver and cast his eyes all over the bus and his colleague walked along the centre passage towards the back seat of the bus looking at each individual passenger fairly closely. Both of them did not sit down as they clearly looked like hunting jackals. I was sitting near a girl, probably in her early twenties (probably same age with my wife). As soon I saw these men approaching the door of the bus, I said to her, in sinNdebele: *"my sister, what is your totem?"* She said *"Ncube"* Such a question was normal when people sat near each other in any public transport. Before she asked me for my totem I whispered to her in siNdebele thus: *"Mancube, could you please do me a favour? From now onwards we will talk to each other as husband and wife and you will refer to me as Seka Nana (Nana's Dad)"* She reacted strongly but with a low voice and said: *"I do not even know you, why should I pretend to be your wife?"* I answered her: *"Please help me my sister because that will be good for me and our country in the end"* She came back with soft whisper: *"Don't you hear what I am saying?"* As the detectives entered the bus I took a gamble and asked her in a low voice like a husband wanting to know what was happening in his home where there were employees paid to work on a project. In this hastily concocted drama, I wished Mancube could respond to my questions like a wife who had just visited me in town and I had no opportunity to talk to her at length about things while at the house in town; now that we were both homeward bound we had the opportunity to discuss in details: *"Mancube, you have not yet told me about progress on our projects at home, how far are the employees close towards completing fencing our garden and preparation for planting?"* Asking this question was a gamble because she had not formally accepted my suggestion. She then looked at me and said *"You know, Seka Nana, I have come to believe that you decided to give your relatives money for nothing because they no longer work on that project yet you continue to pay them."* I breathed a sigh of relief because she acted exactly like a wife reacting to her husband's naive question. I then went on confidently, *"please lower your voice, otherwise people will think we are quarrelling"* She replied quickly: *"You are the one who asked me about domestic matters in the bus because you always came to the house drunk. I have been telling you about the whole situation of wasting money in a project that does not exist but you never listened, instead you just slept and snored and left me talking alone. Now that we are going home together, you will see for yourself that your relatives whom you hired have done nothing to show for. Remember, you ordered me to pay them against my advice."* I chipped in: *"You should have refused to pay them if they did not work"* She replied *"Seka Nana, Have you forgotten that I once withheld payment but one of the employees wrote a letter to you and in reply you ordered me to pay them because that was your money not mine; have you forgotten that, Seka Nana?"* I reacted as in disbelief: *"Ah! Mancube, did you keep that letter because I do not remember using those words."* She said: *"I have got it here, let me show you now* (**making a convincing move towards reaching for it**) *........"* I promptly intervened, holding her hand and said *"No no no you will show me when we get home."* She looked at me with a stern face and said: *"Seka Nana, Do you realise that drinking beer every day has affected you badly because you have no idea of what is happening at home. Yet I have been telling you everything since I came to town. I think you better stop drinking before you are damaged beyond repair."* At this point the bus stopped and the detectives came out of the bus. Was I safe?

Here I do not doubt that if it was not for the bravery of Mancube I would have been arrested by the two detectives because they meticulously looked at every young male person in the bus. Part of my luck was that they were not my regular interrogators. They relied on the photo that they were carrying with them. We were sitting in the middle of the bus and they must have heard us arguing between ourselves because "Mancube" was fairly loud and convincing in her posture. The one in front also seemed to focus on us as we argued with each other so seriously. The more convincing character in the whole drama was Mancube with such impressive creativity at the spur of the moment. She looked genuine and kept her demeanour composed and natural as she spoke with conviction. One man behind us commented: *"Hey, young man, your wife is right you should not discuss your controversial matters in public like that."* Those who heard the conversation nodded in agreement with the man's observation. I was satisfied that the conversation must have sounded real in the ears and eyes of the rest of the passengers, therefore the CIDs took it that way too. I too was amazed by the way Mancube acquitted herself like a wife in dispute with a drunkard of a husband over dysfunctional projects in their home. Especially the way she brought in the issue of intoxication on the part of the husband as a cause of misunderstanding was a master piece as it became the main bone of contention in the misunderstanding. In the eyes of the passengers who heard the argument the problem lay with the husband who had a habit of arriving home drunk and unable to communicate appropriately with his wife who wanted to brief him about the situation in their home. As a matter of fact the conversation was fairly long and ended with the 'husband' apologising for questioning her in a bus full of passengers. In this connection there were many impressive expressions that Mancube used that I have not included here. I merely picked the very crucial ones that seemed strong enough to convince the CIDs that the conversation was a genuine dispute between a husband turned drunkard in town and his wife from the Tribal Trust Lands.

Although the saviour conversation happened forty six years ago, I still remember its key features because it saved my life from going to prison or gallows. No one can tell what was in my mind when I saw detectives entering the bus in which I was sitting hoping to escape prosecution. Sitting near the Ncube girl was a huge blessing because there was no guarantee that an alternative could have delivered me from the hands of my trackers. Supposing I sat near a man or an old woman or a girl who knew nothing about national liberation effort in progress in the country; was I going to survive? The probability is that I could have met my Sharpeville well before attainment of liberation.

Before I got out of the bus, I thanked the girl so much and she wished me well too. Apparently, she thought I was a trained freedom fighter because in the end she said: "Before I went to Bulawayo some of your comrades passed through our home and we gave them full support. My brother, as soon as you mentioned your safety and the country I wandered why until I saw well-dressed fellows walking into the bus looking all over inside it, I realised that you were a freedom fighter whom they were looking for. At the same time I remembered that freedom fighters are busy everywhere. I summoned my courage and decided within seconds that I should help you as you asked. You may feel safe for now, but you never know what is next, just be careful. May God be with you until we achieve our freedom."

For the consumption of the passengers Mancube and I agreed that I would get off at Ntoli School to pick up my brother with whom I would follow by the following bus in four hours' time. I was very touched by her empathy for me, a stranger that she had never known before. It was not a surprise for me to hear that some comrades were sighted in Tsholotsho because battles had been fought in the neighbouring Wankie District in recent months. Clearly Mancube remembered seeing some of them then thought that I was one of them. Since the Wankie battles many rural people believed freedom fighters were massing up in the country in preparation for more battles on a wider scale. So she perceived me as one of them therefore became determined to save a 'lone freedom fighter' from arrest so that he survived to continue with the cause of African liberation.

Our conversation demonstrated an amazing political consciousness of a young woman whose performance showed a commitment in support of a cause that she believed was a just one for Africans. The commitment could be read from the risk she took to defend a political fugitive from his pursuers right in front of them. Her act of brilliance can be seen in her quick grasp of my predicament and to associate me with the freedom fighters who were in battle a couple of months before. Clearly her home area had become accustomed to freedom fighters passing through with the support of the villagers. In the rural villages it became a political tradition that anyone who identified with freedom fighters or as one of them had to be given support to carry out the mission at hand. She did not have to know me personally, but she perceived the cause for which I stood for in my being in the bus because I mentioned the country in my plea for help. So if one believes in justice one does not need personal knowledge of the champions of justice when they seek support to pursue that cause. This is exactly what Mancube did in my case. If she had rejected my request for help, I would have been arrested, tried and probably sentenced to life imprisonment or death penalty. Since she was already politicised she could have suspected that I was a detective or security agent myself and refused to cooperate in fear of becoming trapped. I was lucky that her telepathy picked up my troubled state of mind and became empathetic with the assumption that she was saving a freedom fighter from capture. Above all, if I was captured, there was no guarantee that I could have resisted torture whereby forced confessions could have implicated scores of my colleagues who were in the network of underground activism. By cooperating with me in a hastily cobbled up drama of survival, she saved many people who eventually became some of the most crucial anchors of armed struggle when it intensified in the 1970s. I thanked her many times and got down at Ntoli Primary School where I was received by my first contact, a Head Teacher of the school.

The Head Teacher was my cousin, the son of my uncle, my father's younger brother who had moved to Bechuanaland (Botswana) around 1952, to avoid forced removals of the decade. From Ntoli I took another bus heading to Plumtree, which arrived where I was whisked away by the second contact (cousin) Head Teacher's sister who carried me on a bicycle across the Botswana border to Moroka Village. The moment of the relay started with Phillie Mabena through to Elijah and then Vivian who finally took me to Moroka Village in Botswana. I stayed there for a while hoping that I was hiding safely. This entire dramatic journey took place during the last half of October 1967. The problem I had here was that I felt empty because the kind of work in my uncle's home had nothing to do with the struggle. So I was in some kind of forced holiday. But everything was quite familiar with what I grew up doing at Nkayi. The exception was that the surrounding had no vast forests with huge trees and grassland plateau. When summer arrived in November, I was keen to plough the fields and I did, as soon as the rain started.

Word was sent that on the eve of Christmas my wife Ratie, and daughter, Nonhlanhla, should come to this place secretly. She came with an 11 months old baby strapped on her back and was picked up by bicycle at the border. They stayed until the New Years' Day and returned to Bulawayo safely. During or about February 1968, there was a sudden burst of deafening aircraft sound about 100 metres above the Moroka villages as if they were on a bombing sortie. The noise from two Hawk Hunters was so unnerving and everybody was very afraid. It was on Saturday, when people were just coming out of the Sabbath Service in the late afternoon. All of us had to hide in fear that they might drop some bombs. The following morning it became worse when two helicopters emerging from the eastern horizon, approached the Moroka villages in a battle formation until they reached close to the centre of the village where one of them started hovering over the houses and slowly descending to a few metres above the trees as if in landing mode. It then followed the other one westward. The scenario was more frightening than the previous experience with the aeroplanes. They too, appeared as if they were in a war mission because they first passed over the village in a battle formation and then returned in a single file and disappeared northwards in that formation. To the Mpofu family in Moroka the performance of these machines of war was clearly a sign that the Rhodesian authorities were looking for me or they were frightening me so that I could expose myself by trying to run away in an open field for easy capture. But the family vowed to hide me by all means they could devise. Even at that time I knew that there was a small plane called spotter plane that they could have used to try to locate me and then inform the helicopter-borne security forces to pounce on the identified spot. The puzzling factor was that in this scenario, on the first day large military aircraft zoomed like lightning above the tranquil villages of a neighbouring country and then the following day the villages were 'visited' by another set of military machines consisting combat helicopters. Could they assemble and deploy such a force for one troublesome civilian? Not likely. My suspicion was that there were some guerrillas in that area whom they were trying to flash out into a killing ground. I still think so now because if they were after me they could have sneaked in some security agents under cover to abduct or eliminate me without a hustle.

The day after the helicopters' visit, one local teacher came panting and said he had information that the Rhodesians had reason to believe that someone was hiding in the village preparing to set up a coordinating secret base for the guerrillas. True or not, this could have explained the behaviour of the flying machines the previous day. In this regard it was very disturbing because if they believed that a secret base was being set up at a strategic place like Moroka, they would rather prevent its establishment before it took off. But why use noisy machines instead of investigating first? Anyway, I sensed danger from this information because if they suspected that I was part of a team assigned to play such strategic role in the war zone, they would want to act swiftly to eliminate any such threat to them. I then decided to go to Francistown to declare myself a refugee before they caught up with me. I told my relations that the time had come for me to move on before the entire village got entangled into unjustifiable troubles. Since I did not come to Botswana to hide myself but to seek safe passage to Zambia, I had to proceed. I bade them fare well and left. What a painful departure because everybody was weeping some even sobbing like in moaning. I had rested enough, anyway.

When I got to Francistown I reported at the police station and the junior officers took me to the Officer-in-Charge, Mr Muskel, He looked at me and said "Are you the fellow who has been hiding inside Botswana border villages for three months?" I replied that I did not hide in Botswana for such a long time. He said. "Sergeant, we must send him back, he supports terrorists and comes here lying to me." One African officer strongly advised against my deportation on the grounds of personal safety. Mr Muskel referred me to the CID office. There again the CID Inspector was white and I began to see myself transported back to Rhodesia. Forgive me for my scepticism about white fairness here because it was familiar back home to be treated unfairly by white fellow citizens. He said, "Information available to us suggests that you have been conducting subversive activities against Rhodesia from Botswana territory. That means you entered and stayed in Botswana illegally for three months. What have you to say about that?" Apparently they got the information from the Rhodesian security branch. Anyway, I replied that I was hiding for a long time inside Rhodesia before crossing the Botswana border and never did anything against Rhodesia during my hiding in that country and after crossing into Botswana. I added that if I was sent back I could face a death sentence or life imprisonment for my political activities against the UDI regime. I told them that I was active against illegal UDI since it was declared and now they wanted to arrest me for organising people to fight the regime. An African Detective Inspector immediately intervened saying my political activities against the UDI regime were enough to put me in danger if sent back. He said Botswana would not send back anyone who ran away from his country because of political activities against the Rhodesian UDI regime. The CID officers continued to ask me questions about my future prospects. They seemed satisfied with what I told them then took me to another team of detectives who took my finger prints and finally back to the Officer-Officer-in Charge, Mr Muskel himself, with recommendations for final approval. He had no alternatives because the Detective Inspector of CIDs strongly recommended approval as a genuine refugee.

As soon as the ZAPU office in Lusaka was informed that I was in Francistown, they sent a ticket for me to fly to Zambia. Indeed that happened within a couple of weeks.

CHAPTER EIGHTEEN

IN EXILE: ZAMBIA, TANZANIA, USSR, DEPLOYMENT

On arrival in Zambia I was quickly cleared by a ZAPU official who had credentials to work with Immigration Officials to clear ZAPU immigrants who arrived as refugees without passports. I was quickly whisked from Livingstone town to Lusaka the following day.I found that there was a political Alliance between the African National Congress of South Africa and Zimbabwe Peoples Union .The Military Administration in Lusaka arranged a very intensive programme to visit as many military bases as possible since I had fresh information from the country. There was intensive debriefing process before I settled down. I was taken around the large camps to talk to joint fighters of ZIPRA and Mkhonto weSizwe (MK) throughout the Zambian forestland that provided solid cover for the transit guerrillas of Southern African Liberation Movements. The first camp I stayed in for a long time before I was trained was at the Zambian border with Mozambique and Rhodesia near the Zambezi River at a place called Feira. The camp was manned by a Reconnaissance Detachment made up of ZPRA and Mkhonto weSizwe (MK) guerrillas. The Commander of Reconnaissance, comrade Mbatha, immediately familiarised me with the AK riffle by instructing me how to disassemble and assemble it as well as safety precautions and firing the weapon. That was the first time for me to handle the AK closely as in disassembling and assembling, cleaning and practising to use it. I wished that my father was there to see me holding a pipe that spat fire from a distance. This was what I had been yeaning for since the formation of IBS at Nyathi Secondary School. At Feira I was getting closer to armed struggle that I have been talking about since the days of underground at the aforesaid school and in the Formidable in Makhokhoba Township. Finally I was there but, not yet.

After five weeks of my stay in the camp I was called back in Lusaka to meet comrade Dumiso Dabengwa who gave me two options. The first one was that since I had been very active for a long time inside the country, the Party would like me to rest while I did something constructive in the form of studying for a degree in Industrial Law. The second option was to go for military training that focused on radio communications (signals) in the USSR. He pointed out that the first option would have an element of rest while the second would be quite rigorous and physically taxing for someone who has been intensively busy already with underground work inside the country. After completing the degree in four or five years, I would then go for military training before returning to Lusaka. I replied without hesitation that I preferred the second option of military training because I did not want to break the trend of my involvement in the struggle right from school days. It was always my desire to fight for my country until it attained freedom from colonialism with or without me alive. Above all, I had heard that John Mkandla and Sam Sibanda had fallen in active service for Motherland during the Sipolilo Battles. I therefore wanted to pick up their sword and advance. The way Comrade Dabengwa talked to me gave a clear impression that the Head Office was fully aware of the depth and extent of my underground involvement inside the country since ZAPU was banned. I really felt appreciated by the Party in the role that I played in civilian active service for the liberation of my country using dangerous materials in the face of highly efficient Rhodesian security systems with a dragnet at every level of political activity let alone operations.

Military training in the USSR

In no time a group of twelve men was put together but one, Comrade Mabika, withdrew at the last minute. The rest of us were sent to Moscow for military training specialising in radio communications (signals). I was the leader of the group deputised by Walter Mthimkhulu. The others were Solomon Mujuru (Rex Nhongo), Cain Mthema, John Ndlovu, Pius Mashoko, Elias Mugabe, Mgoli Mathuthu, Bhekuzulu Khumalo, Livingstone Mashengele, William Mugwara. It was an intensive course as it was loaded with technical matters in the military and radio communications.

The course content was as follows:

A. *Political education*

1. Laws of motion for the development of Capitalism
2. Fundamental Principles of Scientific Socialism
3. Just and unjust wars; examples included Zimbabwe liberation struggle as a just war
4. National democratic revolutions against colonialism, eg Zimbabwe, etc

B. *Military science*

1. Introduction to military science and organisational structures
2. Introduction to the principles of guerrilla warfare
3. Origin of classical guerrilla warfare (South Africa)
4. Strategy and tactics in guerrilla warfare and partisan operations (in WW2)
5. Weapons and physical exercises

C. *Radio Communications (Signals)*

1. Specialised in radio communications with base station and many correspondents;
2. Setting up and tuning large base station transmitter and receiver;
3. Setting up and tuning small transmitter and receiver (as a correspondent in the field);
4. Calculation of radio frequencies (using a given formula) according to distance between communicating stations
5. Intensive practice and application of Morse Code ;
6. Transmitting/sending (using a key) and receiving coded messages up to high speed;
7. Ciphering and deciphering messages (coding and decoding systems);
8. Basic principles of Military and General Intelligence

D. Radio Technique: applied physics and maths

1. Technical components of a radio transmitter and receiver
2. Applied physics (for radio transmitters and receivers)
3. Applied mathematics (basic algebra and geometry)

About 70% of the time was spent on C and D modules of the syllabus outlined above. During political studies most comrades felt that our revolution should lead to socialism after victory. But the political instructors asked us to try and apply principles of a socialist revolution and see whether Zimbabwe would fit. We certainly went through analysis of the subjective and objective conditions in Zimbabwe, class composition of the country and whether there was a working class that was politically conscious enough to be a class for itself. After two days' debate, we came to the conclusion that the country was not yet ripe for a socialist revolution. At the same time the question of Intelligentsia that was exposed to Revolutionary theory was addressed. Analyses exhibited low level of revolutionary consciousness all round in respect of being unready for a socialist revolution that should be driven by the proletariat, having developed from a class in itself to a class for itself with leadership in the form of a vanguard party whose membership was well versed with the principles of Scientific Socialism and a sound intellectual capacity through alliance with appropriately enlightened intelligentsia. That is, in Zimbabwe such needed highly developed level of political consciousness was not in vogue at the time of the struggle. Therefore it was a national democratic revolution that embraced all classes which opposed colonialism, including the nascent African Bourgeoisie and the peasantry as well as church and traditional leaders. We all appreciated that but were determined to drive the process towards the development of the progressive forces within ZAPU as a long term project. Contrary to Western propaganda, the Soviets never attempted to indoctrinate us into what they called "Communist dogma." South African Apartheid regime and the Rhodesian Front regime held this fallacy and used it vehemently to convince their followers that they were fighting against Communism. Communist theory is a bundle of scientifically substantiated theory based on dialectical materialism that defines rules of motion of development of socio-economic formations from the lowest to the highest phase. Such a complex theory of synthesis and antithesis takes many years of study to understand it fully (Hegel/Marx/Engels). We had many things to study for only one year and there was no chance to produce fully fledged communists in that package of study in one year. But revolutionary transformative theory could be simplified for ease of application, not communism as propounded by Karl Marx, Frederick Engels, Vladimir Lenin et al. But Lenin's organisational acumen was appropriate for political and military strategy formulation at underground level. Non-racism was one of the key elements of our political lessons. This topic was thoroughly addressed since we were fighting a racist system the question was shall we replace white racism with black racism. The answer was an emphatic no on the basis of upholding basic human rights which the current racist regime was grossly violating by depriving Africans what they themselves enjoyed in the same country.

Our military Instructor asked us as to which of the following was a decisive factor in determining victory in our liberation struggle: a) armed guerrillas, b) International support with weapons and transit bases, and c) support of the oppressed masses inside the country. We came up with varied answers but five of us picked up c) as a decisive factor in the struggle and we had to explain why. For our part we suggested that the masses would always support us by withholding information (about our presence in the country) from the security forces, they informed the fighters about movement of security forces and created a reliable supply system for sustenance of fighters. The important elements of all of this were: information, security, supplies such as food, medicines, clothes, etc. By the way some of us had interacted with guerrillas back home before we left the country. So we knew what we were talking about. The Instructor asked difficult questions on each answer given. At the end he confirmed that c) was the correct answer and went into details why and how that was so. But he did not mention Mao Tse Tung's theory of water and fish yet the principles were similar. For example he described the masses as the oxygen of a freedom fighter without which freedom fighters could not last. The struggle would collapse instantly if the oppressed masses turned against fighters. So freedom fighters should bear in mind that there would come a fierce competition for the support of the masses between guerrillas and the Rhodesian security forces. The latter could use their mighty force to create fear by which to try to put people into line. Guerrillas ought to gain mutual support of the masses without use of force because they were part of that deprived population whereas the government did not belong to them as per principles and practice of racial discrimination and domination that required them to defend a privileged white race that had never experienced repression in their lives. They did not have a voluntary support of the African population and no matter what they did would convince only a few people to betray their own people for short term gratification.

There was also the question of "terrorism" which was described by the Instructor as a directionless adventurism that is applied blindly upon what is called easy targets: civilians. He described it as inhumane as it destroys innocent lives even if they were supporters of enemy should never be made to harden their attitude against fighters whereby they demonize or give them all sorts of monstrous names. They must lose soldiers so heavily that they pressure their government to seek a solution to stop loss of their sons. Supporters of the liberation struggle should not be coerced to give material support or those who could be seen to be reluctant to support. Guerrilla warfare and terrorism are totally different in respect of ideology, short and long term objectives. A guerrilla is a political soldier of the people who is able to cultivate support from the people on the basis of the problem whose solution is not only on his agenda but also on theirs in terms of short and long term goals. At the same time they must be convinced that armed struggle is the only option to achieve such goals of the agenda in hand so that they become part of the whole process of national liberation. For our part, we had already done this before we left Zimbabwe

We were examined on all the four subjects stipulated above and passed with varying grades. In radio transmission and receiving words or signals had to be at high speed because in a war situation the instruments should be used fast and switched off quickly before detection by enemy signal detectors. From the onset of the training the Instructor of Radio Techniques component advised that if anyone found some difficulty in grasping technical formulae should focus on military subjects only. Two of the comrades opted to focus on the military training while the rest of us completed the whole course successfully. Long distance communication was conducted between the base station (Moscow) and the correspondents (Tbilisi) for two months thus marking the end of the training programme in the USSR. We had successfully completed a signals intensive training programme incorporating military component within a year which would have normally taken two years. We worked up to ten hours a day to achieve the required standard of communication under any conditions of field operations. We were ready to go to the field with combat forces equipped with appropriate skills in signals and military proficiency within the principles of guerrilla warfare. Contrary to misinformed distant observers who have spread a wrong notion that ZPRA was essentially trained in conventional warfare. Anyone who believes in this does not know the quality of the Rhodesian security forces in combat. If we trained in conventional warfare and entered Rhodesia with those skills only, we would have never survived conventional warfare with the Rhodesian army under any terrain. Since we were not trained in that kind of warfare, it would be suicidal to apply that method of fighting with the Rhodesian security forces unless attacked before taking initiative. We were prepared for dislocating a regular army by unconventional tactics and manipulation. So this was more or less a form of continuation of the struggle by operating in darkness or at our own choosing like witches of the underground in Nkayi in the mid 1960s. The battles where large detachments clashed with Rhodesian security forces were the result of interception by the Rhodesians rather than part of the strategy or operational plan. Examples of such contacts include Wankie and Sipolilo battles in 1967 and 1968 respectively. But in all planned attacks on the enemy forces the element of surprise was paramount. It was not until the late 1970s that ZPRA began to train regular soldiers for a general attack as the strength of Rhodesian security forces were beginning to be weakened by overstretching themselves trying to counter massive infiltration of guerrillas in all fronts. For instance ZIPA seemed to have succeeded in causing Rhodesian forces to open gaps that enabled guerrillas to infiltrate up to the enemy rear. With that vulnerability of the enemy, Mhanda's concept of "strategic equilibrium" was imminent as guerrillas succeeded in crossing the "search and destroy" first line of defence to spread all over the country. Even though ZIPA was dissolved by ZANU leadership, guerrillas of both movements had already entrenched themselves in virtually every district in the countryside by the late 1970s. Here the Rhodesian regime may have been saved by the Lancaster House Agreement of 1979 because a multipronged general attack, led by mechanised formations and air cover, would have been launched (by both ZPRA and ZANLA) around the end of 1979 in a general attack to secure outright victory. (From conversations with some ex-ZIPRAs, Asafa Ndlela, Nathaniel Mpofu and Phillip Ndlovu).

One of the important elements in our military training was that the army code of conduct should spell out the importance of avoiding civilian casualties as much as possible in a war zone. In fact it had to be quite clear that a civilian shall not be killed by service or any other weapon in the hands of a freedom fighter except under unavoidable cross fire. Any freedom fighter or soldier who acted in breach or defiance of such a code should be eliminated summarily after a brief trial by a military tribunal consisting of senior officers and a couple of combatants. But in post independence Zimbabwe Gukurahundi massacred thousands of civilians in a manner that made many people conclude that no soldier worth his salt could cause mass destruction of civilian lives without official clearance from above. Such a brazen act of gross abuse of human rights by the military must have been dealt with swiftly through a court martial or a board of inquiry should have been set up to investigate and apportion blame for heads to roll on the grounds of war crimes. The question is, if they were not sanctioned from above, why were they not court marshalled under an appropriate code that defines a requirement for the maximum care for civilian life in a war zone? The fact of the matter is that the dissidents who were being tracked by the Gukurahundi were trained personnel who were acting illegally therefore the operational area was a war zone in which the military should have observed a strict code for civilian safety.

Be that as it may, our stay in Moscow was fine although we were heavily occupied by the rigours of military training that consisted of the course content outlined above plus drill and exercises to break down the civilian softness and build a tough soldier. As we started our training at the onset of summer, we spent all summer time in open space training and exercising and in winter we focused on signals and political studies in doors. The instructors seemed to know the capability of the Rhodesian Army because they constantly warned us that if we finished up half-backed fighters Smith forces would easily crush us because they had a high standard of military training in all departments. So we had to be ready to challenge that capability and overcome it but not by frontal attack in the early phase of armed struggle. They pointed out that a guerrilla arsenal should not be located out of the country at all times of need; a well planned guerrilla warfare should create conditions where fighters actually overwhelmed some isolated enemy forces or bases, force them to abandon their weapons in confusion one way or the other. Cubans actually asserted that a guerrilla's arsenal should be in the hands of enemy's armed forces or its arsenals. They emphasised that one of guerrilla tactics in a surprise attack was to cause confusion and disarray in the enemy forces under such attack, capture weapons and other materials of utility value to the struggle and disappear fast from the battle scene. To achieve such a 'golden handshake,' (of seizing weapons from the enemy) should derive from a strategy of how to acquire enemy weapons to sustain the war during the entire phase of guerrilla warfare, taking into account that external supplies might be inaccessible at certain times during a prolonged struggle.

Return to Zambia

Completion of the programme meant our return to Africa to apply our skills in the theatre of operation inside the enemy occupied territory. We certainly came back with high morale and ready to get into the war zone. On arrival in Lusaka we were accommodated in country house in Chelstone, Lusaka then transferred to Nkomo Camp outside Lusaka for six weeks before our radio equipment arrived. I was appointed Camp Commander of the renowned ZPRA Camp deputised by Eliot Dube (specialised in reconnaissance operations). It was an exciting experience to mix with a large detachment of fighters in one base. We spent most of the time on military exercises in preparation for field operations. The comrade in command of the preparatory exercises was Mafu, one of ZPRA Instructors in Morogoro, Tanzania. Mafu was tough and ruthless in the field but kind during recess and own times. When Mafu left, his role was taken over by Cde International Dube, an experienced combatant in several battle fronts. While Mafu's command style was strictly technical, that of Dube was cushioned in humanity in terms of placing focus on maintaining high morale of the fighters by emphasising commander's responsibility to achieve high accomplishment in a given mission with low casualties in the battlefield. That is guerrillas should avoid casualties in any tactical operation because theirs was a swift surprise element in all missions. He was good at creativity concerning tactics in guerrilla warfare.

Nevertheless, while we were in Nkomo Camp we experienced extreme brutality meted out to comrades by the Lusaka based Military Administration. For example one comrade who had sneaked out of the camp to visit a girlfriend was punished by severe flogging with forty lashes on the buttocks. After that he had to be locked up in a dark cell indefinitely yet he was clearly in pain. All this cruelty was supposed to be administered by me, the camp commander at Nkomo camp. My senior commanders from Lusaka just gave me dry orders to do this without giving me a chance to raise questions or to suggest modifications of the sentence. Anyway, after their departure back to Lusaka, I ordered the release of the 'prisoner' comrade because I felt that the measures were far exceeding the lightness of the offence. In the first place it was a minor civil offence, if any, that did not need to attract a harsh sentence of the nature described above. He could not be described as a deserter because he went out and returned to base except that he was sported by a security patrol that did not even apprehend him. They merely reported seeing him "out of bounds" at the wrong time. When asked what he was up to he volunteered the information that he had gone to visit his girlfriend. That was enough to earn him very harsh punishment as if he was a traitor.

The Commander himself returned after four weeks and found his 'should-be-prisoner' a free man among other comrades. He was so annoyed as to threaten to lock me up but I stood my ground and succeeded in demolishing the Chief Commander's grounds of brutality of imposing extremely disproportionate punishment on a freedom fighter for committing a civil offence. He was a seasoned fighter who had been to the front several times and was still determined to be deployed for combat missions. Above all the Commander-in-Chief could not refer me to a rule that stipulated offences and by how much they were punishable. He tried to point out that there were long standing military traditions, norms and conventions but all this could not convince me that such a large army like ZPRA could be governed by "norms and conventions" without its specific code of conduct that should have been universal in all the units. So, prisoner comrade was left free. In essence he did not serve the full sentence (besides prio flogging) as I placed him in a platoon to live a normal life of a guerrilla soldier in the camp. The comrades gave me the name of "Jesus" but I did not wish to be called by that name because I was nowhere near the character of Jesus. They used it in my absence when talking among themselves or comrades from other camps. Instances of a similar brutal treatment of freedom fighters were happening in different camps but not in mine and a few others like C1 and C2.

Owing to their brutality to comrades, the Military Administration earned the name **"Gestapo"** from the freedom fighters. Word spread to all the camps that our military chiefs were now known as Gestapo and the name stuck till for a long time in my generation in the struggle. But no one called them by that name in their faces because that would spell doom for the person concerned. Whether they finally got to know that, I do not know. But most combatants of my generation still refer to them as Gestapo when talking about our days in ZPRA. Eventually comrades all round expressed disquiet on brutal punishment and it was abandoned during our time. Any offending comrade would be punished by serving the community either cooking for them, say for a week or cleaning the camp or digging new toilets or anything that had social utility value not just inflicting pain on a freedom fighter. Hash punishment was preserved for traitors and those who unjustifiably molested or killed civilians in exile or inside Zimbabwe or caused mutiny

Signals Unit in Field Operations

Once the communication equipment landed in Lusaka, the signals troops were deployed in various fronts. Comrades Livingstone Mashengele, Mgoli Mathuthu and I were deployed in the eastern front from April to September 1969. We were in a detachment commanded by Cde Musa Chinyere, a very thoughtful commander with leadership qualities coated with a unique sense of humour to keep everybody in positive mood about the struggle. I was part of the detachment's command structure in charge of communications (signals). The chief of staff was Cde Tsumba, quiet but resolute fellow. The Zambian side transit Camps in the area were called C1 and C2 (located adjacent to each other) near the Zambezi River. At the same time comrades John Ndlovu and Bhekuzulu Khumalo were deployed in the western front. The Zambian side of the transit camp in the west was called DK (opposite the mouth of the Deka River in Wange), commanded by Cde Cephas Cele with Edward Sihwa as chief of staff. Comrades Mathema, Mugwara, Mthimkhulu and Mashoko remained at the base station in Chelstone, Lusaka.

Initially, all deployments of large detachments were effectively countered by the Rhodesian security forces inside the country and this began to affect the morale of the freedom fighters both in the field and rear bases. Apparently, leaders were not aware that most freedom fighters were deeply agitated by what they considered as **"grave strategic misdirection"** exposed by poor performance in field operations. For instance the deployment of large military formations in the country without a clear strategy and tactics to deal with a combined force of heavily armed Rhodesian and South African forces was a tragic miscalculation by ZAPU leadership in exile. We began to wonder whether military operations were properly planned with clear objectives as required by the military science which requires that intelligence should first play a key role in a pre-operation diagnosis that show pros and cons in the enemy occupied territory as well as determining possible supportive and negative factors within the populace. So that decisions would be based on the objective conditions pertaining to military and socio-political intricacies of the situation in the theatre of operation. Many fighters began to suspect that the leadership was merely taking an adventurous gamble hoping that the enemy would be caused to panic upon seeing large numbers of armed men challenging security forces. In other words many comrades did not see any clear direction in the deployment of the freedom fighters in both the eastern, central and western fronts.

During our time and throughout the duration of armed struggle, freedom fighters were trained in guerrilla warfare in such diverse countries as Algeria, Cuba, North Korea, Bulgaria, USSR, Tanzania (by Algerian & Zimbabwean Instructors), GDR and Egypt. From mid 1970s Libya, Zambia and Angola joined the number of countries that trained ZPRA freedom fighters. Most of these countries supplied weapons to all Liberation Movements in Southern Africa and Cape Verde Islands. The USSR was the major supplier of light weapons that were suitable for guerrilla warfare in terms of allowing fast movement because the nature of the war has no room for military vehicles and heavy weapons until the second phase of the struggle. By all accounts our weapons squarely matched those of the enemy if not superior in terms of efficiency and durability (eg AK vs FN) in prolonged use in the battlefield. Once assembled in our transit bases in Zambia, we took part in military exercises under Zimbabwean Instructors where uniformity of content and form were established and incorporated in our scheme of practical application. So we believed that the first phase of the programme of fighting was supposed to be guerrilla warfare in strategy and tactics as this phase of the armed struggle focused on weakening the enemy by disabling its strategic pillars in the military and other physical infrastructure of utility value to the enemy forces. Guerrilla warfare is always irregular in attack and diversions to cause the enemy to chase mirage while opening space for combat guerrillas to strike at will. This was a war of attrition meant to disable enemy forces' strategic lifelines without frontal attack or positional warfare. But none of us could find the appropriate words to describe the kind of war that our leaders were waging against the Smith regime. Noticing too many faulty endeavours in the deployment of fighters, we began to debate the strategic issues very seriously in every camp.

CHAPTER NINETEEN

ERUPTION OF A CRIPPLING CRISIS IN ZAPU LEADERSHIP IN EXILE

The first camp to ask the High Command (JD Chikerema and J Z Moyo), to come and explain matters of military strategy, was C1 and C2 during or about September 1969. They held up the Chief of Staff Comrade Robson Manyika whom they were prepared to keep until the leaders arrived. Comrade Chikerema came alone in response to the request of the fighters and this compounded the problem. Apparently the leaders were not aware that the situation was pregnant with explosive discontent over their misdirection of armed struggle in Zimbabwe. Chikerema discovered the awareness of fighters from the very first speaker who demanded to know what strategy was in place to wage guerrilla warfare to weaken the Smith regime militarily to pave the way for its eventual overthrow. Comrades Chikerema and the Chief of Staff could not give satisfactory answers to all questions on strategic matters with regards the direction and the objectives of the war as driven by the leaders at that time. The fighters put it to the leaders that so far they had failed to prosecute a liberation war against the Smith regime at the cost of high casualties on our side. Speaker after speaker elaborated on the weakness or total lack of strategic direction of armed struggle by the High Command and the Military Administration. Examples of failure focused on several deployments of small and large detachments since 1964 yet no significant progress had been made to weaken the security forces of the Rhodesian regime. A distinct political advantage for a nationalist movement that had existed within the masses since the inception of the African National Congress was that it had gained and retained considerable amount of support for armed struggle inside the country that would enable a prolonged liberation process for decades. Therefore a well thought out strategy should have taken that factor into account after verifying reliability of the underground structures in the country. A large number of freedom fighters of the time were members of the youth wing of ZAPU and PCC before they were banned therefore once they were deployed as fighters they could find it easy to establish themselves fairly easier than stepping into a politically virgin social setting.

At DK camp comrades debated military issues in conjunction with that kind politicised social environment in the country which should have been a catalyst for operating purposes. But they could not understand why leaders were failing to capture that in their strategic planning. In this regard, following a near-rebellion situation at the eastern C camps, comrades at DK camp sent for the leaders to come and address them on what was going on in the whole management of the liberation armed struggle. To our surprise J Z Moyo went to DK alone to hear grievances from comrades there. The same questions were raised and the fighters were left astounded by the lack of clarity on the part of the High Command and the Military Administration on the question of guerrilla warfare for which all of us were trained to carry out in Zimbabwe. Of course the fighters put forward definite demands as to what should be done to improve the thrust of armed struggle in the theatre of operation. The demands were the same from all the camps.

The demands put together read as follows:

1. the military administration to be dissolved and replaced by a new command structure with written code of conduct for governing ZPRA cadres and defining every level of the army
2. once appointed the military administration should move its head quarters out of Lusaka to the bush in some of the thick forests near the Zambezi River
3. the Lusaka office should cease to handle military matters including recruitment and training;
4. Conscription (known as chukuwa) should be abolished altogether and that recruitment should be based on motivating to voluntarily join ZPRA as recruits
5. Lusaka office should focus on resource mobilisation, diplomatic matters, publicity and liaison with civilian members of ZAPU in Zambia because they contributed funds and personnel to the struggle
6. comprehensive revision of the strategy to ensure that the first phase of the struggle takes the course of full scale guerrilla warfare while preparing for the final phase of overthrowing the enemy by **general attack** led by appropriately trained and prepared regular forces
7. there should be a political programme or manifesto spelling out the objectives and goal of liberation war; something similar to the **Freedom Charter** of the African National Congress of South Africa
8. A written code of conduct should bind all military personnel to adhere to a definite standard of discipline at all times where wherever they were
9. Military intelligence to be at high alert along the possible crossing points identified by the reconnaissance unit inside the country
10. Use of explosives and land mines should be given prominence to spearhead sabotage operations to slow down enemy mobility and disable communication networks in the air (telegraph wires) and on the ground

The leaders surprised the fighters by making further deployments of large detachments without addressing the issues raised by the fighters in September 1969. At the onset of rainy season, two detachments were deployed into Zimbabwe in November 1969. One crossed the Zambezi River in the eastern front heading towards the north east of the country. Another was deployed in the western front heading towards the north west of the country with the idea of splitting into small sections once inside the country. Comrade Pius Mashoko took my place in the eastern front in a detachment commanded by Comrade James Chirodza. At this time Comrades Mathema, Mugwara, Mthimkhulu and I were at the main base station in Chelstone, Lusaka where I assumed command of the main base station till end of January1970. From that month I was deployed in the Western front until October 1970. Comrade Mashoko was reported to have fallen in active service in the north eastern Zimbabwe in an encounter with the Rhodesian security forces. Apparently, Comrade Chirodza's detachment was caught in enemy ambush soon after crossing the Zambezi River and they suffered one casualty, comrade Mashoko of signals.

Some of the comrades were captured and others retreated but did not get very far before they were surrounded and captured

In the case of Comrade Mashoko, it would appear that he was spotted by a sniper that he was a signals personnel identified by signals kit. This seemed to confirm what we were trained to do which was that in an ambush the first shot must hit the radioman in order to silence enemy communications before a full scale battle ensures. In this instance the enemy apparently spotted our man first and took the initiative to silence him thus fracturing communication between the detachment in the field and head quarters in Zambia or any other friendly unit. The deployments in both the eastern and western fronts consisted of large detachments in missions that were not clear to all of us including those who were directly involved. These units had some of the best comrades in terms of quality of training and commitment to armed struggle. It was such a waste of human and technical resources by sending not only well trained but also well politicised fighters for an ill- defined mission where there was hardly any preparation in the form of intelligence before field operations. Comparing notes with comrades in the Reconnaissance Units of the eastern and western fronts, we learned that they found the situation to be highly fluid on the entire length of the Zambezi River on the Rhodesian side. It was changing every twelve hours or less in the Zambezi Escarpment making passage extremely constricted and dangerous for large formations crossing all at once. Reconnaissance Units were fully aware that the fluid belt along the Zambezi River was the Rhodesian security forces' first line of defence. It was not unmanageable because it was not entirely watertight. It needed tactful manoeuvres through gaps up to the interior. Then what was the basis of sending these gallant men to face such an entanglement without adopting appropriate format of passing through a restricted passage where the Rhodesian first line of defence was "search and destroy" close to the border crossing point. Only small numbers had successfully sneaked through the enemy dragnet and then reassembled at a convenient spot for whatever reason identified by detachment commander. Information from our intelligence agents and operatives inside the country was not wisely utilised during the first phases of the struggle until so many tragedies had happened in the organisation.

As already stated above, in the western front a detachment was deployed into the country under similar circumstances as in the eastern front. What was more disturbing here was that there was a trend in the handling of the two fronts. The eastern deployment was under the direction of JD Chikerema and the western front by JZ Moyo thus exhibiting an element of tribal division of labour in this whole exercise of national importance. In this connection Tshabangu writes quite extensively on this problem. The deployment of the two detachments compounded the problem rather than alleviate it especially because both of them were intercepted by the enemy forces before they got deep into the country. In the western front comrades scattered themselves in an attempt to evade easy capture. One splinter had a skirmish with security forces but finished up with some comrades captured others, lead by Comrade Philemon Mabuza managed to advance deep to southwards to the Matopo Hills others lead by Jabulani Mazula, headed for Lupane District. The security forces the pursued both splinters until they sneaked out of their hideouts and crossed to Botswana and then back to Zambia. The third splinter, led by Jimy Moyo, was captured by the Rhodesian security forces

The botched deployment described above caused discontent and tension to deepen in all departments of the military forces of ZPRA including Logistics, Intelligence, Reconnaissance, Communications (Signals), and General Combat Forces. ZAPU civilian members in Zambia, too, became disenchanted with the way armed struggle was prosecuted by the ZAPU leadership. Civilian members of ZAPU were always very close to the Party because they provided crucial support to armed struggle in terms of financial contributions for food supplies (in the transit camps) and personnel who were recruited or conscripted into ZPRA in large numbers. With all military departments on the same side about weakness of leadership on strategic matters, there was a move to consult in order to secure a formal approval that would pave the way for the fighters to take the matter into the hands of the military because politicians had made blunders for too long without being checked. Civilian members subscribed to this approach. But before cadres translated their thoughts into action, leaders opened the gates by causing a crisis at their level.

On one April day 1970, we had a surprise visit from Chief Political Commissar, Comrade Roma Nyathi accompanied by Gordon Butshe at D K Camp. They held a meeting with the camp commanding hierarchy of the Camp to deliver bad news from the Head Quarters. The bad news was exactly what freedom fighters did not expect from their commanders at a time when they were waiting to hear about plans to overhaul the entire military strategy in the theatre of operation in Zimbabwe. They told us about the eruption of a crisis within the five members of ZAPU National Executive in Lusaka. It sounded worse than the one experienced during the 1963 split that saw the breakaway group form a new party, ZANU. The two comrades were unsure about whether the rest of the comrades should be informed at that stage. We then urged them to address the entire detachment in the camp about the crisis that they had delivered to us. They had no alternative but drop the bombshell that sparked a fierce debate with comrades demanding the arrest of the two "emissaries of JZ Moyo" as these comrades were representing a JZ faction. The entire camp resolved that the leaders should be summoned to the camp to come immediately. They asked whether all the camps, including C1 and C2 were informed about the crisis or it was JZ trying to get support from us. Apparently the two chiefs were representing JZ Moyo's faction and they sent nobody to the eastern camps. Many comrades demanded the two JZ Emissaries to be arrested right away and then despatch a platoon to seek and arrest the entire leadership of ZAPU in exile.

After a long debate that was punctuated by outburst of anger, the assembly of comrades adopted a modest course of action by assigning four of us to go and take the entire leadership of ZAPU in exile to come and explain what they were up to. The messengers were comrades JZ Mzilethi, Enoch Sebele, Mkandla and myself. We went to Lusaka but only met the JZ faction and were unable to locate JD Chikerema faction as their whereabouts were unknown. Since comrades had instructed us to bring the entire leadership, we could not pick up the JZ Moyo faction alone as it was the only one that submitted itself to us willingly. So our mission was a failure as we returned empty handed to the fury of comrades. If anger could cause people to explode, every comrade at DK could have exploded into powder when they saw us without the feuding leaders. Hearing disappointing report, they adopted a motion that the leaders should be arrested and be forcibly transported to the camps. We had to debate these issues every day until we became cool and free from anger. We then agreed that we should first assess the situation in all the camps of ZPRA before catching the bull by the horns. Also we should take into account that we were on the Zambian territory whose sovereignty we had to respect unreservedly. How did the crisis erupt in the first place?

J Z Moyo's Observations in Our Struggle and JD Chikerema's Reply to the Observations in Our Struggle

The crisis at leadership level erupted when they found themselves overwhelmed by the demands of the freedom fighters to explain the direction of the struggle that had wasted so many lives with very little impact on the enemy strength. Since they were empty, instead of giving a reasonable answer, they cracked. It was at this point that JZ Moyo burst their catacomb in an open document entitled **"The Observations in Our Struggle"** In this document dated 25 February 1970, Moyo was lamenting and **admitting that the fighters were right to say there was no strategy for prosecuting the liberation struggle**. He stressed the decline in morale and breakdown of discipline in the camps from the middle of 1969 culminating into mutiny in the eastern camps. The mutiny was exemplified by the detention of the Chief of Staff by the fighters at C2. He proposed a time table for the deployment of fighters in the country without saying the basis of those numbers. He did not even provide an analysis of the situation in the theatre of operation in terms of the enemy strength and weaknesses in general terms and specific strategic issues. Observable deployment of forces on the surface and under-cover as well as the resources available to the enemy's security forces meant for "counter-insurgents" etc. The time table looked like some statistical figures for plotting a graph forecasting some trend of some sort. He thought he was putting forward a new strategic plan for ZPRA over a period of time. That was inadequate for the purpose of military strategy from which could be derived operational plans. The question was, if it was important, why publish it instead of discussing it with his colleagues, Chikerema, Silundika, Nyandoro and Ndlovu plus the Military Administration?

J Z Moyo must have appreciated JD Chikerema's response which was quite a comprehensive critique of his claims and observations, ending up with seizure of presidential powers and administration of Party and military affairs. JD Chikerema's response came out on 17 March 1970 titled **"Reply to the Observations in Our Struggle"** What a drama. What is important about the reply is that it too, admitted that the struggle was not guerrilla warfare but sabotage to frighten the enemy into submission to dialoguing with the African Nationalists for the purpose of reaching an agreement on majority rule. What a pipe dream on the part of J D Chikerema. What a waste of fighters in a gamble that was so ill-defined from 1964 to 1970. So the concerns of the fighters were finally confirmed by both J Z Moyo and JD Chikerema. So there were no revolutionary leaders in exile for ZAPU. It was now up to the cadres to produce revolutionary leadership to drive the revolution forward to its logical conclusion.

The admission of lack of strategy by JZ Moyo and that there was no guerrilla warfare by JD Chikerema, confirmed the fighters' long standing suspicion that the leaders were interested in getting to power using fighters as cannon fodder. To achieve this shallow ambition, they avoided building a strong army moulded by the struggle and tested in liberation battles with the support of the masses. They would be happy with a compromise situation where the Rhodesian security forces would remain intact thus forming a backbone for a future national army that would defend the government of the day if the liberation 'saboteurs' attempted to challenge their power. That could have been the scenario if the Rhodesian regime was brought down by mere 'scare tactics' derived from a 'sabotage' strategy. This was so because if the negotiations were accepted while the liberation forces were still weak, the Rhodesian Army would have been kept intact as a National Army and the 'saboteurs' would be so weak that they could have had no influence in the direction of transformation of an oppressive system to a people-focused system of governance. In their own admission, they did not have the strategy to wage guerrilla warfare. They wanted to frighten the regime into submission through making haphazard gunfire noises and bangs which they called 'sabotage operations' before there was a strong liberation army led by the African revolutionary movement. They were hoping that the few noises of the 'saboteurs' would catapult them to power where they could have joined the colonial masters without changing state apparatus. The fact that they sent people for fully fledged military training thinking that they would return to pursue a sabotage strategy shows severe limitations in their strategic conceptualisation of a war of liberation because they had no military training themselves. But the regimes's racicist outlook prevented it to see that this whole nationalist weakness would have provided the whites a glaring opportunity to keep their privileges intact under a weak African government "anchored" by an intact Rhodesian Army. The Rhodesian regime took the war seriously because it fully prepared its forces to take advantage of strategic loop holes so as to maintain the initiative at every stage of the war. For our part, only guerrilla warfare could puncture any conventional strategy intended to counter guerrilla warfare no matter how watertight it was constructed in terms of application of technical and professional proficiency of the security forces in the field. But this is not to deny that sabotage is one of the key destroyers of enemy strategic pillars when applied simultaneously or in conjunction with other anti-regular army tactics that are not entirely conventionally.

The fact of the matter is that ZPRA freedom fighters of the post 1964 phase of the struggle were not trained as saboteurs; they were trained as soldiers of a guerrilla capability to fight well trained Rhodesian armed forces led by a professional regular army consisting of a variety of ground forces fully trained in counter-insurgency tactics, backed by a well equipped air force and a mechanised regiment. As would be expected, fighters were prepared to use appropriate guerrilla tactics and to be creative once they became tested in the heat of warfare. But when they finished training, got ready to enter the theatre of operation only to find it difficult to define what kind of warfare they were waging against the Smith regime because the deployment was not met with expectations of the fighters. For instance they noticed lack of proper planning from the way they were being pumped into the country in large numbers in a method that was not compatible with guerrilla warfare as they easily landed into the entanglement of the Rhodesian security forces on the enemy's first line of defence which was defined as "search and destroy zone." Even if they fought gallantly to win the initial encounters, fighters were eventually overcome by the enemy forces because the enemy had the initiative as the "search and destroy zone" was a battlefield of elimination that was deliberately created by the enemy forces to keep all of Rhodesia clear of "insurgents." Leaders were informed by Intelligence and Reconnaissance that Rhodesian strategy was meant to deny guerrillas the initiative by eliminating them at the crossing points before they infiltrated the country. In guerrilla warfare, initiative and the element of surprise are inseparable twins that sustain an offensive over the enemy in terms of maximising time to take well thought out decisions and space to manoeuvre without much pressure from enemy forces. After all guerrillas are always fewer and less equipped than the army they fight, therefore their survival lies in guerrilla tactics of destroy and disappear to avoid confrontation with a large and well armed regular force. Professionally applied guerrilla tactics are meant to disable the enemy capabilities in a war of attrition that starts off by destroying infrastructure and other strategic resources such as communications and transport systems. But if they become exposed to a regular army on frontal attacks or conventional warfare, the danger is that they are the ones who get worn down fast even if they suffered light casualties in every battle. In any military organisation, the first line of contact (at pre-combat level) in a war situation is intelligence and the Rhodesians made good use of intelligence during the initial phase of armed struggle. This way, they were able to deploy their security forces in appropriate formations and military technology to push guerrillas to a killing ground where they could route or force them to surrender by inflicting heavy casualties.

The decisive factor in all of this was the people in the villages who gave full support to the freedom fighters in spite of the fact that the Rhodesian authorities threatened to deal with those who supported what they called "terrorists." What the Rhodesians ignored at their own peril here was that in canvassing for national consensus on UDI and in spelling out actual principles of their declaration of independence they did not include Africans. No reasonable African would

163

forget such a blatant display of racial arrogance by Ian Douglas Smith regime. Both African and European citizens were aware that the power was in European hands therefore it would be terribly unrealistic to expect Africans to do nothing about such a socially insensitive system where they were deprived of everything that became the preserve of a minority race in the country. In essence to transform such a system into a just and fair society, Africans had no alternative but to fight a just war. The freedom fighters with guns were seen as representing those who were deprived therefore it became imperative to support them until power shifted to the majority Africans in a democratic way. The Rhodesian regime placed all its hopes on its mighty military machine to crush resistance from the deprived Africans who had no say in the running of the country whatsoever. On the other hand the liberation movement enjoyed overwhelming support of the deprived majority of the African Rhodesian citizens. But when questioned by authorities Africans denied vehemently that they supported guerrillas for their own safety, thus giving the regime false impression that guerrillas had no support until they realised the falsehood when it was too late. Therefore there was no surprise that the white minority political system eventually became militarily indefensible in spite of their command of massive counterinsurgents outfit.

However, on the part of leaders of ZAPU the mistake was that they attempted to challenge the Rhodesian system by driving armed struggle without military skills that would have enabled them to understand the principles that are spelt out above. This was exactly what led the leaders to fail to cause a dent on the Rhodesian security forces. They waged a war that was not in accord with principles of guerrilla warfare in the context of the Rhodesian social composition of society in terms of utilizing comparative advantage with effect. The fact that appropriate guerrilla war fare, or any other military strategy, was not adhered to as described above was because armed struggle was led by military illiterates during the 1960s until the leaders could no longer proceed in the old way by 1970.

So by their own admission, the leaders were not suitable to command armed liberation struggle as they believed they were sabotaging the enemy while the fighters believed that they were fighting guerrilla war towards the overthrow of the Smith regime thus operating at cross purposes with their leaders. A major problem here was that leaders and fighters were not on the same wavelength because the former were civilians and the latter guerrilla soldiers. It was a huge mistake to assign civilians to direct militarily trained personnel in a warfare that was characterised by contradictory perceptions of strategic directions and objectives of armed struggle. A civilian formulated war strategy could not work for a military operation without input from the military wizards. If a plan originated from civilian leadership, it should have been submitted to military strategists to translate it into a military strategy, taking into account all aspects of information provided by intelligence service and reconnaissance units as well as the observations of the masses and friendly sources in the theatre of operation.

The Aftermath of the Observations and their Reply

Many revolutionaries propound that once an old order becomes moribund it begins to be dysfunctional because it can no longer manage new forces of change in the old way. That is, the development of the new forces of change help to sharpen antagonistic contradictions that make it impossible for the two forces to reconcile using the old model of running the country or organisation. The new forces of change arise as a consequence of the decay of the underpinnings that give life and strength to the old order in question. The pressure of the development of the new progressive forces cause irreparable cracks, subsequently tearing asunder its antique anchors thus causing the old order to collapse and a new era of progress sets in. The rapture that happened in ZAPU at the beginning of the 1970s was exactly an indication of a decayed old order that could not match with the pressure and tension generated by new progressive forces that had to set themselves free to operate in a new way without impediment. After the outburst of the two documents, the leaders became powerless because the majority of the fighters rejected both factions decisively. Above all, the freedom fighters felt vindicated that the leaders in exile were not in tandem with the requirements of armed liberation struggle against a determined and well resourced regime in Rhodesia. The fighters were trained in guerrilla warfare and the leaders were not trained in anything related to waging war. This marked the first line of fundamental differences of approach to the strategic definition and execution of the struggle whereby the leaders believed they were pursuing a 'sabotage' campaign whilst the fighters believed that they were pursuing a revolutionary transformation of colonialism in the country through armed guerrilla warfare with the support of the masses. Those people we left at home in the underground structures were waiting for us to return and continue the struggle with real fire power and tactics to outclass the enemy security forces with tactical strikes.

The fact that the leaders lived in the glittering City of Lusaka was enough to reinforce their distance not only from the fighters, but also from the heat of warfare itself. Such a detached way of driving the struggle by remote control was an indication that they were not a suitable brand for waging a rigorous armed struggle let alone a thoroughgoing transformation of the socio-economic system obtaining in Rhodesia at the time. Their documents showed that they had degenerated to the lowest level of political discourse with a clear indication that they were nowhere near the requirements of leadership of a movement in armed struggle. Clearly, J Z Moyo's Observations and JD Chikerema's Reply had a potential to cause a self-consumption of the Party in the form of splitting the fighters into taking sides to the point of shooting each other on tribal lines as **Owen Tshabangu (1979)** captures this threat very well. Indeed a few of the fighters fell for this by taking sides blindly without a full diagnosis of the political behaviour of the two members of the National Executive of the High Command. Especially the members of the Military Administration who were trained cadres of ZPRA did not show any sign of congruent stance with the general combat forces in terms of deciphering the hidden agenda (of sabotage) of the leaders in terms of the nature of the struggle being waged. It was not surprising to see them easily falling into factions without discerning harmful consequences of tribalising a national liberation movement like ZAPU.

Some of us who became politicians from the school days and spent the good part of our youth more in non-combatant active service than in the armed struggle, found such infantile disorderly behaviour extremely despicable to say the least. We did not see any value in tribal affiliation while in the pursuit of a national cause that was fraught with massive challenges that needed farsighted thinkers and strategists rather than haulers of tribal wagons of doom. We had the political culture of national cohesion that we inherited from the National Democratic Party in the underground in the early 1960s and functioned in it during the life of ZAPU until the split of 1963. In that culture there could never be any thought of placing a tribe over a nation of Zimbabwe. From the days of Aleke Banda at Nyathi Scool (debates on pan-Africanism) via the NDP and ZAPU under Michel Mawema and Joshua Nkomo respectively, we were socialised in a culture of regarding one another as sons and daughters of the same soil of Mother Africa, from Cape Agulhas to Casablanca. Alas! Our leaders were part of the founding fathers of that culture yet they were now tearing it apart as if it was their personal pair of overalls. Something needed to be done to avert the impending demise of ZAPU and its military arm, ZPRA if the armed struggle was to be revived.

However, it was encouraging to find that most fighters did not see value in either JZ Moyo's Observations or JD Chikerema's Reply. Initially the fighters wanted them to come to the camps and explain their problem. But some of us thought there was nothing to explain because the leaders did not only have differences, they had also become irredeemable casualties of a political syndrome of tribal chauvinism in an effort to cover up failures at national leadership level. Any national leader who finds comfort in retreating to a tribal enclave should not be allowed to lead a national movement because he would have alienated himself from the common cause of all tribal groups who are the components of a united nation. Such a leader should forfeit leadership without any compromise to avoid creating divisions in the movement. That is why we called for a conference where all the fighters would attend with civilian branches in Zambia sending delegates. From inside Zimbabwe, our intelligence network could have been instructed to identify the underground branches (through the semi-surface officials) and use the crossing routes to ship them across.

Meanwhile the JZ Moyo faction organised themselves into what they called **Dengezi**[29] which was nearly all-Ndebele and Kalanga. **NB: *In olden days uDengezi was a large frying pan used to fry some portions of muti*[30] *that was believed to provide a protective "shield" to soldiers from any spell of mishap unleashed by the adversarial army. In a single file soldiers would bend towards udengezi, place both palms on a furiously simmering concoction of muti in udengezi on fire, lick hot dripping substance from their palms, jump over udengezi and march forward without looking back up to a designated stopping point some metres away. Then they would be deemed ready to go to war by a conducting sangoma (traditional healer) (Folktale from elders)***

With regard the faction's concept of **uDengezi,** it has never been clear to some of us why these comrades chose the name **Dengezi t**o distinguish themselves from the J D Chikerema's faction which, too, had its share of tribal outlook as it was entirely Shona, especially Zezuru. By the way **Dengezi** members had invited Walter Mthimkhulu and I to attend their meetings. We questioned the status of such a meeting and strongly objected to use the name of ZAPU to promote **Dengezi.** They did not stop calling us to meetings but we kept our comrades fully informed about the whole confusion. They stopped inviting us when they came to know that we wrote a letter to the President of the Republic of Zambia pleading to him to intervene in the crisis and get it fixed or permit general combat forces and civilian members solve it through a conference of ZAPU. The formalization of u Dengezi compounded the crisis because it existed as a faction that seemed to grow towards becoming an organization within ZAPU. The Party was in murky waters in a way that I had never seen ZAPU looking so much in tartars the way I saw it in exile in 1970 since I joined it in 1962. I had never seen it displaying tribes as key elements of the Party of national architecture that was supposed to play a leading role not only in liberation but also in nation building after victory. Of course tribes have a place as building blocks of a nation that anchor the entire edifice of nationhood as it thrives in diversity. If a tribe begins to take over the national mantle of leadership, the fabric of nationhood is bound to disintegrate in a dismally antagonistic fashion which is often fraught with deadly consequences. Using the model of the NDP (which laid the foundation of national unity) the whole thing looked so alien and un-Zimbabwean to me because I grew up with the political language of Pan-Africanism propounded by Kwame Nkrumah, and simplified by Aleke Banda and strengthened further by the African

---

[29]   *frying pan*

[30]   *for luck to win battles*

Nationalism championed by the said NDP and ZAPU under the leadership of Michael Mawema and the Joshua Nkomo respectively. How was I going to accommodate a dark outlook of political primitivism of James Chikerema and J Z Moyo?

In addition to that accumulated political knowledge inside the country, many of us had read quite a lot in the camps and during training where we read revolutionary theory as propounded by Lenin and other Marxists including, Che Guevara, Mao Tse Tung, etc and some African works like, African Nationalism by Ndabaningi Sithole, Auto Biography of Kwame Nkrumah, Wretched of the Earth by Franz Fanon, etc. The bulk of ZPRA comrades were trained in Algeria, Cuba, Tanzania (Morogoro by Algerians and Zimbabwean Instructors) and Zambia. A minority of us were trained in USSR, Bulgaria, North Korea and GDR. But because we all went through the same political theory and political culture we were in the same wavelength in our understanding of the weaknesses displayed by our leaders in the execution of the struggle. It was a huge relief to find that we all saw this fiasco as a degenerative shambles of both the Party and the military to be stopped. In our communication across all the transit camps in Zambia we found that the overwhelming majority of comrades who were in the camps at the beginning of the crisis, agreed that we should press for a conference where the exiled leaders should be suspended for the duration of the struggle or until the elective congress was held, whichever came first. The big camps here were DK, C2, C1, Nkomo Camp, F Camp, Kariba (Reconnaissance), Luthuli (Logistics, Intelligence and Communications), Vietnam (Chunga River), Garden, Morogoro in Tanzania. But there were many comrades that were overseas in training whose views we could not solicit at this stage. When they finally arrived there was confusion during the early days of arrival because they got relevant information in drips and drabs. Owen Tshabangu (1979) delves into this state of confusion very well.

Nevertheless, the JZ Moyo-JD Chikerema fiasco had damaging consequences for ZAPU as a liberation movement and ZPRA as a liberation army of the same. In some camps tribalism exploded beyond control as comrades dispersed in different directions with some joining ZANU and others melted away into the Zambian population. Owen Tshabangu (1979) spells this tribal poison quite explicitly in his book.

CHAPTER TWENTY

REVOLUTION WITHIN A REVOLUTION: THE RISE OF THE MARCH 11 MOVEMENT

Faced by a crisis of huge ramifications for our party and country, we had to come up with a plan to regenerate a massively fractured organisation. Comrades began to ask very serious questions about the way out of the mess. Some of us took it upon ourselves to rapidly seek the opinions of the comrades in all camps in Zambia and Tanzania. Most comrades were suggesting drastic action in the form of an outright military coup d'état. Those of us who had already taken the lead in searching for a solution, pointed out that it was essential to first organise ourselves politically and proceed to solicit the support of the Zambian government for whatever we wanted to do with the exiled leaders of ZAPU. Comrades supported the move to contact the Zambian Government on the question of the conference. We then proposed and comrades agreed to create a structure to make ourselves well organised so as to be able to reach every one we wanted to communicate with on this matter. We then met at F Camp and elected a leading structure which we called the **Revolutionary Council (RC)**. The RC consisted of twenty three members who elected a three member **Triumvirate** which was charged with day to day matters of the RC. The three were, J Z Mzilethi, Philemon Mabuza and I, Joshua Mpofu, with Mzilethi as Chairman of the Triumvirate and RC. Setting up an R C within ZAPU meant that we were waging a revolution within a revolution because we had to operate clandestinely with the aim of removing both factions from leadership of ZAPU and ZPRA. The act of setting up a Revolutionary Council was an act of courage and determination to rejuvenate ZAPU that had become moribund in exile. There was one objective for the Revolutionary Council: to deliver the five exiled members of the ZAPU National Executive Committee together with the Military Administration to an assembly of freedom fighters at one of the camps for the purpose of holding an all-inclusive ZAPU conference of all ZPRA fighters and civilian branches in Zambia and Zimbabwe. The purpose of the conference was to resolve the crisis in ZAPU by suspending the entire exiled five members of the National Executive with their Military Administration and adopt a revolutionary programme and strategy that would allow us to wage a well planned guerrilla warfare strategy with a clear vision for the future in Zimbabwe.

To pursue its assignment the Triumvirate identified comrade Eli Mthethwa as having many contacts in the Zambian Government circles therefore an essential resource for establishing contacts on behalf of the Revolutionary Council. So we agreed that Mthethwa and I should approach as many Government Ministers and officials as possible to solicit support for our proposal for ZAPU conference of all fighters in exile and civilian branches plus some comrades to be smuggled out of Rhodesia by our intelligence operatives.

Comrade Mthethwa and I started with junior government officials, moved upwards reached the Governor of Lusaka who sounded very sympathetic to our cause. We proceeded to meet with some Permanent Secretaries and Cabinet Ministers. It was encouraging to find that all Ministers and officials that we met individually understood the fighters' case and expressed their support as long as we did not use brute force against the leaders. In conversation with us, they showed cnsiderable understanding of the fighters' dilemma regarding the fact that they wanted to fight but there was no united leadership any more in ZAPU; at the same time it was difficult to persuade the two factions to meet the fighters jointly to explain their problem. As we were based on the Zambian soil, it was not very easy to take drastic action without breaking the Zambian law and damaging our credibility in the eyes of the OAU and the Frontline States. They appreciated our desire to go the whole hog in seeking ways of finding a solution to the ZAPU crisis including pressing them hard without outright military force, to come to our camp for a conflict resolution conference.

We gained the impression that the Zambian Government was terribly disappointed and embarrassed to witness the disintegration of ZAPU, a movement that was believed to have the potential to overthrow the Rhodesian regime through armed struggle because it had the support of the masses inside the country as well as from the Socialist countries and the Organisation of African Unity (OAU). In the final analysis we were satisfied find that all the key Ministers and officials did not like the ugly picture of the J Z Moyo/JD Chikerema leadership mess as exhibited by their documents and astonishing political behaviour unbecoming of revolutionary leaders. The Ministers and officials expressed utter disappointment that something like that had happened at the expense of the struggle. Here many pointed out that whatever we did would have the support of the Zambian Government provided such a move excluded use of violence of any sort. We appreciated that stance and obliged.

After mounting an intensive and extensive lobbying in Government offices we reported to the Revolutionary Council that the mission was successful in convincing senior government officials about the danger of the situation if left unresolved through a conference. It turned out that the Zambian Government was fed up with those leaders who had become a disgrace in Southern Africa. So we were flogging a dead horse here. To reinforce our diplomatic offensive, the Revolutionary Council assigned Walter Mthimkhulu and I to write a well substantiated letter to His Excellency the President of the Republic of Zambia. Mthimkhulu was an invaluable resource in the choice of appropriate phrases for sensitive situations needing some tint of diplomatic language when writing to distinguished authorities in high places. I was good at formulating salient points of an issue at stake, especially on political matters like the very one in our case. We drafted it meticulously and brought it back for approval by Revolutionary Council and submitted it to the President via appropriate channels. Owen Tshabangu has quoted from it to illustrate the revolutionary intensions of the fighters.

Although the fighters had resolved that there should be no military showdown with the Zambian security forces, the Revolutionary Council decided that fighters should be armed in the operation to take the leaders to Camp F. A special task force was set up to procure a consignment of light fire arms from the frontline camps in order to arm all the comrades at F Camp for this mission. The task force consisted of JZ Mzilethi (Commander), Walter Mthimkhulu, Job Maphosa and Stolom Ndlovu.

At this point we realised that our weakness was lack of resources, especially transport. We decided to approach the Chikerema faction and pretended to be on their side. Philemon Mabuza and I became the contacts with JD Chikerema and we succeeded to convince him that we were on his side. He too was busy wanting to seize the weapons from Dengezi so we encouraged him to work with us on that one. We told him that we knew of a big weapons dump in the western front but we needed transport to carry the weapons. He asked a friend of his to provide us with a 40 tonne lorry to carry the weapons to Lusaka. Here our aim was to carry them all, separate those we needed and unload them (without his knowledge) and leave heavy stuff 'for him' with a proviso that we were to know the consignment's final destination so that we could remove them at an appropriate time after arresting the leaders. The comrades who travelled to the Zambezi Valley found the weapons and loaded them on to the lorry. On their way back disaster struck. A land rover accompanying the lorry carrying the weapons from the Zambezi Valley overturned and Job Maphosa fractured his hip. Maphosa was an officer in the military intelligence of ZPRA therefore the cause of his injury had to be a well concealed case from the eyes and ears of Dengezi. The incident almost exposed us to both the Zambian Government and the two factions.

At the point of pick-up, the driver was not present because the comrades had entered a security zone where no civilian was required so he had to meet the comrades at a designated point on their return from the Zambezi Valley. The light weapons were loaded towards the back end of the trailer (because they were supposed to be unloaded first) while the rest were towards the front as they were to be unloaded last. Many civilian branches and individuals funded our operations generously as they, too, were eager to see the leadership crisis resolved and armed struggle resumed. After hearing the reports about the twin missions of assembling weapons and the diplomatic manoeuvres, the Revolutionary Council was satisfied that the time for action had arrived.

In laying a lot of emphasis on diplomatic cultivation with government, we were trying to avoid the use of blatant force to get the leaders to face the ZPRA cadres in the camps. More importantly it became clear to us that even if the Government sympathised with our desire to resolve the problem peacefully through a conference, it found it too sensitive to compel unwilling leaders to convene such a conference. At the same time the comrades in the camps wanted positive results from the Revolutionary Council. Actually they put pressure that the Council should bring the leaders to the camps under armed escort without spilling blood. On this account the Revolutionary Council decided that the Triumvirate should look into the possibility of seizing the leaders secretly, transport them to the camps without harming them and then inform the Zambian Government about the action after completing the operation. A detailed assessment of the feasibility of such an action was done by the Triumvirate. The fighters did not run short of intellectual capacity with capability to provide in-depth insights into complex socio-economic, political and military imponderables within our country and out of it. In this connection we had comrades like Matsikidze Gutu, Walter Mthimkhulu, Eli Mthethwa, Charles Gwenzi, Phineas Bepura, Owen Tshabangu, Gershon Phangwana, Jabulani Mazula, J Z Mzilethi, Cain Mathema, Joshua Mpofu and several others who held qualifications ranging from four years secondary education to hard sciences at tertiary level. In this regard all our presentations to government were well articulated and reasonably loaded with factual accounts of events that caused leaders to quarrel and split.

As some of us were political animals from juvenile age, we were able to communicate with civilians and easily mobilised them for support and provision of resources. In this way we ensured that civilian members of ZAPU were on the same wavelength with the fighters in every aspect of our agenda. We consulted them every step of the way and they were satisfied that their input was incorporated in our plans. They urged us to take drastic action against the leaders by arresting them and transport them to the Zambezi valley. Many of them contributed funds to support a 'new' revolutionary transformation of ZAPU to remove archaic ways of directing the struggle and bring about revolutionary changes and strategies of waging well planned guerrilla warfare. Eli Mthethwa and I were responsible for keeping the civilian members on the mode of a two-way communication with the fighters through regular meetings with them in this connection. By the way when we refer to civilian members in Zambia we mean working people, rural peasantry, middle classes, intellectuals and students at the University of Zambia. A combination of all of these made up a huge Zimbabwean population in Zambia and they were very alert to the politics of their country. The OAU was informed last about the leadership crisis and the desire of the carders to solve it by a conference of all freedom fighters in external bases. Every possible imponderable was examined and given its due. The Revolutionary Council was satisfied with our report recommending drastic action to force the leaders to the camps as required by the rest of the freedom fighters.

The time had come to take a crucial decision about what the comrades and ordinary members of ZAPU were calling for. At this point, the RC called a general assembly of freedom fighters from the following camps: Nkomo Camp, Vietnam Camp, Luthuli Camp, F Camp, Garden Camp and Zimbabwe House to a meeting at F Camp. Note that the eastern camps, such as C1 and C2 and their Reconnaissance Unit had either defected to ZANLA or melted away into the Zambian population. But those comrades who came to general assembly of combatants were fully aware that the meeting was a top secret matter of the fighters and they alone knew its purpose. It was a well attended general assembly of ZPRA fighters. We were delighted that the comrades from training abroad had arrived and prepared to be part of the action as they, too, were disgusted by the leaders' destructive behaviour. Tshabangu clearly spells out their frustration before they met with us from the transit camps and field operations. After hearing the report they were further informed that there was a secret Revolutionary Council that was responsible for all the work of putting things together (including getting light weapons from the frontlines to the surrounding camps). The time had come for final action on the five leaders and members of the military administration; all was set for that action. The fighters approved the action with enthusiasm.

Having accomplished the preparatory stage of seizing the leaders, the Revolution Council stood dissolved and a smaller one of fifteen members was elected with a specific mission to prepare a plan that would deliver the leaders to F Camp without being harmed. The purpose of dissolving the pioneer leadership was to allow the larger general assembly of freedom fighters to participate in the election of a leadership that would lead the combatants to accomplish the political transformation of ZAPU and its leadership. The new Revolutionary Council was elected by a large number of comrades assembled from many camps within Zambia. It was headed by a Triumvirate consisting of Philemon Mabuza, JZ Mzilethi and Jabulani Mazula. Comrade Philemon Mabuza was chairman of the Triumvirate. His deputy, Comrade Jabulani Mazula was assigned to command the operations to seize all the five leaders in exiled National Executive of ZAPU and all members of the Military Administration. Comrades Mabuza and Mazula had returned from the theatre of operation inside the country where they had spent most of the time on a hide and seek with the Rhodesian security forces. So they returned to base with frustration and anger for having been launched into a mission that had no objective, to find the comrades at the rear bases utterly disgusted by the political misconduct of the leaders in Lusaka. Some of the comrades had just arrived from military training overseas. All the comrades who were out of Zambia when the leaders burst open their strategic shallowness welcomed the efforts that had been initiated by the comrades in the Zambian camps. Comrade Owen Tshabangu was one of those who came from overseas. Unfortunately comrade Rex Nhongo had left to join ZANU at this point. At the big meeting which elected the second Revolutionary Council for operations, all comrades present were upbeat to hear that that plans had reached advanced stage towards addressing the leadership crisis.

The appointed day arrived and the comrades took positions in civilian clothes with small fire arms concealed under their civilian jackets or coats. In one fell swoop the fighters descended on Zimbabwe House in Armersdale and Lusaka office of ZAPU, seized almost all the members of Dengezi and Military Administration on the **11ᵗʰ March 1971**. The following day, Mabuza and I were supposed to deliver the JD Chikerema faction by surprising them in their hideouts in the offices of Oxford Press. George Nyandoro was lured into ZAPU office and captured by comrade Hlabangana's section. When we were on the verge of seizing Chikerema in the City Centre of Lusaka, things terribly went wrong when one key member of JD Chikerma faction, George Nyandoro, after having been captured, pushed away the escorting comrades and escaped in a sprint into the streets of Lusaka City Centre, straight to Oxford Press Offices where JD Chikerema was waiting for us on appointment not knowing that the meeting was intended for his capture. Nyandoro budged in and informed Chikerema about the fighters' operation in progress. So Chikerema immediately cancelled the appointment with us by which we were on the verge of capturing him to join the JZ Moyo faction at F camp. He informed the Zambian Government about the incident. We, too, rushed to Government to inform them about the action that had happened and what all this was about.

Actually we reminded the Government that the action was related to what we had been telling them about and that we were bound to inform them as soon as the operation was completed. We reiterated our intention to resolve the crisis which had badly disabled ZAPU for the past fifteen months. They seemed to understand our predicament and why we acted as we did. When news spread that only the Dengezi faction was seized by freedom fighters disappointment and suspicion set in on the part of those who were not there. They began to think that the JZ Moyo faction was being arrested by the JD Chikerema faction. We had to move swiftly to allay such fears amongst civilians and other comrades who were far away.

In spite of the setback, we never stopped hunting down Chikerema and Nyandoro to join their colleagues in the camps. Likewise a day later we intercepted Chikerema in the company of an Assistant Commissioner of Police, we humbly informed the Assistant Commissioner that Comrade Chikerema was required to join others at F Camp and he obliged, we went further to respectfully ask the Assistant Commissioner to assist us get hold of George Nyandoro and Edward Ndlovu and, indeed, they delivered the following day. On the third day, with all the five NEC members and the entire military administration under the control of the fighters at F camp, President Kaunda sent a senior Minister, the Secretary General to the Government, Mr Aaron Milner to mediate. His initial approach was amicable and showing signs that Government would seize the opportunity to influence things towards a constructive turn in ZAPU. He held a meeting with representatives of the fighters at which an agreement was reached that the leaders would be guarded by the Zambian Paramilitary Police jointly with a couple of fighters. There was a specific close in the note signed by the Minister, to the effect that the military (ei ZPRA) would have a final say in the solution of the ZAPU leadership crisis in exile. The five beleaguered leaders were taken to Kamfinsa Paramilitary Police Camp in the Copper Belt under the joint watch of two fighters and Zambian Paramilitary Forces. The Minister further agreed that a conference, to be attended by all ZPRA freedom fighters, would be held at a venue far away from Lusaka and that the Government would facilitate at the conference to find a solution to the crisis once and for all. The fighters were to leave their military hardware under the watch of a platoon appointed by the Triumvirate. Government would collect all the fighters from every ZPRA camp in Zambia and the ZAPU representative in Tanzania was instructed to prepare for the transportation of the recruits who were waiting at Morogoro Military Training Camp in Tanzania. The Government further agreed to provide supplies to the entire ZPRA fighters where they were due to assemble.

We were not entirely happy about some of the arrangements because control had shifted half way from the fighters to the Government because all supplies were to be provided by the Government including transport and security to and at the venue. The fighters had to leave their weapons and vehicles under the watch of a small unit (platoon) until the conference was over. We were not fully aware that the Government's intention was to make sure that all cadres from all the camps in Zambia had to bring their weapons to Camp F. Once it had satisfied itself that all the ZPRA cadres had brought their weapons to Camp F, it would order our 'watch dog' platoon to surrender the weapons to Zambian security forces and join their comrades at Mboroma. As the rest of us were transported from F camp to Mboroma, a long distance to the north east of Lusaka, the Government moved swiftly to accomplish what is described above. We reached the designated venue not knowing that the Government did not trust us. We were taken aback to see the arrival of our platoon that we had left behind to take care of our weapons at F Camp. That was a signal of something worse to come from the Zambian Government

The conference site at Mboroma was not inhabited by humans except National Parks rangers in an isolated camp in a forest. We settled in a dense forest that was on a slightly elevated ground across an ever-flowing river that was well supplied by small ravines that zigzagged from small hills in the neighbourhood. One of the ravines had a deep pond with fridge-cold water thus making us feel as if we were in town. But still this did not make us lose the feeling of a slippery slope away from a possible solution of the crisis in terms of having the right to take decisions about the course of our struggle. We began to fear that the leaders would continue to pretend to be united in front of the facilitator finishing up with their reinstatement as drivers of the struggle only to fall apart again later.

However, as soon as we arrived at Mboroma, we started to prepare a keynote speech and substantive resolutions to be adopted by the conference. The drafters were Walter Mthimkhulu Gershon Phangwane and I but, the comrades had to be divided into platoons (24 fighters each) to discuss the draft, amend or replace it as they saw fit. The process went well with the final version of the speech presented and unanimously approved by a general assembly of all the fighters present thus rendering it ready for presentation by Walter Mthimkhulu on the day of the conference.

The date for the conference was given to us by the Government and on that day we assembled in an open space. The facilitator, Mr Aaron Milner the Secretary General to the Government, declared that the meeting was not a conference but a meeting of freedom fighters and their leaders to sort out some misunderstanding. The Minister's announcement shocked the fighters because it was a complete departure from the original agreement made at Camp F with the leaders of the new Revolutionary Council. In spite of putting his foot down on the status of the meeting, the Minister allowed the fighters to speak first ahead of leaders. He proceeded to invite speakers from the fighters. In their delivery, every speaker called for the suspension of the leaders. The majority of members of the new Revolutionary Council spoke very strongly against reinstatement of the failed leaders. As we suspected that the leaders would pretend to be united, they were represented by James Chikerema in their presentation.

Comrade Walter Mthimkhulu was recommended by the Triumvirate and approved by the general assembly of freedom fighters to represent them in reading their keynote speech. It was a long and detailed speech in factual ventilation of the causal factors of the crisis in ZAPU and possible way forward. In the absence of the original document, I have attempted to give a summary of what I remember to be the key issues raised in the speech as I was part of the principal architects of the document.

The speech highlighted in detail the failures of the entire exiled leadership of ZAPU as follows:

1. Five ZAPU members of the National Executive in exile with a mission to wage a war of liberation against the Rhodesian Front regime exhibited their strategic shallowness by their outburst in documentary accusations and counter-accusations of each other in public in February and March 1970 respectively.

2. The worst part was their admission, in their documents and in front of the fighters at Camps C1/2 and DK, that there was no strategy and no guerrilla warfare to fight the Rhodesian Front regime; to them all the efforts and human waste to date was sabotage campaign to frighten the Rhodesian Front regime into accepting round table negotiations on majority rule; yet guerrillas thought they were trained and deployed to launch guerrilla warfare as a first phase to wear down the enemy's military power.

3. In doing this, leaders placed their revolutionary myopia in the public domain without giving some thought as to how the fighters and ordinary members of ZAPU would react to such an unashamed destruction of ZAPU.

4. ZAPU was the main vehicle of national liberation in Zimbabwe at the time but the leaders treated the organisation like a private company gone bankrupt.

5. Instead of making some effort to be seen as a constructive team, they lifted high a banner pronouncing their retreat to tribal enclaves from which to seek comfort within narrow parameters of primitivism.

6. Instead of providing an analysis of the situation on the nature of weaknesses and strengths of the belligerent forces in the country and how to strategise on that, they degenerated into the level of antiquated village chiefs in dispute over succession to the throne.

7. So, the fallout was the consequence of inability to find a better and appropriate strategy to overthrow the Smith's Rhodesian Front regime at a time when there was a compelling need for a comprehensive review of whole strategy and tactics in the backdrop of a series of tragic failures in field operations.

8. It was this failure that exploded into a quarrel between them thus disqualifying themselves from leading a revolution of the nature that needed a leadership of depth in thought to plan sound strategies and capability in execution of planned strategies.

9. Their strategic shallowness helped to reveal their concept of freedom fighters that they treated and used them like automatons that did not deserve to know whether they were guerrillas or saboteurs; this further exposed their ignorance in that sabotage in guerrilla warfare is part of core elements for dislocating enemy physical infrastructure

10. Their deliberate pursuit of a hidden agenda of sabotage made them shun to spell out the main goal and fundamental objectives of liberation pertaining to what a liberated Zimbabwe would look like say, like the Freedom Charter of the ANC of South Africa.

11. As far as the fighters were concerned, the time had come to realise and recognise a guerrilla as a politically motivated fighter whose military involvement in the struggle was to rally the masses behind a political programme of national liberation.

12. Such a programme should be based on the premise that liberation was a revolutionary process focusing on attainment of freedom and social justice in a liberated society.

13. Above all, a guerrilla is an angry citizen whose anger is instigated by injustice of a repressive system of governance in his or her country.

14. In this respect a guerrilla is a self-developed politician who volunteers to fight and get crafted into a military freedom fighter for justice wherein lies the need to function within a disciplined military formation under a leadership of sound political and military perspective.

15. In this regard, a guerrilla cannot be treated in a mechanistic fashion like a conventional soldier who is managed through unquestionable orders from above.

16. Our leaders failed to understand the transcendence from a civilian driven struggle for majority rule to a revolutionary process driven by fire power guided by an enlightened revolutionary leadership with clear goals of freedom for a liberated nation.

17. Having torn leadership cohesion apart by taking refuge in tribal cocoons, their positions have become irreconcilable between themselves let alone between themselves and the freedom fighters because tribalism and revolution are dialectically antagonistic to each other as the former reverts to and thrives in primitivism while the latter is propelled by the dynamics of social transformation towards a better society

18. On this account, a proposal was put forward that all five members of the National Executive Committee in exile, consisting of James D Chikerema Deputy President, George B Nyandoro, Secretary General, Jason Z Moyo, Treasurer General, George T Silundika, Information Secretary and Edward Ndlovu Deputy Sevretary General should be suspended from leadership for the duration of the struggle or until a ZAPU elective congress was held (whichever would come first) to decide their fate.

As Comrade Mthimkhulu formally moved a motion to suspend the five leaders for the duration of the struggle or until an elective congress of ZAPU was held, the Minister intervened and declared that the motion implied that the choice was between rejecting Joshua Nkomo's leadership and remaining loyal to him. He therefore declared that those who rejected Joshua Nkomo should stand up and move to the left and those loyal to him to the right. Before they stood up the fighters clarified that they were still loyal to Comrade Joshua Nkomo. But they were going to move to the left to show their rejection of the exiled leadership of five as stated in the motion. Almost the entire force of the freedom fighters present moved to the left and the leaders together with the Minister seemed shocked by the large numbers that moved to the left. They never expected what they saw.

That vote signified a decisive rejection of the divided leadership of ZAPU in exile and an effort to break with the visionless era towards creation of space for revolutionary forces to emerge and lead the armed struggle in a principled direction. That was a chance for ZAPU to transcend the phase of narrow nationalism to enter a phase of broad path of revolutionary transformation of a repressive system into a progressive system based on the will of the people. The removal of sabotage-wedded leadership would enable the movement to decisively discard the degenerative tendencies of tribalism and nepotism. That was supposed to create an opportunity to craft a bundle of principles that would articulate a definite programme of action with definite set of liberation goals. Other parties in Southern Africa cemented diverse ethnic entities into one nation through well spelt out principles on fundamental requirements and entitlements of their free nation as a goal of the struggle. For example in Zambia the United National Independence Party (UNIP) adopted what they called a 'Philosophy of Humanism' upon which the strategy of detribalisation of the Zambian society was pivoted. In spite of the controversial mode of governance of the first President of Zambia, the adoption of the philosophy actually was the product of realisation by the UNIP leadership that society was made up of different tribes with distinct cultures, customs and traditions. To expand the parameters of nationhood they had to lay emphasis and importance on the common denominator of human beings inhabiting a territory called Zambia. So they had to recognise themselves as one Nation sharing the resources of one territory of Zambia. In this regard Humanism was partly defined as social cement that holds together and inspires young people and a varied nation that is Zambia. The Leadership invoked the fundamental principles of **Ubuntu** (a long standing tradition that defines the core values of humanity redefined from an African cultural perspective) to instil nationhood on the basis of human dignity which was seen as the same dress for all not with tribal colours but with one colour of humanity. This way, all Zambians became able to regard each other as atoms of one nation. Hence "One Zambia One Nation" Today, Zambia enjoys a high degree of national cohesion on the basis of the aforesaid Philosophy of Humanism. Zambians hardly talk about their tribes before mentioning their Zambian nationality. Is it the same in Zimbabwe?

The African National Congress of South Africa adopted a Freedom Charter far back in 1955 which became the focus upon which the majority of the anti-Apartheid activists rallied until the attainment of democracy in that country. The Freedom Charter became one of the sources of consultation when a democratic constitution was drafted along the fundamentals that ventilated the Chrter's liberating principles. Unlike the aforesaid examples of creating unifying national programmes or philosophies, ZAPU did not have any scientifically substantiated articulation of a societal developmental agenda that would have accommodated each and every citizen of Zimbabwe during and after the liberation struggle. The absence of such a framework or programme allowed tribal consciousness to easily supersede national consciousness as there were no guiding principles that constituted a unifying catalyst such as in the Freedom Charter and the Philosophy of Humanism. ZANU too suffered from the same lack of vision for a free Zimbabwe.

The 'old' NDP slogan of **Mwanawebvu** was no longer in vogue in our leader's scheme of things. Therefore it was easy for them to tear apart the mighty ZAPU into tribal-oriented factions without shame. In this regard, the Mboroma Speech from the fighters was meant to close this vacuum by developing a revolutionary programme that defined the parameters of what a liberated Zimbabwean society was going to look like in terms of upholding freedoms, peoples' rights, civil liberties and social justice in terms of socioeconomic transformation and development. In this connection, there were sufficient compelling factors to cause the Zambian Government to listen closely to the fighters who displayed remarkable unity of purpose on that fateful day by presenting concrete proposals for solving the crisis and re-craft a new strategy of national liberation. Unfortunately the fighters' plea for constructive change was brushed aside by the facilitating Zambian Minister. That was a lost opportunity to rejuvenate the organisation into a cutting edge to take on the Rhodesian Front regime in a systematic and calculated approach.

CHAPTER TWENTY ONE

THE DECIMATION OF ZIPRA AND THE RISE AND CHALLENGES OF THE MARCH 11 MOVEMENT

At the end of the meeting the Minister seemed to play down the motion that was adopted by the overwhelming majority of the fighters. He merely mentioned that the Government would ensure that the leaders were reunited with a fresh resolve so that they could resume the armed struggle. It became clear to us that the facilitator was not taking us forward in respect of the proposals contained in our keynote speech. We were contemplating sending a delegation to President Kaunda to present our case directly to him about our concern regarding treating the divided leaders with kid gloves and failure to move forward. Before long the Zambian Paramilitary Police assembled us and announced that the trained cadres should be separated from the recruits. So a contingent of trained personnel were taken down the slope of the valley westwards and settled near a river to the east. In the east of us was a small but deep pond which was filled by water flowing down an overarching rock. The water in the pond was clean and very cold. The entire hinterland of the pond was quite cold, which means our new camp was a cold place and we named it **"The Fridge."** Since the camp was close to the recruits' camp, they joined us within days and no one attempted to take them back.

However, after two months of our stay at The Fridge, a gentle talking officer of the Paramilitary Police arrived and went round the camp talking to comrades. On the second day he invited us to an assembly where he called out forty one names of comrades whom he described as a delegation to meet the President in Lusaka. It became clear to us that such a large number of fighters could not be a delegation and we refused to comply until the truth was told. It was quite clear to us that the Government was no longer on the mode of facilitating a conflict resolution process to end the ZAPU leadership crisis. We demanded that they should tell the truth about what was going to happen to that number of fighters. At this point a paramilitary force the strength of about a company in military terms had surrounded us at the assembly point. Many comrades called for defiance and stiff resistance to the order. They even suggested that we should seize weapons from the paramilitary police and escape towards the Zambezi River which was about a thousand kilometres to the south of us. We discouraged such an adventurous proposition but wanted the officer to announce that we were under arrest. Realising that the fighters could not budge, the commanding officer of the paramilitary unit admitted that we were being taken away for detention at an undisclosed place. Tensions rose to the highest but we still persuaded the comrades against use of force against Zambian authorities of any description. As we respected the sovereignty of the

Zambian state, we reluctantly obliged to submit ourselves to government authority. So forty one of us were taken away on a troop carrier, first to an undisclosed destination but it turned out to be Northern Town of Kasama near the border with Tanzania. But before we reached destination two of the comrades had escaped. We proceeded to Kasama and finished up at Milima Prison about two kilometres north of Kasama, 800 kilometres from Lusaka near the Tanzanian border. This (detention of the core leadership of the combat fighters) marked the beginning of the end of the road for ZAPU as a leading engine of national liberation in Zimbabwe. For some of us the Zambian act of detaining us placed a barrier against our resumption of active service in the liberation armed struggle of our country.

The main question here is, in spite of the irrefutable evidence of a huge gap between JZ Moyo's Dengezi and JD Chikerema's group, on what account did the Zambian government stand behind them and disregard the call to assist the fighters to solve the crisis amicably. It might be due to old friendship league where President Kenneth Kaunda was suspicious that the radical fighters might oust his political ally, Joshua Nkomo or he thought the radicalism might develop into a socialist revolutionary movement that could set a precedent in Southern Africa with far reaching ramifications for the region in general and Zambia in particular. For our part, we genuinely expected the Zambian Government to be well informed about our situation and desire to fight for the liberation of our country uninhibited. Then why the negativity without coming up with a constructive alternative proposal to solve the problem at hand? We had made our views and intentions known to the Government, first through the prior diplomatic manoeuvres in every key office of the state including the President's Office. The second phase of our contact with the Government was through the facilitating Minister, Mr Aaron Milner and Secretary General to the Government. Milner was holding a key position (similar to Prime Minister) in the Zambian Government therefore well placed to comprehend the difference between genuine political matters and hypocrisy in terms empty self-glorification. Above all he was a Zimbabwean who immigrated to Northern Rhodesia before independence, participated in the struggle for freedom as a member of UNIP and finished up adopting Zambian citizenship.

When thirty nine of us were taken away to Milima Prison, the rest of the fighters remained in Mboroma. The Government attempted to order the rest of the comrades back to the leaders. They even tried to use force but without success. Some escaped from the camp and mingled with the Zambian population while others joined ZANU. Those who remained at the camp were taken in troop carriers and driven to the Rhodesian border and handed over to the Smith regime on a silver platter. We first heard about the deportations from the BBC Focus on Africa programme news. We could not believe the story because we trusted that the Zambian leadership was passionately dedicated to the freedom of all of Africa at all means including armed struggle. So it was unthinkable that the Government could send freedom fighters to their enemy for slaughter. It was not until a civilian ZAPU member found a way of informing us about the fate of our comrades. We feared that most of the comrades so deported would be sentenced to death for their participation in battles against the Rhodesian security forces. So, that was the price the fighters had to pay for rejecting our counter revolutionary leaders who unwittingly degenerated into tribal cocoons after dismally failing to lead armed struggle.

It was difficult to decipher Zambia's reasons for sending trained and battle tested and seasoned freedom fighters to their enemy knowing full well that they would face a death sentence and that is exactly what happened. Especially at a time when ZAPU leadership in exile was a shambles and the fighters were united and determined to continue the fighting on a better strategy. Some observers went to the extent of suggesting that Zambia exchanged the maize meal with fighters as per agreement with the Rhodesian regime. But there was no evidence of this even though there was maize delivered to Zambia from Rhodesia following the deportations. Another explanation was that the fighters had become too radical for the Zambian Government to tolerate their presence on its soil. There were fears that the fighters had internalised the Marxist-Leninist revolutionary ideology considered to be a threat to capitalism, which was a pearl of Western multi-national corporations in Southern Africa. But did this justify handing over to the enemy people who had fought in Wankie, Sipolilo, Umvukwes, Chirundu, Kariba and many other fronts? Above all the comrades were not violent against the Zambian authorities. The whole effort of trying to resolve the ZAPU leadership crisis was not vicious to the extent that it should have ignited the wrath of the Zambian Government. After all we had done a lot of diplomatic ironing up relations between the Government and fighters by extensive consultations with politicians and senior government officials. Therefore they were well aware that the ZAPU crisis might explode if no action was taken in advance to resolve it amicably. But we made sure that there was no such explosion of violence against any one on the Zambian soil. Every move we took or one forced upon us by the Government it flowed smoothly as if it was not handled by the military personnel. This was deliberately meant to be so because we respected the Zambian sovereignty as well as portray the fighters as capable of producing responsible leadership without use of force where it was not necessary such as on the Zambian soil. The evidence of all this could be seen in the comrades' conduct to maintain a strict line of discipline even under exceedingly trying conditions like the fact that they were deported to Rhodesia without fighting the Zambian Government. The fact that in the ZAPU crisis there were no fatalities nor injuries showed clearly that there was nothing in our plans that included use of military fire power to achieve our objectives as long as we were on the Zambian soil. There is overwhelming evidence to show that ZPRA freedom fighters were drilled to respect the Zambian authorities under all circumstances prevailing over them while they were on the Zambian soil. Surely what else could have we done to deal with leaders who had become a self dissected bunch of incorrigible failures to the point of destroying a liberation movement that had a crucial role in the liberation of Zimbabwe?

The fighters' presentation in Mboroma was vindicated when the divided leaders openly demonstrated their irreconcilable differences by taking their parting ways with one faction forming a Front for the Liberation of Zimbabwe (FROLIZI) and another remaining in the dormant main stream of ZAPU until they were resurrected by teaming up with ZANU to form Joint Military Command (JMC). The FROLIZI faction finished up conniving with the Rhodesian Front regime in what was called "internal settlement" (meaning cooperation with the Rhodesian Front regime). Clearly, the freedom fighters were right to reject the leaders who were already committed to their parting ways, thus abandoning armed struggle and its fighters scattered in various dungeons in Rhodesia and Zambia. Was it really wise for a frontline state of impeccable political credentials to trust the obviously untrustworthy leaders some of whom finished up submitting themselves to the Rhodesian regime in a treacherous internal settlement with cap in hand? All this was done at the expense of the fighters who had come to know the political behaviour of their leaders very closely enough to see through their empty promises to the Zambian government. Everybody in this fiasco made serious blunders. But, with due respect, the Zambian government made a tragic strategic error of judgement that cost ZAPU its viability as an armed liberation movement, thus disabling it to nearly one hundred percent disability that marked the beginning of its demise as a national movement. The Zambian government had all the opportunity to assist the fighters at Mboroma Meeting to pick up the pieces and come up with a revival plan that would have lead to the resumption of armed struggle with a brand new guerrilla war fare strategy by the end of 1971. The situation could have ended differently in Zimbabwean political landscape at independence.

When talking about ZPRA is not the same thing as talking about a regular army whose primary role is to defend a country under the charge of a government. ZPRA freedom fighters were politically motivated fighters who volunteered to fight for the freedom of their country by waging a guerrilla war (which other authorities call 'peoples' war'). In this respect the overwhelming majority in our forces were politicians in our own right who held responsible positions in the structures of our Party before and after it was banned. Before we joined armed struggle we were in the political structures of the Party with or without positions. I, for example, grew up with politics from primary school day's right through the rough times in the youth movement where I experienced both surface politics and underground subversion against Rhodesian repression. In doing all this I went through constant harassment by the Rhodesian Special Branch till I fled the country. There were many others who had similar or worse experience in civilian activism. In this respect, we were seasoned activists who became fighters before we joined armed struggle. We started and developed techniques of planning clandestine operations and managed to link our activities with semi-surface and surface politics in terms of command and accountability. Our prior leaning ahead of military training started with close contacts with freedom fighters inside the country for several years to the extent of acquiring fundamentals of guerrilla warfare in terms of its strength and weaknesses. That is to say ZPRA reached the people and assessed the readiness of the masses far and wide before they began to pull the trigger against the Rhodesian security forces at their own initiative. As the masses were found to be ready as early as 1963, this suggests that if the exiled leadership had a sound strategy, they could have had a profound impact on the Rhodesian security forces by the beginning of the 1970s. After the dismal failure on the part of leadership the mantle was supposed to fall on to the cadres to pick up the flag and drive armed struggle with knowledge and skills that were accumulated over the years of field operations and training.

In this regard, the art of strategic and operational planning were not entirely new to us, we merely perfected them through military training. We had long experience in self acting creation of a machinery to forge a particular political action within the parameters of the requirements of the liberation struggle in the context of civilian activism. Now that, we had added value to our original capabilities, it was time to combine all that experience with new military skills to cause a paradigm shift towards a well designed military strategy and tactics in pursuance of revolutionary transformation of the politics of tribal chauvinism to the politics of national democratic revolution and social cohesion. A replacement of the exiled leaders would have given fighters the opportunity to demonstrate continuity and development from the rudimental operational planning (during the days of Zhanda and the Formidable) to an advanced level of enhanced capability in terms of combining these prior learning experiences with military expertise in both intelligence gathering and combat operations all driven by a political revolutionary machinery. That is why in our keynote speech at the Mboroma meeting we declared that we were not automatons of any sort. To make things even brighter, within our rising movement there were all specialities that made the fighters a self-contained guerrilla army capable of tackling political, social, economical and military matters adequately. Therefore they were capable of assessing the political situation in relation to military requirements in the theatre of operation in terms of identifying the political dynamics that could enable or hinder the process of armed struggle.

In our canvassing the comrades prior to the Mboroma meeting, we had succeeded in winning the support of all departments of ZPRA at the level of foot soldiers and commanders at all levels except Military Administration. These included the very important and key elements such as Intelligence, Logistics, Communications and all Combat Forces and their commanders. So it was possible to obtain all the crucial information through the Intelligence Service that was deployed behind the enemy lines and within the enemy ranks. The support of all these departments of ZPRA fighters meant that we had the entire ZPRA regiment and other resources to address every aspect of preparing and executing a peoples' war until the regime became weak to the extent of losing the initiative. After all the ZAPU Intelligence service was the most successful operating organ of ZPRA in terms infiltration into the country to be able to supply reliable information about the situation regarding deployment of security forces operating in the rural areas. They had succeeded in infiltrating the country and identified the enemy's strengths and weaknesses in a professional way. With all the ready-to-go systems of the fighters, the military capability of ZPRA was in a position to be galvanized into action on the basis of what I have just described. On this account, it was a huge political error for the Zambian Government to treat freedom fighters like common criminals who were caught doing crime. Surely it was not worth it to stand with a leadership that had clearly retreated to tribal enclaves to which they attempted to drag their fellow tribesmen with them; thus, tearing ZAPU apart and diminishing the military viability of ZPRA. The arresting of freedom fighters and sending some of them to enemy hands was inexcusable by any reasonable measure of political consideration. No one would have expected those comrades to be welcomed with bread and butter by the Rhodesian authorities.

We have always wondered what the Zambian Government could have lost if it decided to let ZPRA freedom fighters take responsibility for Zimbabwe's liberation armed struggle at that time. After all, four years after us, in 1975, ZANLA and ZPRA combined to form Zimbabwe Peoples' Army (ZIPA) to resume and continue the struggle without political leaders. They formed a Military Committee to take the role of a High Command. The Military Committee was similar to our Revolutionary Council formed prior to Mboroma Conference in1971. By all accounts, indications are that armed struggle under ZIPA reached unprecedented levels of effectiveness in scale and intensity since fighting was launched in the mid 1960s. ZIPA proved that dedicated fighters with clear military and political objectives did not need armchair political leaders to command them. The way ZIPA was set up and motivated to resume a paralysed armed struggle, was exactly what we wanted to do but were denied it by the Zambian Government. ZIPA was lucky because of their proximity to a President (Samora Machel) who was a seasoned and progressive ex-freedom fighter. **Manda's** account of ZIPA's rise and fall shows a lot of similarity between our endeavour and what they did. The major differences were that they were given a chance to demonstrate that they were committed and capable to fight systematically without political leaders. In our case, even if we were committed and capable, we were not given a chance to prove ourselves in the battlefield. Internal problems notwithstanding, ZIPA scored significant successes in uniting two Zimbabwean liberation armies into one combat force that was able (with blessing from President Machel) to resume the war yet we were prevented (by Zambian Government) from doing a similar thing four years earlier. We finished up deported to different countries including Rhodesia itself and went down flat and bleeding from the hands of our own brothers (Zambians). But other features of their efforts, challenges and fate were similar to our situation. If they had remained in Zambia, the indications are that they could have suffered the same fate that we experienced. The mistake they made was to remain loyal to reactionary politicians with tragic consequences (**Mhanda, 2011**). But, in spite of all of that, armed struggle had become an unstoppable gale storm that engulfed the country in an increasing scale and ferocity.

The comrades, who were deported to Rhodesia, on arrival in the country, were divided into categories ranging from the least dangerous (recruits) to the most dangerous (trained personnel). On trial, some of the latter were sentenced to death and others to life imprisonment, depending on whether the trained person took part in fighting or not. The recruits were given short sentences and released. The question is who gained out of all this mess? We, of ZPRA, lost badly because we did not gain the opportunity to put our strategy into effect. We were defeated because we did not use maximum force to drive home our objectives of transforming ZAPU into a revolutionary movement to lead the masses to victory without allowing our adversaries to dictate terms of how to end the war in Zimbabwe. But we were on foreign land where there were compelling factors against use of maximum force to remove the divided leaders. Another option that we missed was that we could have picked up the leaders, transported them rapidly to the Zambezi valley where we could have negotiated on a position of strength with the Zambian Government, entrenched in our own bases well covered by a terrain suitable for swallowing the entire guerrilla force instantly if matters got to a head (similar to what the ZANLA forces did when the Zambian Army attempted to force them to integrate with Zimbabwe Liberation Council; a baby of detente, they just disappeared into the thicket of a surrounding forest) (Mhanda, 2011).

One of our mistakes is that after arresting the leaders we took them to no more than twenty kilometres from the capital, Lusaka. This put us on a strategically weak position thus giving the Zambian Government an upper hand in all dealings concerning the whole leadership handling. There is an element of truth that this was partly because we trusted that the Government understood our case very well owing to the extensive consultations we made before we took action. Apparently, we were wrong and we paid heavily for the mistake. The fact that we did not fire a short testifies to the fact that ZPRA fighters fully respected the Zambian territory, people and government. We do not regret that we did not adopt a more combative stance against the Zambian government because that would have damaged our ZAPU-UNIP relations beyond repair recollecting what happened to Jonas Savimbi's UNITA movement when it was expelled from Zambia for sabotaging a railway line that was of strategic importance to Zambia. If we adopted the Zambezi Valley option, described above, we could have succeeded without clashing with the Zambian security forces. Our softly handling approach to the whole issue of ZAPU leaders in exile, landed us into prison and ultimately into political oblivion.

Milima Prison

The first step to political oblivion was Milima Prison. Yet we were still optimistic about our possibility to return to armed struggle. We arrived in the morning in the town of Kasama and drove a few kilometres towards the Tanznia border to Milima Prison. It was a medium security complex with two divisions; one for convicted prisoners and the other for detainees. We were the first detainees of the season but there was no sign that the wing was occupied in recent times before us. We were welcomed by the superintendent of the prison, Mr Muyunda, whose demeanour was endowed with gentility that befits a position of principal of a teacher training college rather than a punitive institution. His sense of humour was rich with effervescence of amusement that would ignite laughter even from the hard hearted characters. When turning to official matters he presented himself correctly as a senior officer of the uniformed services of state. Then he unpacked to us a bungle of entitlements and conditions under which we were to be subjected and the limited rights that were in our favour. The rights included the right to send our grievances straight to the

President of the Republic of Zambia via the Prison Senior Superintendent. He left us with clear understanding of what was expected of us and what we expected from the prison officers.

The group of thirty four was divided into two groups with each group allocated a dormitory. We met to brainstorm options regarding how we could find a way out of prison. We decided that the first thing was to formally adopt the name of **March 11 Movement** deriving the name from the date we rounded up our leaders. Since the core of the previous Revolutionary Council was present in the group, we decided to elect a new leadership to lead the movement in its own right as an emerging revolutionary movement. We elected a Revolutionary Council of fifteen comrades who were mandated to elect a an Executive Committee of five with a Chairman, Deputy Chairman, Secretary and two committee members.

The RC met promptly and elected five members with Philemon Mabuza, as Chairman deputised by Masikidze Gutu, Joshua Mpofu Secretary. The other three were Zwelibanzi Mzilethi, and Jabulani Mazula. We returned to the General Assembly for endorsement and it was done. We then appointed one we called Chief of Staff who was responsible for administration and the wellbeing of the comrades in that camp. We appointed Israel Khupe for this task which he performed beyond expectation. Chief of staff's responsibilities included taking care of the welfare of comrades in terms diet, health matters, and all the material needs of the comrades in the camp. He was also responsible for drawing up a time table for man on duty (comrades took turns to be on duty in the camp for a day) addressed the physical fitness of the comrades in terms exercises and morale. At the same time we decided to grow vegetables, sweet potatoes and paw paws for consumption and sale. We appointed comrade Livingstone Mashengele to be in charge of the garden and the plantation as he was the only one with qualifications in Agriculture. Mashengele managed the garden project with amazing efficiency leading to high productivity. Our man-on-duty shifted his time table from exercises to work teams in the garden daily. So each man-on-duty drew a time table of work on the day he was on duty. This provided Mashengele with much needed labour for the garden project. Within a short period of time the garden became a flourishing commercial enterprise by any standard. Paw paws not only added beauty of the garden outlook, they essentially provided a source of nutrition for us. Our garden was the envy of the prison community and neighbourhood. They admired it because there was a local clinic inside our wing of the prison where members of the public came for treatment so they saw the flourishing garden. Above all we were allowed to sell the vegetables to the residents of the prison compound (staffers and families). All of this made life a bit liveable in the circumstances.

Meanwhile we had to address the pressing needs of the comrades regarding finding the ways of returning to the struggle as soon as possible. Some comrades were not convinced that the Zambian government could tolerate those leaders who washed their dirty linen in public with impunity. In this regard the RC assigned the EC to find ways of how we could get out of prison at the possible earliest time to return to armed struggle. We decided to write a letter to the President of the Republic of Zambia asking for release or dialogue with him to spell out our desire to resume armed struggle about which we were on the Zambian soil on transit. We felt that we should not express bitterness for having been detained for rejecting a divisive leadership. The General Assembly deliberated the issue of our fate exhaustively and finally agreed to write such a letter using carefully chosen verbiage. We were given an official form to write on it. The letter was well drafted and despatched via the Senior Prison Superintendent, Mr Mwale.

We were in a very remote part of Zambia where none of us had reached before so we thought of establishing extra-legal channels of correspondence with the outside world. To this end we cultivated good relations between ourselves and the prison warders in order to create such channels of communication and we were delighted that they opened up in no time. Reaching an agreement with some of the warders to handle our mail outside the system opened windows for informing our comrades and other stakeholders about our whereabouts and what our intentions were. Once commenced, correspondence flourished unimpeded to and from the outside world within and outside Zambia.

The easy establishment of communication was an indication that on matters of justice and fairness it is not possible to place a watertight enclosure around a champion of justice who aspires to improve the human condition where there is injustice. The Milima warders were quite aware of the struggle in Zimbabwe and they were genuinely sympathetic to us as they perceived our cause to be a just one as it was propelled by the desire to remove the unjust UDI regime in our country. They felt that the presence of that regime across their borders was a menace to Zambia as well. The quicker it was removed the better not only for Zimbabweans but for Zambians too. In assisting us to correspond with others they believed that they were facilitating our early release so that we could go and challenge the UDI regime in battle. It was interesting to note that some of them were aware of President Kaunda's famous liberation cross-border song which went thus:

"Kaunda tieni, oh! tieni bo, tiyambuke Zambezi nemtima umozi..................."
"Kaunda let us go, oh let us go and cross the Zambezi River in one spirit"

The warders felt that our detention ran counter to the spirit of the song and the official policy of the Government. They therefore believed that it was right for them to help us as much as possible if that was going to facilitate our release to return to armed struggle.

There was a political phenomenon that has been hardly mentioned by any one in their stories on Zimbabwe's war of national liberation. It was a deeply influential stand that crystallised at the same time as the formative phase of the March 11 Movement (M11) just before the arrest of leaders in March 1971. It steadily developed into a nucleus of comrades who were hard core Marxists- Leninists within the M11. They were the ones that masterminded the rise of the M11 but without a formal structure of their own to start with. The M11 embraced almost the entire ZPRA regiment except those who were contaminated by tribal inclinations that made them stick with tribal factions of discredited leaders. The like minded 'progressives' met in Milima Prison after the M11 was formed. We decided that our national revolution would be based on the ideology of Socialism whereupon we encouraged comrades to study Marxist-Leninist literature.

Meanwhile key members of the M11 decided to form a structured core organisation that should politicise the comrades into the Marxist-Leninist Theory behind the scenes then admit those we considered qualified to be part of the core, more or less like the IBS within the student association at Nyathi Secondary School in the early 1960s. About twelve of us met and decided to form a core circle called the TU as a camouflaging name before it was given a proper name when it became larger. I was elected its first Chairman and deputised by Matsikidze Gutu. The task of the TU was to rapidly encourage all comrades to read Marxist literature in order to understand and internalise it as a guide to revolutionary transformation of moribund political and social systems in Zimbabwe after first going through a national democratic revolution, which was on top of the agenda in our national liberation struggle. The TU's first task was to endeavour to engulf the entire M11 into a progressive Marxist Movement without giving it the name of a Marxist name for a long time until the objective and subjective conditions in the country landed themselves to a possibility of the occurrence of a thoroughgoing revolutionary transformation of society. The core group actually grew quite fast within the M11 because there were many comrades who were exposed to the Marxist theory during training or in the camps where literature was in abundance.

However, after spending one year in Milima prison, a serious fissure occurred within the M11. One comrade of the core group leaked the information prematurely about its existence to the non members of the core group. That caused anger that almost led to violent conflict. It was such a serious blow up to the extent that the prison authorities separated us into two groups. The situation actually caused a devastating blow on the M11 strength. We only succeeded to calm the situation on reminding each other that all this should be directed to our common enemy, the Smith regime therefore there was no need to be bedevilled by it to the point of failing to wage the struggle. Comrades seemed to appreciate that approach but not before bitter verbal attack on the leadership of the M11. The issue healed up over a period of time

Visits by political groups

Within a short period of our stay we had visitors from ZAPU delegation consisting of Dumiso Dabengwa and Sikhwili Moyo (a member of the National Executive). Their mission was to persuade us to join JZ Moyo's faction, claiming that they were the main stream of ZAPU as James Chikerema had teamed up with Nathan Shamuyarira to form Front for the Liberation of Zimbabwe (FROLIZI). We found it inconceivable for us to adopt Dengezi as the main stream of ZAPU which was no different from FROLIZI in tribal outlook and shallowness in national goals. We declined decisively to join them. Shamuyarira, too was generous with books most of which were very good literature on African culture and ancient systems. Some of them were text books which were very useful for our studies that we had started.

Soon after their departure we received information from one of our contacts within the Dengezi camp that the delegation wanted us to commit ourselves to ZAPU and they were going to use that commitment to negotiate with the Zambian Government for our release. Thereafter they would take us to the Zambezi Valley to eliminate all of us by a firing squad on charges of treason for arresting them. He said that he was present when the decision to eliminate us by firing squad was taken. He then strongly warned us not to accept their offer because it was a trap. Actually this was confirmation of our suspicion because we could not believe that Dengezi could reconcile with us so fast and easily without prior negotiations and conditions.

Studies in Prison

One of the most important decisions we took was to start a school starting from the lowest grade to "A" Level. All those with "O" Level and above were assigned to teach the rest of the comrades. We had enough teachers to teach all grades in all subjects that the comrades identified. Technical subjects such as mathematics, Biology, Economics, Geography were well covered because they were taught by graduate teachers. English Language, History, Principles of Accounts, and those required by Zambia Junior Certificate were also well resourced, including textbooks which were sent to us by Nathan Shamuyarira. Actually, he sent dozens of books that were of good use for our purposes at the time. Even if we differed with him in politics, we appreciated the amount of help that he provided in the form of books that kept us busy throughout our stay in Zambian prisons. Some comrades went through Zambia Junior Certificate and finished up with "O" Level from London. Those who started at "O" Level finished up with "A" Level. Those with "A" Levels and degrees were busy teaching as well as reading literature of their interest. At the end of the day many comrades attained some qualifications while in prison. In Zimbabwe it was also a tradition for political prisoners to embark on education as soon as they were in prison. Studies tend to alleviate the effect of depression and trauma caused by factors of spending days in and days out under lock and key surrounded by concrete wall or wrought iron fence with spikes at the top.

Some Disturbing Developments

About six or seven months after detention there was an unfortunate incident which threatened to damage our good relations with prison staffers. One of our comrades escaped without notifying us and we were made to suffer for this escape because the authorities believed that it was planned collectively. We were then kept locked up in one cell for twenty four hours until we put forward a very strong protest. Senior officers came from Head office to sort out the crisis that was threatening to get out of hand. We were not happy with one man effort to escape without our knowledge. I say so because we had appointed an escape committee to look into a possibility of escaping by storm. In this regard we had begun to find ways to seize the warders' weapons and use them for mass escape without raising an alarm. Fortunately the authorities read the situation correctly and they defused it by relaxing the stringent restrictions on our day to day movement around the prison precincts. During our exchange of words with officers they could decipher that many people had become so daring that they could do anything in desperation.

At this point we had heard about the comrades who were deported to Rhodesia so the fear factor had diminished to zero as we felt that the worst fate was hovering over our heads. Therefore we were prepared to demonstrate that we could not stand idle by while unjustified punitive measures were imposed on us. In all of this the chain of events had vindicated our position regarding the failure of the Zambian government to unify our leaders without our involvement in the whole process. The deportation of our comrades and the irreparable split of the leaders showed how flawed the Government's decisions were as none of them was constructive in terms of contributing to the resolution of the ZAPU leadership crisis that would have created conditions conducive to resumption of armed struggle. Detaining and deporting freedom fighters must have delighted Ian Douglas Smith and his supporters to the highest degree because it was tantamount to demobilising more than three detachments of a guerrilla army. How could we be expected to celebrate all these man-made tragedies?

However, the escaped comrade was recaptured and that eased the situation a little more until it went back to "normal." A positive aspect of our comrade's escape and recapture was a sudden gelling of the entire group into one as before and this led to healing up the crack that had bedeviled our cohesion. We resumed our normal practices such as working under same leadership and holding meetings in one assembly as before. We then devised a plan that one of us should get out legally in order to fight for our release by involving humanitarian organisations and other countries to put pressure on the Zambian Government to release us so that we could go and fight again. We went on a prolonged hunger strike that took three full weeks. At the end of the third week some of us became ill and were sent to Kasama Hospital. We had to spot-search for a sympathetic doctor and we found one. We assigned one of us, Joe Zwelibanzi Mzilethi, to cultivate close friendship with the doctor and then persuade her to create conditions that would persuade the government to release him soonest. She reluctantly agreed as she noticed that the comrade who approached her was so thin from hunger strike that he looked as though he was on the brink of crossing a "terminal line."

Likewise she recommended that his condition could only be treated overseas. The Zambian Government accepted doctor's recommendations and fast-tracked the issuing of his passport to travel to the UK. Comrade J Z Mzilethi was released for health reasons and deported to the UK. Before he departed we briefed him about what he should do out there on our behalf. The only problem with our comrade was that he did not regard the word compromise as part of his vocabulary in political negotiations. Some comrades feared that he might be unable to strike some deals to get us out, especially if some compromise was required. This appeared quite probable because he emphatically stated to us that he would not like all of us to be deported out of Zambia. He would want the Zambian government to be persuaded to transport us to the Zambezi valley, to our transit camps on the Zambian side and leave us to chart our path to the theatre of operation to deal with the Rhodesian regime. We had to give him an order that he was being given a mission by the fighters to be flexible and reasonable as long as we got out of jail so that we could find our way back to the struggle. He did not comment on this directive from us until he was released and deported to the UK. We remained behind entertaining a lot of optimism about our possible release now that some of our numbers were out and talking to the world on our behalf.

On arrival Mzilethi linked up with my wife, Ratie, who was a student in Birmingham Orthopaedic Hospital, training as a Physiotherapist. Both became a formidable team because Mzilethi had inside knowledge of our situation as a detainee in Zambian prison. Ratie was familiar with the British system of dealing with advocacy. Their campaign gained considerable of momentum.

Sudden transfer to a prison near the border with Rhodesia

Meanwhile our hopes were dashed when we were transferred to Livingstone Prison, nine hundred kilometres south of Milima Prison and seven kilometres from the border with hostile Rhodesia. It was June 1973, about two years since we were detained in Milima Prison. We began to suspect that the Government was preparing to deport us to Rhodesia, like it did to our 129 comrades. The court yard in Livingstone Prison was very small but the dormitories were decent and officers were cautious in managing us and our demands. That is, they paid careful attention to all demands such as the quality of food we ate.

In Livingstone we had three visits from ZANU senior officials. The first was Comrade Henry Hamadziripi, a member of the Central Committee and **Dare reChimrenga** in exile. He was very clear as to what he was up to: that ZANU had opened a vast operational territory inside the country but they lacked experienced commanders to drive an effective guerrilla campaign. They felt that our group had the calibre of the commanders they needed in field operations. It was true we had comrades who had been to operations inside the country before March 11, 1971. Comrade Hamadziripi's visit was followed by that of Comrade Rugare Gumbo, also a member of Dare reChimrenga and Central Committee, who seemed to be on the same wavelength with Hamadziripi. After those two visits came Comrade Mudzingwa who appeared to be talking on behalf of Chairman Herbert Chitepo, a name that the first two did not mention. After the two visitors we debated the implications of what they conveyed to us and felt tempted to join provided they pressed the Government for our release so that we could negotiate our terms as free people negotiating with other free people about the cause of liberation of our country. But after the third visitor from the same Party, we began to feel uncomfortable as we discerned some differences of emphasis. The first two laid emphasis on wanting to bring us on because of our experience in field operations. The third visitor emphasised support for the Chairman by bringing an element that was lacking in ZANU which was fighters from western part of Zimbabwe. After hearing this, we decided to reserve our position until further clarity of the situation in ZANU because we feared to rush joining in case we found ourselves boosting a faction at the expense of the other faction within the same organisation.

We were fully aware that many of our comrades like Rex Nhongo had defected to ZANU soon after the eruption of the ZAPU crisis in 1970. The exodus continued from that time till our detention in June 1971. Such comrades like Rex Nhongo, Robson Manyika (former ZPRA Chief of Staff), Thomas Nhare, Solomon Badza and others, were commanders with a high profile; that is why their move was visible and the gaps they opened, were had to fill up in terms of military skills and experience in the theatre of operation. There were many rank and file comrades who defected to ZANU but were hardly mentioned due to the lower level of their profile. But it cannot be denied that their departure from ZAPU diminished ZPRA's capability and boosted the operational capacity and capability of ZANLA in the execution of armed struggle. This might contribute to explanation regarding a significant rise of ZANU in the field operations following the collapse of ZAPU in 1970. My hypothesis reads thus:

> **"There are observable indications suggesting a distinct likelihood that a dramatic rise in the degree of ZANLA's effectiveness in the theatre of operation from 1972 onwards may have resulted from additional combatants from ZPRA who brought with them a certain amount of ideological direction, military expertise, and experience in field operations."**

Sadomba (2011 p. 14) confirms this observation: **"Credit is due to this group of ZAPU (March 11 Movement) fighters who laid a firm foundation for the radical ideological development of Zimbabwe's anti-colonial struggle"**.

I must hasten to say that owing to the fact that our exiled leaders crippled ZAPU into a comma, with the Zambian Government failing to see their revolutionary shallowness, we saw no future operating under ZAPU anymore. Therefore, we, too, had the appetite to resume armed struggle even if it meant negotiating our entry into ZANU, especially if the ZANU visiting officials had presented to us a united statement of purpose. We could have persuaded our comrades to support that move as long as it was a genuine one in terms enlisting freedom fighters for the cause of freedom for their country rather than rot in a foreign prison unjustifiably. So those comrades who joined ZANU as early as 1971 might be regarded as having taken a wise move for the cause of national liberation.

Meanwhile Mzilethi and Ratie were advised to concentrate their effort on getting me to be released in order to reinforce them. Since my wife was already there, they agreed to make her take the lead in demanding to be joined by her husband who was merely detained without trial in a foreign country. Their strategy finally succeeded. One warm April day in 1974, I was released, escorted on the train to Lusaka, stayed overnight at the Paramilitary Head Quarters and then taken to Lusaka Airport to board a BA plane to London.

CHAPTER TWENTY TWO

STUDYING IN THE UNITED KINGDOM

When I landed at Heathrow International Airport, I was received by Ratie and her friend Patricia Brayden (simply known as Pat). This was the beginning of a brand new and unexpected chapter in my life. My trip to the USSR was no surprise because I knew that all advanced training for the struggle was done in that country and I had hoped to return to it for further professional development. But to enter the UK the way I did felt strange and bewildering. It took me some time wondering how Ratie and Mzilethi succeeded to get me out of a Zambian prison. My wife, Ratie had secured a place and scholarship from Sweeden for me to study in Birmingham Selly Oak Colleges. Indeed she raised the money from the Evangelical Lutheran Church in Sweeden. Ratie grew up within the religious sphere of the Lutheran Church in Mberengwa, Zimbabwe. More importantly, it was at the Lutheran Church that we made our marriage vows to each other on October 16, 1966. So, that connection became my saviour in a moment of need particularly the act of getting me out of detention and landing on a springboard of further studies in the UK. Fircroft College (one of Selly Oak Colleges) was designated a college of Liberal Studies that were the gateway to university education for mature students who had many years out of school. I already had 'O' Level Certificate from Nyathi Secondary and one subject at 'A' Level, which I obtained during our detention in Zambia.

Where was I coming from? I started off as a cattle herder, went through primary and secondary school as a learner, freedom of speech at school enabled acquisition of debating skills in politics, arrest of a student generated anger that begot underground activism at secondary school and inside Rhodesia, refugee in Botswana, a recruit in Zambia, a cadet in the USSR, a fully fledged freedom fighter in action in the field, arresting my leaders for gross political misconduct but finished up in prison in a friendly country, Zambia. Now in Birmingham, UK, in an academic environment and entirely detached from the struggle. What an anticlimax!

However, soon after my arrival in the UK, I joined the team that was campaigning for the release of the comrades in Zambia. There were four of us namely JZ Mzilethi, Ratie, Jacob Moyo and myself. We approached Government Ministers on the matter and they seemed to understand the problem. We approached Joan Lester, who was Minister of State for Foreign Affairs and she appeared to understand the need for British government intervention. Meanwhile we worked tirelessly to find places of study for all of them. We approached every college of adult education in the UK plus universities for those with appropriate qualifications. Eventually we succeeded in securing the sought-after places and funds from the British Council. There was a small point of legality in our favour: that we were British subjects from a British Colony that had a rebellious regime not recognised by Her Majesty's Government. Fortunately, Jacob Moyo was studying Law with University of London. Our team pressed very strongly on the point of the British Government's responsibility for Rhodesian Africans who needed education but had no government to take care of this except the British government. A few days before the Universities and Colleges opened for a new academic year of 1974/75, we were informed that all the comrades were due to be released for deportation to the UK in masses. Indeed they arrived in time to start the year with the rest of the students. But it was not everybody that was comfortable with returning to the desk after many years out of school. At the end of the academic year those who were not keen about schooling found jobs and settled down.

In all of this, we were still optimistic that we could create a chance to sail back to Africa to continue the armed struggle. The leadership of March 11 Movement met to evaluate the situation and attempted to strategise for resumption of armed struggle. We took this opportunity to recruit civilian members into the M11Movement. We also made effort to communicate with comrades inside Rhodesia and Zambia. We were appalled to find that Zimbabweans in the UK were bedevilled by tribalism of the scale similar to that reported by Owen Tshabangu in his book. We had expected to find intellectually enlightened students showing a broader national outlook than some of our misguided comrades in their reaction to the Chikerema-Moyo fiasco in Zambia. We found that it was easier to interact with the British than with our fellow Zimbabweans in terms of exchanging views on pertinent or topical issues concerning human condition in our country. But we managed to pick up a number of candidates for admission into the M11 as we found some young Zimbabweans were quite progressive and revolutionary in their political ideology. Whilst the M11 Movement seemed to be growing in the UK, the chances of its members going back to the struggle hardly brightened.

Nevertheless, in my newly found academic ladder, I rose a step higher when I was admitted to study for a BA Honours in Social Sciences at York University in UK. It turned out to be a very interesting choice in terms of a variety of theoretical perspectives that attempted to explain the development of socio-economic formations from the simplest to the most complex structures that are characterised by highly developed semi autonomous institutional elements in the form of social classes subtended by a bureaucratic machinery of the state with internal and external dynamics that kept together a societal organisation. After graduating in York I went to Swansea University College in Wales where I read for an M Sc (Econ) in Social Planning. I graduated in July 1980, soon after Zimbabwe gained its hard won independence. After this I registered as a Ph D candidate at Leeds University's Department of Politics. I travelled to Zimbabwe to for field research and decided to write up while I was temporary lecture at the University of Zimbabwe. My first chapter got lost before it was evaluated by my supervisor. I rewrote whole thesis and it got lost again and while I was pondering what could be happening I fell ill, went through an operation and the programme steadily slipped away from my scheme of things at that point of rewriting up.

CHAPTER TWENTY THREE

DEVELOPMENTS AFTER OUR DEPARTURE

Meanwhile J Z Moyo of ZAPU attempted to put ZAPU back into armed struggle by first assembling scattered groups of ZPRA in Zambia. In essence they held on to the diminished main stream of ZAPU when Chikerema teamed up with Nathan Shamuyarira to form FROLIZI. At National Executive level, it was JZ Moyo, TG Silundika and Edward Ndlovu who held on to a remaining faction in an effort to revive the entire organisation. They reorganised themselves and set up a new military administration headed by Nikita Mangena, a brilliant but ruthless soldier of high caliber who was wel versed in military science and atrategic planning at macro and micro level. When he was a military instructor in Murogoro Military Training Camp, Tanzania he distinguished himself as with absolute proficiency in guerrilla warfare in both planning and executing it. His Chief of Staff was Lookout Masuku, a dignified and committed freedom fighter with a demeanour of a priest. He had a background of political activism before he trained as a fighter. During his time as a Military Instuctor, Mangena was always sharp in strategic matters but in rank he was far away from the power of ZPRA commanding chiefs until 1972. Now that he was appointed to a strategic position, he took the job with commitment and applied himself with skill of a guerrilla fighter. But he came at a time when ZANLA had established itself in the north east of Rhodesia. It was during his time that ZPRA infiltrated the country on the basis of guerrilla methods and enabled them to establish their presence in the entire western half of the country. For the first time comrades steadily multiplied inside the country to establish themselves in the theatre of operation without being detected by security forces. Fighters were able to recruit large numbers of youngsters for military training outside the country. Between 1975 and 1978 ZPRA had raised and trained over 15000 military personnel half of whom were guerrillas inside the country supported by a well equipped conventional brigade ready to launch a general attack by summer of 1979 (Moorcraft and McLauglhin : 2008)

It is also remarkable that at the formation of ZIPA Mangena was the founding Political Commissar with Rex Nhongo as Commander and Chairman of the Military Committee. Note that Nhongo was trained by Mangeni in Murogoro, Tanzania, in 1969 after finishing from the USSR. Even though they had the mighty Zambezi River barrier to negotiate, Nikita's guerrillas were able to establish themselves in the entire western half of the country in a manner that never happened during our time under Akim Ndlovu's command. During the Nikita era there were clear signs that the strategy was planned by a trained guerrilla soldier because there were less frequent clashes with security forces at the point of crossing near the Zambezi River. In more cases than before contact was initiated by the guerrillas right deep in the country and that was the most significant successful breakthrough in the history of ZPRA operations. But they were unable to cover the whole country because after the Zambian Government demolished ZPRA in 1971, ZAPU, too as a viable Party ceased to exist until it was resurrected through the formation of the Joint Military Command (JMC) with ZANU. It was not until 1975 that ZIPRA adopted a comprehensive guerrilla war strategy which included massive recruitment of cadres inside the country and trained most of them in Zambia and Tanzania. By 1977 ZPRA army had grown phenomenally and able to systematically deploy large numbers inside the country without detection at the search and destroy lines. In spite of large numbers, they could only cover the western half, the south west, the north and middle part of the country because ZANLA forces had occupied the rest of the country from the middle to the east, north east and south east of the country since 1974. Clearly, if the March 11 Movement had succeeded to change ZAPU leadership in 1971, it is likely that they could have finished up in every corner of the country within five years before anyone else did.

Patriotic Front

During or about 1976 ZAPU and ZANU formed a Patriotic Front by which they agreed to cooperate politically when dealing with third parties.

Diplomatic manoeuvres to quench armed struggle

The fall of colonial administrations in Mozambique and Angola removed a huge slice from the strategic defences of Rhodesia and South Africa. It was worse in Rhodesia with a long border with Mozambique which made the regime surrounded by African independent states that supported armed struggle by providing transit bases and unfettered crossing points into Rhodesia. The balance of power shifted away from the regime towards the Nationalists in terms of vulnerability. At the cold war level, the West read the situation as favouring the key backers of the liberation movements, China and the USSR. Thus they became worried about their interests hence Dr Henry Kissinger, US Secretary of State, moved swiftly to Southern Africa on a mission to promote *detente* whose objective was to stop armed struggle by ZAPU and ZANU to stave off a radicalisation tendency in the movements believed to be driven by key struggle backers. In his compliance with detente, Ian Smith unconditionally released the Nationalist Leaders from prison. The Frontline states contributed by deregistering the two movements and declaring a unilateral cease fire (pertaining to fighters of both parties). This action put breaks on armed struggle. South Africa, too, was an active player in Dr Kissinger's shuttle diplomacy of detente in Southern Africa. Most of the released leaders went out of the country and attempted to unite under the umbrella of the United African National Council (UANC). They were pressurised to cobble together a political outfit they called Lusaka Unity Accord which was expected to embrace all Zimbabwean liberation movements, under the leadership of Bishop Abel Muzorewa, president of the UANC. All the fighters were now required by Frontline States to come under the control of this outfit controlled and commanded by its military wing called Zimbabwe Liberation Council.

Nevertheless, during the period of detente, ZANU went through some crippling setbacks similar to those which bedevilled ZAPU in early 1970s. Some members of ZANLA staged a rebellion led by Thomas Nhari (whence Nhari Rebellion) which was instigated by a catalogue of grievances similar to those that caused ZIPRA to arrest their leaders in 1971. The difference was that there was no bloodshed in the ZAPU upheaval but the Nhari rebellion finished up with executions of the ringleaders of the rebellion. Before their blood dried up the Chairman of Dare reChimrenga Advocate Herbert Chitepo was assassinated by a bomb that was placed in his car. It is not quite clear whether it was the Rhodesian Central Intelligence Organisation (CIO) or the bigger powers that took such a huge decision to eliminate a politician of Chitepo's stature. A Commission of Inquiry set up by the Zambian Government made a finding that the members of the ZANLA High Command were responsible and they were arrested; thus, leaving the fighters without political leadership. Some more work needs to be done to find out how much the Western powers played in all these complex but destructive interplay of forces in Zimbabwean liberation movements between 1970 and 1976. **Mhanda (2011)** describes the internal problems as well as expressing suspicion that detente was a Western design to safeguard their interests by causing the replacement of what was believed to be a communist inspired leadership (in exile) with a moderate bunch of nationalists from detention. The Rhodesian whites stood to gain from such a settlement if it was secured. The diplomatic manoeuvres in between the capitals of Southern Africa may suggest that the elimination of Chitepo was part of that agenda (of eliminating hardliners before majority rule was approved by the West). The same might be said about the assassination of JZ Moyo by a parcel bomb two years later. Maybe JZ Moyo too paid the price for shifting from Dengezi shallowness to a certain level of progressive outlook when he teamed up with Chitepo to form Joint Military Command that enabled ZAPU to regain its existence and subsequent strength, especially in the field. Clearly the Rhodesian regime must have felt uncomfortable to see two liberation movements teaming up to fight as a combined force, especially after expectations that the devastating crisis of ZAPU would diminish armed struggle to insignificant level of effectiveness against the regime. So the regime could have a motive to eliminate the two architects of the JMC hoping that their positions might be taken over by moderate ex-detainees from inside the country. The Zambian Government had no motive to do a thing of that sort unless some elements in government acted as agents of a big power that was worried about its interests that were perceived to be under threat from communist elements backed by the USSR and China.

In the main the consequences of both rebellions were identical in that in both occasions the struggle was caused to grind to a standstill, especially because Zambian government played a leading role in disarming the fighters, detaining some and deporting the rest. Armed struggle was paralysed in an unprecedented way because in both cases there was no more command structures to direct the struggle. But in ZANLA **Mhanda's** strategic thinking enabled him to escape arrest by disguising himself as an ordinary fighter therefore his presence with the fighters gave him the opportunity to play a pivotal role in preparing for the resumption of armed struggle under a new name and command structure. He gives a vivid account about his extensive contacts with fighters and President Samora Machel as well as the Organisation of African Unity (OAU) Liberation Committee to secure a green light towards resumption of armed struggle. In our case in ZPRA, there was no one out of prison who could have played a similar role. The worse aspect of this was that the fighters were dispersed in diverse directions such as deportations to Rhodesia, imprisonment in Zambia, self-demobilisation following mass clearance of the military bases in Zambia. In ZANLA there were hundreds of fighters in bases in three countries as well as inside Zimbabwe. Mhanda had personnel at his disposal in several camps including Tanzania and Mozambique. In this regard his extensive manoeuvres led to the formation and successful operations of Zimbabwe Peoples' Army (ZIPA) as deployment of its fighters inside Zimbabwe elevated the struggle to an unprecedented scale and intensity that caused the regime to be nervous as exemplified by its willingness to talk with the African nationalists internally and externally. Many observers described this period (ZIPA military campaign) as a turning point that saw the Rhodesian regime losing the war. This observation is confirmed by **Paul Moocraft (1990)** when he wrote **"From 1976 to1980 the Rhodesians were sucked into a war they were manifestly losing. If the Lancaster House talks did not intervene, military defeat was around the**

corner for white Rhodesians" It was within this period that Ian Douglas Smith talked about majority rule for the first time because he saw for the first time definite signs of the sun showing signs of setting in the white 'dominion' of racialism. In this regard he was prepared to create a façade of majority rule and present it to the world as a legitimate compromise with "responsible" African leaders. Note that Ian Douglas Smith was fond of using this word when describing those who agreed with him but those who didn't he described as "irresponsible". While the detente drivers accelerated their diplomacy by convening the Geneva Conference the ZIPA fighters intensified armed struggle inside Rhodesia and continued to score significant territorial gains inside the country, thus leaving dents on the Rhodesian regime defences as they were able to make breakthrough on the enemy's strategic 'search and destroy' zone that had seemed watertight during the initial phases of the war. The Rhodesians saw their success over the guerrillas through what they called "kill ratio" which appeared to favour them. But the guerrillas relied on mass support from the African populace thus enabling them to outmanoeuvre the security forces in terms of rapidly increasing occupation of space throughout the country.

The regrettable development here was that upon their release from the Zambian prison, the ZANLA High Command disbanded ZIPA by arresting members of the Military Committee and a large number of their supporters (Mhanda, 2011). But at that time the struggle had covered the whole country as evidenced by the fact that at this time 95% of the country was under Martial Law and protected hamlets. But the guerrillas infiltrated every village in the country whether or not it was protected under Martial Law. ZIPRA too, under Nikita Mangena (before he fell in active service), had established itself firmly in the entire western, northern and central parts of Rhodesia and, with ZANLA covering the rest, that left only the big cities lightly unoccupied by the guerrilla fighters from ZANLA and ZIPRA. Earlier on, I mentioned that in 1972, ZANU and JZ Moyo's ZAPU formed what they called Joint Military Command (JMC) headed by Herbert Chitepo and deputised by J Z Moyo to counter the FROLIZI outfit of JD Chikerema and Nathan Shamuyarira. Further to that, four years later, in 1976, ZAPU and ZANU formed a structure, Patriotic Front, that gave some hope that the two parties might be heading towards unification of the liberation movement. In this respect, they were seen as having strengthened their political unity in the new outfit that became their mouth piece at international forum as well as at negotiations with the British Government. Just after the formation of the Patriotic Front JZ Moyo was assassinated by a parcel bomb believed to have originated from the Rhodesian security branch via Botswana. There was a trend of assassinating leaders of liberation movement's right from Dr Mondlane, Amilcar Cabral, Herbert Chitepo, JZ Moyo, Nikita Mangena, possibly Josiah Tongogara. Whoever did these acts was horribly ignorant about struggles for freedom dating back to ancient times in Europe and Asia as well as Latin America and Africa in more recent centuries. In all of them, fighters for progressive change, with support of the majority of the population, triumphed because power and strength lay in the population not in the armament or efficient killer machines. When people say they want to be rid of oppression, it has never made any sense to regard that stance as an individual demand of a leader that could be easy to crush by assassination.

It was at this momentous period that some of the nationalist leaders like Abel Muzorewa, Ndabaningi Sithole, James Chikerema and Goerge Nyandoro fell for Smith's smoke screen and returned to Rhodesia to negotiate with the Smith regime for white controlled 'majority rule.' They reached an agreement which became known as 'Internal Settlement' but excluded the Patriotic Front. They allowed Smith to call the country **"Zimbabwe-Rhodesia"** This was another political short-sightedness by this bunch of African leaders. As for Chikerema and Nyandoro to be seen cooperating with the Rhodesian Front regime was irrefutable proof that they lacked both depth and comprehension of what national democratic revolution was all about. Ndabaniningi Sithole's presumed intellectual sharpness became highly questionable because his decision to participate in the internal settlement without the entire body of the fighters demonstrated his intellectual myopia. Abel Muzorewa was a Methodist Bishop who would be excused on his ignorance of embedded dynamics in the politics of self-preservation on the part of a cunning regime when faced by a multiple array of imponderables. He became a pseudo Prime Minister of what Smith called **Zimbabwe-Rhodesia** in 1978. Unfortunately political myopia did not allow the Honourable Bishop to sense the fragility of the regime that was constructed without the parties that were driving armed struggle with the support of the masses. The internal settlement was fiercely challenged by the forces of the Patriotic Front from ZANLA and ZIPRA to the extent that the international community could not recognise Muzorewa's regime as a legitimate government of the people of Zimbabwe as a whole. Any seasoned politician should have seen that internal settlement would not last the imminent onslaught from a strategy of final general attack by the Patriotic Front forces. But the named bunch of internal settlement architects closed their intellectual acumen for their personal convenience.

Rhodesian UDI regime attempted to externalise a civil war

All these manoeuvres by Western powers and Ian Smith were galvanised by fears that the USSR and China were on the verge of victory in Southern Africa because these powers and their crony, Ian Smith, deliberately informed their citizens that freedom fighters were pawns of the Eastern Block. The truth of the matter lay firmly inside Rhodesia in terms of the underlying causes of violent conflict of citizens against fellow citizens with so much resolve from both sides. Rhodesian violent conflict was between the Rhodesian Front regime and the African Nationalist movements that started off in a peaceful mode of seeking justice and freedom right from the 1950s before the Rhodesian Front came to power. When the Rhodesian Front came to power in 1962 it spelt out some principles that may be seen as their vision of a Rhodesia governed on the basis of fifteen principles whose sum total constituted foundation for a citadel of economic and political power of the white race over the black race for an indefinite period of time. The legalistic anchor of such racially divided system was the Land Apportionment Act 1934 and its successor the Land Tenure Act 1969. The resultant development was a dual economy whereby the 3% of the population (whites) owned nearly 100% of modern industrial and commercial enterprises. In Agriculture 4500 commercial famers owned nearly 50% of the total land area of the country with 97% of the population occupying another 44%. In essence the minority of whites owned and controlled most of the modern economic units and advanced social amenities. In governance, Parliament had sixty five seats sixty of which fifty (A roll) were designated for whites and fifteen (B roll) for Africans by virtue of high qualifications on the A roll. At UDI there was an economic boom and the whites had never had it so good in terms of the standard of living and quality of life in the form of good education, technical skills development and job reservation (for whites) as well as world class health facilities.

In summary, politically, those who opposed the Rhodesian Front regime by demanding democratization of the system through majority rule were regarded as 'Communist' inspired trouble makers therefore sent to jail or caused to flee the country for their safety. There was no room to pursue a progressive political goal for majority rule under the Rhodesian Front government's watch. The African nationalists were demonised as agents of Communist powers who were misleading the African majority with irresponsible political behaviour. Consequently the voice of the Africans was ruthlessly quenched by the regime through stringent legislation, such as the Law and Order (Maintenance) Act which gave the Minister sweeping powers to detain opponents of the regime at will for long periods subject to continuous extension as the Minister deemed necessary. Anyone who challenged the state strongly by mere condemning minority rule in public or private risked a possible detention or imprisonment if the words were found to be inflammatory in court. So the courts had no mercy on those who attacked the government verbally or physically and the Minister of Law and Order, too, had no mercy for those who were arrested but had no case to answer in court because he served them with detention orders. The response to African political demands was given in the form of detention for as long as the Minister of Law and Order saw it fit, but no more than five years subject to further extension at the pleasure of the Minister of Law and Order. The Rhodesian Front regime did not only pursue white domination over the Africans, it customised the political system into an anti-African damper on social, economical and political advancement by confining them in conditions of perpetual underdevelopment and deprivation. As part of measures for control the Africans were made to live under constant fear of the state through its fearful security forces and the Minister of Law and Order. In this regard there was a politically driven imprisonment based on detention without trial for an indefinite period and the justice system also had key clauses designed to send people to jail or to the gallows if they were found guilty of acting against the regime. Testimony to all of this was the detention of the key leaders of ZAPU and ZANU for over ten years without trial and the maximum prison was bursting at the seams with long term political prisoners and the gallows were dripping with blood of those found to have exceeded the mark in challenging the government. A whole lot of us found ourselves with no alternative but to carry arms of war to fighting a regime that was ruling our country without giving the slightest attention to the legitimate desires of the African majority. In essence there was neither freedom nor justice for the Africans to speak about.

Therefore, the Africans hardly enjoyed democratic and human rights under the Rhodesian Front regime of Ian Douglas Smith as they were never considered to be of any human value in the Rhodesian political and juridical culture. Every drastic step taken by the government was directed at Africans as exemplified by their omission in the principles of Unilateral Declaration of Independence (UDI). I do not know why the RF leaders did not give some thought about possible dire consequences of leaving out such a large number of citizens (Africans) out of their scheme on the basis of being African. When the latter upped their method of resisting oppression they were said to have been sponsored by Communists. Another surprise was that in spite of their high level of education the Rhodesian Whites buried their heads in the sand when the government propaganda reached such brazen falsehood of externalising struggle that was waged by oppressed African citizens most of whom had never been to any Socialist (Communist) country. Those who trained in Socialist countries found that those countries did no see any scientific basis for a free Zimbabwe to become a socialist country. The government knew all this through its very efficient Special Branch. Therefore there was no such a thing as Communist involvement in driving armed struggle in the interests of external powers or forces except provdiing us with military training and weapons free of charge.

Earlier on Rhodesian European citizens actually witnessed the rise of resistance in the form of forming the African National Congress, the National Democratic Party, Zimbabwe African Peoples Union and Zimbabwe African National Union. Instead of advising caution and reasonable approach to the resolution of the conflict, they pressured their government to ban these very peaceful parties, especially the ANC and NDP thus pushing white politicians out of the centre to the right in Rhodesian political spectrum. The Zimbabwe African Peoples Union was promptly formed following the banning of the former. When it was banned, compelling circumstances caused the nationalists to form its regent, the Peoples Care Taker Council which was immediately followed by the Zimbabwe African National Union. Both of the latter were also banned. All these successive parties were African nationalist movements that initially committed themselves to peaceful negotiation with the government for a smooth process towards majority rule like it happened in all the British colonies. Trusting the use of brute power instead of peaceful negotiations, the white settler government regarded nationalist parties as undesirables and swept them away from the register under a grossly mistaken view that Africans were incapable of organising anything that works. They did not know that the spirit of wanting to be free was passed over to us by our parents whose fathers were defeated in 1896. In this connection whites also derived their strength from the victory of their fathers in the 1890s as confirmed by *Peter Baxter (2008 p1): Quick Skecth of Zimbabwe/Rhodesia Bush War; African War History*

"The Rhodesian war of the 1970s was a civil war. It was fought for the preservation of the Anglo/Saxon values grafted into the landscape as a consequence of British imperialism of late 19th and early 20th centuries. The territory of Rhodesia comprised Mashonaland and Matabeleland acquired by the British South Africa Company during the 1890, and occupied by a white, mainly British settler community over the course of 90 years that followed."

Clearly, having entrenched themselves on the basis of the values that Ian Douglas Smith propounded, for Africans there was no other option except a Second Chimurenga/Umvukela after 90 years as a follow up to the First Chimrenga/Umvukela that started the anti-colonial agenda which had to be completed by the grandchildren of those first heroes and heroines. It did not need a scientist to determine whether the Africans wanted to be ruled by white settlers with their Anglo/ Saxon values or not in their own country. The two Chimurengas demonstrated the consistence of the nature of rejecting colonialism that proved that these were internal social upheavals as opposed to an imaginary foreign inspired invasion of Rhodesia. This further showed that the two races never socially or politically gelled into one nation since their fathers or grandfathers fought each other in the 1890s. In this regard everybody knew the true nature of the armed conflict of the 1970s that it was rooted in the 1890 loosers who had now acquired matching firepower to face their conquerors.

Rhodesian government's effort to separate the freedom fighters from their parents by dishing out false propaganda that propounded poisonous narration that freedom fighters were a minority bunch of malcontents sponsored by external Communist powers was too thin to convince the oppressed to turn against their children. The problem was that the holders of the Anglo/ Saxon values hardly imagined that the natives who had become accustomed to calling whites **"baas,"** **"madam"** and **"pikinini baas**[31]**"** could rebel against powerful baases and madams because they were assumed to have internalised inferiority complex that rendered their mental faculties incapable of making a distinction between justice and injustices of a white settler system in Rhodesia. Certainly we could never live with those conditions in addition to the scale of deprivation that was loaded with injustices devolving from a white racially dominated system. The national liberation struggle of our time aimed at drastically changing the entire Rhodesian political culture of political intolerance and hatred of opponents to give all citizens civil liberties

---

31

young baas

and freedoms that would be part of the principal elements of a democratic system to enable the nation open to unimpeded progression to the development of a national democratic revolution that would guarantee peace and justice for all regardless of race or creed.

Africans develop 'two faces' for safety reasons

In all these complex mechanisms of manipulation, in an attempt to make Africans accept their oppression, colonial authorities and the entire ruling class in white ruled Rhodesia did not even read African body language to perceive pretentious loyalty to baases and bosses, for their own safety. Africans developed and adopted a habit of displaying a behaviour of two **'faces'**: the first one was to wear safety **'mask'** in the eyes of Europeans (as they were perceived to be agents of the state) and authorities or employers to save their jobs or to avoid victimisation by security branch. Then their true face was displayed well away from white people of any rank. When alone, they looked at themselves as a humiliated race under the control of a white race that had forcibly exalted itself to a level of domineering power so fearsome. In every gathering people were asking each other about their situation of being taken for granted as manageable glorified human misfits in their own country. The unmasked face of bitterness could not be displayed in front of the **baases** and **madams** without the means of countering their wrath. But the anger and bitterness behind the backs of whites was painfully borne by Africans under conditions of concealment from those in power at all times for safety reasons. Most of us were fully aware that such lack of meeting of minds between Africans and whites had created a deep running current that was pregnant with explosives whose consequences subsequently manifested themselves in a bitter war of national liberation. It should be no surprise to any analyst that in spite of an almost airtight Rhodesian anti-insurgency military strategy, freedom fighters could not be annihilated. That was because the overwhelming majority of the African population was angry against deprivation in their own country therefore they supported the freedom struggle without admitting it to the authorities, including chiefs. It was this denialism that gave the impression that freedom fighters had no support in the African population. Living a fragile life "between legality and illegality" on a daily basis became part of life for the majority Africans until Zimbabwe was liberated. That is why when we were asked by our Military Instructor during training we defined a guerrilla as "an angry citizen who was angry against injustices of a colonial system" but our oppressors deliberately ignored all that because they fed themselves with a falsehood of externalising the war so as to make their followers sustain the belief that Africans on their own could not militarily challenge the **baases** and **madams.**

For instance, after hearing that I was arrested for taking part in the struggle, my chief quizzed me angrily about why I involved myself in useless adventures of Joshua Nkomo. I answered him with full respect and denied that I was at all involved in violent struggle, there were some people who were framing me for reasons known to themselves. He was happy to hear that I was not involved in violent activities against the government. He then went on to say: "Europeans are clever and too advanced to be defeated by you boys because they defeated our brave fathers under a brave king. No one can match bravery and wisdom of our fathers except the Europeans. I am glad to hear that you are not involved in Joshua Nkomo and Ndabaningi Sithole's useless efforts to remove Europeans from power. Just keep your job and look after your mother let the foolish ones go ahead, they are looking for serious trouble." The chief said a lot more than I have summarised here. When I informed some elders about the chief's warning they said: **"tshayela**

phansi"[32]. They reminded me of the policy of witches who could not be pinpointed by anyone with evidence of their activities. Without any doubt the majority of the people in my District did not subscribe to the chief's position in relation to the settler government that was regarded as an oppressor government, but we all had to deny our involvement to avoid landing on a hot surface of the law. That is why everybody had to work quietly in darkness 'like the witches' and be ready to deny when suspected.

By all accounts everyone who supported freedom fighters had to behave like witches who never admitted to anyone that they were involved in witchcraft in fear of physical elimination by the community. In the context of the struggle the government eliminated those who were found to be supporters of freedom fighters therefore, in most cases only extreme degree of torture could force them to admit their involvement. That is why it would be grossly erroneous to attribute country-wide guerrilla infiltration entirely own ability of guerrillas without the support of the masses. The decisive force in all of this was the angry African population, who were compelled by circumstances of repression to live pretentious lives for their own safety and for the success of the struggle which was seen as their saviour no matter how cumbersome and risky to sustain. This is exactly what Nelson Mandela meant when he said under white domination Africans lived two lives: one of legality and the other of illegality. The latter remained concealed to the authorities to the extent that they had false impression that Africans never supported freedom fighters until they saw their edifice cracking. The concept of living between legality and illegality was applied countrywide as a survival skill that developed during the days of underground before the advent of freedom fighters on a large scale. The other way of reinforcing concealment of reality entailed the adoption of a habit of: **"amanga mabi, kodwa mahle epoliseni"** (*lies are bad but they are good for survival when questioned by a policeman*)

As an African born in Zimbabwe when it was still called Southern Rhodesia, I am writing mainly what I witnessed and experienced from my younger days up to adulthood. I would not hesitate to say that the Rhodesian white settlers under the leadership of the RF misled themselves by either deliberately keeping themselves ignorant about the true nature of Africans or misreading their day to day desires and grievances that emanated from blatant racial domination that was characterised by deprivation and injustice in all spheres of societal setting. What they saw as happiest Africans were symptoms of deep-seated fear of the mighty power of the white rulers who had already displayed their ruthlessness by arresting and detaining so many African leaders without trial for nothing except demanding justice. When the struggle intensified, the Rhodesians blamed imaginary external powers of communists as drivers of armed struggle for their own gains. Yet many whites, including Ian Douglas Smith, were born and grew up in Rhodesia to the extent that they knew the African conditions of deprivation and how and when such a state of injustice gave rise to domestic African nationalism in the 1950s. The nationalist movement initially called for equal rights in all spheres of public policy in the country followed by progress to majority rule through peaceful negotiations. But owing to the fact that Rhodesian European settlers did not regard Africans as capable of anything, they discounted those demands and removed a Prime Minister who wanted to listen to Nationalists. In fear of the powerful wave of African nationalism, attempts were made by the successor of the deposed Prime Minister to quench that phenomenon but it regenerated itself back to existence determined and stronger than before. The Rhodesian Front came to power determined to crush African resistance by all means it could command. Indeed they adopted the principle of "final act" to sweep away any African organisation that championed the cause of freedom and justice for all citizens of the country. Their racist approach

---

32

go deep underground

to management of public affairs of state and society led them to exclude the Africans from white citadel of power in the form of a unilateral declaration of independence. When the African responded to that extremism by similar means they were seen as agents of external Communist powers, China and the USSR. In this way the Rhodesians and their sympathisers misdirected themselves further by openly externalising the anti-colonial resistance that had become violent. Instead of recognising that the uncontrollable spread of guerrilla warfare in Zimbabwe was facilitated by angry citizens who desired replacement of a white driven repressive system with a free political dispensation that would accord them full democratic rights as enjoyed in all democratic countries. That was exactly the quest for freedom and justice that caused Africans to live between legality and illegality throughout the period of the liberation struggle in Zimbabwe, not external forces of the East or West. Actually it is surprising that Rhodesian whites shifted the blame for their political defeat from their stiff-necked racism to external forces yet their own highly rated military force, the Selous Scouts found that the masses were excited about freedom fighters, thus:

"A team of Security Force pseudo insurgents, when passing as ZANLA were shocked and disillusioned at wild static, sometimes ecstatic receptions ZANLA was getting among the local population" (Cilliers, 1985)

Such was an epitome of what happened countrywide as parents witnessed their brave children putting their lives on the line for their country in the face of mighty killer machine of the Rhodesian security forces. They would comment: **"kufuzile; kulezibindi njengaboyisemkhulu, sizalitha"** (*these youngsters are as brave as their grandfathers; we will win our country back")*. The latter comment was made at Kafusi, Kezi District, when my uncle saw two of his sons and a nephew as part of a ZPRA unit passing through his home armed with AK assault rifles heading to their operational area further south. The whites missed that connection of freedom fighters with their parents and the spirits of their grandfathers who fought gallantly but lost the war because they had no matching fire power. That chain which connected us from 1896 to the time of struggle was crucial in our resolve to be prepared to die for the freedom of our country, not for external Communists or Western powers. In this regard I am tempted to say that no reasonable person anywhere in the world would be so naive as to believe that thousands of us would be prepared to die for external interests rather than for our own country's freedom. On the day of attaining freedom from colonial repression, the Africans looked forward to leading normal lives on a daily basis whereby they could be free to display their true faces in all spheres of social interaction with no more fear of political or juridical victimisation.

Lancaster House Conference: Who won?

The formation of ZIPA in 1976 should be credited with a breakthrough in causing the Rhodesian regime to feel insecure because of the effectiveness of strategy applied by the Military Committee. The extensive coverage and intensity of guerrilla war in Zimbabwe between 1976 and 79 was heralded by ZIPA forces well before the political leaders returned to the helm of the struggle. The Rhodesian security forces had always believed that they were on top of the situation by all accounts. But from 1976 onwards guerrilla warfare spread throughout the country full scale, proving that this nature of war, with the support of the majority, has never been defeated by a regime that is anchored by minority classes in society no matter how well armed it may be. The process of the war reached a level where it became unstoppable as signified by advance of guerrillas beyond their enemy's strategic "search and destroy zone." Apparently the war had reached what Mhanda calls "strategic equilibrium" whereby the Rhodesian security forces had lost the initiative and the ability to defend the entire country with all their multi-complex and intricate military architecture that was crafted to be a watertight counter-insurgency military framework. General Westmoreland of the United States had some of the most advanced military hardware and best trained soldiers to win the Vietnamese war. But he lost the war because he did not have the population's support which was a strategic advantage to General Giap rather than technically sophisticated military hard ware. It is unbelievable that Rhodesian whites could have expected support from the people they oppressed as they seemed surprised why Africans did not support the government. For our part, the oppressed majority, we could never contemplate rallying behind an anti-African regime of Ian Smith in fighting African guerrillas. Those were very unrealistic expectations by any standard of reasonableness on the part of the government and its supporters. The Rhodesians were lucky that Lancaster House came a few months before a "general attack" was unleashed, heralded by heavily armed regular forces backed by mechanised systems with adequate air cover from both ZANLA and ZPRA. In this regard ZANLA was on the verge of launching such a force in 1979 (Sadomba, 2011). ZPRA too, had fully prepared to launch a massive general attack (conventional onslaught) from several fronts in the summer of 1979 (Moorcraft & McLaughlin, 2008). The regime tried all tricks to dribble the Patriotic Front but the impact of the war was so immense that engineering a 'settlement' that bypassed people with guns, and overwhelming support of the masses, proved unrealistic. The impact of the war had wide implications that left not only white Rhodesians, but also the international community no option but to take the path of negotiating with the Patriotic Front to settle the conflict in the country.

On this account, a constitutional conference was convened by the British Government at Lancaster House chaired by Lord Carrington, the Foreign Secretary. The conference lasted from September 10 to December 22, 1979. On the 22nd December the Conference reached agreement on a new constitution for Zimbabwe's independence. The constitution provided for 100 Parliamentary seats 80 of which were for Africans and twenty reserved for whites. The combatants were to assemble at Assemble Places (AP) throughout the country and the Rhodesian forces were to return to the Barracks. Law and order was to be maintained by the regular police force, assisted by a paramilitary force called Support Unit and Commonwealth Monitoring Forces. A British appointed Governor, Lord Soames, was given responsibility to oversee the transition process from the cease fire period to independence. Lord Soames issued a general amnesty for all political prisoners inside the country and outside.

CHAPTER TWENTY FOUR

INDEPENDENCE: TRIUMPH OF NATIONALISM WITHOUT DEMOCRACY

The Lancaster House Constitution provided for a House of Assembly with 100 parliamentary seats, 80 of which were for Africans and 20 preserved for Whites. Following the cease fire the date for a general election was set for three days from 27th , 28th and 29th February 1980. The results of the general election showed that ZANU PF won 57 seats out of 80 African seats in the House of Assembly. Having won a commanding landslide the leader of ZANU PF Robert Gabriel Mugabe was appointed first Prime Minister of a liberated Zimbabwe. The Rhodesian Front won all the 20 white seats. So on 18 April 1980 Zimbabwe was granted independence at which Prince Charles presided as he witnessed the Union Jack being lowered and the Zimbabwean flag taking its place. Thus Zimbabwe joined the family of nations as an independent African state after a prolonged bitter struggle that finished up in a war in the true sense of the meaning of the word. When Robert Mugabe became Prime Minister he formed a Government of National Unity comprising his party ZANU PF, PF ZAPU and a sprinkle of white Ministers from the old order. Joshua Nkomo held the portfolio of Home Affairs.

Attaining independence is one thing but transforming repressive levers of power into a people-centred apparatus for serving the people is another issue. Here it has to be pointed out that at independence we inherited the above described repressive state apparatus lock stock and barrel, with its unlimited powers over its citizens. This begs the question "Did we liberate ourselves from repression in 1980?" To answer this question I will delve into the nature of governance as I have seen it in Zimbabwe since independence.

The fact of the matter is that the national liberation struggle succeeded in causing the demise of colonialism and the installation of a quasi democratic constitution which was crafted at Lancaster House and accepted by all the parties participating in the Conference. The new constitution provided for majority rule that was attained through the ballot in 1980 followed by independence which means we gained our sovereignty as a self-governing African state that joined the family of nations in the world. Without any doubt those of us who were oppressed felt liberated on the day Zimbabwean Flag rose up to replace the Union Jack in Harare. There were celebrations and joy everywhere. The question still remains: After gaining our national freedom did we transform the state apparatus from a repressive machine to a people-serving and development state? I will dwell on this below.

Working as a Civil Servant in a liberated Zimbabwe

I actually arrived on the last day of voting and cast my first vote of my life in my country of forefathers. After that I returned to the UK to graduate for a Masters degree (Economics) in Social Planning. I returned to join the University of Zimbabwe in 1982 as a temporary Lecturer in the Department of Politics and Administration. I soon joined Centre for Applied Social Sciences (CASS) as a Research Fellow. Before I joined the Civil Service, I researched on the possible causes of women's subordination in Zimbabwe and published a pamphlet on those issues. I was then appointed as an Assistant Secretary in the Prime Minister Office with special responsibility for developing a policy on the development of cooperative in Zimbabwe.

I started work as a civil servant on the 1st of April 1983, just three years after independence. Everything was still new and people were still celebrating the attainment of independence. Most people had high qualifications but no experience of working for the government at senior level of management.

When I got the job in the Prime Minister's Office, I was placed under the Deputy Prime Minister's chain of command through a Minister of State for Cooperative Development, Comrade John Landa Nkomo, a member of ZAPU National Executive. My task was to investigate the state of the cooperative movement for the purpose of identifying weaknesses and strengths and then come up with a strategy of how they could be assisted to become alternative mode of collectively owned enterprises on a large scale. I was surprised to find that in the Prime Minister's Office there was no bureaucratic clog of decision and administrative processes such as reports and feedback. Everything seemed to be moving smoothly and fast. But in the Ministries there was excruciating slowness of decision making and feedback to the lower level of government structures. Senior officials spent a lot of time writing concept papers that hardly reached finality until something new developed and the cycle would start all over again and no progress seemed to take place. There was no such a thing in the Prime minister's Office in all structures of the Office.

For my part, I interacted with the cooperative movement throughout the country and finally came up with a document that was widely discussed by all the stakeholders and adopted. It was presented to Cabinet for approval. After a policy on cooperative development was approved by the Cabinet, we then organized a work-shop that focused on relevant legislation with full participation of the cooperative movement and other stake holders. After the workshop a full report was submitted to the Ministry of Justice and Parliamentary Affairs for drafting a bill derived from the principles stipulated in the report. The task was completed fast and went through Cabinet and Parliament to become Law. An Inter-Ministerial Committee was set up by the Prime Minister for mobilising and coordinating technical assistance to cooperatives by appropriate Ministries or other agencies at home or from abroad. Here I succeeded in streamlining various departments and agencies to provide technical and financial assistance to cooperatives, which were collectively owned community enterprises at grassroots level in all sectors of the national economy. By 1989 there was a boom in both the Agricultural and non-Agricultural cooperatives in terms of growth in yield and high returns on investments. This enabled the members of these enterprises to draw handsome monthly allowances (earnings) for a living. Challenges were immense but the calibre of staff in the Prime Minister Office and Ministry of Community and Cooperative Development was sound enough to measure up to the requirements of their tasks. In the end I felt satisfied with what I had come to do in the public service for six years of research, work-shopping, report writing, drafting and polishing documents for final approval by appropriate institutions such as Parliament.

While my job was to focus on cooperative development there were times when I found myself solving numerous community problems that had nothing to do with cooperatives. Some of the problems were caused by some Ministers who attempted to dispossess the cooperative movement of their most flourishing enterprises or prime land allocated to them through a legal process of resettlement. My interventions usually succeeded in preventing those moves by greedy Ministers and that made my office very popular with communities from all over the country because they heard that I hardly failed to resolve the conflicting claims always in favour of the co -operators or ordinary citizens in resettlement areas. My trump card was that after a thorough inquiry, I wrote a clearly articulated memorandum to the Minister of State spelling out the unwarranted moves of an offending Minister in question and recommended specific steps to be taken. He then interacted with the Deputy Prime Minister who took it forward and the matter finished up with such a Minister's inappropriate moves stopped conclusively by the Prime Minister in favour of the appellant.

Extra-duty functions

Dealing with Ministers who wanted to seize cooperative land was not entirely outside the parameters of my job. But there was a political task that I volunteered to take up and I was granted the honour to do it.

We may recall the intense political antagonism between ZAPU and ZANU that persisted throughout the period of armed struggle. At independence this trend exhibited itself along the tribal divide in a scale that had never been known in the history of Zimbabwe since the advent of colonialism. For instance the results of the 1980 elections showed ZANU getting all the support from the Mashonaland regions and ZAPU got support from the Matabeleland regions and parts of Midlands. A political picture that some of us never expected to see because we were still clinging to the NDP nation building slogan of **mwanawebvu**. Anyway, serious effort was made to integrate a combined force of the liberation forces with the Rhodesian army into one National Army. The process seemed to be succeeding but around 1982 a handful (estimated to be about 500 men) of ex-ZIPRA elements opted out on the grounds that they were unfairly treated by the authorities to the extent that they felt unwanted. On this account the dissident elements went around Matabeleland and Midlands provinces telling the villagers that Zimbabwe was not yet free therefore they needed support to fight the government. They further claimed that they were under Dr Joshua Nkomo's orders to fight Zimbabwe government. The Government took exception to that situation and denounced Dr Joshua Nkomo in public until the Prime Minister dismissed him and some of his colleagues from Government of National Unity.

Nevertheless, Dr Joshua Nkomo disassociated himself from the dissidents and dismissed their claims of support from him as false. Government did not accept Nkomo's pronounced position of rejecting dissidents. Matters got to a head when the Government found arms cache in PF ZAPU properties thus leading to suspicion that the party was up to what some people called "zero hour" which was described as a pass word for a war to be waged by ZAPU against Zimbabwe Government of ZANU (PF). I happen to know that the question of arms cache is a long and complex matter that dates back from 1979 in London during the Lancaster House Constitutional Conference. In this connection I was reliably informed by top officers of ZPRA that while in the Conference Room, Lt General Peter Walls, then Commander of the Rhodesian Army, made a statement that indicated that Rhodesian security forces would deal with ZPRA and ZANLA after they laid down their arms inside the country. The statement prompted top commanders of

ZANLA and ZPRA to rush out of the Conference Room to quickly reach an agreement that both ZANLA and ZPRA should stock arms in strategic points so that if the Rhodesian army tried to implement Lt General Peter Wall's plan, they should be ready to counter the move with adequate fire power to foil it. According to these sources, the stocking of arms was official as it was jointly agreed by both liberation movements at High Command level. Some rank and file comrades of ZANLA and ZPRA confirmed to me that they were surprised by the harsh step by Government on ZAPU for caching weapons because both organisations had done it in anticipation of a coup by Rhodesian army, as hinted by Lt General Peter Walls in front of delegations in Lancaster House in London.

In connection with all of this the Government did not indicate that it was aware of such an arrangement as a precautionary measure. Instead it took further tough measures and trained a special crack force called the **Fifth Brigade hereinafter referred to as the Army or Gukurahundi**. Allegations from the operational areas abound that the Fifth Brigade had become the driver of a vicious campaign against those who were suspected of supporting or sympathetic to the dissidents, including ZAPU officials at branch and District levels. Reports persisted that the wrath and venom employed by the **Gukurahudi** in three provinces in the rural areas had no precedent in level and scale of human destruction in our country since the Rhodesian "Selous Scouts allegedly went around disemboweling suspected guerrilla supporter during the war. This then was reminiscent of the violence-laden split between ZAPU and ZANU in 1963 that begot a culture of political intolerance that has bedevilled Zimbabwean political landscape up to post-independence period (Sachikonye, 2011).

Quite a lot of what I have mentioned above was not in my job description yet I did not hesitate to take up ordinary people's grievances and addressed them adequately. But from 1982 there were some dissident elements from ex-ZPRA who refused to recognise the government lead by ZANU PF. As ZAPU was the principal suspect in both the loose dissidents and arms cache, Dr Joshua Nkomo was dismissed from Cabinet and Dumiso Dabengwa and Lookout Masuku, arrested. Dr Nkomo had to flee the country on a tipoff that his life was in danger. Masuku was released to meet his death in his house in Hatfield and Dabengwa was tried for treason but found not guilty at the end of a long trial.

After the 1985 Parliamentary general elections, I visited my home District of Nkayi and found so many people with broken limbs and a District Administrator lying unconscious in his office. The locals alleged that people were assaulted allegedly by the army personnel under the command of a Colonel. As stated above, this seemed to confirm allegations that there were wide spread reports pertaining to mass killing of civilians in the countryside in Matabeleland and the Midlands provinces. When I saw all this with my eyes at Nkayi, and heard that the army was involved, I felt that the allegations might be true. I went to the police station to find out from the station commanding officer as to who was involved in the beating of so many people at Nkayi Growth Point. When I told him I was from the Prime Minister's Office he looked very unease and confused. He merely said they were investigations in progress. I put it to him that when I arrived in the area there were some police details standing at the scene of trouble therefore they must have witnessed the incident. He could not answer that. Outside the police station many people who saw me strongly advised that I should return to Harare immediately because I was in danger of being harmed. I had to comply with my relations and members of the public who urged me to go away fast as there were some gentlemen looking at me through sun glasses eyes of anger as they seemed to perceive my concern about official driven violence at Nkayi.

Upon my arrival in Harare I approached the Deputy Prime Minister Mr Simon Muzenda about what I saw and heard. I went further to mention what many locals were saying about **Gukurahundi,** which was deployed to deal with dissident elements in Matabeleland and Midlands Provinces. I then offered my services to investigate the allegations that were so rampant regarding the brutality of **Gukurahundi.** The Deputy Prime Minister acknowledged that he was aware that it was not all well in that part of the country. He advised me to discuss my mission with Deputy Secretary Willard Chiwewe. I did. Chiwewe readily agreed saying he too had been contemplating sending me to investigate the same problem of violent conflict in the named provinces. Comrade Chiwewe and I drafted the terms of reference covering Matabeleland North Province. I was advised to ask the Provincial Governor to provide me with an unmarked vehicle with a well trusted driver. I wanted to take one month in the countryside but Comrade Chiwewe said in a volatile situation I needed one week. Actually he was wondering how I was going to cover myself to survive in what he called a danger zone. I reminded him that I was a guerrilla fighter capable of changing my image like a chameleon to fit any environment at a given place and time. So that was not a problem. We agreed that having been to Nkayi already, I should cover Tsholotsho and Lupane Districts only. All those three were some of places where the dissidents were operating therefore there was heavy presence of the security forces, especially the army and all other security elements. On request I was given appropriate documents signed by the Senior Secretary in the Prime Minister and Cabinet Office for my safety from security forces. I flew to Bulawayo where I met the Provincial Governor for Matabeleland North Mr Daniel Ngwenya who briefed me about the dangers of the chosen areas and gave me a car and a driver as advised by the higher authorities. Daniel Ngwenya is the man who woke me up to go and dispatch comrades whom we assisted to escape from Gray Street Prison in Bulawayo in 1964.

The investigation of the allegations that Gukurahundi was involved in gross violation of human rights was a very dangerous undertaking. I had to be very careful indeed the way I conducted myself in respect of talking to people who might have been victims or eyewitnesses or even perpetrators. First of all I had to consider the methodology of the inquiry and the need to record factual information only, and to bear in mind that I was assigned by the highest Office of state, Prime Minister and Cabinet Office, therefore its integrity was of paramount importance. In my own esteem I had to be aware that as a freedom fighter a task like that needed patriotic approach in terms of serving my country with maximum honesty in the name of peace and justice. My academic background reminded me to be as objective as possible in approaching the inquiry and presentation of facts to the authorities without covering up or exaggerating anything whatsoever. I therefore adopted this approach in constructing my methodology of inquiry and reporting.

In volatile situations like that it was imperative to be creative and move away from pedantic dogmatism when addressing methodological issues. In this regard I resolved the methodological question by adopting a multiple approach to carry out the inquiry to its successful accomplishment. I started my mission in Lupane District with senior Government staffers where I formally interviewed the officers of security forces, government officials, school teachers, health professionals and politicians. I introduced myself in full by declaring my credentials with documentary proof that I worked in the Prime Minister's Office and my mission was assigned by that Office. I did not know that documents from the Senior Secretary could make officials and officers talk to me with so much respect and maximum honesty because virtually all of them tried had to be as truthful as possible in terms of telling what they saw and heard regarding gross abuse of human rights under their watch. I did not threaten anybody but the very fact that I was from the Prime Minister's Office investigating atrocities was enough to make people wonder how safe it could be to withhold factual information from me. I was impressed by police officers because they did not hesitate to speak out on what they saw and heard in the villages. Other Government officials were also quite cooperative because they thought telling the truth might lead to the end of the conflict. Officials of political parties were equally cooperative as soon as I showed them my credentials. The ordinary villagers, teachers, priests and hospital staff were also very generous with information on the army atrocities. I was advised not to travel more than fifty kilometres from the centre of Lupane Growth Point. I adhered to the advice because I could see for myself that there were so many security agents who were agitated by my presence. I strongly advised senior officers to tell their juniors that I was from the Department of Education investigating whether it would be possible to build new schools in the rural areas in spite of the dissident problem. All senior government officials and officers held to that word. To avoid breach of my identity, I avoided talking to junior officers completely so that even if they might have got to know what I was up to, I had left already. For villagers and folks in a pub I adopted a conversational method of interviewing them instead of going into the villages or in a pub to interview people in a structured way with a paper holder in hand. I merely joined people in their social gatherings such as beer deinking parties or grinding mills or any other place where people were in jovial moods. I introduced myself as visitor from a neighbouring District. I then started a conversation like anyone around and some people also asked me about Nkayi and fortunately I had a story to tell from what I saw when I was there and they opened up more stories than I had for them.

In Lupane virtually everybody, except one nursing sister, cooperated as much as they could do in the circumstances. At the end of the week I had gathered so much information from an area inside 50 kilo metres in diameter in each of the two districts, Lupane and Tsholotsho. I did not cover entire villages in both Districts. In Lupane I covered Daluka area, St Lukes Hospital and a number of surrounding villages and two schools. In all of this I managed to meet District Administrators, Police and security officers, health professionals in hospitals, local ZANU (PF) officials, some councillors (ZAPU), priests, teachers, ordinary peasants and business people. Out of all the people I talked to in Lupane only one nursing sister declined to talk about conflict situation in the area. She merely declared that everything was "perfect, there was peace and happiness." The majority of all the named categories of people gave graphic details of their experiences and what they heard from other distant areas. In every horrendous violation of human rights the main perpetrators were the members of the Gukurahundi who were grinding on the civilians with extreme brutality on the grounds that people were hiding or harbouring armed dissidents.

In Tsholotsho the level of cooperation with information was different. Like I did in Lupane, I started off with Government officials, police officers and security officers. Like their Lupane counterparts they were satisfied with my credentials and opened up as much as could be expected considering that they were face to face with an official from the highest Office in the land. Very few officers of the security forces were a little bit economical with factual accounts of events. But a large majority of officers spilled the beans. As I have stated above, in Tsholotsho ordinary villagers were too afraid to talk to a stranger. My calculation was that 25% of villagers I approached in Tsholotsho refused to say anything at all no matter how much gentility I adopted to solicit cooperation. Fortunately the 75% who cooperated did so with graphic details of what they experienced in the villages. Even so, initially they were reluctant to speak about the army and dissidents. A sign of deep suspicion and fear was so much in evidence in Tsholotsho and many people were still nervous and very unsettled as they spoke about their painful experience. Those who opened up spoke with their tears flowing down their cheeks because they suspected that after my departure they were going to pay a heavy price for telling me the truth. I assured them as much as I could that no such a thing was going to happen to them. Taking the cue from Government officials and Police who were very candid about human rights abuse, I was able to satisfy everyone that no one would be in danger for cooperating in terms of giving some accounts of human rights abuses that they knew to have happened. Teachers and nurses, too, spoke with tears flowing down the cheeks ending up with expression of fear for their lives after my departure. But they spat out all that was making them sob before they were able to talk about it. Those who declined to talk thought I had come to trap them so that the army would come and finish them up after my departure. I did not ask for names as part of assuring them that they would never appear in any report because I did not have the names and addresses. I did not even ask for the name of the Village Head, Headman and Chief, who, together with the individual's name and ID number, normally make it possible to identify and locate where a particular individual resides in the rural areas in Zimbabwe.

With the teachers, nurses, doctors and all other professionals I declared my credentials as I did with security forces officers. The challenge I encountered with them was that they were afraid to speak out about the Gukurtahundi operations in the villages. I pleaded with them and tried to assure them that I was there to find the truth that would help to solve the very problem which made them fear to talk to me. I stressed that the more the truth remained hidden the worse the problem could become and persist with dire consequences for human lives. They eventually opened up with tears and sobbing because of fear that I might be an agent of government who was sent to identify those who exposed how they suffered in the hands of Gukurahundi. They eventually told me things that were hair-raising, even a hardened guerrilla fighter would only stop tears from flowing down the chick by pushing them back by frequent blinking as if that was a mere expression of astonishment about what was told.

The amount of information from two Districts in a Province with six Districts was loaded with horrific acts of human destruction unimaginable in a country that had just got freedom from a repressive colonial system. What was this for? The coverage was not vast but information from that small sample was too ghastly to commit to memory. The important thing now is that most of the atrocities or massacres committed by the Gukuahundi are in the public domain. There is no need to dwell into the details of what the villagers and the police told me 27 years ago. But what is important is to gravitate towards what was the outcome of my report from that very short visit to the affected places, with a few examples of what I heard from Lupane and Tsholotsho Districts.

It was observable that all government officials I spoke to appeared to be in a dilemma regarding how much they could tell or withhold whilst they were also afraid to lie to the Prime Minister's Office because they saw my validation documentation and I encouraged the doubting Thomases to call the Office and speak to Senior Secretary to the Prime Minister and Cabinet Office. So they found themselves compelled to tell what they saw in their capacity as security officers to the extent that their stories were close to what the ordinary people said. I took as factual veracity any report of an incident that was corroborated by no less than any three of the following categories: a Pastor, local officials of political parties, police officers, security officers, government officials, teachers, hospital staffers, ordinary villagers, and business people. In most cases factual stories were easily corroborated by the majority or all of the above categories of people. Why I grouped them like that was because I met them structured in that order.

An example of horrific destruction of life and property concerns reports of brutal massacres that occurred during 1983 in the western part of Tsholotsho around Pumula Mission where villages were burnt up with people inside their huts. While everybody agreed that homes were burned up, they differed as to methods of burning them. A significant difference that emerged from the security officers was that they said the Army told them that some villages were destroyed by gun fire because soldiers were returning hostile fire from dissidents who opened fire first from inside the huts. But villagers contacted gave details of people who were forced into huts that were set alight by the army. The charred bodies found inside the burnt huts were testimony to this fact. Some huts were entirely razed to the ground with people closed inside and in such cases, people were burnt beyond recognition. If the army destroyed all those huts with military hard ware, the rabble would have been different from the charred huts. Army weapons would have destroyed or damaged the huts extensively, especially if hand grenades and bazookas were used. To confirm that they were burnt by matches, some affected huts had charred roofs collapsed inwards leaving the smoked walls standing without bullet marks. Above all villagers did not recall hearing sound of gunfire except in cases where those who tried to run away before the fire was started were shot dead. In all of this, some of the worst hit areas by the Gukurahundi operation of burning people inside their huts included Manala and Phelandaba Lines around Phumula Mission. Eye witnesses saw the smoke of burning huts and people inside screamed as they struggled to escape from the burning inferno. Close examination showed that some of the huts had their doors tied with wire showing intention to prevent occupants from escaping. Some walls remained erect and without trace of bullet marks outside yet inside the villagers found burnt up bodies under charred rafters which had fallen inside with apex razed to the inside floor. There was no trace of bullet marks on the standing walls. In the circumstances it would be reasonable to conclude that there was no exchange of fire between the Army and the dissidents in Manala and other neighbouring Lines where several huts were burnt up with people inside. Also no evidence was found to support the claims that the Army fired at the huts in a return of hostile fire from the dissidents. Therefore as everybody, including the Army, agreed that some fire was directed at the homes by the Army, but since the latter did not use fire arms, indications are that they set the huts alight after forcing the villagers into them for the purpose of eliminating them for any motive known to the army alone.

In another horrific report, a hospital doctor told me thus: "If I pulled out any number of copies of death certificates of six months old babies who died between 1982 and 1985 I would not be surprised if 75% of them died from bayonet wounds inflicted by the Army." Villagers also confirmed that they witnessed soldiers of the Gukurahundi ripping open abdomen of live pregnant women who finished up dead. The army is alleged to have committed all these atrocities on the grounds that they were eliminating dissidents before they were born to prevent them from coming to cause trouble. Other security officers reported that the Army said perpetrators of this kind of killing were the dissidents. But as stated earlier, village eyewitnesses, survivors and doctors discounted this claim. Witness accounts wherever I went reported that ordinary people in the villages experienced the most horrific physical and psychological abuse since the end of armed liberation struggle in 1980. They gave graphic accounts of their own experiences and what they saw happening to other people. The allegations showed that the Army used the presence of dissidents to ruthlessly grind on the villagers claiming that they were paying the price for supporting and hiding dissidents. Even so the methods of destroying life were too ghastly to be witnessed by anyone.

The difference between the Army and the dissidents was that the latter committed isolated acts of murder and harassment of villagers whereas the former often resorted to aggravated mass abuse of human rights including massacres by burning people in their locked huts. The dissidents spent most of their time marauding in the villages, demanding support from the people in the name of Dr Joshua Nkomo. But Dr Nkomo disowned them decisively and urged the people not to recognise them. Here the villagers were between the stone and the grinder as both sides caused so much fear and havoc on the lives of the rural populace in the named Districts. But the Army was worse because it frequented the villages to assemble people for questioning about whereabouts of dissidents and if they got unsatisfactory answers from the villagers, they could resort to a killing spree on the grounds of punishing the people for hiding the dissidents. In a number of instances the Army personnel would pose as dissidents (**like Smith's Selous Scouts/ pseudo insurgents did**) at dusk and obtain supplies from the villagers. The following morning they returned in their correct Army role and asked whether dissidents visited them the previous night. As people had become used to this practice they had to be very observant over their evening guests so that when they returned the following day they would recognise them through any mark or feature or ways of talking or any mannerism that could identify at least one of them. For example they could respond thus "you were here last night and we fed you because we knew that you were members of our Army." They would ask: "how do you know it was us?" Answer: "That one with light complexion was joking a lot to make us laugh." They would laugh and go away. But if the villagers denied seeing dissidents the previous night or failed to identify at least one of the soldiers present, there would be hell-fire that could result in loss of life through beating or severe injuries. On this account they gave them the name "**omaphenduka**" meaning: '*those who came on unofficial uniform posing as dissidents, went away and returned in official army uniform the following day to ask about who visited villagers the previous night*'

My one-man inquiry was done in a lightning speed because of being cautious in case I could be spotted by some dangerous elements of the security forces. I had to look for facts not opinions or evaluations of the Army or dissidents in their handling of people in the selected operational areas. In those difficult circumstances I was relieved that in very short space of time there were people who agreed to tell me what they went through and what they witnessed relating to gross human rights abuses by the Army and dissidents in their localities or places of jurisdiction in the case of government officials or police officers. The small sample of people who gave evidence on atrocities was enough to enable me to see the picture of what was happening on a larger scale. The scale of destruction of human life and the brutality that was employed by Gukurahundi needed a full scale judiciary commission of inquiry with legal powers to summon witnesses as deemed necessary to assist it in its work. The scale of destruction of human life was such that it was impossible for any authority to cover it up by any means because there were too many people still moaning and sobbing over what they experienced. Those who did it in the field operations, if they were reasonable human beings, must have known that what they were doing would explode massively at some point in their life time.

During the period of Gukurahundi operation the situation was so pregnant with high "explosives" in the country in terms of creating ingredients of a potential civil war that could have arisen from anger and hatred caused by ill treatment of citizens by the Army that should have protected them from dissidents who were disowned by Dr Nkomo and rejected by the people. This is to say the country was brewing a civil war by paying little attention to the loud voices that were alleging that the Army was committing such alarming atrocities on innocent citizens with absolute impunity. In my report I summarised my findings and made recommendations for immediate action to end a socially costly conflict to avert a probable eruption of a civil war. Here I was convinced that Government and the affected people must find a formula that would bring them to the same wavelength regarding the question of who sponsored and supported dissidents. I also concluded that a long term high powered inquiry was required to determine the origin and extent of the atrocities and how to remedy the consequences thereof.

The main bone of contention here was that while the Government accused Dr Joshua Nkomo and PF ZAPU for leading the dissidents, the people believed in Dr Nkomo's position of disassociating himself from the dissidents and their actions in the country. Clearly there was a big gap between the people and Government on the perceptions regarding the question of ownership and political leadership of dissidents. So to solve the problem it was imperative to close this gap because people genuinely felt that they were being persecuted together with their leader, Dr Joshua Nkomo, for a crime (of owning the dissidents) they were not committing and they were very bitter about it. The extent of bitterness was beginning to spill over to the elements of the National Army whose relatives were affected by the Gukurahundi operations. That was where I perceived that danger was simmering slowly but surely. My recommendations were aiming at creating a situation where Prime Minister Robert Mugabe and ZAPU leader Dr Joshua Nkomo would meet and find the best way to resolve the raging conflict and quench the chances of a civil war before ingredients for its eruption mixed into a powder keg.

Apparently, the Honourable Prime Minister Robert Mugabe accepted my report and promptly established contact with Dr Joshua Nkomo for a meeting. They did meet on what they called "the unity talks" between ZANU PF and PF ZAPU. When the first meeting took place Deputy Secretary Comrade Willard Chiwewe informed me in a feedback that the contents of my report and recommendations had led to a meeting between the Prime Minister and ZAPU leader, Dr Joshua Nkomo to start talks for resolving the conflict in Matabeleland and Midlands Provinces. He congratulated me for undertaking dutiful task within a very short (one week) time to cause national leadership to seek a solution to the conflict. Indeed the talks started in earnest, raising hopes that they might be concluded without delay. Apparently, as they went deeper in matters of distribution of powers and responsibilities, stumbling blocks emerged and the talks stumbled to a halt for two years.

After resumption of talks, they dragged for a long period of time (punctuated by breakdowns at some stage) until an agreement was reached between the two parties leading to the signing of what was called "Unity Accord" of 22 December 1987. The Deputy Secretary, at the time, in the Prime Minister's Office Comrade Willard Chiwewe called me again to congratulate me emphatically on what he called "your successful national duty in Matabeleland North has yielded a Unity Accord that has resolved the dissident problem. Watch ZTV news tonight for confirmation, well done comrade Mpofu" I did likewise and an announcement was made to that effect. I felt good to hear that Gukurahundi and dissident bloodletting problem was ending; but did the Unity Accord between ZANU PF and PF ZAPU resolve the entire problem caused by the Gukurahundi in terms of mass destruction of life? It certainly addressed the immediate imperative to stop the horrific conflict at a stroke to give people space to live normal lives like the rest of the population. But the long term consequences of that mass scale of life destruction remained unaddressed.

The Unity Accord only stopped the massacre that was being perpetrated by the Gukurahundi and also removed the suffocating menace of dissidents from the people in the rural areas on offer of amnesty by the Prime Minister. Politically ZANU (PF) and PF ZAPU formally merged into one party in a formula that most commentators described as Dr Joshua Nkomo's surrender to Prime Minister Robert Mugabe or the Unity Accord that enabled ZANU (PF) to swallow P FZAPU with the surrender of its leadership. The stated terror was ended by the Unity Accord which provided for removal of both the dissidents and the Gukurahundi from the affected areas after nearly a half a dozen years of a life-consuming military campaign. During the period in question, the Fifth Brigade (Gukurahundi) was a lawful arm of Government deployed to clear armed dissident elements from society but once in the field, Gukurahundi began to act like killer machine on autopilot mode without paying attention to its constitutional responsibility to defend and protect citizens against any illegal armed force claiming to be freedom fighters in a free country. The dissidents were an illegal killer squad yet both forces did illegal things by unorthodox killing of civilians on a scale that should have attracted decisive restoration of justice from the Government of Zimbabwe. But the psychological trauma that was caused by that reign of terror remained unresolved and the worst part is that the villagers believed that they were innocent yet they were made to suffer so much loss of life of loved ones in the hands of their country's army in their own country under the watch of their national government. Subsequent thoroughgoing independent inquiries have excavated startling gross human rights abuses in the affected provinces.

The most disturbing feature of the Fifth Brigade was the fact that senior commanders were ex-freedom fighters. The concept and reality of a freedom fighter, in my understanding, is an individual who cares about and protects life of the people in terms of their wellbeing in every sphere of social action including the right to life as an unquenchable gift of God or nature, freedom from any form of oppression or exploitation, peace, justice, shelter, adequate means of livelihood and safety from all hazards, natural or man-made. A freedom fighter wants to see a free society enjoying a full bungle of rights in conjunction with a full bungle of basic freedoms in a situation of peace and justice. If it was true that commanders were ex-freedom fighters, I wonder whether they were fully trained as guerrilla fighters to understand what a freedom fighter was fighting for as they commanded an army that did not respect any of the rights of citizens including the right to life. A freedom fighter is a fully fledged politician behind the barrel of the gun in pursuit of a qualitatively better political system than the one that has caused war. Any freedom fighter who did not understand this simple notion was a danger to the people and other comrades because he or she would have no idea about the rights and freedoms that the people were looking forward to in a free Zimbabwe.

Did we achieve what we fought for?

This is the most difficult question to tackle because it needs answers that should address the objectives and goals of national liberation and their achievement in terms of liberation bringing a qualitative change to the peoples' lives that would be distinguished by the absence of all repressive features that prevailed under a white settler regime. The starting point is to revisit the beginning of the African demands regarding change of power relations in the country. The Southern Rhodesia African National Congress (SRANC) demanded loosely defined abolition of racial discrimination by leaders based on equal rights in education, health provision and political representation in Parliament and town councils for all citizens with an electoral system based on one man one vote or universal adult suffrage. Its successor, the National Democratic Party (NDP) improved on this by emphasising that it wanted freedom from an oppressive colonial state to be sorted out at a constitutional conference convened and chaired by the colonial power, the British Government. NDP demanded that there should be a new constitution with principles that guaranteed freedoms and rights of all citizens in the country run on the basis of majority rule. A powerful motivating slogan of **Mwanawebvu** was adopted and well taken by the majority of Africans and helped to elevate the nationalistic solidarity well beyond ethnic consideration in a more visible way than historians doubted about national consciousness in 1896. In the early 1960s the **Mwanawebvu** slogan tore apart the boundaries of tribalism as it cast a bright light that enabled every African to recognise another African as African not an intra-tribesman or extra-tribesman. This was reinforced by appropriate freedom songs that were sung nationwide about **"we want freedom now"** or **"freedom yauya, yauya navatungamiri"** (freedom has come with our leaders) and people were now able to translate this into their own mother tongue (**inkululeko/rusununkuko**[33]). The leaders also tried to explain that freedom entailed many freedoms that would enable people to function without impediment in any sphere of life but they did not unpack the concept of freedom enouph to show that it has extensive properties.

Even so, to premise 'freedom' ahead of other demands of the struggle was qualitatively better and easy to be internalised by the masses as could be seen through the way they sang so much about "freedom now." But, as stated above, there were no clearly elucidated principles of what the substance of our destination, **"freedom,"** was all about. That is, leaders did not unpack the fundamental properties of the concept of freedom in juridical and political terms and context. But its propagation in the population signified that freedom was an embodiment of fundamental enablers that would allow society to manage its affairs to the joy of every citizen as defined and safeguarded by such enablers. But the unpacked concept of freedom left everybody advancing their own properties of freedoms that could be deemed as enablers. For instance for people to exercise freedom they must have rights which are the key enablers in a free society. The problem here was that we were left to use our own discretion to offer elucidation of the enabling properties of freedom and this left us nowhere near something like the South African ANC **Freedom Charter** which spells out a clear vision of a free South Africa Nation.

The slogan **"mwanawebvu" (child of the soil of Motherland)** was one of the best notions in terms of its high social value that made ethnic groups feel cemented into one nation whereby they regarded each other as part of one nation originating from the same mother, the soil of the same African land. This was a strong political pronouncement that laid a practical foundation introduced by the National Democratic Party (NDP) and inherited by Zimbabwe African Union (ZAPU). Proceeding from this notion, it was possible to decipher the complexity of diverse social entities that make up Zimbabwean nation from whence cometh a definition of our relationships as we focus on the original common battle cry: **"freedom now"** that should combine with the aforesaid slogan to enable us to reach and enjoy our legitimate aspirations as "children of the soil of Motherland" **(Vana vebvu: children of the same soil)**. This could be closest to fulfilling what we were aspiring for since the early 1960s in terms of guaranteeing a bundle of freedoms and a reasonable standard of social cohesion in the context of the unpacked bundle of freedoms. Bundles of freedom and rights can only be guaranteed by spelling them out and defining their enabling properties in the context of a system of democracy. On this basis democracy would have been possible as an embodiment of such freedoms that we sang about since we were school children. This would be so because democracy is an embodiment of freedoms without which there can be no bundle of rights and freedoms for citizens to enjoy. If a bundle of enabling freedoms comes into play, it gives rise to the need to recognise a bundle of rights which is an inseparable twin of the bundle of freedoms. These twin bundles are the fundamental basis of a free democratic society because it is from these that all forms of social enablers of peace and justice are derived.

Nevertheless, winds of retrogression began to blow steadily against social cohesion of the African people when the unifying slogan was undermined by the painful split between ZAPU and ZANU in 1963. From that occasion things began to degenerate into incomprehensible primitivism that was characterised by anger, intolerance, bitterness and hatred based on political party lines, which in the long run, demarcated Zimbabwean politics along ethnic lines. Since then Zimbabwean politics have been contaminated by impurities of national self destruction caused by

---

[33] *freedom*

bloodshed flowing from violent conflict between political opponents who angrily regarded each other as traitors for causing split at a time when a more formidable force, Rhodesian Front, had come to power with guns blazing against African nationalism. At the beginning of that painful chapter, the aforesaid conflict was between ZAPU and ZANU lasting throughout armed struggle period but increasing in scope and intensity after independence in 1980. It was not until 1987 when a Unity Accord was signed between the two liberation movements that the conflict ended but leaving tens of thousands of civilians dead in Matabeleland and Midlands in the hands of the 5th Brigade which was deployed by the Government of Zimbabwe, under the watch of ZANU PF, to deal with armed dissidents in those provinces.

However, over a decade later, in 1999, the country witnessed the rise of a new party, the Movement for Democratic Change (MDC) into the Zimbabwean political landscape. This phenomenon switched on ZANU PF's live wire of fury and political intolerance on a scale reminiscent of that between the two abovementioned liberation movements. In this new 21st Century conflict, MDC did not split from the ZANU PF but the ferocity and intensity of the conflict resulted into similar tragic consequences in terms of destruction of human life with impunity at every national election since 2000, reaching startling levels in 2008 during the Presidential run-off on 29th June. The only difference is that the MDC has no militia like ZAPU had Zhanda after the split and a military force during armed struggle. In all of these tragic social calamities the concept of freedom was as dead as the unifying slogan of **"mwanawebvu."** In place of the latter slogan, ZANU advanced a destructive one above all others: **"Pasi naningi"**(down with so and so) which took prominence from 1963 up to this day. At first it was **"pasi nemhandu[34]"** but it virtually embraced everybody considered to be enemy to the party. The pronouncers of the slogan have translated it to mean "get rid of" so and so and that is exactly what has been happening in Zimbabwean politics for the past fifty years (from the 1963 mother of all splits). The **"pasi"** slogan has become a political tradition that has been internalised and interpreted by some youths as giving them the right to eliminate their fellow Africans on shear political differences. Conflict between ZAPU and ZANU was because the two regarded each other as enemy worth of destruction, a practice that developed from low key ferocity into a political tradition of inter-party bitter hatred. These two liberation movements had strong militias that faced each other where possible from 1963 onwards. With ZAPU-PCC commanding formally structured militia regiments such as Zhanda, it seemed to have an upper hand in resisting the rise of ZANU by violent means in the townships, especially in Highfields (Salisbury) and Mpopoma South (Bulawayo). At the point of being banned ZANU's counter militias had also become as effective in terms of inflicting similar or worse injuries on ZAPU members, especially in Highfield (e.g. burning of Chifamba family). In that kind of scenario, a situation of battles between the two was in evidence, but in the new interparty conflict the MDC has not got anything like militias yet it has borne the brunt of a one sided grinding more than its fair share in the duel. It stands to reason that ZANU PF being an experienced belligerent in that ugly duel of violent conflict with ZAPU, has felt disturbed by the rise of MDC which it saw as a new enemy worth of destruction like it regarded ZAPU before 1987. That is, it saw it appropriate to reinstate the tradition that kept it and ZAPU in perpetual bloody conflict for decades at a very high social cost whereby ZAPU finished up surrendering to ZANU in 1987. So, a new political complexion of the country which was expected to prove that democracy was maturing in Zimbabwe, on the contrary, it rolled out a tragic trend that tended to gravitate towards the same scale of loss of human life as during the pre-Unity Accord of 1987. There is no doubt that political intolerance this day and age is anathema to national

---

34
down with the enemy

advancement because it causes undesirable political tremors for everybody including business which spins the economy towards growth. Freedom fighters should have felt delighted that the rights and freedoms that we fought for had begun to mature with the rise of a new powerful party that poised as an alternative government in Zimbabwe. Such rights and freedoms did not exist for Africans under the Rhodesian regime of Ian Douglas Smith. In this connection it may not be terribly unreasonable if people began to accuse ZANU PF Government of behaving like Ian Smith's Government that bitterly resented to be opposed on a point of social justice. I would be guilty of terminological misconception if I failed to mention one important difference of how the RF of Ian Douglas Smith and ZANU PF fulfilled or failed to fulfil promises to their supporters: RF was able to deliver to their people as promised during campaign for white support for UDI and thereafter. The Rhodesian whites became very prosperous during UDI thus proving Ian Douglas Smith's honesty to his promise that he would maintain high standard for his people in spite of United Nations comprehensive sanctions against the country. He delivered his promise of job preservation for the white working class, weak commercial farmers were subsidized to ensure their viability and competitiveness in the share of the agricultural produce market. The contrast here is that our own Government of ZANU PF has focused its anger against other African citizens who opposed it and has lost sight of what it was expected to deliver to the people who suffered humiliating deprivation under colonialism. It is not only lack of freedoms and human rights, but also no economic gains for the masses of people who were solid behind the struggle against ferocious power of the Rhodesian Front regime. This is what lawyers call "double jeopardy" which, in political context, pertains to harshness that people have experienced under both authorities.

ZANU and ZAPU were exposed to progressive revolutionary theories during armed struggle. The only evidence to show that we got something from the Socialist countries is political rigidity as if there is a "correct line" outside of which is a parallel precipice each side. The content of our system is neither socialist nor feudal yet the politics of intolerance and brutality borrows characteristics of both. Socialists justified their rigidity on the grounds of defending economic gains of the working class and peasantry, who were the leading productive forces in society. Our rigidity has absolutely no justification because the country gained its sovereignty but without freedoms and rights, without economic gains and human security. Feudalists defended their monarch who was believed to have divine rights to rule his or her subjects. Anyone who challenged this authority did so at their own peril if his challenge was regarded as a threat to the Monarch's authority. This is a characteristic feature that seems like it was borrowed from Feudalism by Zimbabwe and we call that revolution! We behave as if we are in a feudal system of yester year when everything was in the name of the king and any slightest provocation of the king would promptly trigger ruthless retribution from the state.

Zimbabwe is a Republic in the 21st Century with a new and fairly democratic constitution which is yet to be tested in terms of whether the authorities will adhere to it since its adoption in 2012. But from 1980 to the time of adoption of the new constitution it was a political blasphemy to criticise the President and this portrayed the system of governance as if it was a feudalist one thus pushing the country back to the 18th Century. It was blasphemy to belong to a political party that threatened to overtake the ruling party at the polls. It was a blasphemy to criticise the government for its dismal failure to run a modern state for the past thirty years. Since elections took place at the end of July 2013, it is too early to indicate whether the government is now adhering to the democratic principles that are enshrined in the new constitution.

CONCLUSION

This narrative has spelt out the journey that I traversed from childhood to adulthood in both the biological growth and political maturity as a freedom fighter in the context of the whole stream of freedom fighters in Zimbabwe, who came from all corners of the country and social classes of the African population.

Having gone through so many phases that nurtured my political growth path with a variety of factors that made it possible for me to become a freedom fighter with full readiness to face risky challenges of the struggle during civilian period of activism up to the actual armed struggle; a career that was cut short by the collapse of ZAPU in 1970.

Out of all the phases mentioned here as inputs into moulding a freedom fighter, my father's candid talk around the fire about how Africans lost their country to European settlers, provided more material foundation upon which my political awareness was generated. The rest of the inputs constituted an element of enlightenment and preparatory phases that progressively provided knowledge and skills that became enablers for facing extremely hazardous challenges of the liberation struggle. For instance when I took part in tough boxing games in the forest, for me were mere young boys' games with no notion that they could be of physical value to me at some point of my life. I had no idea that such games could contribute an element of courage to face belligerent opponents without flinching. The only thing that was missing was practice on how to use fire arms in the same manner that young Europeans did at an early age to the extent that they got to military training already familiar with basics in the use of fire arms with accuracy. Most of us began to use firearms for the first time when we were over twenty five years or even thirty. But the aforesaid antecedent factors made it possible for us to forge ahead for Motherland's liberation

However, information from a primary school teachers gave us food for thought with regards the political situation in Africa during our time in school. That was the dawn of hope because the information had practical examples of changes in the rest of Africa in general and Zimbabwe in particular. Inyathi Secondary School elevated the whole platform of politics to a level at which I began to see and internalize issues of justice and injustice in my country and how the contradictory dichotomy could be sorted out regardless of immensity of challenges. Owing to the fact that I became politically fully aware at this point I was able to team up with other students to form an underground organization that turned that school into an "academy" of political knowledge and debate. Knowledge help us to accumulate facts from the real political arena and debates helped to share the knowledge with the rest of the school which enabled us to develop and adopt appropriate underground techniques that eventually equipped us with skills for planning and executing a strategy to fight an unjust system of governance. Full scale participation as an underground activist in the face of the power of the security branch was the peak of preparedness to face more challenging phase of the liberation struggle. Escaping out of the country opened the way to military training that produced guerrilla freedom fighters driven by anger against injustices of racial domination in our country. Having completed the training that specialized in radio communications (signals), we were deployed to various fronts where we found that deployments were not based on strategy for guerrilla warfare. Awareness on this anomaly was so wide spread thus culminating in freedom fighters summoning leaders to the camps to explain the whole war strategy for national liberation. Leaders admitted in front of freedom fighters that there was no strategy for waging guerrilla warfare. Following this startling admission, they accused each other for the strategic discrepancy and this 'automatically' triggered the emergence of a revolutionary force of freedom fighters within ZAPU that staged a rebellion and arrested the leaders to force them to attend a general assembly of freedom fighters with the facilitation of the Zambian Government. Freedom fighters demanded that the leaders be suspended for the duration of the struggle or until an elective congress takes place. But Government was not keen on resolving the crisis and finished up arresting those they believed were ringleaders of the rebellion. All this shows that my experience from childhood was typical for the majority of us in the struggle, variations notwithstanding in parental upbringing. For instance after those of my generation were neutralised by the Zambian Government many more still came up to join armed struggle in larger numbers than they were during our time. In essence, all of those who came forward to sacrifice their lives for their country were part of the deprived citizens who fought against our privileged fellow citizens, who defended a white minority racist regime had marginalised African citizens for decades with minimal genuine compromise to meet their legitimate aspirations.

Nevertheless, I have also brought out the internal strategic blunders and internal conflicts that occurred in the struggle to show that it was not smooth sailing. Internal upheavals were more serious threats to the struggle than our adversaries because that was tantamount to internal combustion of a crucial engine that was designed to drive the process to fruition. But eventually, patriotism prevailed leading to thoroughgoing transformation of the liberation movements by uniting them into a Patriotic Front whose massive deployments weakened the Rhodesian regime into political capitulation.

However, my father's narration was proved accurate because only fire power in the hands of the oppressed Africans helped them to humble their politically stiff-necked white rulers. Freedom from racial domination came home because of the barrel of the gun without which Africans in Zimbabwe would still be languishing under the yolk of injustices of racism based on the fifteen principles of the Rhodesian Front.

Africa, G. G. (n.d.). *Map of Zimbabwe.* Retrieved May 25, 2014, from geographicguide: http:// www.geographicguide.com/africa-maps/zimbabwe.htm

Baxter, P. (2011, August 08). *A Quick Sketch of the Zimbabwe/Rhodesia Bush War.* Retrieved February 26, 2014, from peterbaxterafrica: http://peterbaxterafrica.com/index. php/2011/08/08/a-thumbnail-sketch-of-the-zimbabwerhodesia-bush-war/

Blake, R. (1977). *A history of Rhodesia.* New York: Knopf.

Cilliers, J. (1985). *Counter-insurgency in Rhodesia.* Sydney: Croom Helm.

Crowder, M. (1975). The Second World War: Prelude to Decolonization in Africa. *The Cambridge History of Africa*, 8-44.

Dawson, S. (2011). The First Chimurenga: 1896-1897 Uprising in Matabeleland and. *Constellations*, 144-153.

Gunther, J. (1955). *Inside Africa.* New York: Harper.

Mandela, N. (2004). *Long Walk to Freedom.* Johannesburg: Macdonald Purnell.

Mhanda, W. (2011). *DZINO: Memories of a freedom fighter.* Harare: Weaver Press.

Moorcraft, P., & McLaughlin, P. (2008). *The Rhodesian war: A Military History.* Johannesburg: Jonathan Ball Publishers.

Mzilethi, J. Z. (2014, February 20). Colleague in the Struggle. (J. Mpofu, Interviewer)

Nkrumah, K. (1957). *Ghana: Autobiography of Kwame Nkrumah.* New York: International Publishers.

Palmer, P. R. (1977). Land and Racial Domination in Rhodesia. *Journal of Southern African Studies*, 266-268.

Peck, A. (1966). *Rhodesia Accusses.* Salisbury: Three Sisters Books.

Ranger, T. O. (1967). Revolt in Southern Rhodesia 1896-7. *Africa* , 174-175.

Sachikonye, L. (2011). *When a State Turns on its Citizens.* Harare: Weaver Press.

Gukurahundi in Zimbabwe: A Report On Disturbances in Matabelaland and The Midlands 1980 -1988. By The Catholic Commission for Justice and Peace, Harare: 1997

Sadomba, Z. W. (2011). *War Veterans in Zimbabwe's Revolution: Challenging neo- colonialism and settler and international capital.* Suffolk: James Currey.

M. -m. (n.d.). *Rhodesia - Physical / Altitude - 1973.* Retrieved May 25, 2014, from Rhodesia: http://www.rhodesia.me.uk/documents/RSRmap1973smallscale final 001.pdf

Tshabangu, O. (1979). *The March 11 Movement of ZAPU.* York: Tiger Papers Publications.

Unkown. (1963, August). Report on the National Conference of ZAPU. *African Daily News*, p. unknown.

Wikipedia. (2013, September 07). *Cuban Revolution.* Retrieved Maty 13, 2014, from Wikipedia: http://en.wikipedia.org/wiki/Cuban Revolution

Wikipedia. (2013, September 21). *Mau Mau Uprising.* Retrieved April 29, 2014, from Wikipedia: http://en.wikipedia.org/wiki/Mau Mau Uprising

Wikipedia. (2013, October 18). *Politics of Rhodesia*. Retrieved February 10, 2014, from Wikipedia: http://en.wikipedia.org/wiki/Politics of Rhodesia

Wikipedia. (2013, May 2013). *Rhodesia*. Retrieved MAy 21, 2014, from Wikipedia: http://en.wikipedia.org/wiki/Rhodesia

Wikipedia. (2014, April 21). *National Liberation Front (Algeria)*. Retrieved April 27, 2014, from Wikipedia: http://en.wikipedia.org/wiki/National Liberation Front %28Algeria%29

Wikipedia. (2014, March 29). *Tichafa Samuel Parirenyatwa*. Retrieved April 11, 2014, from Wikipedia: http://en.wikipedia.org/wiki/Tichafa Samuel Parirenyatwa

Windrow, M. (1997). *The Algerian War 1954-62*. Botley: Osprey Publishing.